# Praise For Lowfat Cooking For Dummies!

"This is a wonderful, easily digested book to help anyone when it comes to cutting the fat from their diets — and maybe their waistlines!"

> — Michael Jacobson, Ph.D., Executive Director, Center for Science in the Public Interest, and Publisher, Nutrition Action Healthletter

"Lynn provides you with key information without emphasizing a quick weight loss. She shows you that anyone can trim fat by readjusting their diet."

> — Mark White, Television Director, "Low Cholesterol Gourmet" Show

"*Lowfat Cooking For Dummies* provides a unique, positive approach to eating and cooking light in the '90s . . ."

> — Dr. W. Virgil Brown, Former President, American Heart Association

# Praise For Lynn Fischer's The Better Sex Diet

"We are all fortunate to have someone of Lynn Fischer's skill and talent who can translate hard science into delicious meals. I congratulate her on *The Better Sex Diet* and recommend it as a potent regimen for preserving health and sexual vitality."

> — Irwin Goldstein, M.D., Professor of Urology, Boston University School of Medicine and Co-author of *The Massachusetts Male Aging Study* and *The Potent Male*

# More Praise For Lynn Fischer's The Better Sex Diet

"Comprehensive changes in diet and lifestyle can improve blood flow not only to the heart, but to other organs as well. In *The Better Sex Diet,* Lynn Fisher demonstrates what a meaningful difference these changes can make in the quality of our lives."

> — Dean Ornish, M.D., Director, Preventative Medicine Research Institute and Author, *Dr. Dean Ornish's Program for Reversing Heart Disease*

"Lynn Fischer is right on target! No one has written a clearer or more user-friendly guide to the way food can affect sexuality for both men and women."

> — Neal Barnard, M.D., President, Physicians Committee for Responsible Medicine

# Praise For Lynn Fischer and W. Virgil Brown's The Fischer/Brown Low Cholesterol Gourmet

"If you like good health and love delicious food, this is the only book you need."

> — Larry King

# by Lynn Fischer

## Foreword by W. Virgil Brown, M.D.

IDG Books Worldwide, Inc.
An International Data Group Company

Foster City, CA ♦ Chicago, IL ♦ Indianapolis, IN ♦ Southlake, TX

**Lowfat Cooking For Dummies**™

Published by
**IDG Books Worldwide, Inc.**
An International Data Group Company
919 E. Hillsdale Blvd.
Suite 400
Foster City, CA 94404
www.idgbooks.com (IDG Books Worldwide Web site)
www.dummies.com (Dummies Press Web site)

Library of Congress Catalog Card No.: 97-70748

ISBN: 0-7645-5035-7

Printed in the United States of America

10 9 8 7 6 5 4 3 2

1DD/SR/RS/ZX/IN

Distributed in the United States by IDG Books Worldwide, Inc.

Distributed by Macmillan Canada for Canada; by Transworld Publishers Limited in the United Kingdom; by IDG Norge Books for Norway; by IDG Sweden Books for Sweden; by Woodslane Pty. Ltd. for Australia; by Woodslane Enterprises Ltd. for New Zealand; by Longman Singapore Publishers Ltd. for Singapore, Malaysia, Thailand, and Indonesia; by Simron Pty. Ltd. for South Africa; by Toppan Company Ltd. for Japan; by Distribuidora Cuspide for Argentina; by Livraria Cultura for Brazil; by Ediciencia S.A. for Ecuador; by Addison-Wesley Publishing Company for Korea; by Ediciones ZETA S.C.R. Ltda. for Peru; by WS Computer Publishing Corporation, Inc., for the Philippines; by Unalis Corporation for Taiwan; by Contemporanea de Ediciones for Venezuela; by Computer Book & Magazine Store for Puerto Rico; by Express Computer Distributors for the Caribbean and West Indies. Authorized Sales Agent: Anthony Rudkin Associates for the Middle East and North Africa.

For general information on IDG Books Worldwide's books in the U.S., please call our Consumer Customer Service department at 800-762-2974. For reseller information, including discounts and premium sales, please call our Reseller Customer Service department at 800-434-3422.

For information on where to purchase IDG Books Worldwide's books outside the U.S., please contact our International Sales department at 415-655-3200 or fax 415-655-3295.

For information on foreign language translations, please contact our Foreign & Subsidiary Rights department at 415-655-3021 or fax 415-655-3281.

For sales inquiries and special prices for bulk quantities, please contact our Sales department at 415-655-3200 or write to the address above.

For information on using IDG Books Worldwide's books in the classroom or for ordering examination copies, please contact our Educational Sales department at 800-434-2086 or fax 817-251-8174.

For press review copies, author interviews, or other publicity information, please contact our Public Relations department at 415-655-3000 or fax 415-655-3299.

For authorization to photocopy items for corporate, personal, or educational use, please contact Copyright Clearance Center, 222 Rosewood Drive, Danvers, MA 01923, or fax 508-750-4470.

 is a trademark under exclusive license to IDG Books Worldwide, Inc., from International Data Group, Inc.

# About the Author

 The recipe for Lynn Fischer's success began in the sleepy resort town of Virginia Beach, where her first starring roles were as homemaker, mother, marketing executive, and co-host of a local TV talk show. During these years, Lynn discovered that her husband was running the risk of coronary artery disease as a result of a dangerously high cholesterol level. Responding to her husband's immediate health needs, Lynn set out to learn all that she could to help him get his numbers under control. Her meticulous research led her to the conclusion that a diet low in saturated fat and cholesterol was the first line of defense in curing and preventing heart disease.

The next step was to cut the fat from her family's diet by changing methods of food preparation and food selection, while maintaining flavor, variety, and flexibility. It wasn't long before Lynn realized just how important her role of chief chef was in impacting her family's health and quality of life. From lower cholesterol numbers (her husband's fell by a dramatic 100 points!) and lower medical bills to higher energy and better moods, Lynn's hard work in the kitchen paid off handsomely. Ultimately, Lynn's concern for healthy lifestyles extended far beyond her own family's dinner table and has propelled her to her current position as a nationally recognized health expert, best-selling cookbook author, and host of over 200 national cooking shows.

Lynn, who now lives in Washington, D.C., founded the National Women's Health Awareness Forum and is a former medical anchor at WTTG (Fox) in Washington. She hosts the popular cooking series "Healthy Indulgences" on PBS and was formerly known as "The Low Cholesterol Gourmet" on The Discovery Channel. She is coauthor of the bestseller *The Low Cholesterol Gourmet* with Dr. W. Virgil Brown, former president of the American Heart Association, and has also written *The Quick Low Cholesterol Gourmet, Healthy Indulgences, The Better Sex Diet,* and *Fabulous Fat-Free.*

Pasta cecca, Caesar salad, and tart cherry pie are the special foods that tickle Lynn's taste buds. Friends and family touch her heart and fill her life. This enthusiastic proponent of healthy lifestyles strives each day to learn new skills, embrace new ideas, and through her professional efforts on television and in writing books, make a positive impact on the health and welfare of the world around her.

# ABOUT IDG BOOKS WORLDWIDE

Welcome to the world of IDG Books Worldwide.

IDG Books Worldwide, Inc., is a subsidiary of International Data Group, the world's largest publisher of computer-related information and the leading global provider of information services on information technology. IDG was founded more than 25 years ago and now employs more than 8,500 people worldwide. IDG publishes more than 275 computer publications in over 75 countries (see listing below). More than 60 million people read one or more IDG publications each month.

Launched in 1990, IDG Books Worldwide is today the #1 publisher of best-selling computer books in the United States. We are proud to have received eight awards from the Computer Press Association in recognition of editorial excellence and three from *Computer Currents'* First Annual Readers' Choice Awards. Our best-selling *...For Dummies*® series has more than 30 million copies in print with translations in 30 languages. IDG Books Worldwide, through a joint venture with IDG's Hi-Tech Beijing, became the first U.S. publisher to publish a computer book in the People's Republic of China. In record time, IDG Books Worldwide has become the first choice for millions of readers around the world who want to learn how to better manage their businesses.

Our mission is simple: Every one of our books is designed to bring extra value and skill-building instructions to the reader. Our books are written by experts who understand and care about our readers. The knowledge base of our editorial staff comes from years of experience in publishing, education, and journalism — experience we use to produce books for the '90s. In short, we care about books, so we attract the best people. We devote special attention to details such as audience, interior design, use of icons, and illustrations. And because we use an efficient process of authoring, editing, and desktop publishing our books electronically, we can spend more time ensuring superior content and spend less time on the technicalities of making books.

You can count on our commitment to deliver high-quality books at competitive prices on topics you want to read about. At IDG Books Worldwide, we continue in the IDG tradition of delivering quality for more than 25 years. You'll find no better book on a subject than one from IDG Books Worldwide.

John Kilcullen
CEO
IDG Books Worldwide, Inc.

Steven Berkowitz
President and Publisher
IDG Books Worldwide, Inc.

*Eighth Annual
Computer Press
Awards ≥1992*

*Ninth Annual
Computer Press
Awards ≥1993*

*Tenth Annual
Computer Press
Awards ≥1994*

*Eleventh Annual
Computer Press
Awards ≥1995*

IDG Books Worldwide, Inc., is a subsidiary of International Data Group, the world's largest publisher of computer-related information and the leading global provider of information services on information technology. International Data Group publishes over 275 computer publications in over 75 countries. Sixty million people read one or more International Data Group publications each month. International Data Group's publications include: **ARGENTINA:** Buyer's Guide, Computerworld Argentina, PC World Argentina; **AUSTRALIA:** Australian Macworld, Australian PC World, Australian Reseller News, Computerworld, IT Casebook, Network World, Publish, Webmaster; **AUSTRIA:** Computerwelt Österreich, Networks Austria, PC Tip Austria; **BANGLADESH:** PC World Bangladesh; **BELARUS:** PC World Belarus; **BELGIUM:** Data News; **BRAZIL:** Annuário de Informática, Computerworld, Connections, Macworld, PC Player, PC World, Publish, Reseller News, Supergamepower; **BULGARIA:** Computerworld Bulgaria, Network World Bulgaria, PC & MacWorld Bulgaria; **CANADA:** CIO Canada, Client/Server World, ComputerWorld Canada, InfoWorld Canada, NetworkWorld Canada, WebWorld; **CHILE:** Computerworld Chile, PC World Chile; **COLOMBIA:** Computerworld Colombia, PC World Colombia; **COSTA RICA:** PC World Centro America; **THE CZECH AND SLOVAK REPUBLICS:** Computerworld Czechoslovakia, Macworld Czech Republic, PC World Czechoslovakia; **DENMARK:** Communications World Danmark, Computerworld Danmark, Macworld Danmark, PC World Danmark, Techworld Danmark; **DOMINICAN REPUBLIC:** PC World Republica Dominicana; **ECUADOR:** PC World Ecuador; **EGYPT:** Computerworld Middle East, PC World Middle East; **EL SALVADOR:** PC World Centro America; **FINLAND:** MikroPC, Tietoverkko, Tietoviikko; **FRANCE:** Distributique, Hebdo, Info PC, Le Monde Informatique, Macworld, Reseaux & Telecoms, WebMaster France; **GERMANY:** Computer Partner, Computerwoche, Computerwoche Extra, Computerwoche FOCUS, Global Online, Macwelt, PC Welt; **GREECE:** Amiga Computing, GamePro Greece, Multimedia World; **GUATEMALA:** PC World Centro America; **HONDURAS:** PC World Centro America; **HONG KONG:** Computerworld Hong Kong, PC World Hong Kong, Publish in Asia; **HUNGARY:** ABCD CD-ROM, Computerworld Szamitastechnika, Internetto online Magazine, PC World Hungary, PC-X Magazin Hungary; **ICELAND:** Tolvuheimur PC World Island; **INDIA:** Information Communications World, Information Systems Computerworld, PC World India, Publish in Asia; **INDONESIA:** InfoKomputer PC World, Komputek Computerworld, Publish in Asia; **IRELAND:** ComputerScope, PC Live!; **ISRAEL:** Macworld Israel, People & Computers/Computerworld; **ITALY:** Computerworld Italia, Macworld Italia, Networking Italia, PC World Italia; **JAPAN:** DTP World, Macworld Japan, Nikkei Personal Computing, OS/2 World Japan, SunWorld Japan, Windows NT World, Windows World Japan; **KENYA:** PC World East African; **KOREA:** Hi-Tech Information, Macworld Korea, PC World Korea; **MACEDONIA:** PC World Macedonia; **MALAYSIA:** Computerworld Malaysia, PC World Malaysia, Publish in Asia; **MALTA:** PC World Malta; **MEXICO:** Computerworld Mexico, PC World Mexico; **MYANMAR:** PC World Myanmar; **NETHERLANDS:** Computer! Totaal, LAN Internetworking Magazine, LAN World Buyers Guide, Macworld Netherlands, Net, WebWereld; **NEW ZEALAND:** Absolute Beginners Guide and Plain & Simple Series, Computer Buyer, Computer Industry Directory, Computerworld New Zealand, MTB, Network World, PC World New Zealand; **NICARAGUA:** PC World Centro America; **NORWAY:** Computerworld Norge, CW Rapport, Datamagasinet, Financial Rapport, Kursguide Norge, Macworld Norge, Multimediaworld Norge, PC World Ekspress Norge, PC World Nettverk, PC World Norge, PC World Produkt/Guide Norge; **PAKISTAN:** Computerworld Pakistan; **PANAMA:** PC World Panama; **PEOPLE'S REPUBLIC OF CHINA:** China Computer Users, China Computerworld, China InfoWorld, China Telecom World Weekly, Computer & Communication, Electronic Design China, Electronics Today, Electronics Weekly, Game Software, PC World China, Popular Computer Week, Software Weekly, Software World, Telecom World; **PERU:** Computerworld Peru, PC World Profesional Peru, PC World SoHo Peru; **PHILIPPINES:** Click!, Computerworld Philippines, PC World Philippines, Publish in Asia; **POLAND:** Computerworld Poland, Computerworld Special Report Poland, Cyber, Macworld Poland, Networld Poland, PC World Komputer; **PORTUGAL:** Cerebro/PC World, Computerworld/Correio Informático, Dealer World Portugal, Mac*In/PC*In Portugal, Multimedia World; **PUERTO RICO:** PC World Puerto Rico; **ROMANIA:** Computerworld Romania, PC World Romania, Telecom Romania; **RUSSIA:** Computerworld Russia, Mir PK, Publish, Seti; **SINGAPORE:** Computerworld Singapore, PC World Singapore, Publish in Asia; **SLOVENIA:** Monitor; **SOUTH AFRICA:** Computing SA, Network World SA, Software World SA; **SPAIN:** Communicaciones World España, Computerworld España, Dealer World España, Macworld España, PC World España, PC World Sweden; **SRI LANKA:** Infolink PC World; **SWEDEN:** CAP&Design, Computer Sweden, Corporate Computing Sweden, Internetworld Sweden, it.branschen, Macworld Sweden, MaxiData Sweden, MikroDatorn, Nätverk & Kommunikation, PC World Sweden, PCaktiv, Windows World Sweden; **SWITZERLAND:** Computerworld Schweiz, Macworld Schweiz, PCtip; **TAIWAN:** Computerworld Taiwan, Macworld Taiwan, NEW ViSiON/Publish, PC World Taiwan, Windows World Taiwan; **THAILAND:** Publish in Asia, Thai Computerworld; **TURKEY:** Computerworld Turkiye, Macworld Turkiye, Network World Turkiye, PC World Turkiye; **UKRAINE:** Computerworld Kiev, Multimedia World Ukraine, PC World Ukraine; **UNITED KINGDOM:** Acorn User UK, Amiga Action UK, Amiga Computing UK, Apple Talk UK, Computing, Macworld, Parents and Computers UK, PC Advisor, PC Home, PSX Pro, The WEB; **UNITED STATES:** Cable in the Classroom, CIO Magazine, Computerworld, DOS World, Federal Computer Week, GamePro Magazine, InfoWorld, I-Way, Macworld, Network World, PC Games, PC World, Publish, Video Event, THE WEB Magazine, and WebMaster; online webzines: JavaWorld, NetscapeWorld, and SunWorld Online; **URUGUAY:** InfoWorld Uruguay; **VENEZUELA:** Computerworld Venezuela, PC World Venezuela; and **VIETNAM:** PC World Vietnam.           3/24/97

# Author's Acknowledgments

I love to write recipes and give tips and hints on how to eat lowfat. You type what you made the night before, some interesting food combination; then, from the recipe, you remake it again exactly the way you typed it. You realize what you left out or what would make it better and rewrite it with the corrections. Then you give your "perfect" recipe to a professional tester.

Then the testers work their magic. My testers for this book, whom I thank profusely, were registered dietitian Christin Loudon (who also did most of the nutritional analysis for this book and most of my other books, as well as suggesting recipe ideas); Andrea Goodman, former assistant and associate producer of my television show, who offered recipes and writing ideas from the perspective of a busy new mother and cook; Rita Calvert, cookbook writer, food columnist, and food stylist for nearly all my 200 *Low Cholesterol Gourmet* television shows on The Discovery Channel and the 26 *Lynn Fischer's Healthy Indulgences* shows on public television (APS through Maryland Public Television); and Lynda Gunn, an incredibly experienced food person from New York who's new to the Washington area.

You can't do a cookbook without testers, and they tell you the truth — this recipe is great, this one (which we can change or drop) only so-so. Money really isn't enough for what they do, and Chris's hours were extraordinary. Every single number for every one of the thousands of nutrient values, statements, claims, assertions, and government guidelines had to be checked and rechecked for accuracy.

Thanking people after I write a book is fun. Gail Ross is always first. She's my literary agent, lawyer, adviser, and friend who initiated the relationship with IDG Books Worldwide Executive Editor Sarah Kennedy. I sincerely thank Sarah for giving me the chance to introduce lowfat cooking to this wide audience of ...*For Dummies* book lovers, and especially for giving me IDG Books editor Pam Mourouzis. What a pleasure Pam is.

In my office, my media supervisor Beth Hays has been fabulous, as have interns Kathleen Daly, Annie Musumeci, junior intern Danielle Schwartz, and long-time intern (and soon to be medical intern, I hope) Terry Gerace. These people do terrific work, and both are terrific people. I am fortunate to be in a creative business and to have such an imaginative and enthusiastic staff.

Family and friends always mentioned in my books are my dear Ginnie (Virginia Von Fremd, and son Joey); Bethela (Beth Mendelson); Andrea and Marty Kalin and Yonnie; Diana Ingraham; Linda Ringe; Kathy McClain; Terry and Bob McKenzie; my dad Addison Connor, who at 92 has finally hung up his Rollerblades; daughter Lisa Jehle; grandchild Wolf; son Cary Bialac; niece Susie Fischer McGarry (and Mark); and brothers Tom Connor (and Mary, and their kids Matt and Scot), Bob Connor, Ann Connor Taylor (and husband Bill), and Jim Connor (and wife Trudy, and kids Jimmie and Annie). Especially I thank my companion Chris Gillette and the whole Gillette family, including Chris's little daughter Haley, mom Dixie (and husband Gene), and sibs Rocky, Billie, Jeannie, Terry, and Kathy (and husband Cole and daughter Kasie).

# Publisher's Acknowledgments

We're proud of this book; please register your comments through our IDG Books Worldwide Online Registration Form located at http://my2cents.dummies.com.

Some of the people who helped bring this book to market include the following:

### Acquisitions, Development, and Editorial

**Senior Project Editor:** Pamela Mourouzis

**Acquisitions Editor:** Sarah Kennedy, Executive Editor

**Copy Editor:** Susan Diane Smith

**Professional Recipe Testing:** Christin Loudon, R.D., Rita Calvert, Andrea Goodman, Lynda S. Gunn

**Technical Reviewers:** Christin Loudon, R.D., Lynda S. Gunn

**Editorial Manager:** Kristin A. Cocks

**Editorial Coordinator:** Ann Miller

### Production

**Project Coordinator:** Sherry Gomoll

**Layout and Graphics:** J. Tyler Connor, Maridee V. Ennis, Todd Klemme, Jane E. Martin, Tom Missler, Anna Rohrer, Brent Savage, Kate Snell

**Special Art:** Elizabeth Kurtzman

**Proofreaders:** Christine D. Berman, Carrie Voorhis, Joel K. Draper, Rachel Garvey, Rob Springer, Karen York

**Indexer:** Steve Rath

### Special Help

Jamie Klobuchar, Assistant Brand Manager; Dummies Recipe Testers Tina Carter, Gwenette Gaddis, Sherry Gomoll, Janet Huebner, Cheryl Knapp, Stephanie Koutek, Pat O'Brien, Brenda Patterson, Jackie Pennywell, Sarah Rehberg, Pat Rickett, Cindy Schmith, Christine Whetstone, Nazan Wolfe

---

### General and Administrative

**IDG Books Worldwide, Inc.:** John Kilcullen, CEO; Steven Berkowitz, President and Publisher

**IDG Books Technology Publishing:** Brenda McLaughlin, Senior Vice President and Group Publisher

**Dummies Technology Press and Dummies Editorial:** Diane Graves Steele, Vice President and Associate Publisher; Mary Bednarek, Acquisitions and Product Development Director; Kristin A. Cocks, Editorial Director

**Dummies Trade Press:** Kathleen A. Welton, Vice President and Publisher; Kevin Thornton, Acquisitions Manager; Maureen F. Kelly, Editorial Coordinator

**IDG Books Production for Dummies Press:** Beth Jenkins, Production Director; Cindy L. Phipps, Manager of Project Coordination, Production Proofreading, and Indexing; Kathie S. Schutte, Supervisor of Page Layout; Shelley Lea, Supervisor of Graphics and Design; Debbie J. Gates, Production Systems Specialist; Robert Springer, Supervisor of Proofreading; Debbie Stailey, Special Projects Coordinator; Tony Augsburger, Supervisor of Reprints and Bluelines; Leslie Popplewell, Media Archive Coordinator

**Dummies Packaging and Book Design:** Patti Crane, Packaging Specialist; Lance Kayser, Packaging Assistant; Kavish + Kavish, Cover Design

♦

The publisher would like to give special thanks to Patrick J. McGovern, without whom this book would not have been possible.

♦

# Contents at a Glance

# Recipes at a Glance

# Table of Contents

# Foreword

When asked to write the foreword for Lynn's new book, *Lowfat Cooking For Dummies,* I was very enthusiastic because I worked with Lynn on the book *The Low Cholesterol Gourmet.* Not to my surprise, I found that the book is packed with excellent tips and advice for people who want to trim the fat out of their diet and prepare healthy, flavorful meals for their family, their friends, or themselves.

*Lowfat Cooking For Dummies* provides a unique, positive approach to eating and cooking light in the '90s, with recommendations for foods and serving suggestions that are consistent with dietary guidelines of the American Heart Association and the American Cancer Society. Each chapter provides you with straightforward, easy-to-follow, delicious recipes that use lowfat cooking techniques that add spice and flavor without contributing to your waistline.

Not only does Lynn provide you with zesty lowfat recipes, but she also has compiled information for how to slenderize your kitchen, interpret and understand nutrition labels, and trim the fat from your shopping lists. There is even up-to-date information about lowfat packaged foods, with the real story of health benefits and downfalls.

Everyone knows that reducing saturated fat and cholesterol rich foods from your diet can reduce the risk of heart disease, and that eating less fat reduces calories, which in turn helps you to maintain a slimmer and trimmer waistline. But remember, if you've changed your diet by eliminating the foods that you like, it may be hard to sustain because you may be tempted to eat those not-so-good-for-you foods. However, in *Lowfat Cooking For Dummies,* Lynn Fischer provides you with sound, heart-healthy advice so you don't have to eliminate the foods you like, but instead use tips, tricks, and techniques to cut the fat and cholesterol from your favorite foods and still enjoy them!

Here's to healthy eating!

W. Virgil Brown, MD
Former President of the American Heart Association

# Introduction

. . . . . . . . . . . . . . . . . . . . . . . . . . . . . . . . . . . . . . . . . . . . . . . . .

*1* wrote *Lowfat Cooking For Dummies* because, after 30 years of cooking and eating lowfat, I decided that I really know the tricks to make it easy for others. Plus, great new lowfat and fat-free products — especially dairy foods — are available. And better labeling has taken away some of the confusion and made it easier.

This book shows you that cooking and eating lowfat are really pretty easy. When my former husband had a dangerously high cholesterol level, I changed our whole eating plan while raising kids, training a new dog, building a house, and working outside the home full-time. My husband's cholesterol level came down 100 points, largely through a change in diet. My lowfat foods also helped my television director Mark White lose 100 pounds (which he's kept off for five years). And writing six lowfat cookbooks since 1989 has given me an understanding of how easy it can be *and* how hard it can seem. Changing any habit is difficult.

## About This Book

In this book, you can find out how to prepare fresh produce, such as peaches, green beans, eggplant, blueberries, carrots, and potatoes; healthy grains, such as rice, pasta, and beans; and other foods with natural fats, such as nuts and avocados (used in limited amounts) simply but with great taste and appeal. This is the right and natural way to eat, according to all the scientific information we have — and we have plenty. Being able to eat a wide variety of fresh foods, not gorging yourself on fat-smothered foods so that you have to struggle to get up from the table, is the *real* luxury.

Learning how to cook and eat lowfat, whether through new recipes or by adapting your own favorites, is an important step in giving your body the best chance for optimum health. When you eat lowfat, you may notice that you have more vitality, that you can keep your weight in check or lose weight, that your blood cholesterol drops, and that a host of other diet-related problems fade. Because you are reading this book, you are on your way to healthier eating this very day. Plus, I think I've made it fun.

Eating lowfat can be a challenge. That cheesecake is always there, but so are wonderful recipes using fruits, vegetables, healthy grains, lowfat dairy products, and lean meats, fish, and poultry — the foods that humans were meant to eat. The recipes in this book, which are lowfat (some fat-free), are here to entice you to eat those foods, even in the face of cheesecake or a cream-filled doughnut. Finding beautiful, fresh produce is a thrill for me, as is anticipating how fresh peaches, grapes, or artichokes will taste, or tearing off a piece from a crusty and fragrant loaf of fresh bread. I hope that this book helps you feel that way about food — especially lowfat food — too (if you don't already).

Good lowfat cooking and eating isn't deprivation; it includes many of the foods you are used to eating. From fajitas to fettuccine, French fries to frankfurters, frosting to fudge, lowfat eating plans can include them (although some of these items should not be eaten often). Changing your diet is usually an adaptive process, not an all-or-nothing one.

**Note:** Honesty is necessary in writing a lowfat guide. Lowfat doesn't taste the same as high-fat. Some lowfat and fat-free foods don't taste good (and some high-fat foods don't, either!). A few ready-made lowfat and fat-free dairy products are terrific and make it very easy, and a few (such as cream cheese) aren't just right yet.

Occasionally, you hear conflicting information, such as that eggs, butter, and steak, even if eaten daily, can lower cholesterol; that if you're on a weight-loss plan, avocados should be avoided because of fat content; or that you can get too little fat. You can find the answers to your questions about what's true and what's trendy right here. This book makes it very clear that lowfat can be tricky. I explain what to watch out for, because what you previously thought was lowfat (or high in fat), or what you thought you should or shouldn't eat, isn't necessarily so.

Because some people eat lowfat not for weight control but for reducing heart disease, I include saturated fat and cholesterol information as well as information about fat. I provide a little medical information, too. (I used to be a television medical anchor and headed a women's health awareness organization.)

Use *Lowfat Cooking For Dummies* as a reference book, a recipe book, and an enthusiastic friend encouraging you to love lowfat food. Read what interests you, what surprises you, what amuses you, and what is useful to you. You don't have to read the book in any order, such as from front to back, to understand lowfat cooking. I don't expect you to remember everything you read, either; if you need to know something, I explain it right there or provide a cross-reference to the chapter that explains the topic in detail.

## Conventions Used in This Book

Every cookbook has its own way of doing things. Before you begin, you need to know a few things about my lowfat approach:

✔ All dairy products — milk, yogurt, cottage cheese, and so on — are fat-free or labeled lowfat.

✔ All mayonnaise, other spreads, and salad dressings are fat-free or labeled lowfat.

✔ All meat and poultry are lean, and fish and turkey are extra lean. All are completely trimmed of visible fat. Remove the skin from all poultry.

✔ All fatty broths and stocks are defatted.

✔ All commercially prepared foods and canned goods need to be labeled lowfat or fat-free, meaning that they contain 3 grams or less total fat for each labeled serving.

✔ I call for substitute eggs in many recipes because they have no fat or cholesterol and are safer for many uses because they are pasteurized. (I also call for fresh eggs or egg whites in some recipes.)

✔ I use butter substitutes. These products taste good and have far less fat than butter. (I do use butter and other fats in some recipes.)

✔ I always use no-stick vegetable oil spray to cut down on the amount of hidden fats for browning. You can fill your own spray bottle with olive oil, but the nozzle may become clogged.

Get an idea of what the recipe is like before making too many changes. Lowfat recipes can be tricky, and some of the measuring needs to be exact. You can almost always add more vegetables and mushrooms or substitute turkey or even fish for lean pork or beef, though, and when you don't like something, you can usually omit it.

Finally, read through every recipe at least once before you begin. Get out the pots and pans you need. Understand how long the recipe may take, because cooking lowfat is different — better, but different. Shopping is different, too. Most recipes are written to serve four people, but some serve more, and a few, such as beverages, serve fewer.

# Foolish Assumptions (Or, Who This Book Is For)

Whether you have a degree in nutrition and are foraging for a few new tips to provide lowfat cooking and eating information to your clients, you are an experienced cook who wants to buy and prepare healthy meals for yourself or your family, or you have never even boiled water but want to start paying attention to what you put in your mouth and how it affects your health, this book can guide you. *Lowfat Cooking For Dummies* is the perfect solution if you want to both save money and control what you eat by making your food at home instead of eating high-fat meals at often high-priced restaurants.

# How This Book Is Organized

This book is divided into *parts,* and each part is further divided into *chapters.* The following sections tell you what you can find in each part.

## Part I: Getting Started with Lowfat Eating

The whole subject of lowfat can seem overwhelming, so in this part, I give you an overview to clear up some of the confusion. Food labeling can be a particularly confusing part of cooking and eating lowfat (yet labels are very clear when you know what you're reading), so I explain labels in their own chapter.

## Part II: Setting Up a Lowfat Kitchen

Having lowfat foods handy is half the battle in lowfat cooking. This part of the book talks about stocking your pantry, helping you to get rid of the bad stuff and buy more of the good. It also talks about purchasing and cooking meats, poultry, fish, eggs and substitute eggs, and dairy products, some of which have lots of fat and some of which have very little fat but taste pretty much the same. Tables enable you to compare the fat in various foods so that you can make your own decisions about where you want to cut down on fat.

This part also includes a chapter that tells you how and where to use herbs, spices, and other flavorings, which can make all the difference in lowfat cooking.

## Part III: Over 150 Delicious and Lowfat Recipes Made Easy

The recipe chapters are grouped together in Part III. At the head of each chapter is a little history, sometimes going back thousands of years, so that you know you aren't doing something new by cooking and eating lowfat. Then I talk a little about what you can do to cut down the fat in the particular type of dish discussed in that chapter. So that you're armed with information when you eat out, I list the dishes that are typically high in total fat, saturated fat, and cholesterol, and those that are usually lower in fats and cholesterol.

Finally come the delicious and easy-to-prepare recipes. A header for each recipe helps you know what to expect, such as what it looks and tastes like. At the beginning of each recipe, I list the pots, pans, and other tools you'll need, the number of people the recipe serves, and the number 1, 2, or 3, which tells you about how long it takes to make the dish. A 1 means fast, and a 2 means not so fast. If the recipe takes more than an hour or two or involves marinating or soaking, even if the cooking time is short, I give it a 3.

At the end of each recipe are the nutritional values in each serving: total fat, saturated fat, protein, dietary fiber, carbohydrate, cholesterol, sodium, percentage of calories from fat, and calories. The terrific and exacting Christin Loudon, a registered dietitian who served as the reviewer for this book, used a special computer program called Genesis R&D to make sure that every single recipe falls under the government definition of lowfat, because how could I call my book lowfat and not meet the government definition? You can have confidence in every thing I say — every number, every suggestion — because it all has scientific backing. When I'm stating my opinion, I say so.

At the end of most of the recipes, you also find a lowfat tip, a cooking hint, or information about an ingredient in the recipe that may be of interest to you.

## Part IV: The Part of Tens

Each quick chapter in Part IV gives you tips that make cooking and eating lowfat fun and easy. In this part, I tell you ten ways to lower your fat intake immediately, dispel ten myths about fat, and give you information about resources you can use to expand your knowledge of healthful cooking and eating.

## Appendix: Glossary

If you aren't sure of a term, such as *RACC,* look it up in the glossary. (Who can remember all this scientific jargon?) After someone explained everything to me, it was easy, so I wrote the glossary the easy way (and had my "resident scientist" Christin Loudon check every fact).

## Icons Used in This Book

I use icons aplenty in this book because they are handy visual signals. Look for the following icons:

Lowfat can be easy when you know how. This icon marks tips that make lowfat cooking easier.

These days, everyone can use a few extra minutes. This icon points out time-saving shortcuts.

When you see this icon, beware! (Actually, *beware* means to be aware.) Many items look like they may be low in fat but aren't *necessarily* low in fat, such as some foods marked "Reduced in Fat."

Some things are more important than others. Because no one can remember everything, I mark the most important pieces of information (such as looking for the grams of fat per serving on each food package) with this icon.

A little icon that gives you a big tip for lowering the fat.

I place this icon where you might substitute a different ingredient or throw something together using whatever ingredients you have on hand.

When I tell you a story to illustrate a point, you see this icon.

# *Where to Go from Here*

Enjoy your food to the max. Eat when you're hungry; stop eating when you're full. Eating is great fun — much more so when you don't feel gorged after every meal, a path that can be self-destructive. Changing to a lowfat path is always an adaptive process . . . and a new adventure.

Start your journey at Chapter 1, which explains the lowfat basics. Or head for your kitchen and jump right into some recipes. Where you begin is up to you!

Take small steps and make small changes when changing your eating plan. If you stumble, just get up and go at it again. Welcome to your new path!

# Part I

# Getting Started with Lowfat Eating

The 5th Wave                    By Rich Tennant

Because of his parents' practice of serving lowfat meals by carving melons into the shapes of high-fat foods, it wasn't until college that Dennis discovered that fried chicken didn't come with seeds.

AND WHAT THE HECK IS THIS...?

# In this part . . .

Y ou bought this book, so you must want to make wise decisions about your eating habits. This part provides you with all the basic information you need to know to make the best choices.

I decipher some potentially confusing terms for you — no-fat, high-fat, lowfat, reduced-fat, and so on. So you won't be misled, I tell you the actual fat content of many foods that display these terms on the labels.

Speaking of labels, I also unravel the mysteries of product labeling. Read this part, and you can understand nutrient claims, ingredient lists, and Nutrition Facts panels. Armed with this solid information, you can choose foods that promote health and boost energy.

# Chapter 1

# Where Fat Really Lurks

## In This Chapter

▶ Shedding light on the no-fat, lowfat, so-so fat, and "just how much fat is that?" lingo

▶ Recognizing that all foods have fat, and you need to be alert to those tricky little globules

▶ Fat and cholesterol, that mutually exclusive duo — sometimes

▶ Understanding how dietary fat relates to weight and metabolism

*I*'ve been studying this high-fat, lowfat, no-fat, saturated fat, and cholesterol subject as it relates to good-tasting food for 30 years, and I learn something new every day. But I learned the basics of lowfat eating in an hour or two, and you can, too. Fat can seem confusing, yet it's actually quite simple. After you understand the terms and start reading Nutrition Facts panels on foods, you really do begin to get it.

And I want you to get it. I want you to know how to lower your fat intake, be healthy, and enjoy your food. After all, you should know exactly what you're putting in your mouth. Your body is your life, and probably the only thing you really have a little control over. So find where fat lurks and drive it out — and save that body!

This chapter talks about what fat is and where it's at. You need to know these things because fat is in everything from bananas (minimal) to butter (maximal), and unless you can figure out how much fat is there, you don't know whether it's worth worrying about. With a little sleuthing, you usually can find and remove those pesky, gooey globules. They do you no good if they're in large amounts.

I also explain how fat is most often added to basically healthy foods and that it doesn't need to be there, at least not in the amounts that are added to many common foods and dishes. After reading this book, you'll understand that even the little things count when it comes to fat.

# All That Lingo Can Make You Loco!

The word *lowfat* is easy to understand. What else could it mean but that there isn't much fat in this or that food? In fact, to be called lowfat, a product must have 3 grams of fat or less per labeled serving.

Every day, though, I hear mistaken ideas about what has fat, what has saturated fat, and what has cholesterol. People think that one food is lowfat when it isn't, and that another food isn't lowfat when it is. And no wonder! Food labels can contain a baffling collection of jargon. In addition to the more straightforward terms like *lowfat* and *fat-free,* some labels say such things as *lean, lite,* and *reduced in fat.* "Is reduced in fat also lowfat?" you may ask. "What does *reduced* mean? Reduced from what?"

Most confusing of all are those labels that say what you may think is the same thing in so many different ways. You go to buy a can, jar, box, or frozen entree, and none of the jargon is recognizable. A product that has less than 0.5 grams of fat per serving can legally claim to be fat-free, free of fat, no fat, zero fat, without fat, nonfat, a trivial source of fat, a negligible source of fat, and a dietarily insignificant source of fat. The claims on lowfat products can say "Lowfat," "Low in Fat," "Contains a Small Amount of Fat," "Low Source of Fat," and "Little Fat." Products that have 25 percent less fat than the product they're being compared with might say "Reduced Fat," "Reduced in Fat," "Fat Reduced," "Less Fat," "Lower Fat," or "Lower in Fat." I've seen "No Added Fat," too (which doesn't meet government guidelines) — and of course that plain old word *free,* which isn't government approved but can be used in the name of a product (such as Oscar Mayer Free, which is fat-free, of course).

Why are there so many terms, many of which look like they mean exactly the same thing? Is it really that complicated? No! I'll begin at the beginning because it is really pretty simple after you understand a few basic facts.

# A Simple Exercise in Labels and Fat

The first thing to understand is that even when a label on a food says "Fat-Free," it isn't. When Aunt Bessie advises you, "You need to eat a little fat or you won't be healthy," she's right. But fat is in everything — even radishes, tomatoes, corn, apples, flour, lettuce, artichokes, grapes, and fat-free granola, albeit in trace amounts. Every time you eat, you're eating fat.

*Added* fat is the fat you need to be concerned about. In the United States, chances are you can never get either too little fat or too little protein in your diet. Too little fat, especially, is not the problem.

Take the classic dish Chicken à la King, for example. It's poured over noodles, rice, or biscuits — usually something starchy. All the foods in that delicious traditional sauce, even those cute little green peas, mushrooms, red pimentos, and green peppers, have fat — again, most only in trace amounts.

These vegetables are relatively fat-free, but the sauce for this unkingly dish can contain enormous amounts of fat in the form of cream and butter. This amount is in addition to the chicken breast, which also contains fat. Even the food you pour the sauce over, whether it's rice, potatoes, pasta, toast slices, polenta wedges, crepes, or biscuits, contains fat. (The rice has the least fat, going incrementally up to the biscuits, which, depending upon how they are made and whether you put butter or margarine on them before pouring sauce over them, can contain a whole lot of fat.)

When you're grocery shopping and see an attractively packaged jar of thick, creamy, delicious-looking Chicken à la King sauce with hunks of chicken, pretty red pimentos, flecks of green peppers, several mushroom slices, and maybe even a few peas, you may get hungry. If you're fat-conscious, a little bell goes off, and you may think that this rich, creamy sauce contains lots of fat. You may be right. But you can't know until you read the label.

This particular Chicken à la King may be made with just a few chunks of skinned chicken breast with all visible fat removed, the creamy sauce thickened with cornstarch or flour in evaporated skimmed milk. It may also have a few more pimentos, peas, and mushrooms than usual, and the whole entree may be nearly fat-free.

If the sauce is made with 2 percent milk instead of skim milk and contains just a tad of butter and a few more pieces of chicken, that serving might contain 3 grams of fat (which is still lowfat). But if you eat two or three servings, the Chicken à la King doesn't have only 3 grams of fat anymore. You may be consuming 6 to 9 grams of fat.

Lowfat always means 3 grams or less per labeled serving, regardless of whether it is describing Chicken à la King or Pie à la Mode. That's nice to know. The Nutrition Facts panel on the package label always tells you how much fat the food contains. (See Chapter 2 for more information about the Nutrition Facts panel.)

---

# More color may mean less fat

Look for lots of bright colors in prepared foods. Chances are that the product contains less fat if it's filled with green, red, yellow, and orange vegetables. If a food contains a lot of white stuff that's not rice, pasta, or hard-cooked egg whites, it may be a fat trap.

If you eat three servings of fat-free Chicken à la King, it isn't fat-free anymore. The tiny bits of fat that didn't add up to half a gram in one serving can add up to 1.5 grams in three servings — certainly not high in fat, but no longer fat-free. And if you pour the whole jar of fat-free or lowfat à la King sauce over an extra-large, butter-smothered baked potato or a hefty serving of egg noodles, the dish may not even be lowfat. One serving could contain 8 or 9 grams of fat, depending upon the amount of butter on the potato or the fat content of the noodles.

Even 8 or 9 grams isn't terrible, and the sauce being fat-free helps to keep the calories and overall fat content of the dish under control. But if you buy traditional Chicken à la King, noticing that it contains far fewer naturally lowfat peas, pimentos, and mushrooms and more sauce, and the front label doesn't say "Fat-Free" or "Lowfat," chances are that the sauce is chock-full of butter, cream, and untrimmed chicken. The fat content of one serving of this sauce could be 20 or 30 grams. (See Figure 1-1.)

As you can see, label reading (which Chapter 2 explains in detail) is a must. The Nutrition Facts panel tells you exactly how much fat, cholesterol, vitamins, sodium, and other nutrients are in your Chicken à La King.

The point is that you can eat the dishes you want in all kinds of ways, and food doesn't need to have that much fat to taste good and satisfy you. You can make tradeoffs. For example, you see the difference that one lowfat sauce can make in a whole meal. With a lowfat sauce, you can swing with, say, a great-tasting egg noodle, which is slightly higher in fat than rice.

**Figure 1-1:**
Chicken à la King can be low or high in fat.

# *Adding Cholesterol and Saturated Fat to the Mix*

You may wonder how cholesterol fits into all this. "Is it fat? Are there good and bad types of cholesterol? Can I eat as much 'good' cholesterol as I want?"

*Cholesterol* is an odorless, white, waxy substance that your body needs to build cell walls and make certain hormones. Cholesterol is needed to maintain life itself. When you have too much, either what your body makes (which is rare) or the cumulative amount you eat, it turns into cholesterol plaque, which builds up on your artery walls. The saturated fat you eat causes this cholesterol plaque buildup more than the cholesterol you eat does, but both substances are destructive to most people.

This plaque is cumulative, meaning that you may have collected a little at age 10 and more at age 24 (in the U.S., half of all men and a third of all women at this age have a cholesterol level that is too high). If you don't keep your intake of saturated fat and cholesterol low, this plaque can eventually choke off the tiny arteries that supply blood to your heart (or brain). This is heart and artery disease, from which half a million people each year die prematurely and another million or so are incapacitated. Having a cholesterol test performed gives you some indication of how much cholesterol you have in your blood supply so that you can take appropriate action. A blood cholesterol of over 200 milligrams per deciliter is a risk factor for heart disease, says the National Cholesterol Education Program. See Table 1-1 for more information about recommended cholesterol levels. (Of course, you should consult with your doctor to find the ideal level for you.)

| Table 1-1 | Cholesterol | | |
|-----------|-------------------|-----------|---------------|
| *Risk* | *Total Cholesterol* | *LDL* | *HDL* |
| High | Above 240 | Above 160 | Less than 35 |
| Borderline | 200 to 239 | 130 to 159 | |
| Desirable | Below 200 | Below 130 | Above 60 |

## *Where do cholesterol and saturated fat come from?*

All animals and animal products, including minnows, shrimp, quail, sheep, and aardvarks, have cholesterol. Of these animals, shrimp have the most cholesterol. (I don't know about aardvarks.) You have cholesterol, too; you make it naturally every day right in your liver. You don't need more cholesterol. Your body has all it needs.

All animal products, all fats, and all oils also contain saturated fat in varying amounts. Shrimp contain almost no saturated fat and almost no total fat. Coconut oil has extraordinary amounts, braunschweiger has a lot, and eggs and milk have some.

## Does "good" cholesterol really exist?

If you eat it, no cholesterol is good. Your body makes a good cholesterol called *high density lipoproteins,* or *HDL.* You want HDL in your body because it helps to eliminate the bad cholesterol you eat. The higher your HDL number, the healthier your heart and arteries are, according to most experts, even if your cholesterol level is slightly over the recommended 200. (Be aware that you can have some risk of heart disease even if your cholesterol level is slightly under 200.)

HDL acts like little garbage trucks in your arteries, removing the cholesterol from your blood before it can weasel its way into your arteries, making them narrower. How do you get or make more HDL garbage trucks? Eating little saturated fat and cholesterol and exercising regularly are the known factors that raise HDL. And the exercise usually doesn't have to be much more than brisk walking a couple of miles three or four days a week. However, if you exercise more, you may make more garbage trucks.

## When should I have my cholesterol level checked?

The National Cholesterol Education Program says that all people over age 20 should have their cholesterol checked. I think children should be checked, too. One-fourth of American children over age 12 have a blood cholesterol level that is higher than is considered normal.

### A snack dilemma

Ounce for ounce, shrimp has more cholesterol than red meat. Should you eat it? Your other option, a package of cookies, sports a label that says "Cholesterol Free" (but not "Fat-Free" or "Lowfat"). You are hungry and want to dip that succulent shrimp in some cocktail sauce for a yummy snack. But the sugary soft cookies look so good with chocolate oozing from the chips, crispy on the edge. Which to eat, cookies or shrimp?

Eat the shrimp. The saturated fat in the cookies has a greater effect on your cholesterol level because saturated fat is more important than cholesterol in cholesterol plaque buildup. But don't eat too much shrimp – it's a better choice, but it should be eaten only occasionally.

Have your cholesterol checked by your doctor after you fast for eight hours so that you can get your HDL reading, too. Be sure to get your own copy of your results. Although levels are established, not all doctors are informed in interpreting them, and some labs aren't up-to-date. My own lab checked my HDL reading of 93 under the "abnormal" or "too high" column. You *want* your HDL number to be high.

## Can I avoid dietary cholesterol altogether?

Yes! Some people eat no cholesterol as a matter of preference. Vegans consume no cholesterol because they eat no animal products at all, including even gelatin and Worcestershire sauce, both of which contain animal products. A small amount of dietary cholesterol is okay for most people, but researchers have found that vegans and Seventh-Day Adventists (who eat no meat but, unlike vegans, do eat dairy) tend to live longer and have significantly less heart disease, which can mean better health and a better quality of life. Experts who do studies, like the leaders of the Framingham study that has tracked thousands of men for decades, now say that high-saturated-fat and high-cholesterol diets lead to more heart disease, and that reducing saturated fat and cholesterol intake leads to less heart disease.

What is really confusing is that some people can eat all the saturated fat and cholesterol they want with no cholesterol plaque buildup. Who doesn't have an Uncle Harry or a Cousin Martha who ate four steaks and at least six eggs, smoked a pack of cigarillos, and drank a fifth of Scotch every day for 80 years and lived to be 95? But this situation really is rare. Most people need to keep their saturated fat and cholesterol intake low because doing so tends to decrease the risk of premature heart disease.

A diet low in total fat, saturated fat, and cholesterol is always the first line of defense for heart disease and the first line of defense for weight control.

# Debating over Trans Fatty Acids

Trans fatty acids are formed when oils are partially hydrogenated during the process of hydrogenation. This process chemically changes oils (which are liquids at room temperature) into solid fats and changes the mixture into a saturated fat. Trans fatty acids are found in foods that contain hydrogenated oils or partially hydrogenated oils in their ingredient lists. Sources of trans fatty acids may include margarines and baked goods; the amount of trans fatty acids varies depending on how hydrogenated the fat is.

## A few words about moderation

Many times I hear a friend say, "I don't eat lowfat. I don't need to. I eat in moderation — fat, meat, oils, eggs, cheese, desserts, you name it. I eat them all in moderation."

Moderation is neither a good nor a workable word when it comes to food. It's relative and can't be trusted to really mean anything. What *you* think is moderation may not be moderation to your doctor. The following figure shows some examples of moderation that do *not* lead to good health.

Instead, read the Nutrition Facts panel on each product you consider purchasing for information about fat and other nutritional values so that you know what you're putting in your body. Chapter 2 explains how to interpret all that label information so that you can make smart (or at least informed!) choices.

Because food labels usually do not list trans fatty acid content, the following can help you control your trans fatty acid intake:

- ✔ Check ingredient lists on packages and avoid foods that contain vegetable shortening or partially hydrogenated oil.
- ✔ Look for lower-fat margarines, snack foods, and baked goods. Tub margarines are lower in trans fatty acids than stick margarines.
- ✔ In place of butter, margarine, or shortening, use olive or canola oil when possible.

Some research studies show that trans fatty acids can raise blood cholesterol levels as much as saturated fat does. Other researchers argue that the evidence is inconclusive and that trans fatty acids are not worse than saturated fat. Whatever the case, if you eat a lowfat diet, you are consuming less trans fatty acids.

# *Metabolizing It All*

It is primarily excessive dietary calories that people eat, usually in the form of fat, that cause them to become fat or gain weight. But people *metabolize,* or process, food differently — some at a high rate, some at a lower rate. You hear things like, "She has a slow metabolism," presumably meaning that she eats a radish and thinks she'll gain weight.

*Metabolism* is actually the sum of the physical and chemical processes in a cell or organism, in this case the human body, by which complex substances are synthesized and broken down and growth and energy-production are sustained. In other words, metabolism is the process that changes the food you eat into a form your body can use. Metabolism of food is required for maintaining all human and animal life.

Food contains calories, and metabolizing food takes calories. Dietary fat has more calories than the other energy-providing nutrients, like protein and carbohydrates, and it takes fewer calories to make body fat from drinking a high-fat milkshake than it does to make body fat from eating, say, celery. In other words, the milkshake goes from your lips to your hips in a flash. The celery, however, is thrashed about, fiber removed, pushed here and there, smooshed through the intestines, more stuff removed, and the rest eliminated, all of which takes quite a few calories to metabolize and then hang on your hips.

Now you know why you should immediately lower your fat intake if you're not watching it already. Whether you want to maintain good health, reduce your weight, put off heart disease, lower your cholesterol level, or reverse heart disease, lowfat eating always makes good sense. High-fat eating almost never does.

# Chapter 2

# Reading Labels

• • • • • • • • • • • • • • • • • • • • • • • • • • • • • • • • • • • • • • •

• • • • • • • • • • • • • • • • • • • • • • • • • • • • • • • • • • • • • • •

*1f the box has no label,*
*Keep it off your table.*
*If you can't read the fat,*
*Who knows where it's at?*

My poem is true. If you don't know how much fat is in, say, a bran muffin, you don't realize that when you buy a big, hot, fragrant bran muffin from the corner bakery and thoroughly enjoy every bite, you may be ingesting 10 grams of fat and 390 calories. If you miss lunch and snack on two or three muffins, along with a few cups of steaming hot coffee with hazelnut cream and a tablespoon or so of sugar, your snack can easily add up to close to 100 fat grams and more than 1,000 calories.

If you are female and eat about 2,000 calories a day, you have just eaten more than half your daily calories in a single snack. No wonder gaining weight is so easy, and all because you didn't have a few facts. Reading the labels on the package would tell you that the muffin is full of fat — and more.

## The Labels Tell All

Labels not only list exactly how much fat a product contains — including saturated fat (the fat that is associated with heart and artery disease) — but they also tell you the number of calories and the amount of dietary fiber, total carbohydrate, sodium, sugars, vitamins, minerals, and protein the product contains. They include the percentage of the daily values for some of the nutrients.

Labels can tell you that a better snack is air-popped popcorn, which contains one-fourth the calories and one-tenth the fat of the muffin. Even with a little butter-type coating and salt, popcorn isn't as high in fat or calories as the muffin, and you usually can control some of the fat and salt on popcorn. Eating popcorn at least exercises your jaws, keeping your teeth healthy and firmly embedded. Drink some orange or tomato juice with the popcorn, and you increase the nutritional value of your snack. The labels tell it all — if you know how to read them.

## Most Products Carry Labels

Except for fruits, vegetables, fresh meats, and other products packaged within the store, such as store-made deli and bakery items, all foods must have labels.

If a muffin comes commercially packaged from the supermarket instead of from the corner bakery (which doesn't have to tell you what it puts in its products), it boasts many different labels with copious amounts of useful information. These labels must conform to strict government guidelines. You may even find several different kinds of muffins, enabling you to select the type that contains the ingredients and fat content you're comfortable with.

In a few cases, bakery goods do have labels. Shop owners recognize that consumers often prefer the freshness and ambiance of a bakery, but they want information, too. If your bakery doesn't provide nutrition information, let the management know that labels are valuable to you.

## Confronting the Front Label

The first label is on the front of the package and tells you what the package contains — for example, bran muffins. One muffin package you pick up may be called "Jones's Old Fashioned Bran Muffins." Jones is the manufacturer's name. Old Fashioned could be a brand, with several different products using the same brand name. The Jones company may also offer "Jones's Old Fashioned English Muffins," or doughnuts, or corn bread, for example.

The manufacturer's name and the brand name are often identical. For example, Campbell's is the name of a manufacturer, and Campbell's is also the brand name of a line of soups. Sub-brands (for example, Campbell's V8 Juice) may also be available. Special designations, such as "Spicy Hot" or "Low Sodium," may also appear on the label to tell you which of the several types of V8 you are selecting.

The Jones company may claim health benefits on the label, such as, "Jones's Reduced-Fat Bran Muffins." A label on the front could also read, "Contains No Cholesterol." These claims, as well as the phrases *fat-free, low sodium, no saturated fat,* and many others, are government controlled, and the products have to conform to strict guidelines. The manufacturer can't claim that a product is "Reduced in Fat" if it doesn't meet the guidelines. And if a label reads, "Contains No Cholesterol," the product must also meet specified criteria for saturated fat content (2 grams or less per labeled serving).

## Claims

Companies can make health claims and nutrient claims on food packages. A *health claim* is a food label message. This message defines the relationship between a nutrient — such as fat, calcium, or fiber — and a disease — such as cancer or heart disease. A health claim on a package may read as follows:

- ✔ "While many factors affect heart disease, diets low in saturated fat and cholesterol may reduce the risk of this disease."

- ✔ "Lowfat diets rich in fruits and vegetables (foods that are low in fat and may contain dietary fiber, vitamin A, and vitamin C) may reduce risk for some types of cancer, a disease associated with many factors. Broccoli is high in vitamins A and C and is a good source of dietary fiber."

*Nutrient claims* usually include the words free or reduced/less. These claims can refer to calories, fats, saturated fats, cholesterol, and sodium (which can also be called *very low*). Sugar can be associated with only the words free or reduced/less.

## When reduced fat means high fat

Knowing what front label terms mean is important. The word *lowfat* can't be used indiscriminately on a food label — by government definition, it means that a product contains 3 grams or less of total fat per labeled serving and per RACC, or Reference Amount Customarily Consumed (serving sizes vary depending upon the product).

To qualify as *reduced fat,* a product must contain 25 percent less fat than the food it's being compared to. For example, if a regular Jones's Old Fashioned Bran Muffin has 20 grams of fat, the "Reduced Fat" version can contain no more than 15 grams of fat. But lowering the fat content of one muffin from an incredibly high fat 20 grams to 15 grams doesn't mean much. The product is still high in fat, although "Reduced Fat" legally appears right on the front of the package. This labeling can be confusing.

The term *reduced fat* is the most misleading item on the label. Many people misinterpret it to mean that the product is low in fat when it may not be and often isn't. Look at the label for a concrete number of fat grams per serving. The amount of fat removed is a percentage of the amount of fat that was originally in the product, not a number you can use to determine how much fat the food contains.

## What other front label words mean

The word *low* may be used on foods that meet government guidelines. Table 2-1 defines other label words as they apply per serving of food.

| Table 2-1 | Definitions of Label Terms |
| --- | --- |
| *Term* | *Definition (Based on Labeled Serving and RACC)* |
| Lowfat | 3 grams or less total fat |
| Low saturated fat | 1 gram or less saturated fat and 15 percent or less calories from saturated fat |
| Low sodium | 140 milligrams or less sodium |
| Low cholesterol | 20 milligrams or less cholesterol and 2 grams or less saturated fat |
| Low calorie | 40 calories or less |
| Lean | Less than 10 grams fat, less than 4.5 grams saturated fat, and less than 95 milligrams cholesterol (describes meat, game meat, poultry, and seafood only) |
| Extra lean | Less than 5 grams fat, less than 2 grams saturated fat, and less than 95 milligrams cholesterol (describes meat, game meat, poultry, and seafood only) |

## Bottom grazing

The bottom of the front label displays the product weight in ounces and/or pounds (such as 1 pound, 2 ounces, or sometimes 18 ounces). The weight is also given in grams. One pound equals about 453 grams, and 1 ounce equals about 28 grams.

If a package contains four muffins and the weight totals 18 ounces, each muffin weighs about 4$^1$/$_2$ ounces — pretty big for a muffin. This large size can mean lots of fat and calories. If you check the label on the back of the package (the Nutrition Facts panel, which I talk about later in this chapter), you may find that each muffin contains 390 calories and 10 grams of fat. You can find good information on every side of a package if you know what to look for.

# Now for More Substance: The Ingredients Label

Another important label on the package, usually on the back, lists the exact ingredients. Ingredients appear in order according to how much is in the product according to weight. Ingredients at the beginning of the list (which are usually preservatives) make up the biggest percentage of the food by weight. Those at the end of the list (which are usually preservatives) are present in smaller amounts. In a muffin package, sugar may be listed first, telling you that the largest single ingredient in the muffins is sugar.

After getting into the habit of reading ingredient lists, I got lots of surprises. For example, the first ingredient in my three kinds of mustard is vinegar, then water, and then mustard. I always thought mustard was mustard. I also discovered that some mustards contain egg yolks.

My browsing brought to light that dry crackers contain fat, sometimes lots of it. But most pretzels have no fat. I found that anchovies are in Worcestershire sauce, no oysters are in oyster sauce, and no butter is in apple butter. Some potato chips are fried in high-saturated-fat oils. Cream sherry contains no cream, but Irish cream does. Ketchup contains sugar. Most mincemeat for pies has no meat (some contain meat suet, which is 100 percent fat). My taco shells contain lime (not the juice but the kind you put on lawns, which I investigated and found was perfectly safe, especially in such small amounts). Reading ingredient lists can tell you a great deal about the food you are putting in your mouth.

## Sugar by any other name . . .

Sugar is often listed in the ingredient lists of baked goods in several ways, which can be deceiving. Molasses, honey, maple syrup, corn syrup, fructose, glucose, sucrose, and fruit concentrate (fructose) are all forms of sugar. When combinations of these ingredients are present in products, the total amount of sugar can be substantial. You may not want that much sugar, so read ingredient lists carefully.

## Fat

Fat can also be listed several ways. Hydrogenated safflower oil, partially hydrogenated cottonseed oil, palm oil, canola oil, walnut oil, grapeseed oil, almond oil, tallow, suet, margarine, butter, and lard are forms of fat, and others exist, too. Fat has more calories than any other food, so it pays to keep an eye out for fats in the ingredient list.

# The Newest Member of the Label Club: The Nutrition Facts Panel

The Nutrition Facts panel is another — and the newest — important label component. It is usually located on the back or the side of a package. Look for a black border with a thick, horizontal bar across the middle. The Nutrition Facts panel gives you enormous amounts of useful information, such as how many servings are in the package, the size of each serving, how many calories each serving contains, and especially how much total fat the food contains.

Getting a requirement for accurate and useful nutrition labels on packaged foods in the U.S. took a 1990 act of Congress, lots of pressure from public interest lobbying groups, such as the Center for Science in the Public Interest, headed by Dr. Michael Jacobson, and advocacy by Dr. David Kessler (who was the director of the Food and Drug Administration at the time). Some food manufacturers and producers were reluctant and fought the measure, but the labels provide extremely useful information and are necessary for consumers.

## The regulators

Labeling, like ingredient lists and package claims, is carefully regulated in the U.S. both by the United States Department of Agriculture (USDA) and by the Food and Drug Administration (FDA), a complicated and sometimes overlapping procedure. One food may fall under the jurisdiction of one agency, another food, a different agency.

For example, different agencies regulate pizza. A cheese pizza that doesn't contain any meat is regulated by the FDA; a pepperoni pizza, because it contains meat, is regulated by the USDA. However, all food manufacturers and producers must conform to strict guidelines, and both agencies make sure that manufacturers follow these guidelines.

## Ten reasons to read labels

✔ You have an accurate idea of what is in the food you eat.

✔ You can control your fat and saturated fat intake.

✔ You can make a knowledgeable decision about buying cheesecake.

✔ You can switch foods on the kids and spouse by dumping the high-fat, 22 gram ice cream and filling the empty carton with lowfat, 3 gram vanilla praline frozen yogurt.

✔ You now realize that just because a product doesn't have fat, it can still have a gazillion calories.

✔ Fiber takes on a new meaning when you know how much to look for.

✔ You can eat the candy bar that has the least fat and feel a little less guilty.

✔ You can now buy Dove chocolate sauce, which contains only 4 grams of fat in 2 tablespoons, or Hershey's chocolate syrup, which has no fat.

✔ You can purchase lower-fat Brie (called reduced-fat Brie).

✔ You know more than you ever thought you wanted to — which can be good for your health.

## *Anatomy of a cereal label*

Even on similar cereal boxes, the Nutrition Facts panel data are different, but they all offer the same general information. If a nutrient is in the food, the producers usually must list it and the corresponding amount. (They don't have to list magnesium or potassium, among other nutrients.) Certain nutrients are required; others are voluntary.

Figure 2-1 shows Nutrition Facts panels from three boxes of cereal.

### *The serving size game*

Cereal labeling is complicated because of regulations. It took a while to get the government to use common household measurements that everybody can relate to, such as $^1/_2$ cup (instead of 2 ounces).

You can find the serving size at the top of the cereal Nutrition Facts panel. Although the U.S. government standardized serving sizes for better comparisons of values and nutrients, serving sizes for cereal still differ slightly. Some cereals weigh just a little, such as a puffed cereal, and others weigh a great deal, such as granola, so the serving size is smaller. Oatmeal is in its own category because it's unprepared. A $^1/_2$ cup serving of dry cereal such as oatmeal, when cooked, is close to 1 cup.

Weight in grams is listed in parentheses next to the serving size on the Nutrition Facts panel, just as it is on the front label.

Corn flakes

**Nutrition Facts**
Serving Size 1 CUP (27g)
Servings Per Container about 25

| Amount Per Serving | 1 Cup Cereal | Cereal with 1/2 cup Skim Milk |
|---|---|---|
| Calories | 100 | 140 |
| Calories from Fat | 0 | 0 |

| | % Daily Value* | |
|---|---|---|
| **Total Fat** 0g | 0% | 1% |
| Saturated Fat 0g | 0% | 1% |
| **Cholesterol** 0mg | 0% | 1% |
| **Sodium** 280mg | 12% | 14% |
| **Potassium** 25mg | 1% | 6% |
| **Total Carbohydrate** 23g | 8% | 10% |
| Dietary Fiber 1g | 4% | 4% |
| Sugars 2g | | |
| **Protein** 2g | | |

| Vitamin A | 25% | 30% |
|---|---|---|
| Vitamin C | 25% | 25% |
| Calcium | 0% | 15% |
| Iron | 15% | 15% |
| Vitamin D | 10% | 20% |
| Thiamin | 25% | 25% |
| Riboflavin | 25% | 35% |
| Niacin | 25% | 25% |
| Vitamin B6 | 25% | 25% |
| Folate | 25% | 25% |
| Zinc | 10% | 10% |

\* Percent Daily Values are based on a 2,000 calorie diet.
Your daily values may be higher or lower depending
on your calorie needs:

| | Calories: | 2,000 | 2,500 |
|---|---|---|---|
| Total Fat | Less than | 65g | 80g |
| Sat Fat | Less than | 20g | 25g |
| Cholesterol | Less than | 300mg | 300mg |
| Sodium | Less than | 2,400mg | 2,400mg |
| Potassium | | 3,500mg | 3,500mg |
| Total Carbohydrate | | 300g | 375g |
| Dietary Fiber | | 25g | 30g |

Calories per gram:
Fat 9 • Carbohydrate 4 • Protein 4

**INGREDIENTS:** CORN, SUGAR, MALT SYRUP,
SALT, CORN SYRUP, SODIUM ASCORBATE
(VITAMIN C), NIACINAMIDE (NIACIN),
REDUCED IRON, ZINC OXIDE, VITAMIN A
(PALMITATE), PYRIDOXINE HYDROCHLORIDE
(VITAMIN B6), RIBOFLAVIN (VITAMIN B2),
THIAMIN MONONITRATE (VITAMIN B1),
FOLIC ACID AND VITAMIN D.

DISTRIBUTED BY SAFEWAY INC.
HEAD OFFICE OAKLAND, CA 94660
PRODUCT OF U.S.A.

100% GUARANTEED OR YOUR MONEY BACK.
When writing to us, please include the box top
with the embossed code and write to:
Safeway Inc., P.O. Box 28846,
Oakland, CA 94604-8846.

Whole Grain Total

**Nutrition Facts**
Serving Size 3/4 cup (30g)
Servings Per Container About 11

| Amount Per Serving | Whole Grain Total | with 1/2 cup skim milk |
|---|---|---|
| Calories | 110 | 150 |
| Calories from Fat | 10 | 10 |

| | % Daily Value** | |
|---|---|---|
| **Total Fat** 1g* | 1% | 2% |
| Saturated Fat 0g | 0% | 0% |
| **Cholesterol** 0mg | 0% | 1% |
| **Sodium** 200mg | 8% | 11% |
| **Potassium** 100mg | 3% | 9% |
| **Total Carbohydrate** 24g | 8% | 10% |
| Dietary Fiber 3g | 10% | 10% |
| Sugars 5g | | |
| Other Carbohydrate 16g | | |
| **Protein** 3g | | |

| Vitamin A | 25% | 30% |
|---|---|---|
| Vitamin C | 100% | 100% |
| Calcium | 25% | 40% |
| Iron | 100% | 100% |
| Vitamin D | 10% | 25% |
| Vitamin E | 100% | 100% |
| Thiamin | 100% | 100% |
| Riboflavin | 100% | 110% |
| Niacin | 100% | 100% |
| Vitamin B6 | 100% | 100% |
| Folic Acid | 100% | 100% |
| Vitamin B12 | 100% | 110% |
| Pantothenic Acid | 100% | 100% |
| Phosphorus | 20% | 30% |
| Magnesium | 6% | 10% |
| Zinc | 100% | 100% |
| Copper | 4% | 4% |

*Amount in Cereal. A serving of cereal plus skim milk
provides 1g fat, less than 5mg cholesterol, 260mg sodium,
300mg potassium, 30g carbohydrate (11g sugars) and
7g protein.
**Percent Daily Values are based on a 2,000 calorie diet.
Your daily values may be higher or lower depending on
your calorie needs:

| | Calories | 2,000 | 2,500 |
|---|---|---|---|
| Total Fat | Less than | 65g | 80g |
| Sat Fat | Less than | 20g | 25g |
| Cholesterol | Less than | 300mg | 300mg |
| Sodium | Less than | 2,400mg | 2,400mg |
| Potassium | | 3,500mg | 3,500mg |
| Total Carbohydrate | | 300g | 375g |
| Dietary Fiber | | 25g | 30g |

INGREDIENTS: WHOLE GRAIN WHEAT, SUGAR, WHOLE GRAIN
BROWN RICE, TRICALCIUM AND DICALCIUM PHOSPHATE
(PROVIDES CALCIUM), SALT, CORN SYRUP, VITAMINC (SODIUM
ASCORBATE), ZINC AND IRON (MINERAL NUTRIENTS), VIT-
AMIN E (TOCOPHERYL ACETATE), TRISODIUM PHOSPHATE,
A B VITAMIN (NIACINAMIDE), A B VITAMIN CALCIUM PAN-
TOTHENATE), VITAMIN B6 (PYRIDOXINE HYDROCHLORIDE),
VITAMIN B2 (RIBOFLAVIN), VITAMIN B1 (THIAMIN MONO-
NITRATE), VITAMIN A (PALMITATE), A VITAMIN (FOLIC ACID),
VITAMIN B12, VITAMIN D. FRESHNESS PRESERVED BY BHT.

Oatmeal

**Nutrition Facts**
Serving Size 1/2 cup (40g dry)
Servings Per Container about 30

| Amount Per Serving | Cereal | Cereal with 1/2 cup Skim Milk |
|---|---|---|
| Calories | 150 | 190 |
| Calories from Fat | 25 | 30 |

| | % Daily Value** | |
|---|---|---|
| **Total Fat** 3g* | 5% | 5% |
| Saturated Fat 0.5g | 3% | 3% |
| **Sodium** 0mg | 0% | 3% |
| **Total Carbohydrate** 27g | 9% | 11% |
| Dietary Fiber 4g | 16% | 16% |
| Soluble Fiber 2g | | |
| Insoluble Fiber 2g | | |
| Other Carbohydrate 23g | | |
| **Protein** 5g | | |

| Iron | 10% | 10% |
|---|---|---|
| Thiamin | 15% | 20% |
| Riboflavin | 2% | 15% |
| Folate | 4% | 6% |
| Pantothenic Acid | 4% | 8% |
| Phosphorus | 15% | 30% |
| Magnesium | 10% | 15% |
| Zinc | 8% | 10% |
| Copper | 8% | 8% |

Not a significant source of cholesterol, sugars, vitamin
A, vitamin C and calcium.

*Amount in cereal. One half cup skim milk contributes an additional
40 calories, less than 5mg cholesterol, 65mg sodium, 6g total carbohydrate (6g sugars) and 4g protein.
**Percent Daily Values are based on a 2,000 calorie diet. Your daily
values may be higher or lower depending on your calorie needs:

| | Calories: | 2,000 | 2,500 |
|---|---|---|---|
| Total Fat | Less than | 65g | 80g |
| Sat Fat | Less than | 20g | 25g |
| Cholesterol | Less than | 300mg | 300mg |
| Sodium | Less than | 2,400mg | 2,400mg |
| Total Carbohydrate | | 300g | 375g |
| Dietary Fiber | | 25g | 30g |

Calories per gram:
Fat 9 • Carbohydrate 4 • Protein 4

**INGREDIENTS:** 100% ROLLED OATS.

**Figure 2-1:**
Nutrition Facts panels from the boxes of three popular cereals: oatmeal, corn flakes, and Whole Grain Total.

## Additions to the realm

You can find another practical addition to the cereal information. Cereal panels provide values for the cereal with and without milk. Because cereal companies are now more health conscious, the values on the panel are for skim milk, not whole milk. The amount of milk they use is the same on all three packages in Figure 2-1, 1/2 cup per serving.

Another reason for the manufacturer to add skim milk to the Nutrition Facts panel is because the addition boosts the cereal's calcium, thiamin, riboflavin, and a few other values slightly. (Skim milk has slightly more calcium than whole milk.)

You may notice that, of the three in the figure, only the oatmeal is "pure" cereal. The other types all have added vitamins, malt syrup, and corn syrup; the second ingredient on both dry cereal packages is sugar. The panels also list folic acid (or folate) and pantothenic acid, which sound terrible but are actually only vitamins.

## When a serving isn't a serving

You need to examine the serving sizes on labels, because they may not equal the amount you're used to eating. You can still eat a larger or smaller portion, but you should adjust the numbers. The serving amount may be far too small to be realistic, or just too small for an active male weighing 240 pounds who needs 2,500 or even 3,000 calories a day instead of 2,000.

Serving sizes are based on food consumption studies. Manufacturers can make larger servings, though, if they adhere to certain criteria. For example, the standard serving size for a muffin is 2 ounces, but some manufacturers make one-serving muffins that weigh 4 ounces, which are probably too large. And I've seen bagels that weigh 6 ounces, almost the size of a small loaf of bread. On the other hand, a whipped cream label that defines a serving as 2 tablespoons may be a little illusory, because few people add just 2 tablespoons of whipped cream. One-fourth cup, which is 4 tablespoons, is more like it, at least for me.

To give you another example of misleading serving sizes, I noticed that the label for Pasta Alfredo Broccoli and Chicken frozen dinner entree said that it contained two servings and weighed 13 ounces. However, when I heated it and sat down to eat, the nice, plump, frozen stuff, which looked bigger on the picture and in the package, seemed to melt and flatten with all the sauce. Little actual food remained; much of the content was liquid. The total amount of food — noodles, broccoli, a few bits of chicken, and lots of sauce — measured just over $1\frac{1}{2}$ cups. It was supposed to be 2 cups.

The Nutrition Facts panel on the back of the package said that the total fat, per serving, was 24 grams and 410 calories. To get an accurate measurement of fat and calorie content ( plus the other nutritional values) for the amount I ate, I needed to multiply the listed totals by two (48 grams of fat and 820 calories). Wow! And I was still hungry.

By eating these kinds of processed, ready-made, often very high-fat, high-calorie, high-sodium foods, I can easily eat more than 3,000 calories and 3,000 milligrams of sodium a day, far too many for my 5'1" height and petite bone structure. Knowing what's in a package lets you know what you're eating and can help you keep fat and calories within desired limits.

# The members of the panel

The top of the Nutrition Facts panel shows the number of calories in the product, as well as the number of calories from fat. Then you find a bold black line followed by the total fat and saturated fat content. Sometimes, the panel provides totals for polyunsaturated fat and monounsaturated fat (these amounts are not mandatory). The listing must include sodium, even if sodium is not present in the product. An entry for total carbohydrate is mandatory. Dietary fiber is listed only if present. The soluble and insoluble fiber content may be included. Information about sugars and protein content follows on the label. If cholesterol isn't in the product, it doesn't have to be listed. (These rules are very complicated. I've just tried to give you an overview here.)

After another bold black line, you can find the names of the nutrients in the product with the corresponding nutritional values. However, the following totals are mandatory:

- ✔ Vitamins A and C (percentage only)
- ✔ Calcium and iron (percentage only)

In some cases, if there's an insignificant amount, it may not be shown on the label.

Most values are listed in grams (g); sodium and cholesterol appear in milligrams (mg). Calories are a unit of measurement, so they don't have a designation after them. Most people are pretty familiar with what calorie numbers mean.

## The big picture: percent daily values

The percent daily values (%DV) on the Nutrition Facts panel tell you what percentage of each nutrient you've eaten in the food, based on 100 percent for one day. For example, if the label says 30% DV for vitamin A, you've consumed 30 percent of the USRDI (United States Recommended Daily Intake) of vitamin A you need for the day in that product.

The percent daily values listed on the Nutrition Facts label for fat, saturated fat, and total carbohydrate are based on a 2,000-calorie-a-day diet. The totals for cholesterol, sodium, vitamins and minerals are static numbers.

If the calcium content in Total cereal is listed as 40 percent of the USRDI, or 1,000 milligrams (far right number on the Nutrition Facts panel in Figure 2-1), $\frac{1}{2}$ cup of Total and skim milk gives you 40 percent of the calcium you need. The oatmeal panel doesn't even list calcium, because oatmeal isn't a significant source. Although the corn flakes panel says that the flakes contain no calcium, you get 15 percent of the USRDI when you add milk.

# Changing an apple, or mixing labeled and nonlabeled foods

Many people know that a plain, pretty red apple, which doesn't have a label, is fairly low in calories (it contains about 100 calories). Now come the additions.

A sweetened baked apple is a little higher in calories because it also contains brown sugar and perhaps a sprinkle of chopped walnuts and is often served with a little cream or lowfat creamer. Now the apple provides about 200 calories.

A piece of apple strudel with butter-brushed layers of filo dough, pecans, and butter topping is quite a bit higher in calories, closer to 400. The additional calories are due, in part, to the nuts and butter.

The whopper of all apple dishes is a nice, big serving of thick double-crusted deep-dish apple pie topped with two scoops of Häagen-Dazs Vanilla Ice Cream and a wedge of Cheddar cheese — over 1,000 calories and 60 grams of fat in one serving.

Using the numbers on the packages, you can make some knowledgeable decisions about what you should eat. For example, you may want to select the baked apple and some Häagen-Dazs Lowfat Vanilla Ice Cream. Bakers may want to make a deep-dish tart apple pie with only a top crust, or individual miniature apple pies with the only pastry being a carved apple on top.

### Fat, more fat, and calories from fat

The calories from fat number is of disputable value but is interesting to know. All the calories in olive oil are from fat, but that doesn't mean that you must never use olive oil. Adding up your calories from fat, and especially total calories, over a week or month is more important. (And adding up fat grams is probably more meaningful than trying to make wise food choices based on the calories from fat.) The American Heart Association recommends that people eat no more than 30 percent of their calories from fat. Other sources suggest that the number should be lower, from 10 to 25 percent.

Paying attention to the calories from fat number *can* tell you when avoiding a certain food may be a good idea. For example, if a product provides 250 calories and 200 are from fat, you know that 80 percent of the calories are from fat, and the product probably offers little nutritive value. High-fat cheeses do provide nutrients, but the fat content is still detrimental if you eat cheese often.

You can get the same nutritive value, including calcium and protein, from lowfat cheese.

### Saturated fat, polyunsaturated fat, monounsaturated fat, and cholesterol

Saturated fat, polyunsaturated fat, monounsaturated fat, and cholesterol are closely connected with heart and artery disease. Two of them, saturated fat and cholesterol, are mandatory listings on the Nutrition Facts panel (but only if the product contains them) because they are so important to your health.

Yet many people may understand that dietary cholesterol — what they eat in foods like shrimp and eggs — and the cholesterol that accumulates in their bloodstream and causes narrowing of the arteries are different. There is a connection but a much stronger connection with the amount of saturated fat in your diet.

Eating saturated fat (or more accurately, saturated fatty acids) stimulates your body's production of low-density lipoproteins, or LDL (for "bad" cholesterol). The body mistakenly makes more of its own cholesterol. That cholesterol, and some of the dietary cholesterol, ends up in forms that accumulate on arterial walls.

Saturated fat is found mainly in animal products, especially beef, pork, poultry skin, whole milk, cream, cheese, and butter. Some vegetable oils, such as coconut, palm, and palm kernel oil, also contain saturated fat.

The other two types of fats, polyunsaturated fat and monounsaturated fat apparently neither cause nor exacerbate heart disease, although they are filled with calories and cause weight gain just as saturated fat does.

### Salt and sodium

Though the ingredients list says salt, the Nutrition Facts panel says sodium. Why use two different words? Salt is 40 percent sodium and 60 percent chloride. Sodium is a component of salt. The sodium content of a food may not just come from the salt. It may also come from sodium found naturally, such as in that found in celery.

### Dietary fiber and carbohydrates

A daily intake of 25 to 30 grams of fiber from oat bran, fruits (such as pears, apples, and grapefruit or orange chunks), peas, dried beans, lentils, carrots, and barley works chemically to reduce the absorption of certain substances into the bloodstream and may lower cholesterol.

Try to keep carbohydrates under 90 grams per meal, depending on your calorie level. Carbohydrates are usually 50 to 60 percent of a person's calorie intake. Often when people lower fat consumption, they raise their intake of carbohydrates by eating foods such as lowfat pasta, beans, bread, potatoes, and rice. If those carbs contain a lot of calories and people eat large portions or put fatty things on them, people gain weight.

### Other stuff, like hydrogenated

The term *hydrogenated* means that hydrogen has been added to the product to artificially harden fats. Hydrogenation causes fat, even largely unsaturated fat, such as soybean oil, to become saturated and solid at room temperature. Still, most hydrogenated or partially hydrogenated products, such as margarine, contain far fewer saturated fats than butter, which is not hydrogenated.

# How Label Reading Can Help You Eat Less Fat

If you understand the Nutrition Facts panels on the foods you eat, you can lower your fat intake immediately. Look at a whole day's meals and snacks. Here's what you may have during a regular day.

### Daily menu number 1

**Breakfast:**
Breakfast cereal
Milk
White toast with butter or margarine and preserves
Coffee with cream

**Lunch:**
Chicken salad on croissant with mayonnaise
Potato chips
Cole slaw
Carrot cake
Iced coffee with sugar and cream

**Afternoon Snack:**
Oatmeal cookies, 2
Apple
Coffee with cream

*(continued)*

### Daily menu number 2

**Breakfast:**
High-fiber, lowfat cereal
Skim milk
Whole grain toast with fat-free spray and preserves
Coffee with liquid fat-free non-dairy creamer

**Lunch:**
Chicken breast sandwich, 1 slice chicken, plenty of lettuce and tomato, on whole grain bread with fat-free spread
Pretzels
Cole slaw with lowfat dressing
Sorbet with fruit on top
Iced coffee with sugar substitute and liquid fat-free non-dairy creamer

**Afternoon Snack:**
Fat-free oatmeal cookies, 2
Apple
Coffee with liquid fat-free non-dairy creamer

*(continued)*

## *Daily menu number 1*

**Dinner:**
Braised beef over pasta, with carrots in butter
Garlic toast, 2 pieces
Caesar salad
Cherry pie à la mode
Coffee with cream

**Evening Snack:**
Butter toffee candy, 1 piece

*(continued)*

## *Daily menu number 2*

**Dinner:**
2 or 3 ounces braised lean beef over pasta, with carrots with fat-free butter spray
Garlic toast with fat-free butter spray
Caesar salad with half the dressing or lowfat dressing
Cherry pudding with fat-free topping
Coffee with liquid fat-free non-dairy creamer

**Evening Snack:**
Sour balls

Menu 1 doesn't look too bad: an apple, coffee, a little beef, oatmeal cookies, and pasta. This sample menu is actually pretty typical of the way most people eat each day, especially if they eat out. You may rationalize that the beef wasn't too fatty, the scoop of ice cream was small, and you didn't eat the crust on the pie. But look at Table 2-2, which gives the fat, calorie, and other totals for these foods. How easily the fat adds up!

Compare the totals for the lower-fat, higher-fiber, lower-sodium Menu 2 with the totals for the "pretty typical" day.

| Table 2-2 | Daily Totals for Menus 1 and 2 | |
| --- | --- | --- |
| | *Daily Menu 1* | *Daily Menu 2* |
| Calories | 4280 | 2322 |
| % of calories from fat | 55 | 15 |
| Total fat | 267 g | 39 g |
| Saturated fat | 94 g | 10 g |
| Cholesterol | 546 mg | 156 mg |
| Sodium | 4639 mg | 4000 mg |
| Total carbohydrate | 396 g | 401 g |
| Dietary fiber | 21 g | 29 g |
| Sugars | 181 g | 178 g |
| Protein | 94 g | 104 g |

Even with the dramatic results from the suggested changes, the type, taste, volume, and amount of the food in the two menus changed very little. (The creamer, for example, is made of soybean or cottonseed oil and tastes like cream.)

Although you don't have a Nutrition Facts panel for a whole day's meals, you can use the labels on foods to add up the nutritional information for everything you eat. A small notebook helps you keep track and can help you lose weight.

# 2,000 Calories and the Daily Values

As I mentioned earlier in this chapter, the percent daily values (%DV) on the Nutrition Facts panel are based on 2,000 calories a day. Not everyone needs exactly 2,000 calories a day. Some people, such as football players, teenage boys, pregnant women, and heavy laborers, need more. Some people, such as children, elderly people, or people trying to lose weight, need less.

U.S. government guidelines suggest these amounts based on a 2,000-calories-a-day diet:

- ✔ **Total Fat:** Less than 65 grams (30 percent of calories from fat)
- ✔ **Saturated Fat:** Less than 20 grams
- ✔ **Cholesterol:** Less than 300 milligrams
- ✔ **Sodium:** Less than 2,400 milligrams
- ✔ **Total Carbohydrate:** 300 grams
- ✔ **Dietary Fiber:** 25 grams

Because not all of us are alike, here are my own nutritional gram and milligram goals based on 1,800 calories a day. I am a 5'1", 108-pound female, active, and in my 50s. My goals are much lower than the preceding recommendations:

- ✔ **Total Fat:** Less than 30 grams (15 percent of calories from fat)
- ✔ **Saturated Fat:** Less than 10 grams
- ✔ **Cholesterol:** Less than 100 milligrams
- ✔ **Sodium:** Less than 2,000 milligrams
- ✔ **Total Carbohydrate:** 300 grams
- ✔ **Dietary Fiber:** 30 grams

When I know my own goals, I find it difficult to rationalize eating full-fat spreads, high-fat cheese, whole milk, egg yolks, and fatty meat or poultry on any but an occasional basis.

Here are the Nutrition Facts panel recommendations for a 2,500-calories-per-day diet:

✔ **Total Fat:** Less than 80 grams (30 percent of calories from fat)

✔ **Saturated Fat:** Less than 25 grams

✔ **Cholesterol:** Less than 300 milligrams

✔ **Sodium:** Less than 2,400 milligrams

✔ **Total Carbohydrate:** 375 grams

✔ **Dietary Fiber:** 30 grams

The following are my recommendations based on 2,500 calories a day for a male who is 6', 180 pounds, semi-active, in his early 40s, and doesn't have hypertension but does have a tendency to gain weight. These totals are lower than the preceding government recommendations:

✔ **Total Fat:** Less than 50 grams (18 percent of calories from fat)

✔ **Saturated Fat:** Less than 15 grams

✔ **Cholesterol:** Less than 200 milligrams

✔ **Sodium:** Less than 2,400 milligrams

✔ **Total Carbohydrate:** 400 grams

✔ **Dietary Fiber:** 30 grams

# The Food Guide Pyramid

The United States Department of Agriculture (USDA) has developed the Food Guide Pyramid (see Figure 2-2), which is a visual companion to the dietary recommendations listed in the preceding section. The pyramid is made up of six food groups, and the placement of these groups corresponds with the recommended number of servings. The base of the pyramid is made up of the largest group — breads, cereals, rice, and pasta, and you should strive to eat the most servings from this particular group. The tip of the pyramid is formed by the smallest group — fats, oils, and sweets, which you should consume sparingly. If you follow the pyramid and make wise choices, you will most likely follow a lowfat eating plan.

After reading all those labels, claims, and guidelines, you may find that nutritional information can be a little overwhelming. I hope that this chapter helps you understand how to use these tools to make more informed choices about the foods you eat. By paying attention to these details, you can avoid enormous amounts of fat and vast numbers of calories — without feeling deprived.

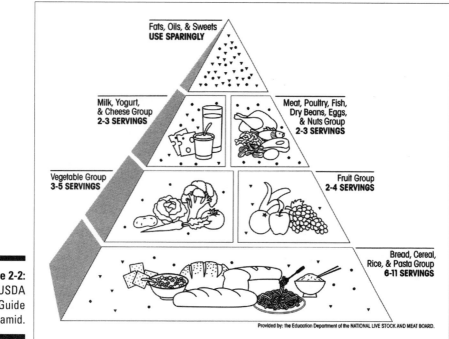

**Figure 2-2:**
The USDA
Food Guide
Pyramid.

# Part II
# Setting Up a Lowfat Kitchen

The 5th Wave    By Rich Tennant

ICE CREAM MAKER

DEEP FAT FRYER

CHOCOLATE MELTER

YARD SALE

"Purchase at your own risk."

## In this part . . .

In this part, I explain the practical steps for shifting from a high-fat to a lowfat diet. I help you take a critical look at your kitchen pantry and decide which foods to enjoy regularly on your lowfat eating plan — and which foods to avoid like a tax audit.

Read this part to find out how to use lowfat flavorings to make food more pleasurable. I also provide some helpful advice on including meat, poultry, fish, eggs, and dairy products in a lowfat diet.

# Chapter 3

# Slenderizing Your Kitchen Pantry

· · · · · · · · · · · · · · · · · · · · · · · · · · · · · · · · · · · · · · ·

## In This Chapter

▶ Filling your pantry with lowfat foods

▶ Making a lowfat grocery list

▶ Choosing canned and bottled goods

▶ Selecting lowfat packaged and dried foods

▶ Discovering lowfat snacks

▶ Asking your store to stock the products you want

· · · · · · · · · · · · · · · · · · · · · · · · · · · · · · · · · · · · · · ·

Starting with your pantry, getting your kitchen into a lowfat mode is pretty easy. The majority of us are collectors, pack rats, hoarders — whatever label you choose — and if we find space in our lives for stuff (including kitchen cabinets, refrigerators, cupboards, and drawers), we seek to fill it.

What happens is that we tend to use and re-use the items that are most accessible. The rest are — well, you know the saying — "out of sight, out of mind." When you dig, you discover the junk and the good stuff. "Gosh, I didn't know I still had that nifty no-stick, fold-over French omelet pan that I got for my birthday ten years ago. I haven't seen it for years."

You can use that omelet pan for lowfat cooking. But much of the hidden-away stuff you can't use, and the clutter just takes up room that you don't have enough of anyway. As for the deep-fat fryer — out!

So take some time to explore. Get out your rubber gloves, the Goodwill box, and a garbage bag, and take a load off your cabinets, refrigerator, body, and mind. The idea here is simple: Simplify!

# Lowfat Food Smarts: Cleaning Out Your Pantry

"What should I buy, and what should I keep?" you may ask. The following foods are keepers. These items have great shelf lives; chances are they're still usable if they're canned. If you don't already have some of them, use these as suggestions for your grocery list of lowfat foods. The list is important because "in the buying is the eating." If you have corn dogs, you'll eat them. But if you have great lowfat or fat-free dogs, good buns, and the best mustard and relish, you'll eat those instead. The latter choice has 50 percent fewer calories and one-fourth the fat — and these differences count. With fat, every little bit counts.

Here's what you want to keep in your lowfat pantry. All products (except the oils, nuts, and seeds) should be as close to lowfat or fat-free as possible. You should have predominantly lowfat foods.

- ✔ Canned or bottled vegetables, fruits, and juices
- ✔ Canned or bottled soups, stews, pastas, sauces, and gravies
- ✔ Canned or bottled beans, lentils, garbanzos, and peas
- ✔ Canned poultry, fish, and shellfish packed in water
- ✔ Packaged dried beans, lentils, and barley
- ✔ Packaged pasta, rice, bulgur wheat, and other grains
- ✔ Cereals, breads, rolls, and other bakery goods
- ✔ Flour, cornstarch, biscuit and pancake mixes, gravy mixes, instant soup cups and mixes, bouillon cubes and flavor granules, and cocoa
- ✔ Sugar, honey, syrup, jams, preserves, and other sweeteners (these products are discussed in Chapter 4)
- ✔ Spreads, mayonnaise, salad dressings, oils (the regular high-fat kind), vinegars, and herbs and spices
- ✔ Pretzels, popcorn, chips, crackers, cookies, nuts, seeds, and other lowfat snacks
- ✔ Dried fruits such as raisins and cranberries

When you're cleaning and tossing, don't be a saver like me. If you see even one tiny critter running around on your pasta or flour shelf, you have a thousand, and they may be inside your packages. If the ends of a can are a bit rusted or rounded, throw it out (unless your child is a budding scientist or a collector of exploding cans).

Here's what you want to throw or give away to create a lowfat pantry:

- Canned meats, such as Spam, Vienna sausages, meat pâté, marinated herring, and deviled ham (you haven't even unwrapped that little red devil!)
- Two-year-old popcorn packages with butter in a greasy microwave-able bag
- Gravy and biscuit mixes that have dark stains that come from escaping oil
- Bottled tamales, high-fat pork and beans, Alfredo sauce, and cream of lobster bisque
- Any package that doesn't carry a Nutrition Facts panel, which means that it was packaged before 1990
- Lard-fried potato chips and corn chips
- Chocolate bars and chocolate-covered nuts
- Cheese puffs
- Velveeta and Cheez Whiz (trade for the lowfat varieties)
- Evaporated milk (unless it's skimmed)
- Packaged macaroni and cheese (if you have to keep it, make it with skim milk, no butter, and double the pasta)
- Salad dressings with oil or mayonnaise

Toss out any other high-fat products or give them to someone you don't like.

# Lowfat Shopping Tips

Lowfat shopping is slightly different, but it gets easier with time. The following tips can help you ensure that the items you have on hand fit into your lowfat eating plan. Remember, if you don't buy it, you won't eat it!

- Consider store brands only if they are low in fat. They are cheaper, but you may prefer higher quality.
- Buy packages of dried beans, rice, pasta, peas, lentils, and barley and use these terrific foods rather than so much meat and poultry. They're cheaper, too!
- Try TVP (textured vegetable protein) in place of meat and poultry.
- If you need oil, buy the oils with the most monounsaturated and polyunsaturated fats and the least saturated fat, and use them sparingly anywhere you use oil for cooking and in salads. Use no-stick spray when you can.

✔ Although canned mackerel is cheaper than tuna, it contains double the amount of fat.

✔ Purchase fat-free or lowfat ready-made puddings, diet dressings, toppings, sandwich spreads, sour cream, American cheese, Swiss cheese, Cheddar, mozzarella, ricotta, and farmer cheese, reduced-fat cream cheese, and lower-fat feta, plus lowfat or fat-free ice cream, frozen yogurt, and yogurt. Get skim milk and fat-free "cream," which is a liquid non-dairy creamer available in the dairy case. Fat-free and lowfat whipped cream and whipped toppings are available, too.

✔ Buy plenty of fresh fruits and vegetables and lots of canned fruits and vegetables. If you have them handy in the refrigerator or in a can, you'll eat them.

✔ Purchase desserts and bakery goods that are fat-free or lowfat. Plenty are available now, including the Entenmann's brand. Get English muffins, crumpets, bagels, most breads, buns, and angel food cake, which are already very low in fat; check the labels. Omit doughnuts, croissants, and cream- or cheese-filled stuff.

# Doing the Can-Can: Canned, Tinned, and Bottled Goods

Canned foods are a part of every pantry and a necessity in every lowfat kitchen. While you juggle your life between cheering at your kid's soccer game and rushing to a candlelit dinner for two (or for me, rushing to my computer to write the next recipe), canned foods can be challenging and rewarding. You need them, and they help you.

After you come home from work, the last thing you want to think about is what to make for dinner. So if you don't have fresh vegetables, using canned peas and carrots is okay. The nutrition is there. All you need are a few tips on how to mix and match, maybe add a touch of herbs and a pinch of spices, and you can transform a meal buttressed with handy canned stuff into a gastronomical wonder. (You can read more about that topic later in this chapter.)

Obviously, if you don't like something, don't buy it; get the lowfat extras that you do like. The following canned vegetables are all lowfat or fat-free, so use these foods freely. You may want several cans or jars of one food that you eat often. The idea is to have lowfat products handy, handy, handy.

✔ Artichoke hearts in water (if in oil, rinse well and pat with paper towels)

✔ Asparagus

- Butter beans
- Carrots
- Corn
- Green beans
- Hearts of palm (for salads)
- Lima beans
- Mushrooms (whole, bits and pieces, sliced, and Chinese)
- Pasta sauce (several kinds, all lowfat)
- Pearl onions
- Peas
- Pimentos
- Red beets
- Roasted red peppers in water or vinegar (mainly for salads)
- Tomatoes (whole, crushed, and diced), tomato paste, and tomato sauce

## Canned corn — a lowfat essential

Corn adds flavor, starch, and bulk to foods while adding little fat. Add canned corn to creamed pasta sauces, rice dishes, chowders, soups, Mexican dishes, mashed potatoes, salads, or meat loaf. You can add canned corn to stretch the servings of fresh-cut corn from the cob, too. Canned corn, unlike tomatoes, comes just a few ways:

- **Creamed corn:** Can be low in fat

- **Whole kernels:** Always low in fat; good hot as a side and in soups, macaroni, or chili, and good cold in salads

- **Corn with peppers, limas (succotash), or other vegetables:** Good for a quickie hot vegetable side or in salads

- **Baby corn:** Whole cobs that go well in Chinese dishes and salads

- **White hominy:** Bleached, white corn kernels; good hot as a vegetable side or with breakfast

- **Yellow hominy:** For salads, as a side, and to add to soups

# A little bit about canned tomatoes

Vine-ripened tomatoes are wonderful but are not always available. If a recipe calls for fresh tomatoes when they're out of season, shriveled, bruised, or $4.99 a pound, use canned instead.

A canned tomato is simply a fresh tomato that is cooked for a short time right in the can. It is first blanched, by steaming or immersing in boiling water for 30 seconds, and then plunged into cold water so that the skin can be removed easily. You can do this simple process at home with fresh tomatoes — if you have the time, great! Most people don't, so they use them unskinned, which is better, or canned.

Why are canned tomatoes a staple? You can create a myriad of dishes from a single can: for example, salsa, pasta sauces, chilies, stews, soups, omelets, salads, salad dressings, casseroles, dips, appetizers, and probably more.

Occasionally I spot boxed tomatoes, which can stay on the shelf almost as long as canned tomatoes and are just as useful. If you're on a sodium-reduced diet, buy low-sodium varieties.

Here are some, but not all, of the forms of canned tomatoes:

- **Whole tomatoes:** Whole tomatoes come in several can sizes. Cans may contain a variety of tomato types, but the most common is Roma. Cut whole tomatoes into pieces and use them for chunky sauces, soups, stews, roasts, chili, and casseroles.

- **Crushed tomatoes:** Tomatoes that went splat! Crushed tomatoes come in several can sizes, from 14.5 ounces on up. You can use them right from the can for pasta sauce.

- **Tomato paste:** To make paste tomatoes are cooked for several hours, which reduces them to a thick form. The seeds and skins are strained out. Tomato paste comes in a convenient tube, but more often is found in 6-ounce cans, sometimes larger. You usually thin the paste when using it in sauces.

- **Tomato puree:** Tomatoes are briefly cooked and strained, resulting in a thick liquid that needs thinning. Puree comes in 14.5-ounce (or larger) cans and boxes and is used for soups, chili, and sauces.

- **Tomato sauce:** The sauce is also tomato puree, but more watery (meaning that it doesn't need thinning with water or other liquids). Tomato sauce is sometimes flavored with Italian seasonings or green peppers (the label lists any added ingredients) and can be used for pasta sauce, casseroles, soups, and pizza.

- **Diced tomatoes:** Tomatoes are cut into ¼-inch pieces for easy use in pasta sauces, casseroles, omelets, salsas, and soups.

- **Tomato wedges:** Tomatoes are cut into wedges — good for chunky pasta sauce, salsas, and using drained, right from the can, for salads.

# Canned fruits

Whether fruit is in syrup or is *lite,* meaning that it contains less sugar, is your choice, but fruit is popular and good for you. You can eat fruit right from the can, or you can dress up beans with a peach salsa, add pineapple wedges to stir-fries, pop apricots into the skillet with chicken or turkey fillets (see Chapter 12), sprinkle some berries on cereals, throw any variety into a cake batter, or poach and pour over fat-free or lowfat ice cream or frozen yogurt. People who eat lots of fruit, even canned, tend to have better weight management and lower cholesterol. No fruit contains fat (except in trace amounts almost too small to measure).

Any canned fruit in its natural juices with minimal additives (such as sugar, salt, or cream) is a welcome addition to a lowfat pantry. The important rule is to read the label and make sure that the product contains little or no added fat. (See Chapter 2 for more information about labels.)

All foods contain some natural fat, even if the label says that one serving has less than 1 gram. If a serving is labeled 0 grams of fat, it can have a very small amount of fat, but still less than 0.5 grams. The following canned fruits don't contain artery-clogging saturated fat and have too little fat to measure:

- ✔ Apricots
- ✔ Berries
- ✔ Cherries
- ✔ Fruit cocktail
- ✔ Mandarin oranges
- ✔ Mangoes
- ✔ Peaches
- ✔ Pears
- ✔ Pineapple rings, crushed pineapple, and pineapple wedges
- ✔ Plums
- ✔ Prunes
- ✔ Spiced or candied apple rings and apple sauce

# Canned soups

Canned soups are quick, easy, hearty, and nutritious ways of happily filling yourself when you don't want to cook from scratch. Freshening canned soups with parsley, chopped onions, tomatoes, carrots, noodles, rice, celery, potatoes, garlic, fresh herbs, and spices is easy. Just precook them (except for parsley, herbs, spices, and tomatoes).

Try to purchase only lowfat canned soups — you have plenty to choose from. Just close your eyes at the lobster bisque with cheese. If you're unsure of the fat content, look at the Nutrition Facts panel on the back of the can. Because almost all soups are lowfat or come in lowfat versions, even when creamed, why not?

Several of these soups come not lowfat but fat-free, so purchase them. You may want to add your own favorite soups to the list, but check the label for total fat content and keep it under 3 grams per serving. (I keep it under 2.)

✔ Bean soup

✔ Chicken or beef and vegetable soup

✔ Chicken or beef noodle or rice soup

✔ Chowder and stew

✔ Cream soup (broccoli, celery, mushroom, seafood, and so on)

✔ Tomato soup

## Canned broth or stock

Fat-free canned broth or stock has many uses in lowfat cooking. Broth or stock is a strained liquid that results from cooking vegetables, poultry, meat, bones, or fish and condensing it slightly. Lowfat cooks should buy stock in stocks and broths. Not only can you use stock or broth as a base for soups, stews, casseroles, entrees, basting liquids, and sauces, but you can also use these products to sauté, steam, boil, and stir-fry, as well as to flavor and enhance just about everything from salad dressing to shrimp étouffée.

You can't beat homemade stock. You can make it yourself easily, but who has the time? The ease, simplicity, and taste of canned are almost as good. You can find fat-free broths in the soup aisle of your supermarket. Be sure to buy fat-free or defat it at home.

Following are some common handy stocks:

✔ **Canned beef stock or beef bouillon:** Generally made with beef bone marrow, water, onions, carrots, celery, and spices

✔ **Canned chicken stock or broth:** Generally made from chicken (the back and wings), water, onions, carrots, salt, celery, and spices

✔ **Clam juice:** Made from none other than clams; a great fat-free substitute for stock or broth when making Bloody Marys, linguine with clams, or bouillabaisse

> ✔ **Fish stock:** Generally made with fresh fish (including the head and bones), water, onion, wine, and spices
>
> ✔ **Vegetable stock:** Generally made with water and a variety of vegetables, including carrots, celery, onions, mushrooms, and leeks — spices, too

Instead of water, you can use canned broth to make stir-fries, to cook rice and potatoes, for soup bases, and to extend homemade soups.

## Canned beans

I suggest that you keep a wide variety of canned beans on hand. You want to have them readily available in case you want to increase your use, which experts have said everyone should. Canned beans make a quick and easy meal.

I always invest in the direction I want to go. Having ten cans of beans on my shelf at first may look daunting, but sooner or later I use them. For me, this approach works. I'm a slow mover when establishing new habits. If my cupboard is full of the foods I want to begin eating, one day I always break down and say, "Go ahead, it won't hurt — and I'm too hungry to argue."

Usually, I'm so surprised at how good the beans (or whatever I'm trying to add to my regimen) are that the good experience encourages me to try the food again, only sooner. I exercise resolve when selecting and purchasing at the store. Nature takes care of itself after that.

I've discovered many uses for canned beans. Use drained navy beans as a tasty salad addition, add field peas to a rice dish (see Chapter 13), add cannellini beans to fresh or canned soups or salads, and heat pinto beans (with a few raw scallions on top, a lime wedge, and some hot sauce) for a great side dish. Garbanzos, pintos, and black beans can be pureed with onions or garlic and herbs and spices for an appetizer or dip.

I have all the following beans in my cupboard and more. When I feel adventurous, I purchase an unfamiliar type of bean. They're cheap, and even if I don't love the taste of that particular bean, in salads all beans add a nice texture. If I really hate them, I add them to the juice that remains in my bottled three-bean salad after the three beans and pickles are gone. Refrigerate for a day, and the beans taste better.

Always check the fat content; some beans are cooked with salt pork and contain ridiculous amounts of fat.

> ✔ Adzuki beans
>
> ✔ Black beans
>
> ✔ Black-eyed peas

✓ Butter beans

✓ Cannellini beans

✓ Field peas (seasoned and unseasoned)

✓ Garbanzo beans

✓ Kidney beans (dark)

✓ Lentils (not really beans)

✓ Navy beans

✓ Pigeon peas

✓ Pinto beans

✓ Red beans

✓ Refried beans (the fat-free variety)

✓ Soybeans

✓ Three-bean salad (comes in jars)

✓ Vegetarian baked beans (the fat-free variety)

# Canned meats, poultry, fish, and shellfish

That 6-ounce can of tuna, chicken, crab, or shrimp, that teeny can of deviled ham wrapped in paper, or the Vienna sausages tucked away in your pantry can be terrific or terrible, depending on both their fat content and their taste. Crab, shrimp, tuna, or sometimes chicken are all you need to top off a really spectacular salad, pop in a stew for extra flavor, or finish an elegant sauce. Ladle tiny shrimp over a fish fillet. Or add crab chunks to an appetizer dip. Canned meats and seafood can be very handy.

Want more proof? Salmon and tuna make great casseroles, and tuna is necessary for tuna fish sandwiches (see Chapter 14). Place tuna in chunks in Niçoise salads along with the lettuce, green beans, and potatoes (see Chapter 9). Anchovy paste, although you'll have it forever, keeps well, and you need it for fantastic Caesar salads (see Chapter 9) and some sauces.

In addition to the following items, I keep smoked oysters and several other kinds of tinned fish and shellfish to help me out in a pinch or to add to something or other.

✓ **Anchovies:** Tiny, salt-cured fish canned in oil, mustard, or tomato sauce — so salty, in fact, that you should use them sparingly, usually to flavor or garnish sauces and pizza, and in canapés (savory appetizers) and Caesar salads.

✓ **Anchovy paste:** For Caesar salads and, occasionally, other dishes.

- ✔ **Chicken:** Use in soups or for a quick chicken salad; it's great to take on camping trips. Pick the lowest-fat brand.

- ✔ **Clams:** Great added to homemade or canned clam chowder, linguine with clam sauce, and dips.

- ✔ **Crab:** Great for last-minute dips, pastas, and cold soups like gazpacho. But when it comes to crab, fresh is always better.

- ✔ **Salmon:** Sometimes comes packed with pieces of skin and edible bones. If this is appetizing to you, use canned salmon on a bed of greens sprinkled with wine vinegar; or mix some salmon with yogurt, red onions, and chopped fresh dill; or make a salmon mousse ring for an appetizer. Pick the lowest-fat brand.

- ✔ **Sardines:** Come packed in oil, tomato sauce, or mustard sauce. These small, soft-boned, salt-water fish are great to serve with crusty rye bread, but use them sparingly because they're high in fat.

- ✔ **Shrimp:** Tiny baby ones come ready to toss into tomato soup, dips, cold shrimp salad, or hot fish stew, or use as an elegant garnish.

- ✔ **Tuna packed in water:** Pick the product with the lowest fat content; even when packed in water, tuna's fat content can vary. Does the tuna need to be albacore? No! It's cheaper in chunks. In addition to making tuna fish sandwiches, tuna is great served in salads, tonnato (or tuna) dip, and, shant I forget, the lowly tuna casserole.

# Dried Beans

Jack was a savvy businessman when he traded in the family cow for a handful of beans. Little did he know the value of those beans! They are rich in nutritive value, are easy to store — not to mention a real bargain — and have almost no fat (now about that cow . . .). No other food gives you so much fiber, iron, protein, and nutrition with so little fat for so few francs.

Beans in the pantry are terrific because they keep forever, need no refrigeration, and are rehydrated only when cooked, so they don't take up much space. They also don't tend to get buggy. If you're suspicious of bugs, freeze beans immediately after you purchase them and then put them in glass jars and store in the pantry.

Unlike canned beans, dried beans come in boxes and bags and have to be rehydrated and cooked. But like canned beans, you'll use them if you have them. Cooked dried beans make great soups, baked beans, dips or appetizers (pureed), salads, stews, and casseroles. You can also use cooked dried beans as a bed for a small piece of fish, pork, turkey, or chicken for a fancy presentation, or to bulk up salsa.

Hundreds of bean varieties exist. Except for lima beans, fava beans, and black-eyed peas (which, although called peas, are really beans), the majority of beans are purchased dried, not fresh. Some specialty food stores do carry fresh beans, though. You can buy fancy dried beans at most markets, especially specialty markets.

Here are the dried beans I have (shown in Figure 3-1). Long-cooking ones take 3 hours; short-cooking beans or lentils require 30 minutes to an hour. The rest take 2 hours or so to cook. (Chapter 13 offers more information about cooking times.)

- Barley (a grain that cooks like a bean)
- Black beans (long-cooking if large)
- Black-eyed peas
- Garbanzo beans (long-cooking)
- Kidney beans (long-cooking)
- Lentils (brown and red; short-cooking)
- Lima beans (long-cooking)
- Mung beans
- Navy beans
- Pinto beans
- Red beans
- Soybeans
- Split peas (short-cooking)

# Pasta

A wide variety of pasta is available, and it's all lowfat — unless it is fresh or ready-made with Alfredo sauce or filled with cheese or sausage. From tiny orzo or couscous (I mention couscous under the pasta category because it's made of wheat pasta) to huge manicotti tubes for stuffing with lowfat ricotta to wide lasagna noodles, pasta is good, good, good.

Dried pasta comes ready to rehydrate and eat in about 20 minutes. You can find fresh-made pasta in store refrigerators or make it yourself; it takes about 3 minutes to cook. Neither type is better, fancier, or more useful than the other. They have different purposes.

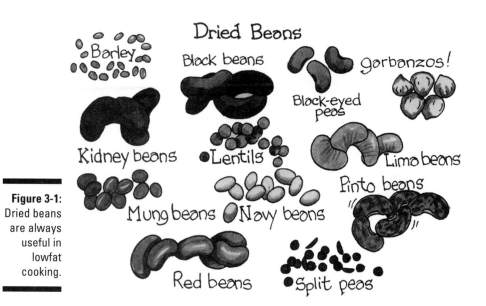

**Figure 3-1:**
Dried beans
are always
useful in
lowfat
cooking.

✔ **Dried pasta** can be used for any dish but holds up better than fresh pasta in soups, stews, casseroles, or dishes that are recooked after the pasta is originally cooked and softened. Dried pasta has a firmer, more al dente texture than fresh.

✔ **Fresh pasta** is better for ravioli, wrapped manicotti, and sheet-pasta lasagna. Homemade fresh pasta doesn't have to contain eggs (which add fat and cholesterol), but fresh store-bought pasta always seems to include eggs.

One serving, or 2 ounces, of dried pasta generally contains 1 gram of fat, but you can find it with half that amount. If the taste and texture are the same, use the lower-fat version. Every gram counts!

# Rice

Rice is a must on a lowfat diet, and it's very easy to make. Purchase several types because rice is the grain that is lowest in fat. Well over a dozen varieties are available in most stores, and each has a slightly different flavor, color, texture, and size. You'll find subtle but unique differences among aromatic jasmine or pecan rice, delicate-tasting but firm-feeling basmati, short-grained white rice, long-grained white rice, nutty-flavored brown rice, rich wild rice, and creamy Arborio rice.

White rice doesn't have much fiber, but it contains slightly less fat than pasta and beans, which don't have much anyway. Nutrition-wise, rice falls between pasta and beans.

Short-grain rice should be cooked within weeks of purchase; long-grain rice, such as basmati, can be shelved or stored for decades in covered glass jars. I suggest the following rice types for your lowfat pantry (Chapter 13 talks about a number of additional varieties):

- ✔ Arborio rice
- ✔ Brown rice
- ✔ White rice
- ✔ Wild rice

## Other Grains

Instead of just rice, you can try some of the following interesting and delicious grains to spice up your cooking repertoire (see Figure 3-2):

- ✔ **Bulgur:** A sweet wheat that is fluffy and can be eaten cold in salads (tabbouleh) or as a hot side dish, much like rice. Add seasonings or other vegetables in addition to bulgur to bulk up a tomato or vegetable soup or stuff in peppers with rice. You can also eat bulgur as a breakfast cereal with sugar. (Wheatena is similar.)

- ✔ **Couscous:** A tiny pasta made from wheat that is a favorite in Middle Eastern food. Most couscous sold in the U.S. is precooked and takes only 5 minutes to steam. If you're lucky enough to own a couscoussière, make it with that. If not, pour boiling water over the couscous, cover it with a plate, let it steam for 5 minutes, and enjoy.

- ✔ **Kamut:** Looks like long brown rice grains when cooked, is very nutritious, and offers great flavor (like wild rice). Kamut does take 2 hours to cook, although you can leave it more or less unattended — just a covered pot with kamut and water and maybe some vegetables and seasonings all simmering on low. Put it on the stove on Saturday morning, and you'll have good eating that afternoon.

- ✔ **Quinoa (pronounced "KEEN-wa"):** Quinoa is relatively new on the market, provides all eight essential amino acids, and contains no fat. It tastes like rice and looks like tiny, white BBs. This grain can be made into appetizers and salads, served hot with salt or pepper, or eaten as a dessert with fruit and cream (not real cream but fat-free liquid non-dairy creamer, which tastes like cream and can be found in the dairy section). Use quinoa exactly like you do rice.

**Figure 3-2:**
Bulgur,
couscous,
kamut,
quinoa, and
wheat
berries
offer good
nutrition
and great
taste.

Other grains

Bulgur  Couscous  Kamut  Quinoa  Wheat berries

✔ **Wheat berries:** Whole wheat kernels that provide the most nutrition of any wheat type. They can be eaten as a cereal, served plain with salt and pepper, or placed in soups and stews. If cooked first, wheat berries add a nice texture to bread. Wheat berries take $1^1/_2$ to 2 hours to cook.

# *Cereals*

Here's the cereal scoop. If you have a large cereal serving, say 2 cups or more of certain brands, and the milk is whole instead of skim, you can easily consume 20 grams of fat just in your breakfast cereal, which doesn't count toast, butter or margarine, cream in your coffee, or whatever else you have for breakfast. Yuck!

Here's what I do: I use only skim milk or liquid fat-free creamer and eat the cereal I want in the amount I want. On my English muffin, I use fat-free I Can't Believe It's Not Butter! spray and the best preserves I can find. This way, I get nutrients and fiber without fat. Then I drink my orange juice, take my vitamins, down my coffee, and I'm off.

Plain corn flakes, which have no fat, are okay. So are the fruit and nut varieties that do have fat — the largest amount. Eat your fat in the flakes, not the butter or milk. Corn flakes don't contain much in calories, fiber, and vitamins, so they're better than sausage but not as good as bran flakes. If you want fiber, raisin bran contains the most at 7 grams, or eat a pear or add raisins or berries. Many cereals have added vitamins, which I don't particularly want. I take a vitamin pill every day, and one can become "overvitamined." (All wheat products, including the grains from which all cereals are made, plus the flour in crackers, bread, doughnuts, cookies, and pasta, are "enriched" with vitamins anyway, and most people eat different grain products, such as cookies, rolls, pies, and pretzels, constantly.)

Really, nearly any cereal is fine, but check the labels — fat content and serving sizes vary widely. If you are desperately trying to lower your fat intake, buy corn flakes or shredded wheat. Here's a general list of cereals that you may want to consider:

- ✔ Bran flakes or wheat bran
- ✔ Corn flakes
- ✔ Grains, nuts, and fruit or granola
- ✔ Multigrain cereal
- ✔ Oat bran flakes
- ✔ Oatmeal
- ✔ Puffed grains
- ✔ Shredded wheat

Oatmeal is one of your best cereal bets. It contains small amounts of fat, fills you up, provides some fiber, and may lower your cholesterol. It comes instant, quick-cooking, or Irish-style long-cooking. I like the longer-cooking varieties because they have more texture, but in time crunches, the 5-minute variety does fine.

# Breads, Rolls, and Bakery Goods

Most plain commercial and bakery breads, and nearly all bagels, crumpets, English muffins, and plain rolls, contain the same amount of fat: very little. However, croissants, doughnuts, danishes, scones, biscuits, muffins, bear claws, and coffee cakes are a different story. You can ingest an enormous amount of fat in one croissant, probably more than is recommended for a whole day (at least my day). Some really good lowfat and fat-free coffee cakes, cookies, and other baked goods are available — and so are some really bad ones. These products contain calories, but less fat. They also offer no real nutritive value. But the fat-free and lowfat products are better than those with a high fat content because those items provide no nutritive value, either, and at least the lowfat versions don't have as much fat.

Because they're so low in fat, you may be tempted to eat more lowfat and fat-free baked goods, both because you're trying to find the taste (which they often lack) and because you think, "Why not? They're fat-free, so I can eat 20." Well, the reduced-fat varieties often contain more sugar and salt than the higher-fat versions of these products. Although sugar has less than half the calories of fat, calories are calories.

Some pastries are cleverly made lowfat or fat-free, and the changes in flavor and texture aren't important (although you can tell a difference). With other bakery goods, they are. Lowering the fat in croissants, which usually derive 40 to 50 percent of their calories from fat, and doughnuts, which are made with fat and sometimes even filled with fat, loses the essence of the pastry. Fat does have a taste, and we are used to its flavor and texture. So, if you can, forget croissants and doughnuts. There's enough other stuff, including the following:

- ✔ **Bagels:** Check the size; 2 ounces is very different from some of the 6-ounce monsters I've seen. Bagels come in a variety of sizes and flavors.

- ✔ **Crumpets:** A chewy, round, bread-like food, usually served toasted for breakfast or lunch.

- ✔ **Diet breads:** Smaller slices of white or brown bread that sometimes have less fat and sodium because they're smaller.

- ✔ **English muffins:** A round white bread, usually served toasted. English muffins taste better if they are the refrigerated kind (Bays is a favorite brand of mine).

- ✔ **White bread:** Enriched with vitamins and made from bleached wheat flour.

- ✔ **Whole wheat, multigrain, or high-fiber bread:** Made from the un-bleached grain, sometimes with bits and pieces of wheat berries or bran or with many grains. These breads contain double the fiber of white bread, or about 2 grams.

# Flours and Other Extras

You'll need flour and will want some of the following extras; they make lowfat cooking easier and much more fun.

- ✔ **Flour:** *All-purpose flour* is for everything. It contains a modicum of fat and is a sturdy, hard flour. *Self-rising flour* is all-purpose flour that contains baking powder, which contains baking soda; this flour rises when mixed with liquids. You can use self-rising flour in most recipes. *Whole wheat flour* contains a few more nutrients and fiber.

  Even if you aren't a baker, you need flour in your pantry. You can use a tablespoon or two to thicken soups, coat skinless lean chicken or turkey for lowfat frying, dredge meat cubes for a stew, make lowfat gravy (it's great even fat-free; see Chapter 16), and dust a baking sheet. If you have used flour a few times within the last month, get a 1-pound bag, if you used it only once about six months ago, borrow some and keep it in a jar.

- ✔ **Winter soft-wheat flour or cake flour:** Winter soft-wheat flour is for bakers who want to bake soft and tender foods without adding extra fats and oils. Winter soft-wheat flour creates a different texture than all-purpose flour.

- ✔ **Corn meal:** If you make corn bread, you may want corn meal in your pantry; it also comes in a self-rising form.

- ✔ **Cornstarch:** Cornstarch can thicken almost anything and is necessary in lowfat cooking. If a Chinese sweet and sour sauce or a pasta sauce needs thickening, use cornstarch. If a gravy (see Chapter 16) is too thin and you don't have 4 minutes to thicken it with flour, use cornstarch. It takes the place of fat.

- ✔ **Biscuit and pancake mixes:** Lowfat biscuit mixes are handy for pancakes, waffles, cinnamon rolls, dumplings, and shortcake. Several lower-fat brands are available, such as Lowfat Pioneer and Reduced Fat Bisquick. You can make good lower-fat biscuits with both products.

- ✔ **Gravy mix:** You can find very good lowfat and fat-free gravy packets and bottled gravy. When you add your own small amount of defatted meat drippings to white or brown gravy, you have terrific, old-fashioned stuff to put on potatoes, meat loaf, or biscuits or to moisten those one or two slices of beef, pork, chicken, or turkey.

- ✔ **Instant soup cups:** These lowfat soup mixes come with beans, noodles, rice, beef, chicken, and vegetables and are good for quick-fix lunches and dinners. Add more steamed veggies to freshen the taste.

- ✔ **Bouillon cubes and flavor granules:** Bouillon cubes, which are condensed stock bases, have been around forever. In lowfat cooking, they are tremendously useful for giving the extra boost of flavor that so much of lowfat cooking lacks. They come in cubes, powders, and granules; Wyler's offers a low-sodium brand. Use them to season bland or canned soups, rices, and stews; to add flavor to baste potatoes, carrots, and beans; and to add a soupçon (flavor) to any sauce. Stock up on flavor cubes and granules!

- ✔ **Cocoa:** Cocoa provides chocolate flavor without the fat. Use it when you want pure chocolate flavor. Some cocoa mixes contain added sugar. Use cocoa in cookies, cakes, and hot chocolate. In baking, adding instant coffee granules enhances the cocoa flavor.

# *Snacks*

The snacks described in this section are always good for the grabbin'. A portion is usually pretty generous, but checking out the labeled serving size doesn't hurt. Calories do add up!

Several lowfat snack foods are available now, including Frito-Lay products; Frito-Lay recently put $32 million into developing lowfat foods, mostly chips and stuff. You can find lowfat potato chips, corn chips, and cheese puffs. Many crackers, including Ritz, Triscuits, and Wheat Thins, offer reduced-fat versions.

Pretzels and air-popped popcorn without oil flavoring are nearly fat-free naturally. The best lowfat snacks are fresh fruits and vegetables.

## Dried fruits

Dried fruit contains very little fat and keeps for six months. In humid weather, apricots and raisins get softer; in dry weather, they are chewier. I keep some of the following dried fruits around. To remoisten, cook them.

- ✔ Apples
- ✔ Apricots
- ✔ Cranberries
- ✔ Dates
- ✔ Figs
- ✔ Prunes
- ✔ Raisins
- ✔ Tart cherries

## Nuts

Nuts have fat, but the fat they contain is natural fat and not added fat, plus they have fiber and nutrients — so I think they're okay as long as you aren't eating a half pound at a time. Not counting coconut, the nuts with the most fat and saturated fat are the macadamia and the Brazil nut. (Wouldn't you know it?)

Nuts spoil rather quickly if not eaten within two weeks, so transfer them to the refrigerator or freezer (in glass jars with lids) if you don't use them up quickly. Frozen nuts placed on a plate defrost in 10 minutes — ready for you or guests.

Try the following nuts (listed in order from least to most saturated fat), which are pictured in Figure 3-3:

- ✔ Chestnuts
- ✔ Hazelnuts
- ✔ Almonds

- ✔ Pecans
- ✔ Walnuts
- ✔ Pistachio nuts
- ✔ Peanuts
- ✔ Cashews
- ✔ Pine nuts
- ✔ Macadamia nuts
- ✔ Brazil nuts
- ✔ Coconut

**Figure 3-3:**
Although they have fat, nuts also provide fiber and nutrients.

## Seeds

Seed types are a personal choice. I like sunflower seeds and a few others for their flavor and use in some dishes. Plus, seeds are fun to snack on. When I make squash (see Chapter 15), I cook it with the seeds and serve them as part of the dish. The following seeds offer quick and handy fiber and flavor:

- ✔ Poppy seeds
- ✔ Pumpkin seeds
- ✔ Sesame seeds
- ✔ Sunflower seeds

# Getting the Lowfat Products You Want

Perhaps when you skied in New Hampshire or went to a music festival in Aspen, you saw a terrific lowfat or fat-free product. Why can't you get it at your store? With the form on the following page (photocopy it), you can better guarantee that you get the products you want. If you don't tell your store's managers which products you prefer, they won't know. And in writing, your request will be remembered.

# One Last Note on Lowfat Shopping

Although many experts advise against it, try shopping for lowfat foods like fruits and vegetables when you're hungry. Your senses are heightened when your stomach is on the empty side, and even the foods you usually thumb your nose at become more appealing. For example, succulent Georgia peaches may seem to fit rather nicely in the grocery cart, or ruby red tomatoes still on the vine may seem worthwhile. How about freshly picked sweet corn on the cob or that foot-long Asian-style bean? Go with it! How can you deny yourself these simple pleasures?

Lowfat and fat-free products all look good when you're hungry. Just control those impulses and pass on the doughnuts.

After you read this chapter, make your shopping list. Shopping wisely can mean savings in money and fat. Read labels (see Chapter 2) and don't use food coupons unless they are for lowfat or fat-free products.

Date:

Dear Store Manager:

Below is a product that I would like you to carry for me. Would you call me as soon as it arrives so that I can purchase it immediately? I appreciate your efforts to get the lowfat products I want and need.

If you are unable to get the product, would you please save this form for me and make a notation as to why it is unavailable so that I may take another approach? You may make notations on the lines with the asterisks (*). Thank you for your help.

Product name: _____

Type of product: _____

Product manufacturer: _____

_____

*Comments from manager: _____

_____

*Results: _____

_____

Thank you again for your time and effort in helping me. May I call your supervisor to tell him or her how responsive you were?

*Supervisor's name: _____

*Phone: _____

Sincerely,

My name: _____

Address: _____

Phone: _____

# Chapter 4

# Cooking with Oils, Condiments, and Other Flavorings

. . . . . . . . . . . . . . . . . . . . . . . . . . . . . . . . . . . . . . . . . . . . . . . . . . .

*In This Chapter*

▶ Getting the skinny on fats, oils, and vinegars

▶ Finding out everything you ever wanted to know about herbs and spices

▶ Adding flavor but not fat with liquids, pastes, extracts, and other essentials

. . . . . . . . . . . . . . . . . . . . . . . . . . . . . . . . . . . . . . . . . . . . . . . . . . .

*T*he oils, condiments, herbs, spices, and other flavorings you use to prepare and season dishes can have a big impact on the fat content of the foods you eat. Fortunately, you can control the amount of added fat easily, and you can use a huge variety of fat-free flavorings to enhance the taste of lowfat dishes.

This chapter talks about those all-important but often unnecessary fats and oils that you use for cooking, and it explains how you can reduce the amount of oil you use during preparation. I also describe the various herbs, spices, and other things you can use to add flavor so that you don't even miss the fat.

*Note:* Although butter is a dairy product, it is pure fat. In a lowfat eating plan, you should treat it as a fat, not as a nutritive food or even a flavoring. Therefore, for the purposes of this book, I am lumping butter with the vegetable fats, such as olive oil, vegetable oil, and margarine.

## Oil Is Oil Is Oil . . . or Is It?

All oils are 100 percent fat, and all fats — bacon fat, butter, canola oil, olive oil, and so on — are identical when it comes to calories: about 120 for 1 tablespoon, with close to 13 grams of fat in each tablespoon. These items are not identical, however, in makeup or type of fat.

Canola and olive oils contain more *monounsaturated fat.* Although canola and olive oil can cause you to become fat, most of it isn't saturated and doesn't accumulate inside your arteries, unlike butter, which is high in saturated fat, the fat that causes the problem. Canola oil contains very little saturated fat — less than any other oil. And like all vegetable products, the tablespoon of canola oil contains no cholesterol, unlike butter.

The tablespoon of bacon fat contains a great deal of *saturated fat,* which is the fat that causes the plaque inside the highways that carry your blood. However, any fat is stored on your body if you take in more calories than your system needs.

So what distinguishes one oil from another (besides flavor) is the amount of saturated fat, monounsaturated fat, and polyunsaturated fat each oil contains. Because saturated fat affects the level of cholesterol in the body more than any other fat does, you should use the oils that are low in saturated fat. Plenty of good ones are available, as Table 4-1 shows.

| Table 4-1 | Saturated Fat Per ¼ Cup |
|---|---|
| *Oil* | *Saturated Fat* |
| Canola oil | 3.5 g |
| Safflower oil | 4 g |
| Hazelnut oil | 5 g |
| Walnut oil | 5 g |
| Grapeseed oil | 5 g |
| Olive oil | 7 g |
| Corn oil | 7 g |
| Liquid margarine | 8 g |
| Partially hydrogenated tub margarine | 8 g |
| Sesame oil (dark or light) | 8 g |
| Peanut oil | 9 g |
| Partially hydrogenated stick margarine | 9 g |
| Hydrogenated shortening | 13 g |
| Lard | 20 g |
| Palm oil | 27 g |
| Butter | 29 g |
| Palm kernel oil | 44 g |
| Coconut oil | 47 g |

# Cooking with Oils in a Lowfat Kitchen

The single most important oil in a lowfat kitchen is no-stick vegetable oil spray. Instead of coating a pan with 2 tablespoons of oil, you can use a spray to keep foods from sticking without adding all that fat.

But sometimes you just have to use pourable oil. For these times, keep oils such as canola and safflower on hand because they are lowest in saturated fats. Olive oil contains nearly twice as much saturated fat as canola or safflower oil, but it's still low and has a flavor that many people like. The trick is to use oils *sparingly*.

The following are descriptions of some oils that are good for using in lowfat cooking:

- ✔ **No-stick vegetable oil spray:** Whether in an aerosol can or your own pump bottle, no-stick spray is great because you use far less oil than you can carefully pour out of a bottle. Use spray oil for sautéing, stir-frying, roasting vegetables, making your own pita chips, and greasing baking sheets and cake pans. A vegetable oil spray stays fresh in the pantry for about six months.

- ✔ **Canola and safflower oil:** Use for salads, sautéing, and whenever you use oil. Some people mix these two oils with a strong olive oil for less saturated fat than pure olive oil but an olive oil flavor. These products can be kept in the pantry, but they become rancid after several months. You can also refrigerate them.

- ✔ **Olive oil:** The important feature to look for in olive oil is its grade, usually printed on the front of the bottle: extra-virgin, superfine, fine, or pure (virgin). Olive oils are graded according to the degree of acidity they contain, with the finest oils containing the least acidity. Extra-virgin olive oil is the result of the first pressing (the crushing process that releases the oil from the olives), and consequently has the richest aroma, the strongest flavor, and the least acidity.

  Olive oil can be stored in a cool, dark place for up to one month after opening. Its shelf life is even longer in the refrigerator (one year or more), although the oil becomes cloudy and too thick to pour. Running it under hot water or letting it sit at room temperature liquifies it again.

- ✔ **Flavored oils (chili, garlic, basil, and lemon oils):** A little bit of one of these oils goes a long way. Instead of sautéing or cooking with them, you can use a drop or so to enhance a dish — and add much less fat. Flavored oils are only fair in taste, in my opinion.

✔ **Nut oils (such as walnut and hazelnut):** Light, sweet, and delicate, these oils are great on salads, sprinkled over freshly cooked vegetables, and in cookies and cakes.

✔ **Peanut oil:** A clear oil pressed from peanuts. I listed this oil separately from nut oils because of its mild flavor and high smoke point, meaning that it's great for deep-fat frying (which is unheard of in a lowfat kitchen). Peanut oil is high in saturated fat, although far below palm kernel and coconut oils, which top the list.

## Choosing a no-stick spray oil

When using small amounts of spray oil, you can't discern a difference in taste between corn, canola, olive, and butter-flavored oil. You may want to pick up a can of olive oil spray for coating lettuce for salads. If you spray the lettuce leaves, you consume less fat than if you use a bottled olive-oil-based dressing.

Consider two or three spritzes of an aerosol can or pump bottle oil to be one serving; too many spritzes equal too much fat. One spritz means that you depress the nozzle for about 1 second. Eight spritzes equal about $1/2$ teaspoon of oil.

## Storing oils

Some oils, like sesame oil, stay fresh indefinitely in the pantry, even after you open them. But nut oils quickly lose their flavor and become rancid, so buy them in small amounts and store them in your refrigerator.

In general, you should store oils in the refrigerator after opening them, because they turn rancid quickly. What's a good way to tell whether your oil's gone bad? Have yourself a smell!

# Using Vinegars for Flavor

Vinegars, which contain no fat or cholesterol, are helpful when you're trying to reduce your fat intake because they add big flavor without adding fat. They vary greatly, and you don't have to use just one at a time. This section describes some of the most popular types of vinegar; you may come across many more. I recommend that you buy several varieties. Vinegar is inexpensive, easy to store, and tasty in salads, soups, stews, and sweet and sour sauces.

*Vinegar* is derived from the French word *vinaigre,* meaning "sour wine." Many vinegars are wine vinegars, but some, such as cider, are made from fruit. Anything that can be fermented to produce alcohol can be used to make vinegar. The British prefer malt vinegar, which is made from malted barley, on their fish and chips. A key element in sushi rice is rice vinegar, made from fermented rice.

Specialty vinegars, usually made from wine with added herbs, spices, and fruits, are also available. A few examples of these infused or steeped vinegars are garlic, tarragon, lemon and herb, and raspberry. You can even find vinegars made from potatoes and beets. (See Chapter 9 for recipes for making flavored vinegars at home.)

Unopened bottles of vinegar keep forever; store them airtight in a cool, dark place. After opening, experts say that a bottle's shelf life is about six or seven months.

These vinegars appear in order of my own personal preference and degree of use, although I confess to having Asian black vinegar, honey vinegar, and, somewhere, Champagne vinegar as well.

- ✔ **Cider vinegar** is amber in color, strong, and clean-tasting. It is made from apples and has their rich smell. Quality is fairly consistent from brand to brand.

- ✔ **Balsamic vinegar** is a strong, sweet but mellow, highly aromatic, dark vinegar. All balsamic vinegar is from the Modena province in Italy, but it is not all equal in quality. Traditionally, balsamic is aged for years in wooden casks, which gives it an unusual flavor. Different brands vary widely in flavor, and pure balsamic vinegar is very costly.

- ✔ **Wine vinegar** can be made from red or white wine, such as Burgundy or Chablis. It varies in consistency, taste, and color and can range from very strong for some of the reds to more mild. Sherry vinegar is especially tasty.

- ✔ **Rice vinegar** is Asian, and is clear and mild. Brown rice vinegar and sweet rice vinegar, called *mirin,* are also available. Rice vinegar is ideal for those who like a less pungent or acidic vinegar flavor.

- ✔ **Malt vinegar**, made from barley, is actually mild, but with a husky taste and aroma. It is excellent on fish, spinach, and greens. The English serve it on potatoes.

- ✔ **Flavored or herbed vinegars** are made by adding herbs, fruits, and spices to the vinegar. These vinegars often don't require accompanying oil.

- ✔ **Distilled white vinegar** is clear and strong. It is made from grains, such as corn and rye, and can be diluted with water, tomato juice, or fruit juice. It's the vinegar of choice for adding fresh herbs or fruits.

# Flavoring Foods with Herbs and Spices

Herbs are leaves, and spices are ground seeds, flowers, and bark. Herbs and spices are essential in lowfat cooking because they help to add flavor when you're reducing fat.

When using herbs and spices, be aware that some have special cooking requirements. For example, dried oregano can get bitter when cooked too long (over 10 minutes); saffron should be cooked for 30 minutes or more to bring out the flavor. When using fresh herbs, remember that 1/4 teaspoon dried equals 1 teaspoon fresh.

The following list should increase your enjoyment of lowfat food. You can use the list to look up suggestions for herbs and spices you can add to a dish. Try using a little at a time, because overdoing it is easy.

- ✔ **Allspice:** A mild and aromatic ground spice resembling a blend of cinnamon, cloves, and nutmeg. Use allspice for roasts, chicken, duck, fish, ham, stews, consommés, potatoes, tomatoes, and, more often, fruit dishes (apple pie, chutney, and fruit juice).

- ✔ **Anise and anise seed:** A mild whole-seed spice that tastes like faint licorice. Use anise for beef, pork, sausage, shellfish, soups, beets, turnips, cabbage, cauliflower, cucumber salads, slaw, pasta, sauces, coffee cakes, cookies, and fruit juice. Add during or after cooking.

- ✔ **Basil or sweet basil:** A mild and aromatic fresh, dried, or flaked herb. Several kinds are sold in the United States, but sweet Italian is considered the best. Use basil for meat, poultry, fish, seafood, omelets, soups, stews, sauces (especially pasta or Italian sauce), vinegar, stuffing, dips, salad dressings, and vegetable juice. Add basil before, during, or after cooking in sprigs or chopped as a garnish.

- ✔ **Bay leaf:** A mild aromatic herb that is usually a whole dried leaf. Use for roasts, fish, bean dishes, bouillabaisse, chowders, potatoes, vinegar, rice, tomato juice, gravies, and marinades. Always remove the leaves from the dish before eating.

- ✔ **Caraway seed:** A mild, tingly spice, usually purchased as whole seeds. Caraway seed is one of the oldest seeds in recorded history and is used for German dishes, goose, onions, potatoes, noodles, sauces, dips, stews, stuffing, salads, sauerkraut, cabbage, vegetable juice, and rye and wheat breads. Can be added before, during, or after cooking and can be sprinkled on as a garnish.

- ✔ **Cardamom:** An expensive, mild whole or ground spice. Use cardamom with meats, curried fish, melon, fruit salads, pea soup, bean dishes, salad dressings, cookies, cakes, breads, and Danish pastry. It is that elusive spice that you smell and taste in doughnuts.

- **Cayenne pepper:** A spicy hot ground spice. Use cayenne for chili, meat, fish, pasta, soups, vegetables, macaroni, and Tex-Mex, Cajun, and Asian cuisine. Can be added before, during, or after cooking and can be sprinkled on as a garnish.

- **Celery seed:** A mild dried spice. Use celery seed in meat and poultry recipes, soups, stews, salads, vegetables, vinegar, sauces, dips, slaw, herb breads, relishes, and vegetable juice. Celery seed can be used as a garnish.

- **Chervil:** A mild fresh or dried herb that is similar to tarragon. Use chervil for lamb, sausage, poultry, fish, shellfish, bouillon, cottage cheese, soups, sauces, avocado recipes, omelets, vegetables, salads, salad dressings, and vegetable juice. Chervil is hard to find.

- **Chili pepper:** A (usually) spicy hot capsicum or vegetable in fresh, dried whole, flaked, powdered, and paste form. Many kinds are available, including ancho, habañero, chipotle, serrano, Scotch bonnet, hari mirch, and jalapeño. You can add chilies before, during, or after cooking.

- **Chili powder:** A medium spicy ground spice that varies greatly. Chili powder is sometimes a combination of a variety of spices and is used for chili, chili sauce, onions, guacamole, barbecue sauce, tomato and other soups, beans, potato salad, salad dressings, cottage cheese, eggs, and vegetable juice. Add during cooking.

- **Chives:** A medium spicy fresh or dried form of onion. Use chives with meat, poultry, fish, and shellfish; in soups, stews, chowders, sauces, dips, vegetables, and vinegars; or anywhere onions can be used. You can add chives before, during, or after cooking and use them whole or chopped as a garnish.

- **Cilantro or Chinese parsley:** A medium spicy fresh herb (the fresh, whole version of coriander). Use cilantro for salsas, salads, guacamole, Asian dishes, curries, soups, stews, onions, spinach, tomatoes, cauliflower, vinegar, cakes, cookies, gingerbread, and fruit.

- **Cinnamon or cassia:** A medium spicy and aromatic spice in ground and stick form. Use cinnamon for pork, ham, chicken, lamb, relishes, fruit pies and tarts, sauces, cookies, spiced and mulled wine, punch, coffee, toast, coffee cake, apple sauce, chutneys, pickles, gingerbread, pumpkin bread, onions, squash, tomatoes, sweet potatoes, yams, beets, noodles, rice, and desserts with chocolate. This spice can be added before, during, or after cooking. Use it ground as a garnish or add whole sticks to hot and cold drinks.

- **Cloves:** A spicy, but not hot, usually aromatic ground or whole spice (whole cloves are the dried part of a flower). Use cloves with beef, ham, pork, lamb, or vegetables, or in stews, stocks, hot mulled wine, relishes, chutneys, cranberry juice, potpourri, cakes, fruit pies, and cookies.

- ✔ **Coriander:** A medium spicy whole, seed, dried leaf, or ground spice (the dried or seed version of cilantro). Use in beef, chicken, lamb, and pork dishes, salsas, guacamole, soups, stews, curries, cakes, cookies, and vinegars, and with onions, spinach, tomatoes, cauliflower, and fruit. Can be added before, during, or after cooking.

- ✔ **Cumin:** A spicy ground spice in Tex-Mex, Middle Eastern, and East Indian dishes. Cumin is often used with chili powder and curry powder in beef, lamb, or pork dishes, soups, stews, beans, chili, curries, sauces, dips, vinegar, breads, cakes, and salad dressings. Add during cooking.

- ✔ **Dill:** A medium spicy and aromatic fresh, dried, or seed herb. Use dill for meats, poultry, seafood, pickles, vegetables, salads, salad dressings, marinades, sauces, dips, vinegar, cottage cheese, omelets, slaw, bean soup, chicken soup, and breads. Dill can be added before, during, or after cooking. If fresh, it can be used whole or chopped as a garnish.

- ✔ **Fennel:** A seed spice, sometimes ground, with a mild to medium spicy licorice flavor. Use fennel for meats, poultry, sausage, seafood, stews, sauces, dips, cabbage, cucumbers, onions, salads, salad dressings, pickles, breads, vinegar, pasta, cookies, and cakes. Add fennel during cooking.

- ✔ **Garlic powder:** A spicy and aromatic root powder, usually made with added salt and sugar. Use garlic powder for meats, poultry, seafood, stews, beans, pasta, rice, breads, sauces, dips, vegetables, salads, salad dressings, and marinades. Add this powder during cooking.

- ✔ **Ginger:** A spicy fresh, ground, pickled, or candied *rhizome* (or underground stem). Use ginger for Thai, Japanese, Chinese, and other Asian dishes, meats, chicken, duck, fish, shellfish, vegetables, soups, stews, stir-fries, sweet and sour dishes, cakes, cookies, gingerbread, pies, candy, chutney, mulled or spiced wine, or pickled as a condiment for sushi. Add ginger before, during, or after cooking.

- ✔ **Juniper berries:** A mild fresh or dried berry seed. Use juniper berries for game, pork, poultry, stuffing, stews, sauces, potatoes, apples, sauerkraut, gin, and beer.

- ✔ **Lemon grass:** A mild fresh and dried aromatic grass. Use lemon grass for Asian and Middle Eastern soups, stews, rice, noodles, and vegetables. Add lemon grass during cooking and remove before serving.

- ✔ **Mace:** A medium spicy ground spice (the lining of the nutmeg). Use mace for fish, poultry, rabbit, sausage, soups, beans, pasta, fruit, brussels sprouts, cabbage, broccoli, chutney, sweet-style breads, cakes, cookies, and spiced wines.

- ✔ **Marjoram:** A medium spicy fresh or dried herb. Use marjoram for meats, poultry, seafood, stews, sauces, dips, spinach, onions, carrots, squash, oyster stew, herb breads, stuffing, omelets, salads, and tomato juice. Use whole as a garnish.

✔ **Mint:** A medium spicy fresh or dried aromatic herb. Many varieties are available, such as peppermint, wintergreen, spearmint, curly mint, apple mint, garden mint, pennyroyal, water mint, pineapple mint, and Corsican mint. Use mint for lamb, fish, poultry, ham, vegetables, salads, desserts, fruits, sauces, Middle Eastern foods, beverages such as mint julep, sorbet, jelly, tea, and yogurt. Can be added before, during, or after cooking. Use whole or chopped as a garnish.

✔ **Mustard:** A spicy ground or whole-seed spice. Use mustard dry, mixed, or prepared (commercial mustard), American or Dijon style, for meat, poultry, fish, shellfish, potatoes, relishes, deviled eggs, salads, salad dressings, mayonnaises, marinades, sauces, dips, and cheese dishes. Add before, during, or after cooking. Seeds can be used as a garnish.

✔ **Nutmeg:** A mild whole or ground aromatic spice. Use nutmeg for meat loaf, meatballs, poultry, ham, pork, sausage, onions, squash, eggplant, mushrooms, potatoes, black beans, pea soup, sauces, fruit, quiches, pasta dishes, cream soups, eggnog, coffee, cakes, cookies, doughnuts, and pies. Add before, during, or after cooking, or sprinkle on as a garnish.

✔ **Onion powder:** A medium spicy and aromatic ground root, often with added salt and sugar. Use onion powder for meat, fish, poultry, soups, stews, beans, vegetables, dips, sauces, marinades, and salad dressings.

✔ **Oregano:** A mild and aromatic fresh, ground, or dried herb. (European oregano is wild marjoram.) Use oregano for lamb, beef, pork, fish, poultry, salads, mushrooms, onions, sorbets, vegetable juice, sauces, vinegar, and omelets. Add before, during, or after cooking, but don't cook for more than 10 minutes. Oregano can be used whole as a garnish.

✔ **Paprika:** A mild ground spice. Use paprika for beef, chicken, turkey, duck, pheasant, stews, chowders, Hungarian foods, deviled eggs, vegetables (especially potatoes, carrots, onions, and cauliflower), sauces, barbecue, salads, and salad dressings. Add before, during, or after cooking, or sprinkle on as a garnish.

✔ **Parsley:** A mild fresh or dried flaked herb. Use parsley for beef, fish, shellfish, poultry, salads, salad dressings, soups, stews, vegetables, vegetable juices, cottage cheese, omelets, grains, stuffing, vinegar, and sauces. Add before, during, or after cooking. Use parsley whole or chopped as a garnish.

✔ **Pepper:** A spicy hot whole, pickled, cracked, or ground spice that comes in several varieties. Use pepper on meats, fish, shellfish, poultry, vegetables, salads, prosciutto and melon, sauces, dips, grains, pasta, vegetable juice, barbecue, savory and spicy dishes, marinades, and spice cake. Add just before eating because its flavor develops with heat and time.

- **Black pepper:** Underripe whole berries.

- **Brazilian black:** The most prevalent pepper in the United States, but not considered the best.

- **Green pepper:** Fresh, pickled, or freeze-dried. Can be used as a garnish.

- **Lampong:** Usually the whole black pepper.

- **Malabar:** Reportedly the best pepper until tellicherry pepper came along.

- **Sarawak:** Reported to be the best white pepper but is only occasionally available.

- **Szechwan:** Often a combination or blend of predominantly red and reddish brown berries, or peppercorns.

- **Tellicherry:** Whole or ground. The best, boldest, blackest, most flavorful black pepper.

- **White pepper or Montoc:** The core of the ripest, mature berries. White pepper is made by washing off the outer shell of the berry. White pepper is less aromatic, has a different flavor, and is preferred in some foods for its lack of color.

✔ **Poppy seed:** A mild seed spice. Use poppy seeds in vegetables, salad dressings, breads, pasta, potato salad, egg dishes, vinegar, and coffee cakes. Add before, during, or after cooking. Can be used for garnish.

✔ **Purple basil:** A mild fresh herb that doesn't hold its flavor when cooked. Purple basil can be used whole, but only as a garnish.

✔ **Red pepper flakes:** A spicy hot, flaked form of red chili peppers. Red pepper flakes are used in Mexican, Middle Eastern, Asian, and Cajun cuisines. Use for fish, beef, curries, pizza, sauces, soups, noodles, dips, and French dressing. Add before, during, or after cooking. Red pepper flakes can be used as a garnish.

✔ **Rosemary:** A mild and aromatic fresh, dried, or ground herb. Use rosemary for beef, poultry, lamb, fish, spinach, tomatoes, potatoes, salads, fruits, soups with potatoes, sauces, macaroni, marinades, stuffing, vinegar, vegetable juice, and focaccia. Rosemary can be used whole or chopped as a garnish and can be added before, during, or after cooking.

✔ **Saffron:** The most expensive of all spices, mild, in threads or a powder. Use saffron for bouillabaisse, tomato soup, turkey, duck, chicken, seafood, squash, paella, curries, risotto, couscous, pilaf, stuffing, breads, cakes, cookies, and tea. Saffron needs a long cooking time to develop in flavor. Add before or during the early stages of cooking.

✔ **Sage:** A mild fresh, dried ground, or crumbled aromatic herb. Use sage for beef, rabbit, lamb, pork, sausage, poultry, pâté, soups, stews, sauces, onions, peas, tomatoes, bulgur, vinegar, casseroles, pasta, bread, stuffing, cottage cheese, fondue, omelets, and tomato juice. Use whole or as a garnish.

✔ **Savory:** A mild and aromatic fresh or dried herb. Use savory for meat, poultry, fish, shellfish, soups, stews, casseroles, beans, artichokes, asparagus, green beans, beans, pasta, vegetable juice, and fish sauce.

✔ **Sesame seed (also called benne or sesame paste):** A mild spice or seed. Use sesame seed for beef, poultry, fish, salads, vegetables, Asian and Middle Eastern dishes, noodles, breads, rice, cakes, and cookies. Seeds can be sprinkled on as a garnish. Ground seeds are called tahini.

✔ **Star anise:** A medium spicy spice, usually dried in the form of sliced pods that contain licorice-flavored seeds. Use star anise in soups, stews, sauces, and Asian dishes. This spice can be used whole as a garnish.

✔ **Tarragon:** A mild and aromatic fresh or dried herb. Use tarragon for meat, poultry, fish, pasta, rice, grains, stuffing, asparagus, beets, carrots, green beans, onions, squash, mushrooms, vegetable juice, marinades, mayonnaise, mustard, and vinegar. Tarragon can be used whole as a garnish.

✔ **Thyme:** A mild and aromatic fresh or dried herb of many varieties. Use thyme with beef, venison, rabbit, poultry, fish, shellfish, vegetables, pasta, cornbread, cottage cheese, omelets, gumbo, pea soup, tomato soup, vegetable soup, vinegar, stuffing, stews, salads, and Benedictine liqueur. Thyme can be used whole as a garnish and can be added before, during, or after cooking.

✔ **Turmeric:** A yellow, very mild (you can hardly taste it) powdered, fresh, or dried rhizome. Often called Indian saffron, it is used to enhance or boost saffron or to give foods a yellow color. Use turmeric in curries, deviled eggs, squash, couscous, rice, chutney, mustard, relish, poultry or fish dishes, salad dressings, and soups. Can be added anytime, before, during, or after cooking.

Spice mixtures and blends are handy, too. I keep the following blends on hand:

✔ Barbecue seasoning

✔ Bouquet garni

✔ Cajun spice mix

✔ Chinese five-spice powder

✔ Curry powder

✔ Fish herbs

✔ Herbes de Provence

✔ Mexican seasoning

# Taking Advantage of Lowfat Spreads, Salad Dressings, and Other Condiments

I probably have more condiments than any other type of food in my refrigerator. Most condiments have no fat and keep forever, and a meal isn't a meal unless pickles, relish, olives (which have some fat), or some bottled sauce adds a fillip of flavor. Following are some of the items that I keep on hand:

- Chili sauce
- Chowchow
- Chutney
- Dijonnaise
- Hot sauce
- Ketchup
- Mayonnaise (fat-free)
- Peppers (hot, red, and pickled)
- Pickles
- Prepared mustard
- Prepared Dijon mustard
- Relish
- Salsa
- Salsa ketchup
- Soy sauce (the low-sodium variety)
- Worcestershire sauce

Some of the new sandwich spreads, mayonnaises, and Dijonnaises are terrific, and many are fat-free. You can use them as a salad dressing base, too. Bottled salsas are excellent.

Most fat-free salad dressings are terrible, but some fat-free Italian dressings, though not good on salads, make a fine poaching sauce for turkey and fish cutlets (see Chapters 11 and 12). Fat-free and lowfat dressings are getting better, however. With just a little more effort, you can make your own tasty and lowfat dressings — flip to Chapter 9 for a variety of recipes.

# Using Liquids, Extracts, Pastes, and Other Flavorings

All these items are useful when cooking lowfat because concentrating on flavor instead of fat is important.

✔ **Barbecue sauce:** A medium spicy mixture of tomatoes, syrup, paprika, cayenne, sugar, garlic salt, black and white pepper, chili powder, and onion. (Celery salt is more Southern than Texan; in Tennessee, many people use Worcestershire sauce; in North Carolina folks often use mustard, vinegar, cumin, lemon juice, and no chili powder.) Use barbecue sauce for salad dressings, vegetables, beans, ribs, pork, and beef.

- ✔ **Hot sauce:** A spicy hot liquid made up of several kinds of hot chilies in a carrying liquid of water, vinegar, extract, oil, or juice. Good for soups, stews, guacamole, and pasta sauce.

- ✔ **Liquid smoke:** Adds great flavor to baked beans, bean soups, or pea soup when you don't want the fat from ham.

- ✔ **Vanilla:** An expensive, mild, and aromatic liquid, bean, pod, or extract that is used in puddings, cakes, cookies, pastries, sweet-style breads, ice cream, and milkshakes. Can be added before, during, or after cooking. (Vanillin artificial flavoring is not as full-flavored and may taste slightly bitter.)

# Sweetening the Deal with Sugar, Honey, Syrups, and Other Sweeteners

No sugar contains fat, but sugars do contain calories: 16 per teaspoon. Fat contains about 40 calories per teaspoon.

Many types of sugars are available. All sugars react in your body the same way, so don't think that brown sugar and honey are better for you or provide appreciably more nutrients. Sugar of any type offers little or no nutritional value.

In my pantry, I keep the following sweeteners:

- ✔ **Chocolate syrup:** Believe it or not, you can buy really good chocolate syrup that contains very little fat, and Hershey's makes one that is fat-free. Check the labels. Chocolate syrups do add calories, however, because they contain sugar.

- ✔ **Confectioners' or powdered sugar:** For sprinkling over baked goods and cookies or for quick frostings.

- ✔ **Dark and light brown sugars:** For baked goods, baked beans, quick syrups (heat first), and meat glazes. Dark brown sugar is more intense in flavor than light brown.

To keep brown sugar soft after you open it, store the whole box in a tightly sealed glass jar. If it hardens, place the sugar in a microwaveable dish and microwave on high for 10 seconds or until softened. If you don't have a microwave, place half an apple in a sealable plastic bag containing the box of sugar. Leave the apple there for several hours or overnight and then remove it.

- ✔ **Granulated sugar:** An all-purpose sweetener. Store it in a canister with a tight-fitting lid. Also comes in finely granulated form.

- ✔ **Honey:** A natural sweetener for glazes, dressings, and syrups.

  To thin crystallized honey, place $1/4$ cup in a microwaveable container and microwave on high for 10 seconds or until smooth. If you don't have a microwave, place the bottle or container of honey in a pan of hot tap water.

- ✔ **Jelly, jam, preserves, conserves, and apple butter:** Mixtures of fruit or fruit juice, sugar, and sometimes *pectin* (a thickening agent derived from fruit). Jelly is gelatinous, jam is a thick fruit puree, preserves are jam with chunky fruit, and conserves are usually a mixture of fruit, sugar, and nuts. Apple butter, which contains no butter, is thickened, pureed apple sauce and is good on toast, baked yams, and pork (see Chapter 12). All these products can be used as bread spreads, in pastries, and in cakes.

- ✔ **Maple syrup:** For pancakes and waffles or, more uncommonly but just as delicious, as a glaze for baked acorn squash or a base for sautéing bananas.

- ✔ **Marshmallows or marshmallow fluff:** A quick, no-fat frosting base; also good dolloped in hot cocoa.

- ✔ **Molasses:** A thick syrup that's great in baked goods, baked beans, and — believe it or not — wild rice dishes. Add a tablespoon or two to the cooking liquid before adding the rice. I keep both light and dark molasses on hand.

# Chapter 5

# Using Meat, Poultry, Fish, and Eggs in a Lowfat Eating Plan

. . . . . . . . . . . . . . . . . . . . . . . . . . . . . . . . . . . . . . . . . . . . . . . . . . . . . . . . .

. . . . . . . . . . . . . . . . . . . . . . . . . . . . . . . . . . . . . . . . . . . . . . . . . . . . . . . . .

*M*eat is a major source of dietary fat, saturated fat, and cholesterol. But many cuts of meat, not just poultry, are absolutely fine on a lowfat, low-saturated-fat, and low-cholesterol eating plan.

Meat, poultry, and other animal products such as eggs, cheese, and milk make up a large part of good daily nutrition. There's no medical reason not to continue eating animal products on a lowfat eating plan if the portions are small, they aren't eaten at every meal, and the visible fat is removed. However, reducing the fat in meat and poultry isn't as easy as reducing it in dairy products, where the many fat-free and lowfat dairy products available do the job for you. (See Chapter 6 for more information about the dairy side of things.) This chapter blows the whistle on a few myths and shows you what to look for when selecting meat, poultry, fish, and eggs.

## Does Red Meat Really Deserve Such a Bad Rap?

About 99 percent of animal products contain fat and saturated fat. Most meat and poultry, whether steak or chicken, turkey or pork, can be high in fat.

Knowing this, many people who are trying to cut down on fat or just eat more healthfully say that they don't eat red meat and stick to chicken, turkey, and fish. Most don't know exactly *why* they're switching, or for sure whether the switch will bring them better health, but they have a vague feeling that red meat isn't good for them. I want to make it clear right now that in many cases, just switching from red meat to chicken, especially if the chicken is the thigh or it isn't cooked with a lowfat method, doesn't do much.

Here's why: If you make the switch to lower your cholesterol intake, you're not doing anything because all meats (except organ meats), poultry, and seafood contain generally the same amount of cholesterol. (Organ meats contain more.)

If you make the switch to lower your fat intake, you may be on the right track. Fat contains more calories than any other substance you consume, and saturated fat is the major cause of cholesterol plaque in the arteries. But switching from red meat to chicken still may not reduce fat; it may even be harmful if you think that eating chicken is healthier without paying attention to how it's prepared and how much you eat. If beef is lean and simply prepared, then switching to fried, creamed, or butter-sautéed chicken is a bad move, raising fat, saturated fat, and cholesterol intake.

Switching from both red meat and batter-fried chicken to turkey breast prepared without fat can lower saturated fat and total fat. Skinless turkey breast contains less fat and saturated fat than any other meat. What's more significant is that skinless, almost fat-free turkey breast fillets can have almost half the saturated fat of the same amount of lean chicken, lean beef, lamb, or pork. Table 5-1 compares the fat and cholesterol contents of various cuts of chicken and turkey cooked in various ways.

| Table 5-1 | Chicken and Turkey (Per 3-Ounce Serving) | | | |
|---|---|---|---|---|
| | Calories | Fat g | Saturated Fat g | Cholesterol mg |
| Batter-fried whole chicken | 245 | 15 | 4 | 75 |
| Batter-fried chicken drumstick | 230 | 13 | 4 | 75 |
| Flour-fried whole chicken | 230 | 13 | 3 | 75 |
| Flour-fried chicken drumstick | 210 | 12 | 3 | 75 |
| Roasted whole chicken | 205 | 12 | 3 | 75 |
| Batter-fried chicken breast | 220 | 11 | 3 | 70 |
| Stewed whole chicken | 185 | 11 | 3 | 65 |

| | Calories | Fat g | Saturated Fat g | Cholesterol mg |
|---|---|---|---|---|
| Roasted chicken drumstick | 185 | 10 | 3 | 75 |
| Stewed chicken drumstick | 175 | 9 | 2 | 70 |
| Roasted whole hen turkey | 185 | 9 | 3 | 80 |
| Flour-fried chicken breast | 190 | 8 | 2 | 75 |
| Roasted whole Tom turkey | 170 | 8 | 2 | 80 |
| Roasted chicken breast | 170 | 7 | 2 | 70 |
| Fried skinless chicken drumstick | 165 | 7 | 2 | 80 |
| Roasted skinless dark turkey | 160 | 6 | 2 | 70 |
| Stewed chicken breast | 155 | 6 | 2 | 65 |
| Roasted skinless chicken drumstick | 145 | 5 | 1 | 80 |
| Roasted skinless hen turkey | 150 | 5 | 2 | 60 |
| Roasted whole fryer/roaster turkey | 145 | 5 | 1 | 100 |
| Stewed skinless chicken drumstick | 145 | 5 | 1 | 75 |
| Fried skinless chicken breast | 160 | 4 | 1 | 75 |
| Roasted skinless Tom turkey | 145 | 4 | 1 | 65 |
| Roasted skinless dark and light turkey | 145 | 4 | 1 | 65 |
| Roasted skinless chicken breast | 140 | 3 | 1 | 70 |
| Stewed skinless chicken breast | 130 | 3 | 1 | 65 |
| Roasted skinless white turkey | 120 | 1 | < 1 | 75 |

*Source:* Genesis R&D Product Development & Labeling Software

But 3 ounces of lean beef, lamb, or pork, with all visible fat removed and prepared without added fat, can be lower in fat than chicken, or even turkey, if the turkey or chicken is batter-fried and the skin is left on. Table 5-2 shows how much fat, saturated fat, and cholesterol are usually in a 3-ounce portion of various cuts of red meat trimmed of all visible fat. (Meat that has 1/8-inch fat trim can have twice as much fat and many more calories.)

| Table 5-2 | Beef, Pork, and Lamb (Per 3-Ounce Serving) | | | |
|---|---|---|---|---|
| | Calories | Fat g | Saturated Fat g | Cholesterol mg |
| **Beef** | | | | |
| Ground beef, broiled, well done (27% fat*) | 250 | 17 | 6 | 85 |
| Ground beef, broiled, well done (17% fat*) | 230 | 13 | 5 | 85 |
| Ground beef, broiled, well done (10% fat*) | 210 | 11 | 4 | 85 |
| Chuck, blade roast, braised | 210 | 11 | 4 | 90 |
| Brisket, whole, braised | 210 | 11 | 4 | 80 |
| Rib roast, large end, roasted | 200 | 11 | 4 | 70 |
| Rib steak, small end, broiled | 190 | 10 | 4 | 70 |
| Loin, tenderloin steak, broiled | 180 | 9 | 3 | 70 |
| Top loin, steak, broiled | 180 | 8 | 3 | 65 |
| Chuck, arm pot roast, braised | 180 | 7 | 3 | 85 |
| Bottom round, steak, braised | 180 | 7 | 2 | 80 |
| Loin, sirloin steak, broiled | 170 | 6 | 2 | 75 |
| Round tip roast, roasted | 160 | 6 | 2 | 70 |
| Eye of the round roast, roasted | 140 | 4 | 2 | 60 |
| Top round steak, broiled | 150 | 4 | 1 | 70 |
| **Pork** | | | | |
| Spareribs, braised | 340 | 26 | 9 | 105 |
| Ground pork, broiled | 250 | 18 | 7 | 80 |
| Loin, country-style ribs, roasted | 210 | 13 | 5 | 80 |
| Shoulder, blade steak, broiled | 190 | 11 | 4 | 80 |
| Loin, sirloin roast, roasted | 180 | 9 | 3 | 75 |
| Loin, rib chop, broiled | 190 | 8 | 3 | 70 |
| Loin, center chop, broiled | 170 | 7 | 3 | 70 |
| Top loin, chop, boneless, broiled | 170 | 7 | 2 | 70 |
| Top loin, roast, boneless, roasted | 170 | 6 | 2 | 65 |
| Loin, tenderloin roast, roasted | 140 | 4 | 1 | 65 |

*Fat before cooking

| | Calories | Fat g | Saturated Fat g | Cholesterol mg |
|---|---|---|---|---|
| **Lamb** | | | | |
| Rib roast, roasted | 200 | 11 | 4 | 75 |
| Loin chop, broiled | 180 | 8 | 3 | 80 |
| Shoulder, blade chop, broiled | 180 | 10 | 3 | 80 |
| Shoulder, arm chop, broiled | 170 | 8 | 3 | 80 |
| Leg, whole, roasted | 160 | 7 | 2 | 75 |
| Shank, braised | 160 | 5 | 2 | 90 |

*Sources:* Nutri-Facts; Genesis R&D Product Development & Labeling Software

Switching from red meat to fish is advisable if the fish isn't batter-laden, butter-sautéed, or fried. Fish is generally lower in fat and saturated fat than red meat and poultry. Except for cod and scallops, which are even lower in fat, fish has about the same amount of fat as turkey. (You can find a table of lean and fatty fish later in this chapter.)

Health-conscious fast-food patrons got quite a surprise a few years ago when they switched from burgers to fish sandwiches after reading about fish being better for them than beef. Unfortunately, they discovered that fast-food fish, which is batter-fried, contains far more fat than fast-food fried chicken sandwiches. Reading that chicken is better than beef, they then switched to fast-food chicken, not realizing that most is breaded and fried. So they discovered that a fast-food chicken sandwich contains more fat than a burger. The single burger has the least fat of all.

So switching, especially from red meat to chicken, may not help you reach your goal of more healthful, lower-fat eating if you aren't knowledgeable about the cut of chicken, how it's prepared, how big the serving is, and how often you eat it.

# Good lower-fat meat and animal products: they do exist!

All is not lost in the effort to include meat and other animal products in a lowfat diet. Some of the fat and sometimes all the fat from animal products can be removed. It can be eliminated enough to call it fat-free in substitute eggs, milk, yogurt, ice cream, sour cream, cheese, and some lunch meat slices, including ham, turkey, and chicken. Fat-free cheeses are made by Alpine Lace, Borden, Healthy Choice, Kraft, and Smart Beat, as well as a few others.

Esskay and other regional brands make a chipped beef that only has half a gram of fat

*(continued)*

*(continued)*

per serving. Louis Rich makes deli-style sliced ham, chicken, and turkey breast that are 98 percent fat-free, plus fat-free hot dogs. The trick is to search and seize. Sometimes products are here today and gone tomorrow. (See Chapter 3 for a way to get stores to order the products you want.)

Fat can also be significantly reduced in unprocessed meats, such as pork, beef, lamb, and poultry, by breeding leaner animals to begin with, raising them in a leaner way, not fattening animals before slaughter, and then zero-trimming meat at the market. To zero-trim, the meat cutter takes off all the edge fat on slices or roasts of pork, beef, or lamb, including chops, tenderloins, and fillets. Even though red meat may have *marbling* (white strands of fat throughout the meat), there is no fat on the edge. Zero. Nada. The meat cutter removes all of it, so you aren't tempted to cook with it and eat it. Some cuts are leaner naturally.

# *You Can Eat Red Meat and Still Eat Lowfat*

According to the most trustworthy groups and respected experts, such as the American Heart Association, the Surgeon General of the United States, and the National Research Council of the National Academy of Sciences, red meat is an important food source. One reason not to omit red meat from your diet is that it has great nutritional value. Beef, for example, has more zinc, vitamin B-12, and iron than chicken.

Even the consumer watchdog group the Center for Science in the Public Interest says that lean red meat, depending on how often you eat it and how big the serving is, is fine as part of a healthful diet. This group doesn't approve of hamburger, however, which, if store bought, and even if lean, still contains a lot of fat.

You can get around that, though. Make your own hamburger by purchasing a lean cut of beef such as top round, have the edge fat removed, and have it ground at the store (or do it at home). Then your hamburger contains very little fat. However, it won't hold together for a burger unless you add rehydrated TVP (textured vegetable protein), bread crumbs, an egg white, water, or some combination of these. Still, the leanest possible ground sirloin or ground round, plus onions, celery, and/or a soy extender, is excellent for meat loaf, tacos, chili, sloppy Joes, and other dishes that call for ground meat.

Experts differ on how often to eat red meat such as beef. Many people eat meat twice a day (a sandwich for lunch and a pork chop for dinner, for example), but changing to four or five times a week would be greatly beneficial in terms of eating less total fat, as well as less saturated fat and cholesterol.

The ideal portion size for red meat, or any meat, for that matter, is 3 ounces — about the size of a deck of cards. When you're served more at restaurants, and you always are, take half home. Add a few vegetables and you have another meal on the same dollar. If you have four in your family, 1 pound of raw meat gives each person 3 ounces cooked.

# Pork

Pork, which has the worst reputation for fat, is actually the leanest red meat if the cut is Canadian bacon or lean ham. But pork is the fattiest meat if the cut is fatty bacon, salt pork, or ribs. Again, with pork, fat content depends upon the cut, the breed, and how the pig was raised.

The saturated fat content of some pork is higher by about 1 gram per serving than it is in similar cuts of most other red meats.

Ounce for ounce, pork has about the same cholesterol content as poultry, fish, lamb, and beef, but a 6-ounce serving of pork ribs can contain 52 grams of total fat and as much as 18 grams of saturated fat. Canadian bacon and lean ham, on the other hand, contain about 12 grams of total fat and less than 4 grams of saturated fat.

Sliced fat-free ham is available from brand-name manufacturers, such as Oscar Mayer, Louise Rich, and Hillshire Farms at most major markets. It is presliced and comes in small packages. Some are ham loafs, but they are primarily pure ham, although they do contain *carrageenan,* a product made from seaweed that helps bind the meat when it doesn't contain fat.

# Lamb

Lamb *can* be lean and somewhat low in fat, but generally it isn't. Fat content depends on the cut and how the lamb is raised. Most lamb contains 46 percent calories from fat. Ounce for ounce, lamb generally contains the same amount of cholesterol as beef, pork, chicken, turkey, and fish do.

Instead of ordering lamb at a restaurant, where you can't control the fat content and the cut is often selected only for taste, buy it yourself, cook it at home, and trim away the fat, which you can see. Much, if not all, of the fat can be removed with determination and a sharp knife. Chops don't fall apart when you remove the fat.

As for a leg of lamb, have the meat cutter *butterfly* (cut open and flatten) it and remove the bone. Then marinate the whole flat leg, season it, and grill or roast it in a slow oven (see Chapter 12). When the leg is butterflied, the fat is especially easy to see. I remove every single bit of fat with a sharp knife and scissors.

# All Poultry Is Lowfat, Right?

Even a breast of chicken or turkey that it is skinned and trimmed of all visible fat gets about 20 percent of its calories from fat if chicken, 13 if turkey. But a 3-ounce serving of skinless and defatted poultry breast generally has 1 gram less total fat and $1/2$ gram less saturated fat than 3 ounces of lean red meat. Poultry contains about the same amount of cholesterol as most fish and lean red meat do.

Fat-free chicken and turkey slices are available from brand-name manufacturers such as Oscar Mayer and Louis Rich at most major chain markets. Note that some fat-free poultry slices contain carrageenan, a harmless substance (see the sidebar "Chemicals in your food" for more information).

---

## Chemicals in your food

Food manufacturers and producers have to mention every product or additive that's in their food on the label, beginning with the ingredient that's present in the largest amount by weight. From sodium to seaweed, whether the amount is trace or half of the total weight, it is listed. Many ingredients, although strange-sounding, such as carrageenan or locus beans, are nutritious, and if not nutritious, are used in such small amounts that they are generally harmless. Some ingredients are chemicals, such as citric acid, which is used as a preservative. Others, like calcium disodium EDTA, prolong shelf-life. Color such as beta carotene, deemed safer than the previous red dye #4, is also listed.

Watchful individuals, organizations, and hopefully the government help keep manufacturers on their toes with laws to protect consumers so that food producers and manufacturers aren't allowed to add harmful ingredients. So if you see carrageenan added to a fat-free meat or poultry product, don't be alarmed.

---

# *Chicken*

Ounce for ounce, a lean chicken fillet has about the same amount of cholesterol as does a lean turkey, duck, beef, lamb, pork, or fish fillet. Though the cholesterol is generally the same, the fat content is different. Chicken that is skinned and has all visible fat removed generally has less saturated fat than lean beef, pork, or lamb, but it has more total fat and saturated fat than turkey.

If skinless and completely defatted, 3 ounces of lower leg or drumstick of the chicken is 4 grams fattier than the same amount of chicken breast. The thigh, skinned and defatted, has slightly more fat than the lower leg, but you can lower the fat content by removing the two or three small, almond-sized pieces of fat between the muscle. Butterflying the thigh and cutting the meat off the bone exposes the fat globules, making them easier to remove.

For better-tasting and moister chicken parts, buy the chicken parts with the skin, bone, and fat. Then skin, bone, and defat the breast or thigh at home. If the skinless chicken has been sitting in the store's refrigerator case in its cello-pack, which is porous, it will be drier and lose taste.

If you don't want to remove the skin and fat yourself, have the meat cutter do it when you purchase it. To save myself time, the meat department is the first place I head to when I enter my grocery store. I pick out all my meat, such as lean top round and chicken, and have the meat cutter remove all the edge fat from the top round and grind my own very lean hamburger. Then he or she skins my chicken (I have to do more fat removal at home) and removes any edge fat from a leg of lamb and butterflies it. Meat cutters (as they prefer to be called) do this at no extra cost to you.

Both whole capons and Cornish game hens can be skinned before cooking with no discernible taste difference, but this method doesn't work with quail or turkey, which is leaner to begin with. Because much of the chicken fat resides in the skin, one study suggests that it's okay to cook chicken with the skin and then remove the skin before eating. I always remove it before cooking; then I don't have to be concerned that someone (usually me) will want to eat that good-tasting crispy skin. Why tempt myself or anyone else? I cook the skinned chicken in an oven bag either in the oven or in the microwave. (You can find a recipe in Chapter 12.) And the skin, bones, and fat make great stock — defatted after cooking, of course.

## Turkey

Skinless and defatted white and dark meat turkey (and chicken) has less total fat than duck, duckling, lean beef, pork, such as Canadian bacon or lean ham, or lamb. A 4-ounce boned turkey cutlet trimmed of skin and all visible fat has less than 1 gram of fat. Turkey cutlets can be cooked easily in many ways, all taking less than 5 minutes (you can find the recipe in Chapter 12).

Check the Nutrition Facts panel on packages of ground turkey to be sure of the fat content, as the manufacturer may have added skin, loose fat, thighs, and lower back meat in the grinding process. Turkey hot dogs, too, can have as much or more fat than beef or pork hot dogs. Read the labels carefully. Look for "lowfat" or "97 percent fat-free." Then you know it's only 3 percent fat or less by weight.

Don't let the words *ground turkey* lull you into thinking that it has to be lowfat. Ground turkey can be very high in fat.

## Duck

Ounce for ounce, duck has the same amount of cholesterol as do chicken, turkey, beef, pork, lamb, and fish. The total fat content is different, though. If the duck is wild, it has less fat than domestic duck. Skinning a duck breast is far more difficult than skinning chicken breasts, so have your meat cutter do it. A 3-ounce serving of duckling breast without the skin has 2 grams of fat, whereas 3 ounces of duckling breast with the skin has 9 grams of fat.

# What about Hot Dogs, Lunch Meat, and Other Processed Stuff?

Reading labels is especially important in this category, because you can find everything from fat-free to very-high-fat varieties of these products. The following sections let you know what to look for.

## Hot dogs

Hot dogs can be made from beef, pork, poultry, vegetables, or soy products, and they can be fat-free. The average meat hot dog, whether beef or pork, is about 27 percent fat by weight, and about 75 percent of its calories come from fat. Yuck!

Fat-free hot dogs come in several brands, such as Oscar Mayer and Ball Park. In my market, fat-free dogs come and go. A month ago, I saw four brands of fat-free hot dogs. Now there are only two. Lowfat hot dogs are more plentiful. Healthy Choice has them at 1 gram of fat. Higher in fat are certain Louis Rich hot dogs, which have 8 grams of fat. High-fat dogs are the regular Ball Park and half a dozen other brands, which average about 16 grams of total fat per hot dog. One brand of knockwurst (or knackwurst) — which is precooked beef or pork link that is a little fatter-looking than a hot dog and has more garlic in the mix — has an enormous 26 grams of total fat.

With hot dogs, you can almost get what you want in terms of fat. Just read the labels, as companies change their formulas, adding new ingredients and improving the taste. In my observance, the lower the fat of the dog, the more sodium it contains. But because I'm more concerned about fat than I am about sodium, I go with the product that has the least fat. Your dietary needs may differ.

Yves veggie dogs come in several flavors and are also fat-free. Some canned veggie dogs are not lowfat, however. Again, get into the label-reading habit.

## Lunch meat

Most lunch meats, such as bologna and salami, contain high amounts of both fat and sodium. Ninety-seven percent fat-free bologna and 70 percent fat-free salami are available from at least two major brands, including Oscar Mayer. Hormel offers pepperoni with 70 percent less fat, or 4 grams for 17 slices, so these are good choices for lowering fat.

One way to keep the flavor of lunch meat and yet lower the fat is to go half and half. Because no one uses just one slice of meat in a sandwich, go one slice regular bologna or salami for taste and one slice fat-free for health, or 10 slices regular pepperoni and 15 slices lower fat. You get all the taste with less fat.

## Tofu

Tofu is a good meat substitute. Made from soybeans, tofu comes in several types, silky to firm, with firm having the highest fat content (which isn't very high) and silky the lowest. Tofu also comes fat-free. It's made from a bean and is often used in place of meat in such dishes as stir-fry. Somewhat bland-tasting, it can be diced in salads or soups or crisped by frying or baking. Eaten mainly in Asian communities at first, tofu gains friends every day because it is a good source of protein and low in fat.

# Purchasing Meat and Poultry

In addition to the cut, the fat content in meat such as pork, beef, and lamb, as well as poultry, depends on several factors: breed (some breeds are naturally fattier than others), feed, sex, and age at slaughter. The important thing to remember is to choose meat with your eyes as your guide. You can see fat.

Beef is graded *prime,* which used to mean the fattiest or most marbled, then *choice,* the next fatty, and then *select,* plus there are other commercial grades. But a select grade of a top round from one cow may not have anywhere near the same fat content as a select top round from another cow. Top round has less fat than ribs, but choose the meat that *looks* the leanest.

I've had many a meat cutter look me in the eyes and say, "This is lean hamburger," when I can see a lot of fat. The cutter's training on what tastes best for you may come into play. When I used to request that all edge fat be removed on a very lean top round, ready to be ground into my hamburger, the finished product often came back fatty. I would ask about it, and the cutter would say, "I heard what you said, but you need some fat." After a little coaxing, my regular meat cutter grinds it just the way I want it.

Meat offerings in supermarkets can vary from region to region. I was in several markets in one Florida city where I not only couldn't find any lean meat but also couldn't even find meat lean enough to cut the fat away. In big cities, you usually can find extremely lean meat and a variety of other lowfat or fat-free meat items, such as hot dogs, ham, chicken, turkey, and lunch meat slices, plus lowfat sausage.

Markets and producers are changing because of health-conscious consumers like you. No longer is coconut oil syringed into frozen turkeys (although other oils are). Duck breasts are available skinless in some areas, and quail and other lowfat poultry, like nearly fat-free "tenders" and turkey breast fillets or cutlets, are available in many areas. The only poultry that doesn't change regardless of the store, chain, or region is whole chicken. Everywhere, whole chickens are disgustingly fatty.

The way to get around that is to buy a chicken and have the meat cutter remove the skin. Use the skin to flavor soup, which is defatted. When you get home, remove the unnecessary fat that ridges the thigh, back, and breast. Cook the chicken skinless in an oven bag spiced with rosemary and thyme for a great and fast meal for four. (Whole turkeys, however, need to be cooked with the skin on.)

Today, many breeders of pigs, sheep, and cattle are raising leaner animals and bringing them to market earlier, when they are naturally more tender without extra fat. More meat cutters are *zero-trimming,* meaning that they remove most, if not all, edge fat. Some lowered-fat beef producers or brands are Beefalo, Brae Beef, Coleman Natural, Dakota Beef, Lean and Free, Lean Limousine, Shenandoah Beef, and Stapleman.

For those who eat processed foods or frozen dinners, often because of time constraints or because they don't know how to cook, many more lowfat frozen dinner entrees that contain beef, lamb, pork, chicken, and turkey are available.

## What lean really means

For a meat, poultry, or seafood label to use the term *lean,* each 3¹/₂ ounces of the product must contain less than 10 grams of total fat, less than 4.5 grams of saturated fat, and less than 95 milligrams of cholesterol. *Extra lean* contains less than 5 grams of total fat, less that 2 grams of saturated fat, and less than 95 milligrams of cholesterol. Because 4.5 grams is a lot of saturated fat, go extra lean when you can. In terms of fat, nearly all seafood can be considered extra lean. Preparation methods such as breading and frying and then serving it with a fatty sauce such as tartar sauce make it high in fat, however.

I hear many people say, "I cut out red meat years ago to improve my health." You're fooling yourself by thinking that red meat has to be a high-fat product. It *can* be and often is. But so can chicken and fish! Lean red meat contains the same amount of cholesterol and close to the same amount of fat as lean chicken, fish, and turkey. The point is that you can eat lean red meat such as beef, lamb, or pork. If the red meat doesn't say lean, buy dense cuts, such as top round, or any red meat that looks lean, such as tenderloin, London broil, ham, or Canadian bacon that has no visible fat.

Restaurants are the last to hold out in the fat-lowering push. Few have reduced their meat or poultry portion sizes or lessened the cream, butter, and cheese in their dishes. People no longer eat out once a month as a treat; often they eat out six or seven times a week, daily for weekday lunches and once or twice for dinner. More restaurants and chefs need to take into account that a lowered-fat menu plan is in their customers' best interest. Chefs do an excellent job with substitutions and personal requests on menu changes because of dietary or allergic needs. I think that nutritional information should be on every menu and every cafeteria offering.

# Fish, Fat, and Cholesterol

Except for sardines, herring, mackerel, eel, and a few other varieties, fish contains less fat and saturated fat than lean red meat or poultry — between 1 and 2 grams for 3 ounces. Fish contains about the same amount of cholesterol as red meat and poultry: between 60 and 70 milligrams per 3 ounces. Cod contains the least amount of fat of any fish.

Because omega-3 fatty acids, prevalent in some fish, tend to keep the blood from coagulating in much the same way that aspirin does, eating fish may be good for people who are at risk for heart attacks and strokes.

Shrimp and squid contain almost no fat. These shellfish have about two times the cholesterol of the same amount of meat, fish, and poultry; lobster is similar, somewhat high in cholesterol but also low in fat. Bivalves such as scallops, mussels, and clams contain less cholesterol than lobster, shrimp, and squid, and about the same amount of fat — nearly none. Scallops, the bivalves with the least amount of fat, are an ideal seafood on a lowfat menu plan.

I practically memorized the lists in Table 5-3 because they help me in making restaurant and fish market selections. If I can't decide between scallops, scrod, tuna, or salmon, for example, and I know that scallops and cod have almost no fat and that tuna and salmon are very fatty, my choice is easy when fat is the only consideration.

Usually, the lighter in color the fish, the less fat it contains. The darker the fish, the more fat it has.

✔ **The leanest fish and shellfish:** These fish and shellfish fall into the category of 1 gram of fat, sometimes less, per serving. The lowest in fat are cod, scallops, and clams. Cook extremely lean fish and shellfish with methods that keep in as much moisture as possible, including quick steaming, boiling, braising, and quick sautéing.

- **Extra lean fish and shellfish:** These fish and shellfish are considered extra lean but aren't as lean as the leanest. They should be cooked quickly by steaming, microwaving, braising or poaching in wine or lemon, sautéing, baking in parchment or dough (or other wrappers), foil grilling, or a cooking procedure where the natural moisture is enhanced or can't escape, or where more moisture is added.

- **Lean fish and shellfish:** These fish are considered lean. The best cooking methods for lean fish are the same as for extra lean fish, although some lean types of fish can be grilled, broiled, and if firm, used in kebabs or chowders.

- **The fattiest fish:** You can cook fatty fish by using almost any method, but you'll be especially successful when broiling, grilling, dry frying, barbecuing, smoking, or baking — methods that can make lean fish too dry. You can also use any of the methods for cooking leaner fish, such as poaching or baking.

| Table 5-3 | | Fish from Lean to Fatty | |
|---|---|---|---|
| **Leanest of All** | **Extra Lean** | **Lean** | **Fattiest** |
| Abalone | Anchovies (raw, not in oil) | Butterfish | Anchovies (canned in oil) |
| Ahi | Blue runner | Carp | Atlantic mackerel |
| Burbot | Bluefin tuna | Coho salmon | Chinook salmon |
| Clams | Bluefish | Lake trout | Eel |
| Cod | Bonito | Lake whitefish | Herring |
| Crayfish | Channel catfish | Pompano | Sablefish |
| Dungeness crab | Crab | Sockeye salmon | Sardines |
| Flounder | Crevalle jack | Spanish mackerel | Shad and shad roe |
| Golden king klip | Croaker | Whitefish | Tuna (canned in oil) |
| Grouper | Cusk | Yellow tail | |
| Haddock | Greenland turbot | | |
| King crab | Halibut | | |
| Ling | King mackerel | | |
| Lingcod | Langoustines (small spiny lobster) | | |

*(continued)*

**Table 5-3 (continued)**

| Leanest of All | Extra Lean | Lean | Fattiest |
|---|---|---|---|
| Mahi mahi | Maine lobster* | | |
| Orange roughy | Monkfish | | |
| Pike | Mullet | | |
| Pink snapper | Mussels | | |
| Pollack | Ocean catfish | | |
| Scallops | Ocean perch | | |
| Scrod (baby cod) | Oysters | | |
| Skate | Pink salmon (but belly is fatty) | | |
| Skipjack tuna | Porgy (scup) | | |
| Tuna (canned in water) | Rainbow trout | | |
| Yellowfin tuna | Redfish | | |

\* Indicates fish and shellfish that have more than 95 mg cholesterol per serving

*Sources:* The National Fisheries Institute; Genesis R&D Product Development & Labeling Software

Other extra lean fish include rockfish, sea bass, sea trout, shark, shrimp*, smelt, snails, snapper, sole, spot, squid*, striped bass, sturgeon, swordfish, tilapia, tilefish, wahoo, whiting, and wolffish.

# Telling the "Good" Eggs from the "Bad"

On average, whole fresh eggs contain 5 grams of total fat and 213 to 240 milligrams of cholesterol. Eggs with double yolks contain more fat and cholesterol. The fat and cholesterol are in the yolk, which also contains protein. Egg whites are mostly protein and contain neither fat nor cholesterol.

Just because one fresh egg contains a high amount of cholesterol doesn't mean that you shouldn't use fresh eggs. The trick is not to use the yolks, at least not very often. Because only the yolks contain cholesterol and fat, simply discard them or mix them with water and use them to fertilize outdoor plants (after two days, the smell is unacceptable for indoor use).

You might use one or two fresh eggs (with the yolks) when making an omelet for six people and mix them with substitute eggs for a yellow color. For certain dishes, such as a lowfat cheesecake, you might use one or two whole eggs with yolks, because a cake serves eight or ten and may not have an acceptable texture without the yolks. I eat as few yolks as possible at home so that I can be less stringent about them at restaurants, cocktail parties, and friends' homes. I do not order restaurant foods that contain yolks (or butter or cheese), such as omelets or desserts.

I use fresh eggs in many other ways, however. I often add a fresh egg white or two to substitute egg omelets or scrambled eggs, and I use a half-dozen fresh egg whites for soufflés and a dozen for angel food cake and other chiffon-style cakes. I also add fresh egg whites to baked egg dishes, French toast, or other batters in which I use mainly substitute eggs. They mix together well and cause no problems in cooking or baking.

## *Substitute eggs*

Substitute eggs are an excellent alternative to fresh eggs in most dishes. The substitutes have no fat and no cholesterol, are lactose free, and contain about 100 milligrams of sodium and 6 grams of protein per serving (brands vary slightly). Most important, substitute eggs are pasteurized, meaning that they are heated with a special process long enough to kill salmonella but not long enough to congeal the eggs.

Substitute eggs look just like fresh eggs. They are made primarily of egg whites with some beta carotene for coloring. The package reveals that they also contain certain additives, such as guar gum and other vegetable gums, vitamins, minerals, folic acid, calcium sulfate, and trace amounts of other chemicals for thickening and longevity. Substitute eggs are usually about 99 percent egg and 1 percent all these other ingredients combined. The percentage or amount of chemicals is considered to be too small to significantly affect your health, but they have to be mentioned on each carton even if they are present in trace proportions. In my opinion, the high cholesterol and moderate fat content in fresh egg yolks are far more detrimental to your health than the small amount of chemicals in substitute eggs.

Substitute eggs come in cartons, both frozen and unfrozen. Frozen egg substitutes keep for several months; unfrozen ones keep for about seven days after the sell date on the package, which is often weeks after your purchase, giving them a total refrigerator life of about three weeks. Excellent-tasting substitute egg brands are Egg Beaters, Healthy Choice, Lucerne, Nulaid, Scramblers, and Second Nature.

# The dangers of salmonella

Two thousand people a year die from salmonella bacteria found in eggs, chicken, and other products. Another several hundred thousand become ill with stomachaches and other flu-like symptoms. Heating eggs and chickens to 180° kills salmonella bacteria; washing chicken or eggs with soap and water before cooking does not.

Consider all eggs and chicken to be tainted by this pesky bacteria. No raw egg should be used if it isn't thoroughly heated to a temperature high enough to destroy salmonella. This means that you should not eat soft-cooked or soft-scrambled eggs, eggs fried with loose yolks, egg-based sauces, eggnog,

homemade mayonnaise, hollandaise sauce, Caesar salad, or most meringues. Nearly all these foods can be made with egg substitutes instead, and they're perfectly safe. When eggs are thoroughly cooked, such as in cakes, soufflés, cookies, baked casserole dishes, and hard-cooked eggs, the salmonella bacteria is destroyed.

So be a smart eggie. Cook all fresh eggs and poultry thoroughly, and don't make or eat dishes that contain partially cooked or uncooked eggs. And don't cross-contaminate utensils by using the same ones for raw foods as for cooked.

Some brands of substitute eggs taste or work better than others, depending on what you're using them for. You want especially good-tasting substitute eggs for unadorned scrambled eggs, for example, so compare brands for flavor and texture — they differ widely, and they are continually being improved. The brand doesn't matter for dishes such as pancakes, cakes, and cookies, in which the eggs are incorporated into a batter.

You can use substitute eggs straight from the carton in uncooked or not thoroughly cooked dishes like eggnog, Caesar salad, mayonnaise, hollandaise, and loosely scrambled eggs or soft omelets; you should not use fresh shell eggs for these dishes because of the danger of salmonella poisoning. You can also use substitute eggs in just about any recipe that calls for whites and yolks mixed together, such as puddings, custards, casseroles, soufflés, sauces, omelets, cookies, cakes, pancakes, and French toast. Substitute eggs also work in egg salad sandwiches (see Chapter 14) if you hard-cook them and then chop and mix them with chopped hard-cooked egg whites. You can also make stuffed deviled eggs by pureeing cooked substitute eggs, adding lowfat mayonnaise and other spices, and piping the mixture into hard-cooked egg whites. If you aren't eliminating all egg yolks from your menu plan, you can puree a couple of cooked yolks with 3 cups cooked egg substitutes.

*Note:* Some baked goods take on a slightly different consistency when made with substitute eggs. That's usually because the fat content is lower and the consistency of substitute eggs is slightly different from that of fresh eggs.

## The substitute egg taste test

Some months ago, I suggested that I make an omelet for my friend Bob, who is a true gourmet. He owns more than 30 restaurants and knows all the nuances of fine food. In addition, he is particular and fussy. I remarked that I might make the omelet with substitute eggs because his cholesterol level is high. He scoffed and said that he wouldn't touch an omelet made with "fake" eggs.

I explained that they aren't fake eggs but 99 percent egg product, made of mostly whites, but without the yolk — and therefore without the cholesterol and fat. I also bragged that he wouldn't be able to tell the difference whether the omelet was made with fresh eggs or my eggs in a carton. He insisted that he would.

He said, "Okay. Make one with 'real' eggs and the other with 'chemical' eggs." I told him that both are real eggs; one is simply pasteurized, which kills salmonella.

I made two omelets, both with substitute eggs. I served them on crisp watercress placed on large plates attractively decorated with raspberries, orange wedges, and kiwi slices, and I added a freshly made side of mushrooms and shallots sautéed in white wine. I added a lightly steamed asparagus spear across each omelet to make it really enticing.

While we ate the omelets, I said, "Well, which is which?" He tasted mine, then his, and then mine. He didn't know. First he said, "Fresh," then, "Substitute," then, "Fresh" again, and finally, "Definitely fresh."

When I told him that both were made with egg substitutes and showed him the carton (I was out of fresh eggs), he wasn't annoyed but amazed at how good they were. He ate the whole omelet, which was the true test. (You can find a variety of omelet recipes in Chapter 7.)

You may want to try using substitute eggs that aren't frozen or adding a fresh egg white, which doesn't alter the fat content of the dish. Baked goods made lower in fat always have a slightly different taste and texture than do higher-fat versions. But you get used to the taste of food without fat much like you get used to drinking skim milk instead of whole milk.

## Dried egg whites

Dried egg whites that you reconstitute with water are a terrific product that I recently discovered. Just Whites are a dry, powdered egg white mixture sold in a canister with a vacuum lid. They need no refrigeration even after opening. You mix them with water and use them just like egg whites: unwhipped, beaten until frothy, or whipped into stiff peaks. Just Whites are made of pure egg whites and are manufactured and distributed by Deb El Foods (2 Papetti Plaza, Elizabeth, NJ 07207).

You can use Just Whites for meringues in lemon meringue pie (they brown nicely) and in *whips,* which are delicious old-fashioned desserts made with dried or fresh fruits that are pureed and combined with sugar, sometimes lemon juice or zest, and stiffly beaten egg whites and then chilled and served in tall glasses. They are perfect on a lowfat menu plan because they contain no fat.

Additional uses for Just Whites are for fluffing up frozen fruits for parfaits, making chocolate mousses with cocoa powder (pure chocolate with most of the fat removed), making frostings, or preparing any dish that calls for uncooked egg whites. They cook up quite nicely, too.

## *The Skinny on Cholesterol*

All animals and animal products, from milk to meat, butter to eggs, chorizo to cheese, fish to fowl, contain cholesterol, with egg whites being the one exception. All organ meats, such as liver, brains, and sweetbreads, contain large amounts of cholesterol.

Skinned turkey with all visible fat removed has slightly less total fat and saturated fat than skinned chicken prepared the same way, and fish has slightly less total fat than the turkey, but the turkey, chicken, fish, and red meat all have about the same amount of cholesterol.

Cholesterol is in both muscle and fat, so eating only lean cuts, turkey fillets, or zero-trimmed meat doesn't mean that you get less cholesterol. And dietary cholesterol is a culprit in heart disease, although not the major culprit, which is saturated fat.

# Chapter 6

# Dairy Products: The Easiest Foods to Change to Lowfat

*By switching from regular dairy products to fat-free and having only two servings each day of products such as milk, cheese, cottage cheese, sour cream, and yogurt, you can avoid consuming about 35,000 calories a year, which equates to losing about 10 pounds without changing your volume of food.*

*Changing the usual 3 teaspoons of butter or margarine a day to I Can't Believe It's Not Butter! fat-free spray saves you nearly 33,000 calories and over 9 pounds of weight per year.*

People take for granted that all dairy products are healthful, but it all depends on which dairy products you consume and how much fat is in them. Sure, a glass of skim milk with an afternoon snack is a terrific choice — but choose whole milk instead, and you're consuming *lots* of fat.

In this chapter, I tell you exactly how much fat is in whole-milk dairy products and explain why skim and fat-free products are healthier choices for most people. I also examine 2 percent and 1 percent dairy products, which cause confusion for many people. I include several tables comparing various cheeses, yogurts, sour creams, and other dairy products, enabling you to compare their total fat, saturated fat, cholesterol, and calorie content. Read through this chapter for fat-saving dairy product substitutions, too.

# Fat and Dairy Products

The saturated fat content in such dairy products as milk, cheese, butter, and cream is important because people eat so much of these products. Pizza is a classic American dish, and restaurants now serve pizza with cheese not only on top but stuffed in the crust, too. People think pasta needs cheese. Chili isn't chili unless it has cheese on it, and tacos need cheese and sour cream in them. People think bagels have to have high-fat cream cheese; potato pancakes need sour cream; toast, waffles, pancakes, and bread need butter; and so on. Culture reinforces this desire for high-fat foods. But to make wise choices, you need to know the contents of the foods you eat and the effects of those foods on your body.

Saturated fat and cholesterol that you eat or drink, for example, doesn't just pass through your body. Depending on how your body handles these substances over time, they cause your body to make substances that can accumulate in your heart and arteries. What you eat during your early years can be the beginnings of deposits of cholesterol plaque. In fact, cholesterol plaque is cumulative for half of all American men and a third of all American women. This means that if you're among the half or third of the population that is affected, the fat you ate between ages 5 and 25 can affect your heart and arteries at ages 35, 55, and 75.

Primarily, the fat you eat, including the fat in dairy products, is what makes you fat. Volume also makes you fat. I put this topic into better perspective in the following sections.

## Milk

If you drink two glasses of whole milk each day, you consume almost 13 pounds of solid fat each year, most of it saturated. No wonder people experience problems with weight and heart disease!

You may know that most of the fats in dairy products are saturated fats. But did you know that only slightly reducing the fat in milk and other dairy products may not do much good?

The Center for Science in the Public Interest, a consumer watchdog organization in Washington, D.C., reported that drinking four glasses of 2 percent milk is the equivalent of eating six pieces of bacon a day — something most people wouldn't do on a daily basis. If you drink several glasses of 2 percent milk each day (or put it on cereal or in coffee), you're getting a great deal of fat, much of it saturated. Those four 8-ounce glasses contain 19 grams of fat! Incidentally, the 2 percent milk has over twice as much cholesterol as the bacon — 73 compared to 32 milligrams.

If you read the preceding milk and bacon comparison, you may now realize that even 2 percent milk on a daily basis isn't great for you. Two percent milk is *not* lowfat. But did you know that 1 percent milk has only about 0.5 grams less than the maximum amount of fat a food can contain and still qualify as lowfat? In other words, 1 percent milk is almost *not* lowfat. One percent milk is certainly better than 2 percent, but it's not as good as skim. See Table 6-1 for all the details.

| Table 6-1 | Milk (Per Cup) | | | |
|---|---|---|---|---|
| | **Fat** | **Saturated Fat** | **Cholesterol** | **Calories** |
| Whole milk | 8.1 g | 5.2 g | 33 mg | 150 |
| 2% milk | 4.7 g | 3.1 g | 18 mg | 121 |
| 1% milk | 2.6 g | 1.7 g | 10 mg | 102 |
| Skim milk | 0.4 g | 0.3 g | 4 mg | 86 |
| Buttermilk | 2.2 g | 1.3 g | 9 mg | 99 |
| Fat-free buttermilk | 0 g | 0 g | < 5 mg | 80 |
| Evaporated milk | 19.1 g | 11.6 g | 74 mg | 338 |
| Evaporated skimmed milk | 0.5 g | 0.3 g | 9 mg | 199 |
| Sweetened condensed milk | 24 g | 16 g | 80 mg | 1040 |
| Lowfat sweetened condensed milk* | 12 g | 8 g | 40 mg | 960 |
| Fat-free sweetened condensed milk* | 0 g | 0 g | < 5 mg | 880 |

*These products can be labeled lowfat and fat-free because the serving size is only 2 tablespoons, according to the label.

*Source:* Genesis R&D Nutrient Analysis Software and Food Manufacturers' Data

You can see from the numbers that whole milk has a lot of fat and cholesterol. I personally recommend consuming only skim milk, even if you're on a lowfat menu plan that isn't particularly restrictive. Switching to skim milk is an easy way to lose fat.

When deciding whether to switch to skim milk, to 2 percent, or to stay with the regular whole-fat milk, consider that — like all dairy products — fat-free or lowfat milk contains just a little more calcium than regular milk.

Chocolate milk comes fat-free, but it's hard to find in some areas. Major brands like Carnation have made fat-free chocolate milk for many years, and it tastes so good that it is indiscernible from the high-fat variety.

Sweetened condensed skimmed and lowfat milks are available from Borden, and evaporated skimmed milk also is available fat-free from a couple of major brands. If your store doesn't offer some of these great products, which make lowfat baking so much easier, request them with the form in Chapter 5.

## The milk-labeling controversy

Even after the Nutrition Labeling and Education Act of 1990 said that the "lowfat" label should apply only to foods with 3 grams of fat or less per serving, 2 percent milk was still called lowfat, although it contains 5 grams of fat per serving. Because of the labeling, people thought that 2 percent milk was lowfat and okay. This misrepresentation made the term *lowfat,* with regard to dairy products, unreliable and misleading, because the term meant one thing on one food and something else on another food.

In 1996, under pressure from groups that are usually on opposite sides (the Milk Industry Foundation, the International Dairy Products Foods Association, and the Center for Science in the Public Interest), the Food and Drug Administration decided that all dairy products, except for yogurt, have to be in line with all other food products with regard to labeling the fat content in dairy products. With the new ruling, lowfat now means 3 grams of fat or less per serving. Two percent milk is now called "reduced in fat" because it has been reduced in fat by at least 25 percent from the fat content in whole milk, by which all other products must be reduced to in order to say, "reduced in fat."

## *Butter, margarine, and diet spread*

Stick butter contains about the same amount of fat as stick margarine. But regular stick margarine contains 75 percent less saturated fat than stick butter, so if saturated fat is a concern for you, you should use margarine instead of butter. Also, butter is high in cholesterol and margarine has none. Diet or liquid margarines are even better than stick margarines with an even lower saturated fat content, and using little or no butter or margarine is ideal. Packaged margarine, the kind you buy in the market, doesn't contain animal fat, whereas butter is 100 percent animal fat.

Both butter and margarine can contain pesticides, artificial color, sodium, and other additives, but only butter can contain hormone and antibiotic residuals, and only margarine is hydrogenated and contains trans fatty acids (about which scientists still offer no agreed-upon conclusions regarding possible health risks). All these items are present in relatively small amounts.

Stick margarine is always *hydrogenated,* which is a hardening process that makes the oils in margarine firm. Hydrogenation makes the formerly unsaturated fats saturated, but not as saturated as butter. Look at the labels to find which brand of margarine contains the least saturated fat. Table 6-2 offers a comparison of fat, saturated fat, cholesterol, and calorie contents.

## Table 6-2   Butter, Margarine, and Diet Spreads (Per Tablespoon)

|  | Fat | Saturated Fat | Cholesterol | Calories |
|---|---|---|---|---|
| Butter | 11 g | 8 g | 30 mg | 100 |
| Margarine (stick) | 10 g | 2 g | 0 mg | 90 |
| Margarine (tub) | 10 g | 2 g | 0 mg | 90 |
| Squeeze margarine | 9 g | 1.5 g | 0 mg | 80 |
| Light butter | 6 g | 4 g | 20 mg | 50 |
| Light margarine (stick) | 6 g | 1.5 g | 0 mg | 50 |
| Light margarine (tub) | 5 g | 1 g | 0 mg | 50 |
| Fat-free spread | 0 g | 0 g | 0 mg | 15 |

*Source:* Genesis R&D Nutrient Analysis Software and Food Manufacturers' Data

Weaning yourself from butter and margarine may be difficult, but solutions are available. Diet margarines generally contain 50 percent less total fat than regular margarine, depending upon the brand and how much water or other additives it contains, and some diet margarines have zero fat. Fat-free tub spreads, such as Promise and Smart Beat, are also available. You can find fat-free plastic squirt bottles, such as Fleischmann's (this company also has a fat-free squirt cheese), and fat-free sprays, such as I Can't Believe It's Not Butter! (which, at this writing, doesn't even say it is fat-free on the front label, although "0 total fat" appears on the Nutrition Facts panel on the back).

Changing from butter to diet margarine (which can contain 80 percent less saturated fat than butter) or to a fat-free spread can help lower your cholesterol, too.

Diet margarines can make toast soggy because they contain so much water. If you thought those 2 tablespoons of diet margarine you used to coat your wok for a stir-fry (knowing that the heat wouldn't be high enough to warrant peanut oil, a more highly saturated fat) looked an awful lot like water, you were correct. It was water — expensive water and a tiny bit of fat. But the result from cooking in diet margarine isn't bad. In fact, you can make stir-fry without any fat, using only low-sodium soy sauce or lemon juice.

***Note:*** You don't want to use substitute diet margarine for regular margarine in baking unless you do so with a small amount at a time, determining what effect each $1/4$ cup of substitution will have on the finished product.

## A personal success story

In the past year, my exercise routine remained about the same; because of a change in residence, I dropped my health club membership and worked out at home. My food choices remained about the same in restaurants and at home. My work load is a bit heavier.

About a year ago, I began using I Can't Believe It's Not Butter! fat-free spray on vegetables and toast rather than the usual butter or margarine. This past year I used a dozen or so of the spray bottles and less of my usual fat-free or lowfat tub margarines or butter substitutes, which I still use occasionally. I check my cholesterol and do other doctorly tests in the month of my birthday each year so I don't forget. I was amazed that, although my cholesterol had remained steady for about ten years, it dropped ten points this year. The change to a fat-free spray was most probably the reason.

## *Cheese*

I really hate to break it to you deep-dish double-cheese pizza lovers, eggplant Parmesan paramours, cheese enchilada aficionados, and other cheese cherishers, but cheese has a lot of fat. Cheddar cheese is 33 percent fat by weight and gets 74 percent of its calories from fat. Cheese (like all milk products, whether the milk is from a cow, goat, buffalo, lamb, or another animal) also contains cholesterol — even if it is labeled lowfat or fat-free. The only time cheese doesn't contain cholesterol is when it is made from tofu or another type of plant.

If you can't live without cheese like I can't live without cheese, now is *not* the time to jump off a bridge because you feel that existing with no cheese in your life is unbearable. Understand the seduction of that creamy feel in your mouth, those layers of taste as they roll around your tongue and slide down your throat, and then mentally slap yourself silly. You can't dream about cheese. Cheese is a real rat-trap, and knowing how much fat is in that trap is imperative in helping your break loose from your cheese addiction.

Here's a way to shake loose: Go to the grocery store armed with cheese-avoidance resolve, and don't go near the cheese counter. Go when you're hungry; lowfat foods look better then. (Everything looks good when you're hungry.) If you have to have cheese, pick the variety carefully and buy a small amount.

I confess that I still eat high-fat cheese occasionally, but I insist that it be very, very good. I often ask to taste it under the guise of being a connoisseur, and because they don't give you much, I do get just a taste. Usually, with all my self-imposed roadblocks, I find that the taste and quality aren't worth my buying the cheese anyway. If something is truly irresistible, I may purchase a small amount, and then I savor it. Recently a friend unexpectedly served homemade string cheese, the kind with tiny black seeds. I actually had a difficult time controlling myself and enjoyed several pieces immensely. It had been about eight years. Now I'm satisfied. (At least when it comes to string cheese.)

Some of the highest-fat cheeses, the triple cremes, are my favorites. Brie has slightly more total fat than another delicious triple creme, Camembert. The saturated fat content can run close to 5 grams for 1 ounce of Brie, which is only about 2 tablespoons or a 1-inch cube. Two 1-inch cubes of Brie contain more saturated fat than I personally want in a day. The other highest-fat cheeses are Cheddar, Colby, and cream cheese, which contain 9 grams per 1-inch cube. I probably could eat a quarter-pound block, or 36 grams of fat, at a single sitting, but now that I know how much fat is in cheese, I wisely restrain myself.

### *Reduced-fat and fat-free cheeses*

Reduced-fat or lower-fat versions of feta, Brie, Swiss, mozzarella, Cheddar, and other cheeses are available, but most are still fairly high in fat. However, even without the usual amount of fat, they taste quite good. The slightly lowered-fat Brie is actually excellent. Ask the cheese manager in your market to get it for you. (This request often takes some coaxing.)

As for feta, I can't tell the fatty feta from the less-fatty version, as all feta has only a tiny taste difference. The fattiest variety I've seen contains 9 grams of total fat per ounce; the lowest-fat brand contains 5 grams. If the fat content of one brand of feta is 100 percent greater than another, for me, a lower-fat feta is an easy trade-off. Reading the Nutrition Facts panel is a must.

TIP

## Checking the Facts

When you see wrapped cheese wedges in the market without a label stating how much fat they contain, ask the cheese manager for the Nutrition Facts panel that comes with every box of cheese so that you can see the total fat and saturated fat content. Amounts vary quite a bit. By law, the manufacturer must package Nutrition Facts panels along with nearly every food item, including cheese. Stores often neglect to adhere the stick-on labels to the individual packages. Dozens of these informative little labels come in every carton; I've seen them, and stores have them. You may have to insist on seeing these labels. If the store personnel have thrown them out, tell the manager that you want at least one displayed or kept available for people like you who care about their health and have a right to know what's in the products they buy.

Part-skim mozzarella contains 4.5 grams of fat, and part-skim ricotta contains 2 grams. Reasonably good-tasting brands of fat-free mozzarella and ricotta are available. Other available fat-free cheeses include American, Swiss, Cheddar, mozzarella, string cheese, cream cheese, tofu cheese, and something called "pizza cheese," among a dozen others. Cottage cheese, ricotta cheese, farmer's cheese, and pot cheese also come fat-free. Table 6-3 gives you all the details for a variety of cheeses.

| Table 6-3 | Cheese (Per Ounce) | | | |
|---|---|---|---|---|
| | *Fat* | *Saturated Fat* | *Cholesterol* | *Calories* |
| American | 8.9 g | 5.9 g | 27 mg | 106 |
| Reduced-fat 2% milk American | 4 g | 2.7 g | 13 mg | 67 |
| Brie | 7.9 g | 4.9 g | 28 mg | 95 |
| Lite Brie | 4 g | 3 g | 20 mg | 70 |
| Cheddar | 9.4 g | 7.7 g | 30 mg | 114 |
| 1/3 less fat Cheddar | 5.5 g | 3.7 g | 18 mg | 82 |
| Cream cheese | 9.9 g | 6.2 g | 31 mg | 99 |
| Light Neufchatel (1/3 less fat) | 6.1 g | 4.1 g | 20 mg | 71 |
| Feta | 6 g | 4.2 g | 25 mg | 75 |
| Reduced-fat feta | 4 g | 2.5 g | 10 mg | 60 |
| Monterey Jack | 8.6 g | 5.4 g | 25 mg | 106 |
| 1/3 less fat Monterey Jack | 6 g | 4 g | 20 mg | 80 |
| Mozzarella (whole milk) | 6.1 g | 3.7 g | 22 mg | 80 |
| Part-skim mozzarella | 4.5 g | 2.9 g | 16 mg | 72 |
| Parmesan cheese | 8.5 g | 5.4 g | 22 mg | 129 |
| Ricotta (whole milk) | 3.7 g | 2.4 g | 14 mg | 49 |
| Part-skim ricotta | 2.3 g | 1.4 g | 9 mg | 39 |
| Swiss | 7.8 g | 5.1 g | 26 mg | 107 |
| Lite reduced-fat Swiss | 3.5 g | 2 g | 10 mg | 70 |

*Source:* Genesis R&D Nutrient Analysis Software and Food Manufacturers' Data

Note that fat-free cheeses usually contain more sodium than reduced-fat cheeses, so if reducing the amount of sodium in your diet is important to you, the trade-off may not be worthwhile. If this is the case, you might opt for the slightly higher-fat, lower-sodium version. However, the fat epidemic is so prevalent and so threatening to health that most people are willing to accept slightly more sodium if the fat content in the food is reduced. Most experts agree that the fat is more dangerous for most people than the sodium, but check with your doctor to find out what's best for you, especially if you have high blood pressure.

Most fat-free cheeses don't melt well and don't have much taste, but name brands are generally better tasting and have better melting properties than lesser known brands. I've seen the words "melts well" on fat-free cheese. Look for this label if you want the cheese to melt on pizza or grilled cheese sandwiches, but any fat-free or lowfat brand works well for sprinkling on a steaming dish of chili or a salad.

### Cottage cheese

Regular cottage cheese is a moderately high-fat item, regardless of its reputation as a "diet" food. One-half cup contains 4.5 grams of fat and 15 milligrams of cholesterol. One-half cup of fat-free cottage cheese, on the other hand, contains no fat and only 10 milligrams of cholesterol — a far better choice. The cholesterol is lower in the fat-free variety because cholesterol is in the fat that is removed.

As with other types of cheese, fat-free cottage cheese usually contains more sodium than reduced-fat cottage cheese. Two percent and fat-free cottage cheese contain more calcium than regular, full-fat cottage cheese. Because calcium is a consideration when reducing fat in dairy, Table 6-4 provides the facts.

| Table 6-4 | Calcium Content in Cottage Cheese (Per ½ Cup) |
|---|---|
| *Type of Cottage Cheese* | *Amount of Calcium* |
| 4% cottage cheese | 68 mg |
| 2% cottage cheese | 77 mg |
| 1% cottage cheese | 69 mg |
| Nonfat cottage cheese | 52 mg |

*Source:* Genesis R&D Nutrient Analysis Software and Food Manufacturers' Data

Because fat affects most people more than calcium or sodium and the differences are so small, fat-free is still my choice. Just be aware that you aren't missing much, if any, calcium by purchasing fat-free or lowfat dairy products.

# Cream, whipping cream, and half-and-half

Heavy cream is fat-filled; one cup contains 88 grams of fat and 816 calories. Do you drink 16 cups of coffee during a week? If you add 2 tablespoons of cream to each cup, you are consuming 1,600 calories a week in cream alone. That's a lot of calories!

Half-and-half is a much better choice. However, if you use half-and-half in your six cups of coffee each day, you can easily ingest an extra 10 grams of daily fat that you can avoid by substituting a liquid fat-free non-dairy creamer, available in all dairy cases. Table 6-5 compares fat, saturated fat, cholesterol, and calorie contents for four types of cream.

### Table 6-5    Whipping Cream and Half-and-Half (Per Tablespoon)

| | Fat | Saturated Fat | Cholesterol | Calories |
|---|---|---|---|---|
| Heavy whipping cream | 5.5 g | 3.4 g | 20 mg | 51 |
| Light whipping cream | 4.6 g | 2.9 g | 17 mg | 44 |
| Half-and-half cream | 1.7 g | 1.1 g | 6 mg | 20 |
| Liquid fat-free non-dairy creamer | 0g | 0g | 0g | 10 |

*Source:* Genesis R&D Nutrient Analysis Software and Food Manufacturers' Data

To only slightly reduce the fat in recipes calling for heavy cream, use half-and-half. To reduce the fat somewhat more, use one part whole milk and one part half-and-half. You can also use half regular milk and half evaporated skimmed milk. Or you can use part cream and part fat-free creamer. Using all condensed or evaporated whole milk or skimmed milk gives the dish a caramel-like flavor that you may not want in a casserole but that you may not mind in a custard.

Fat-free non-dairy creamers are made by major brands, such as Carnation, Land O Lakes, and Farm Rich. You can find these creamers in both pint and quart cartons in the dairy cases of most chain stores. These creamers are quite good. I use plain creamers for baking; as a cream substitute in coffee or tea; on my cereal; and in cream soups, casseroles, and desserts. Creamers can be boiled and baked without curdling. They are made from soybean oil, aren't quite as thick as dairy cream, and are slightly sweet.

As for whipping cream, Kraft and Reddi Whip are testing fat-free varieties. At least two major brands of whipped topping are fat-free and lowfat: Lucerne's tastes more like cream, but Cool Whip holds its shape better. The serving size for fat-free Cool Whip is only 2 tablespoons, probably less than most people use. When you use 3 tablespoons, Cool Whip and Lucerne may no longer be fat-free, but lowfat and fat-free whipped toppings and whipped creams are certainly far lower in fat than pure whipping cream.

## Sour cream

Fat-free sour cream, unlike cheese, is one of the products that has most successfully greatly reduced or omitted the fat without losing consistency or taste. Part of that taste is at the cost of additional sodium — more than with most other fat-free dairy products. Fat-free sour cream contains the most sodium, and lowfat and reduced-fat sour creams contain more sodium than regular sour cream does.

***Note:*** Because sodium is sometimes a consideration in lowfat menu plans, I mention it often so that you are informed about the impact of a lower-fat diet on sodium intake. Apparently, manufacturers add sodium to boost the taste in lowered-fat and especially fat-free versions of foods. But unless you are on a drastically sodium-reduced menu plan suggested by your doctor, purchase the lowest-fat product available regardless of sodium content. For most people, excessive fat in foods is far more damaging than sodium.

Regular sour cream is a high-fat item, as you can see in Table 6-6.

| Table 6-6 | Sour Cream (Per 2 Tablespoons) | | | |
|---|---|---|---|---|
| | *Fat* | *Saturated Fat* | *Cholesterol* | *Calories* |
| Sour cream | 6 g | 3.7 g | 13 mg | 62 |
| Light sour cream | 2 g | 1.5 g | 10 mg | 35 |
| Fat-free sour cream | 0 g | 0 g | 0 mg | 31 |

*Source:* Genesis R&D Nutrient Analysis Software and Food Manufacturers' Data

# Yogurt

Regular full-fat yogurt is a high-fat item. A 1-cup serving contains 8 grams of fat and 31 milligrams of cholesterol.

A 1-cup serving of fat-free yogurt contains no fat but still contains 5 milligrams of cholesterol. Table 6-7 gives you the skinny on yogurt's fat, cholesterol, and calorie content. The taste of fat-free yogurt is barely discernible from the medium and high-fat versions. Like all other fat-free dairy products, fat-free yogurt contains more calcium than regular yogurt does.

| Table 6-7 | Plain Yogurt (Per Cup) | | | | |
|---|---|---|---|---|---|
| | *Fat* | *Saturated Fat* | *Cholesterol* | *Calories* | *Calcium* |
| Whole milk yogurt | 8 g | 5.3 g | 31 mg | 150 | 296 mg |
| Lowfat yogurt | 3.5 g | 2.5 g | 15 mg | 155 | 448 mg |
| Fat-free yogurt | 0.4 g | 0.3 g | 4 mg | 137 | 488 mg |

*Source:* Genesis R&D Nutrient Analysis Software and Food Manufacturers' Data

## Diet, dairy products, and heart disease

Several lifestyle components, including what you eat, whether you smoke or drink, how often you exercise, and your heredity, can contribute to premature heart disease. According to some experts, 80 percent is caused by diet and lifestyle and not by heredity, which means that you can take steps to prevent heart disease even if your heredity predisposes you to it. Too much ingested fat, saturated fat, and cholesterol cause much premature heart and artery disease. The shortest-lived people in the world are the Finnish, who eat a diet exceptionally high in high-fat dairy products:

whole milk, cream, butter, and especially cheese. (Not all countries keep careful records, by the way.)

Each year, 1 million adult Americans die, perhaps unnecessarily and prematurely, from heart attacks and heart disease. Apparently, no single group is protected from heart disease, regardless of race or ethnicity, gender, or age. Women often mistakenly believe that they are safer. However, 500,000 heart attack victims a year are women, and heart disease is the leading cause of death for women.

# Difficulties of Change

Making changes is difficult. Many people understandably changed from whole milk to 2 percent, made the switch fairly easily, and thought they were doing a good and healthful thing. But they weren't going far enough. You may think that going from 2 percent to 1 percent is even better and healthier. It is. But then you may think, "Why bother to go skim when it's only a 1 percent change?"

Because the terms are so confusing, some people think that 2 percent milk contains 98 percent less fat than regular milk. Many people may not be sure exactly what 2 percent really means. After all, if you get only 2 percent return on some money you invest, the profit is very little. In fact, 2 percent milk is 2 percent fat *by weight,* and when it comes to fat, that's quite a bit.

Dairy products are nutritious foods; however, whole-fat dairy foods (products that are not modified to reduce the fat content) are extremely high in fat. Many people grow accustomed to whole-fat milk, ice cream, cheese, and yogurt in the formative years of childhood and continue consuming these products throughout their lifetime — despite the high-fat content and resulting health risks. The eating habits that you learn in childhood often carry into adulthood.

## Whole-milk dairy products and children

In 1995, scientists discovered that 25 percent of American kids over the age of 12 have high cholesterol levels. Whole-milk dairy products may be part of the cause, because whole milk is a high-fat food. It's supposed to be. A calf weighs approximately 80 pounds at birth and grows to about 500 pounds at five to eight months old — all on a steady diet of cow's milk. And humans eat and drink whole-milk dairy products far longer than calves do.

Whole-milk dairy products are healthful for very young children. Some experts advise that children need mother's milk or whole milk until the age of two; others extend the age to four. But for most people, whole milk is not beneficial after that. Even if a child has no weight problem, cholesterol accumulation, heart disease, or possible cancer problem, choosing fat-free or lowfat dairy foods is a more healthful alternative for most children.

## Teenage boy diet

One glass of 2 percent milk contains 5 grams of fat. If you drink six glasses of milk a day, you consume a hefty 30 grams of solid fat that you could bounce just in beverages. Drinking six glasses of milk is not unusual for a teenage boy. This boy wants to gain weight and be tall.

He might drink one glass of milk with breakfast, put the equivalent amount on his cereal, drink one glass for lunch or eat the equivalent in dairy fat in macaroni and cheese or a ham and cheese sandwich, and drink one glass at dinner. He might have a glass with dessert, with an after-school snack, or with a bedtime snack. He might also consume milk in baked goods or ice cream. Plus, he might have additional servings of other dairy-rich products, such as cheese on his pizza or burger, or frozen yogurt, or cottage cheese.

At the end of the day, it's possible for this teenage boy to have consumed an enormous amount of fat in dairy products and other foods. His total fat intake could be as much as 133 fat grams based on his 3,000 calories a day. The solid fat he is eating each day is the size of a baseball, and most of that fat can be cumulative. His saturated fat content could be greater than 44 grams and his percentage of calories from fat, 40 percent. He is getting far too much fat and saturated fat for his overall health. But because he is an athlete, wants to gain weight, wants to grow, and wants to be strong, he thinks that he's young and that all this fat is okay. It isn't.

## Teenage girl diet

This section is short because most studies indicate that teenage girls as a group drink little milk and eat few dairy products. However, to better manage weight problems and stave off possible heart disease in later years (heart disease being a major killer of women), girls should switch to fat-free or lowfat yogurt, cheese, and other dairy products.

Because young women need calcium, they should know that lowfat and fat-free dairy products often contain more calcium than high-fat dairy products do.

## Cholesterol, dairy products, and young people

High-fat products, including dairy foods, increase the formation of cholesterol plaque for many people. Both young men and young women should have their cholesterol levels checked. James I. Cleeman, Coordinator of the National Cholesterol Education Program, says that all young adults should be screened for cholesterol. Failure to check cholesterol levels denies 7 million adults under age 35 with elevated cholesterol the chance to reduce their long-term risk. One young person in 500 has heredity-related elevated cholesterol. Attempting to lower cholesterol in middle age, while worthwhile, confers only about half the reduction of coronary risk that can be gained from earlier efforts.

Most experts advise that infants and children under the age of two shouldn't have a diet restricted in fats. Some experts, however, think that a more natural diet of fat-free or very lowfat food should begin at age four.

As for cholesterol testing, the American College of Physicians guidelines say that testing for cholesterol should begin after age 35 for men and 45 for women. Cleeman, however, feels that information and an earlier start can give people 20 extra years to improve their patterns of diet, exercise, and weight control. Why let a problem go unimpeded when a simple test provides valuable data? Because heart and artery diseases are the number-one killers worldwide, I believe that testing should begin at age two. Then you have over 30 years to conterbalance a tendency toward high cholesterol.

# Easy Strategies for Avoiding Extra Calories

When you empty your pockets, do you toss the extra change into a jar or box? If so, you are probably amazed at how quickly those coins add up. Fat and calories are like those pennies, nickels, dimes, and quarters; they add up quickly over time. In the same way, as I explain in the following sections, even small alterations in lifestyle can significantly reduce your fat and calorie intake.

## Avoid almost 7,000 calories each year by switching from 2 percent to 1 percent milk

Here's another way to look at why most adults should drink 1 percent milk (which is lowfat) or, even better, skim milk and use lowfat or fat-free dairy products instead of regular high-fat ones. A one-glass-a-day milk drinker who switches from 2 percent to 1 percent cuts his or her fat intake by almost 2 pounds each year. The milk drinker also loses close to 2 pounds in a year by avoiding almost 7,000 calories and ingesting 2 fewer pounds of solid fat in a year's time.

## Avoid over 12,000 calories each year by switching from 2 percent to skim milk

What if you switch from 2 percent to skim milk? You ingest close to 4 pounds less fat and over 12,000 fewer calories per year.

# Fat-Free or Lowfat Dairy Product Substitutions

The lower-fat dairy product substitutions in Table 6-8 can save you several hundred calories per serving, depending upon the food. You may not have even been aware that some of these products exist.

*Note:* Lowfat or fat-free cheese products still aren't the best-tasting, nor do they always have the best texture, but they're better than they were. Tofu Rella, a tofu-based mozzarella cheese, melts well and tastes good; however, it doesn't have much flavor.

Liquid fat-free and lowfat non-dairy creamers (without sugar or flavors) are really excellent substitutes for creamed dishes, including creamed soups, and they don't curdle when boiled or baked. Although the labels say fat-free, if you use enough, say over 2 tablespoons, non-dairy creamers do have some fat, and some are moderately high in calories.

Fat-free or lowfat cream cheese isn't very good, either, but it's great in cheesecakes and dips in which other flavors and textures predominate.

| Table 6-8 | Lowfat Dairy Substitutions |
|---|---|
| *Instead of This* | *Try This* |
| Butter | Fat-free butter substitute, such as I Can't Believe It's Not Butter! |
| Canned cream soups | Lowfat canned cream soups |
| Cheese | Fat-free or lowfat cheese |

*(continued)*

### Table 6-8 *(continued)*

| Instead of This | Try This |
|---|---|
| Cheese dishes | Fat-free or lowfat cheese dishes, like Healthy Choice or Lean Cuisine macaroni and cheese |
| Cottage cheese | Fat-free or lowfat cottage cheese |
| Cream | Fat-free or lowfat non-dairy creamer |
| Cream cheese | Fat-free or reduced-fat cream cheese |
| Custard made with whole eggs and whole milk | Custard made with fat-free creamer, substitute eggs, and skim milk |
| Evaporated milk | Evaporated skimmed milk |
| Feta cheese | Fat-free or lowfat farmer's cheese |
| Frozen yogurt | Fat-free or lowfat frozen yogurt |
| Half-and-half | Fat-free or lowfat non-dairy creamer |
| Homemade cream soups made with cream | Homemade cream soups made with fat-free non-dairy creamer |
| Ice cream | Fat-free or lowfat ice cream |
| Margarine | Fat-free or reduced-fat (diet) margarine |
| Parmesan cheese | Fat-free Parmesan topping (or mix half fat-free with half regular Parmesan) |
| Part-skim mozzarella (this isn't lowfat) | Fat-free or lowfat mozzarella |
| Part-skim ricotta (this isn't lowfat) | Fat-free or lowfat ricotta |
| Sour cream | Fat-free or lowfat sour cream |
| Sweetened condensed milk | Fat-free sweetened condensed milk |
| Whipped cream | Fat-free or lowfat whipped topping |
| Whole milk | Skim milk or dry nonfat milk |
| Yogurt | Fat-free or lowfat yogurt |

# Ten Lowfat Dairy Dishes, Drinks, and Desserts

I call these ten quick lowfat dairy-product concoctions "fast lowfat assemblies"; they're for when you want something in 10 minutes or less, and you want that homey, comfort-food feeling that you can get only from dairy products. This list is an eclectic one. I hope it gives you ideas of foods you can add to other similar dishes, drinks, and desserts.

- ✔ **Baked potatoes, veggies, and sour cream:** Top potatoes with fat-free sour cream (all brands are good), chopped fresh onions, chopped chives, finely diced tomatoes, and shredded steamed broccoli tops or chopped fresh parsley.

- ✔ **Buttered vegetables:** Top vegetables with I Can't Believe It's Not Butter! spray, which is fat-free, or make a lowfat hollandaise sauce by microwaving the juice of half a lemon, 1 tablespoon diet margarine, $1/2$ teaspoon flour, and 1 cup substitute eggs, whisked together, stopping the microwave to stir every 10 seconds until thick.

- ✔ **Cream of celery, broccoli, or mushroom soup:** To lowfat or fat-free canned cream soup, add 1 cup liquid fat-free non-dairy creamer. Steam 1 cup diced fresh celery, 1 cup finely diced broccoli, or 1 can drained mushrooms separately in a few tablespoons water for 3 to 4 minutes; then add to the soup. Add $1/2$ cup diced onion, $1/2$ cup frozen corn, and $1/2$ cup frozen green beans or peas to add taste and flavor to the convenient canned food, without adding fat.

- ✔ **Cream in coffee:** Use fat-free or lowfat non-dairy creamer, flavored or unflavored (which has more calories), ice cream, frozen yogurt, evaporated skimmed milk, or dry nonfat milk mixed with skim milk.

- ✔ **Desserts and whipped cream:** Use fat-free or lowfat commercial desserts, such as cupcakes and cookies from Entenmann's; lowfat frozen desserts; and angel food cake (which is always fat-free). Top with fat-free or lowfat ice cream or frozen yogurt or whipped topping. Look for fat-free whipped cream soon — several companies are currently testing this product.

- ✔ **Frozen macaroni dinner:** To a serving of Healthy Choice or Lean Cuisine (or other lowfat) macaroni and cheese or stuffed manicotti (which contains a nice amount of cheese), add a small can of drained mushrooms; $1/2$ cup frozen string beans, peas, or corn; and fresh diced tomatoes. Microwave for another 2 minutes. The extra vegetables add fiber and volume to the already small amount of fat.

✔ **Frozen Swedish meatball dinner:** Steam $1/2$ cup frozen peas or string beans, 2 tablespoons chopped onion, and $1/4$ cup white beans or leftover pasta or cooked rice in a few tablespoons water for 3 to 4 minutes. When fully cooked, stir the mixture into a serving of Lean Cuisine Swedish Meatball Dinner (which offers lots of meatballs and a creamy sauce) to add bulk and fiber to the tiny amount of fat.

✔ **Ham and cheese sandwich:** Use fat-free mayonnaise, a slice or two of lowfat or fat-free ham, fat-free or lowfat cheese or a combination of lowfat and regular cheese, and several slices of tomato, lettuce leaves, sprouts, and pickles to add volume and reduce the overall fat content.

✔ **Malted milk, milkshake, or ice cream soda:** Mix fat-free or lowfat ice cream or frozen yogurt and skim milk with fat-free or lowfat flavored non-dairy creamer. For a malted, add malt powder.

✔ **Pizza in or out:** Order (or make) pizzas with double the onions, fresh or sun-dried tomatoes, extra mushrooms, green and red peppers, and diced fresh tomatoes, topped with one-half or one-fourth the cheese, all on a thick crust, to increase the vegetables and grains. The bulk negates the "less food" reputation of lowfat cuisine; the extra vegetables keep you from missing the pepperoni, sausage, and heavy cheese. You can also purchase Hormel's reduced-fat pepperoni for homemade pizza at most markets.

# Putting the Wraps on Dairy Foods

The addition of labeling and conformity in label standards provides better information to the public on exactly what they're eating. In time, many people hope that producers of dairy products, who have done an excellent job of reducing or eliminating the fat in many foods, can improve the consistency, taste, and texture of lowfat and fat-free dairy goods, especially cheese.

The point of all this information about dairy products is that Americans incorporate a lot of these foods into their daily diets. If you want to eat high-fat dairy foods occasionally, you can. Eat a pizza, have a cheeseburger or a small amount of butter now and then, or even a zabaglione sauce over crème brûlée sometime (zabaglione sauce is made of whipped egg yolks and wine, and crème brûlée is made of sugar, cream, and eggs) — especially if the rest of the dairy products and other foods that you regularly eat are either fat-free or very low in fat. Why not? The balance is what counts — balance means what you ate for the whole week or the whole month. Lowfat or fat-free dairy products, eaten regularly, are terrific foods. Knowledge is power.

# Part III
## Over 150 Delicious and Lowfat Recipes Made Easy

The 5th Wave    By Rich Tennant

"We're trying to use more lowfat cooking methods, so Barbara's grilling tonight. How do you like your lasagna?"

## In this part . . .

Turn to this part when you are ready to roll up your sleeves and cook. I offer lowfat recipes for everyday meals and special-occasion dishes. Do you need a warm soup after a cold walk with the dog? Or maybe you want to prepare a fancy brunch for some new friends? And, yes, I even include desserts. With my recipes, your lowfat menu can be diverse, fulfilling, and easy to prepare. The best part is that these dishes taste terrific — really, I promise.

# Chapter 7

# Breakfasts and Brunches

· · · · · · · · · · · · · · · · · · · · · · · · · · · · · · · · · · · · · · · · ·

## In This Chapter

▶ Strategies for eating a quick, easy, lowfat, and healthful breakfast or sumptious brunch

▶ Quick lowfat breakfasts

▶ Breakfasts that are usually high or low in total fat, saturated fat, and cholesterol

· · · · · · · · · · · · · · · · · · · · · · · · · · · · · · · · · · · · · · · · ·

*E*nglish novelist Charles Dickens writes while visiting America on March 28, 1843 (his 30th birthday), while en route to Pittsburgh: For breakfast "there are upon the table tea and coffee, and bread and butter, and salmon, and shad, and liver, and steak, potatoes, and pickles."

Breakfast is often said to be the most important meal of the day. But is eating traditional breakfast fare — bacon, eggs, and pancakes — a good idea?

This chapter explains how to make wise decisions about your breakfast menu. I offer 16 recipes, including 9 omelet and egg scramble variations, with exact instructions for making each dish. I provide a handy list of lower-fat breakfast substitutions — good for when you're eating out or at home. And I give you quick lowfat breakfast suggestions, as well as a list of breakfast foods that are usually high in total fat, saturated fat, and cholesterol. I also include a list of lowfat alternatives.

## Recipes in This Chapter

▶ Basic Fluffy Omelet or Egg Scramble

▶ Cheese and Potato Omelet or Egg Scramble with Cheese and Potatoes

▶ Eggs Carbonara (Ham, Peas, and Pasta)

▶ Eggs with Confetti Peppers, Mushrooms, and Veggies

▶ Feta and Spinach Omelet or Egg Scramble with Feta and Spinach

▶ Ham and Cheese Omelet or Egg Scramble with Ham and Cheese

▶ Jelly Omelet or Egg Scramble with Jelly

▶ Onion Omelet or Egg Scramble with Onions

▶ Western Omelet or Huevos Rancheros (or Egg Scramble with Salsa)

▶ Baked Apples

▶ Blueberry Pancakes

▶ French Toast

▶ Hash Browns or Potato Pancakes

▶ Hearty Roast Beef Hash

▶ Oat Bran Muffins

▶ Pineapple Upside Down Cake

🍴 🍳 🥄 🍴 💥 🌿

# The Breakfast Dilemma: Should You Eat Traditional Breakfast Foods?

"What should I eat for a lowfat breakfast?" is probably the question I'm most often asked. If you look at any restaurant menu or think about typical breakfast foods, such as bacon and eggs, pancakes, and sausage, you can easily see why people are concerned about their fat intake at breakfast.

I give them an honest answer. First, divide breakfast into two types: everyday and Sunday (because many people work on Saturday). Breakfast is the easiest meal to eat lowfat. It's also the easiest lowfat meal to plan and buy food for. Here's an everyday lowfat menu, which is just one obvious and simple solution: Eat a lowfat cereal (such as shredded wheat or oatmeal), any fruit you like (including berries, bananas, or raisins), and skim milk. Add juice (and coffee or tea) and you have an excellent breakfast that's full of fiber, vitamins, fruit, and little fat. And it tastes good.

But, at least sometimes, you may want something more interesting than shredded wheat or oatmeal. Bacon and eggs, omelets, sausage, pancakes, and waffles always come up as typical breakfast foods — at least when you have the time. Plus, if you're a traveler, those foods are almost all that is available on planes and trains. Hotels do offer cereals, and you can request a lowfat breakfast from any airline. Travel makes staying on a lowfat breakfast plan more difficult but not impossible.

The major cause of weight gain from breakfast foods is doughnuts. Doughnuts are followed by butter, regular margarine, meat (such as bacon and sausage), cream cheese, cheese, and other breakfast breads (such as danishes, bear claws, and coffee cakes). The substitution list later in this chapter can help you make healthier choices.

Instead of eating a 2-ounce doughnut every day, try a 2-ounce bagel and avoid 4,380 grams of fat and 28,105 calories per year. Instead of 1 teaspoon of butter, use I Can't Believe It's Not Butter! fat-free spray and save 3.8 grams of fat and 34 calories each day.

I know that when you eat cream cheese, you want "real" cream cheese with the taste that is familiar. Fat-free cream cheese still isn't very good. But after you get used to a food prepared a certain way, you like it that way. Try the fat-free and mix it with the regular type. This option offers less fat than the "$1/3$ Less Fat" types and more taste. The bright side is that preserves, jelly, jam, conserves, honey, and apple butter — all the things you can put on a bagel over the lower-fat cream cheese — contain no fat. You can also put these condiments on English muffins, toast, or crumpets, which contain very little or no fat.

Eating pancakes and waffles occasionally is fine on a lowfat diet, even though waffles, in particular, contain some fat. The scoop of butter on top is the problem. One pat of butter or margarine is not only high in fat, but butter also contains cholesterol and an enormous amount of saturated fat, ranging from 7 to 14 grams, depending on the size of the pat or scoop.

Fourteen grams of saturated fat is more than many people want to consume in a whole day, and you may not want your daily "butter fix" on a pancake or waffle. Margarine contains one-fourth as much saturated fat as butter (and a small amount of trans fatty acids). One to 2 tablespoons of diet margarine supplies only 2 grams of saturated fat, depending on the brand. Several butterlike spreads that contain no fat are available.

Most breakfast meats are extraordinarily high in fat. Canadian bacon and very lean ham with all visible fat removed contain the least fat. If you really want bacon, cut off all the fat. As for sausage links, patties, or scrapple, I occasionally eat a bite of someone else's, but I never order or buy it so that I won't be tempted to indulge. Healthy Choice offers a great sausage patty; the links are only fair. Turkey bacon always has less saturated fat, but the total fat is often the same.

# The Scoop on Cereals

Another common breakfast food is cereal. If you compare Nutrition Facts panels on packages, you find that fat in cereals ranges from 0 to 6 grams per serving. (Hot cereals, such as Cream of Wheat, Wheatena, and oatmeal contain small amounts of fat.) If you put 1 cup of whole milk or cream on your cereal, you add up to 8 grams of fat for whole milk and 94 grams of fat for cream. If you put whole milk or cream on your cereal each day for a year, you consume a total of 2,940 grams of fat for whole milk and 34,310 grams of fat for cream.

Cereals often contain many other ingredients besides grains. Even "health-ful" bran cereals and muesli include ingredients such as sugar, sodium (which you may not want), nuts (to which you may be allergic), zinc oxide, vitamins (such as pyridoxine hydrochloride and folic acid), partially hydrogenated cottonseed and/or soybean oil, dried whey, malt syrup, BHT (a preservative), and a lot of other stuff. In my cupboard, only oatmeal contains 100 percent rolled oats and nothing else.

What's my recommendation? Buy the lowfat cereal you like — just remem-ber to use skim milk instead of whole milk or cream. Getting up each morn-ing is hard enough for some people, and how you feel in the morning can set the tone of your day. You can make your own cereal mix, too. Try oat bran, rice flakes, a few currants, or dried cranberries (for some, raisins are too sweet), and you have your own designer cereal. In a few months, blend a new and different mixture.

# A Few Words about Eggs

Egg yolks contain about 215 to 240 milligrams of cholesterol; egg whites contain no cholesterol. Egg yolks have 5 grams of fat, and 1½ grams is saturated. Both egg yolks and whites contain protein; the egg white offers a little more.

A reason not to eat eggs that are lightly fried (so that the center remains runny), scrambled, soft-boiled, or in certain sauces (like hollandaise), is that unless eggs are cooked for a long time, they are unsafe. Uncooked eggs contain a nasty bacteria called salmonella. This bacteria kills many people each year and makes hundreds of thousands sick. That day you thought you had the flu, you could have been suffering from salmonella poisoning.

Two thousand people in New York fell ill at the same time after exposure to salmonella-tainted eggs. New York even passed a law prohibiting restaurants from serving soft-boiled or soft-scrambled eggs. Unfortunately, the law has since been repealed. More people (82 percent from 1984 to 1989) become sick from eggs, versus other foods contaminated with salmonella, than from all other sources.

I use primarily substitute eggs for omelets, scrambles, and baked goods. Substitute eggs are 99 percent egg. The other 1 percent consists of a few chemicals, starches, and a safe yellow coloring that includes beta carotene. You may not like chemicals, but "real" eggs contain chemicals, too. Whatever the farmer fed the chicken, such as hormones and antibiotics, is in the egg.

Salmonella bacteria is killed during pasteurization. The real egg material in substitute eggs is pasteurized, so they are completely safe for all egg dishes.

# Lowfat Breakfasts When Eating Out (or at Home)

The following are lowfat alternatives to traditional breakfast fare:

- ✔ Bacon (all fat removed), lean Canadian bacon, or lean ham (under 2 ounces)
- ✔ Bagel with reduced fat or fat-free cream cheese or lower-fat margarine or butterlike spread, jelly, jam, or preserves
- ✔ Cereals or granola (look at the fat content), hot or cold with skim milk, with or without sugar, or with fruit or lowfat or fat-free yogurt
- ✔ Crumpet with lowfat or fat-free spread and plus jelly, jam, or preserves
- ✔ English muffin with reduced-fat or fat-free cream cheese or lower-fat margarine or butterlike spread, plus jelly, jam, or preserves

# Ten quick lowfat breakfasts

Knowing which breakfast foods are low in fat helps you make wise choices. But if you eat a lot of any one of these foods, say 2 or 3 cups of the potato and onion breakfast or two whole bagels, the meal can still be high in calories.

**Bagel breakfast:** Toast a bagel (bagels have almost no fat, but if they are larger than 3 inches or 2 ounces, they can contain 300 calories or more). Spread with lowfat or fat-free cream cheese and preserves or 1 slice lox or salmon.

**Cold cereal breakfast with fruit:** To any lowfat, high-fiber cereal, add a cup of skim milk or a mixture of skim milk and liquid fat-free non-dairy creamer (it's thick like cream and is located in the dairy department). Top with bananas, peaches, or berries.

**Crumpet breakfast:** Did you know that crumpets have almost no fat and really taste great? Try toasting two crumpets rather than ordinary bread. For no fat, spray on I Can't Believe It's Not Butter! fat-free spray. For lowfat, use diet margarine and add preserves. Butter almost always makes a dish high in fat if you use enough to taste it.

**Fruit breakfast:** Fill a plate or bowl with several fruits (such as melon, peaches, grapefruit, canned apricots, and fresh or canned pears) and juice. In summer, enjoy the fruit fresh and cool. In winter, place in an ovenproof pie plate a bag of frozen dark bing cherries, a can of drained peaches, $1/4$ cup each chopped dried apricots and prunes, a tablespoon or two of lemon juice, several tablespoons of sugar, a shake or two of cinnamon, 1 teaspoon orange or lemon zest, and $1/2$ cup orange juice in which you've dissolved 1 tablespoon cornstarch. Bake for 45 minutes at 350°. For more food, toast an English muffin.

**Hot cereal with hot fruit:** In an ovenproof plastic bag or covered dish, place $1/2$ cup fruit, such as a diced tart apple, blueberries, raspberries, or peaches. Add 2 teaspoons each sugar, lemon juice, and cinnamon and heat for 15 minutes on high, turning once. In a nonstick saucepan, prepare the oatmeal (the 5-minute type rather than quick oats provides more texture) and add the hot fruit to the cereal before serving.

**Mushroom breakfast:** Lightly coat a nonstick skillet with no-stick vegetable oil spray. Combine 1 cup sliced mushrooms, salt (if desired) and pepper, and 2 teaspoons diced onion. Heat for about 7 minutes. Put the mushrooms on an omelet or eat them plain.

**Potato and onion breakfast:** Lightly coat a nonstick skillet with no-stick vegetable oil spray. In the skillet, place a medium sliced potato and a small onion (and half a red or green bell pepper if you have one), salt (if desired) and pepper, and a few teaspoons water. Cook for 20 minutes, tossing often. The mixture will brown if you leave the lid off and turn often, or steam and cook faster if you cover it.

You can also cover the potatoes and vegetables and bake them in the oven for 50 minutes at 350°. Drink a glass of carrot juice to top off the vegetable theme.

**Tomato breakfast:** This option is my current favorite. After removing a slice or two of tomato for the lunch sandwiches I make each morning, I eat the rest of the tomato and find it refreshing and less acidic than orange juice or half a grapefruit. Then I have toast and hazelnut coffee half and half (my ground mixture of half regular coffee and half decaf).

*(continued)*

*(continued)*

> **Vegetable breakfast:** To a generous portion of romaine lettuce, add a cup of diced or sliced celery or fennel (including leaves or ferns), drained baby corn, chopped scallions or onions, and red and green bell pepper slices. Make a dressing of the juice of half a lemon, minced garlic, cider vinegar, a teaspoon of olive oil, a sprinkle of Parmesan cheese, and salt (if desired) and coarsely ground black pepper.
>
> **Wake-up breakfast:** Are you particularly sleepy and worn out, or did you have a little too much to drink the night before? Try one tall, cold glass of tomato or V8 juice with 10 shakes of hot sauce (if you aren't nauseous), 1 shake Worcestershire sauce, and the juice of half a lemon. Then drink 2 cups of strong black coffee and eat a rice cake. The crunch wakes up your body, the coffee wires you, and the tomato juice nourishes you (just be aware of the salt in the juice).

- ✔ Fruit: fresh or cooked, plain or with skim milk or lowfat or fat-free yogurt
- ✔ Grits or cornmeal mush (with no butter or margarine) with syrup or salt and pepper
- ✔ Lowfat pancakes or waffles and syrup (with no butter or margarine)
- ✔ Lox, smoked salmon, or trout (under 2 ounces) and a bagel or toast
- ✔ Toast with reduced-fat or fat-free cream cheese or diet margarine or butterlike spread, plus jelly, jam, or preserves

Keeping breakfast simple but enjoyable seems to work for most people. Cooking lowfat breakfasts is easy when you know how — and now you do.

# Breakfast Foods That Are Usually Low or High in Total Fat, Saturated Fat, and Cholesterol

The fat damage in most of these foods usually comes from what you put on them: cheese on the apple, cream cheese on the bagel, cream or whole milk in the cereal, butter on the coffee cake, and so on. The starred items contain the least fat.

- Bacon (microwaved in paper towels and completely defatted)
- Bagels (with lowfat spread and jelly)*
- Blinis (the lowfat variety)
- Canadian bacon (under 2 ounces)

- Cereal (hot or cold, with skim milk — check the fat content on cold varieties)*

- Cornbread (some varieties qualify as lowfat)

- Cornmeal mush*

- Cream of wheat or rice*

- Crumpets*

- Egg whites or substitute eggs (scrambled, hard-cooked, or in omelets, if little or no fat is used)*

- English muffins (with lowfat spread and jelly)

- Farina*

- Fish, broiled (under 2 ounces)

- Fruit*

- Grits or groats (without butter or other fatty additions)*

- Hash browns (if made with little fat)

- Jam, jelly, and preserves*

- Lean ham (under 2 ounces and not fried)

- Lean top round steak (under 2 ounces and not fried)

- Lox or salmon (under 2 ounces)

- Muffins (depending upon size and ingredients)

- Oatmeal*

- Pancakes or waffles and syrup (with no butter or margarine and little fat in the batter)

- Postum*

- Strudel (made without butter or margarine)

- Syrup*

- Toast (with fat-free or lowfat spread)*

- Vegetables*

The foods in the following list are almost always high in fat. Occasionally, you can find biscuits made without fat. Pioneer flour makes a lowfat biscuit and baking mix. Bisquick makes a reduced-fat variety that has considerably more fat than the Pioneer brand. These two brands contain half the fat of the regular variety.

You may notice that I list turkey bacon, and you may think that because it contains turkey, the fat content is lower. However, the Nutrition Facts panel on the package claims that the total fat in one slice of Louis Rich turkey bacon is 2.5 grams. Regular Center Cut Oscar Mayer bacon contains 4.5 grams of total fat in two slices, according to the package. The turkey bacon contains more fat than the regular bacon! The amount of saturated fat is less for the turkey bacon: 1 gram, versus 2 grams for the same number of slices. If total fat reduction is more important to you, eat regular bacon. If saturated fat reduction is more significant, go for turkey bacon.

- Bacon, marbled ham, sausage, or steak
- Bear claws
- Biscuits
- Blintzes or blinis (containing cheese)
- Casseroles with eggs and cheese
- Cereal (with whole milk or cream)
- Cheese toast
- Clotted or Devon cream
- Coffee cake
- Corned beef hash (canned or fresh, especially if topped with an egg)
- Cream cheese
- Creamed eggs
- Crepes
- Croissants
- Crullers
- Danishes
- Doughnuts
- Egg breads or challah
- Eggs and egg dishes
- Fritters
- Granola (although lowfat and fat-free are available)
- Muffins (with added fat in the batter and butter on top)
- Omelets
- Pancakes and waffles (with excessive oil in the batter and with butter)
- Quiches
- Scones
- Yogurt (whole milk or 2 percent)

# Easy Lowfat Omelet Recipes

Personally, I don't care whether I eat an omelet with a filling or an egg scramble with a topping as long as it's lowfat and low in cholesterol. Scrambled eggs with a topping are easier to make and taste just as good. In the following recipes, I include instructions for preparing both options.

You can make a great plain omelet or scramble with jelly, ham and cheese, cheese and potato, pasta, feta cheese and spinach, onion, or a mixture of vegetables. The recipes are all here, building on the basic recipe.

These omelets are delicious. Even better, no one can tell that they aren't made with higher-fat, high-cholesterol eggs. If you are cooking more or less than four servings, adjust the recipe so that you always use twice as many substitute eggs as fresh egg whites.

## Basic Fluffy Omelet or Egg Scramble

**Tools:** *Large nonstick skillet with lid, or four small nonstick skillets with lids*

**Preparation time:** *1*

**Yield:** *4 servings*

*3 fresh egg whites*

*Pinch of cream of tartar or flour (optional)*

*1 cup substitute eggs*

*1 teaspoon butter*

*Chopped fresh parsley for garnish*

*Salt (optional) and freshly ground black pepper*

In a small bowl, beat the egg whites and cream of tartar or flour (if desired) until very fluffy. Add the substitute eggs, blending well.

### Omelet

*1* If you're making one large omelet, melt the butter in a medium-hot large skillet with a lid. If you're making individual omelets, use 4 small skillets with lids. Pour the egg mixture into the pan(s) and reduce the heat to low. Cover the eggs and cook for 2 to 3 minutes.

*2* When the edges are firm, use a rubber spatula to lift several times to make sure that the bottom isn't getting too brown. (If it is, turn down the heat drastically.) Fold the omlet as shown in Figure 7-1.

*3* Sprinkle on the parsley (or other topping) and season to taste with salt and pepper.

### Egg Scramble

*1* To scramble the eggs, melt the butter in a medium-hot, large nonstick skillet with a lid. Pour the egg mixture into the pan and reduce the heat to low. With a fork, gently mix the eggs every few minutes for about 6 minutes.

*2* Sprinkle on the parsley or other topping and season to taste with salt and pepper.

**Nutrition at a glance (per serving):** *Total fat 1 g; Saturated fat 0.5 g; Protein 12 g; Dietary fiber 0 g; Carbohydrate 2 g; Cholesterol 3 mg; Sodium 239 mg; % of calories from fat 14; Calories 66.*

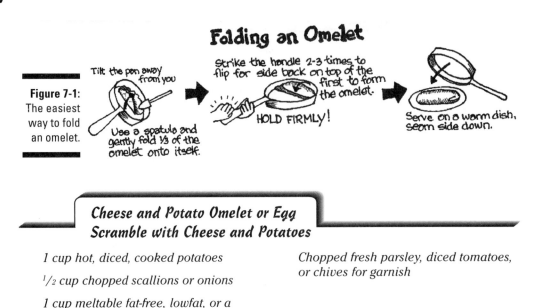

**Figure 7-1:**
The easiest way to fold an omelet.

## Cheese and Potato Omelet or Egg Scramble with Cheese and Potatoes

1 cup hot, diced, cooked potatoes

$^1/_2$ cup chopped scallions or onions

1 cup meltable fat-free, lowfat, or a mixture of fat-free and regular cheese

Chopped fresh parsley, diced tomatoes, or chives for garnish

### Omelet

*1* Prepare the omelet according to the Basic Fluffy Omelet recipe at the beginning of this section.

*2* Lightly coat a separate skillet with no-stick vegetable oil spray. Combine the potatoes, scallions or onions, and cheese and toss. Cook over low heat for 10 minutes, stirring, and adding a few tablespoons water for moisture if necessary.

*3* When the omelet is ready to fold, loosen the bottom with a rubber spatula, place the cheese, potatoes, and scallions or onions on one side of each omelet and fold over. Briefly cover to melt the cheese, which should slightly run out.

*4* Garnish with chopped parsley, diced tomatoes, or chives.

### Egg Scramble

*1* Prepare the egg scramble according to the Basic Egg Scramble recipe at the beginning of this section.

*2* Lightly coat a separate skillet with no-stick vegetable oil spray. Combine the potatoes, scallions or onions, and cheese and toss. Cook over low heat for 10 minutes, stirring, adding a few tablespoons water for moisture if necessary.

*3* Place the eggs on a plate. When the cheese begins to melt, place the mixture on top or to the side of the egg scramble.

*(continued)*

**4** Garnish with chopped parsley, diced tomatoes, or chives.

**Nutrition at a glance (per serving):** *Total fat 1 g; Saturated fat 0.5 g; Protein 22 g; Dietary fiber 1 g; Carbohydrate 12 g; Cholesterol 5 mg; Sodium 523 mg; % of calories from fat 6; Calories 154.*

## Eggs Carbonara (Ham, Peas, and Pasta)

*¹/₂ cup hot diced lean ham*

*¹/₂ cup frozen but separated peas*

*¹/₂ cup hot leftover pasta (such as orzo, shells, or noodles)*

*¹/₄ cup fat-free Parmesan topping or grated Parmesan cheese*

*Chopped fresh parsley or scallions for garnish*

### Omelet

**1** Prepare the omelet according to the Basic Fluffy Omelet recipe at the beginning of this section.

**2** When the cooked omelet is ready to fold, loosen the bottom with a rubber spatula. Place the ham, peas, and pasta on one side. Fold over and briefly cover to heat the peas.

**3** Garnish with the Parmesan cheese and chopped parsley or scallions.

### Egg Scramble

**1** Prepare the egg scramble according to the Basic Egg Scramble recipe at the beginning of this section.

**2** Add the ham, peas, and pasta to the skillet with the eggs and scramble.

**3** Garnish with the Parmesan cheese and chopped parsley or scallions.

**Nutrition at a glance (per serving):** *Total fat 2 g; Saturated fat 1 g; Protein 20 g; Dietary fiber 1 g; Carbohydrate 13 g; Cholesterol 11 mg; Sodium 605 mg; % of calories from fat 12; Calories 152.*

## Eggs with Confetti Peppers, Mushrooms, and Veggies

1 medium onion, peeled and chopped

1 medium tomato, chopped

$^1/_2$ green bell pepper, slivered or chopped

$^1/_2$ red bell pepper, slivered or chopped

$^1/_2$ yellow bell pepper, slivered or chopped

1 8-ounce can sliced mushrooms, drained, or 1 cup steamed fresh mushrooms

$^1/_2$ teaspoon cumin

$^1/_2$ teaspoon dried basil

$^1/_2$ teaspoon dried oregano

### Omelet

**1** Prepare the omelet according to the Basic Fluffy Omelet recipe at the beginning of this section.

**2** Lightly coat a separate large nonstick skillet with no-stick vegetable oil spray. Combine the onion; tomato; green, red, and yellow peppers; mushrooms; cumin; basil; and oregano. Cook over low heat for 10 minutes, stirring, adding a few tablespoons water for moisture if necessary.

**3** When the omelet is ready to fold, loosen the bottom with a rubber spatula, place several tablespoons of the filling on the omelet, fold, and place several more tablespoons on top.

### Egg Scramble

**1** Cook the vegetables as directed for the omelet and prepare the egg mixture according to the Basic Fluffy Omelet or Egg Scramble recipe at the beginning of this section.

**2** When eggs are ready to scramble, add them to the vegetable mixture — reserving some for garnish — and cook until the eggs are solid, about 8 minutes.

*Nutrition at a glance (per serving):* Total fat 1.5 g; Saturated fat 0.5 g; Protein 14 g; Dietary fiber 3 g; Carbohydrate 13 g; Cholesterol 3 mg; Sodium 322 mg; % of calories from fat 11; Calories 116.

## *Feta and Spinach Omelet or Egg Scramble with Feta and Spinach*

4 ounces raw greens (spinach, chard, collards, kale, or beet greens), chopped or thinly sliced

$^1/_2$ cup chopped scallions, or 1 small onion, peeled and chopped

1 clove garlic, peeled and minced

2 tablespoons fat-free or lowfat sour cream

2 tablespoons feta cheese

$^1/_4$ cup diced tomatoes for garnish

Salt (optional)

### *Omelet*

**1** Prepare the omelet according to the Basic Fluffy Omelet recipe at the beginning of this section.

**2** Place the spinach, chard, collards, kale, or beet greens; chopped scallions or onion; and garlic in a saucepan in $^1/_2$ inch of boiling water. Steam, covered, for 5 minutes. Drain.

**3** Toss the spinach with the sour cream and feta cheese.

**4** Place the mixture on one side of the cooked omelet and sprinkle with salt (if desired). Fold and garnish with diced tomatoes.

### *Egg Scramble*

**1** Prepare the egg scramble according to the Basic Egg Scramble recipe at the beginning of this section.

**2** Follow the omelet directions for cooking the vegetables. Place the vegetables on a plate and cover with the scrambled eggs. Garnish with diced tomatoes.

***Nutrition at a glance (per serving):*** *Total fat 2.5 g; Saturated fat 2 g; Protein 14 g; Dietary fiber 1 g; Carbohydrate 6 g; Cholesterol 9 mg; Sodium 349 mg; % of calories from fat 23; Calories 107.*

## Ham and Cheese Omelet or Egg Scramble with Ham and Cheese

*1 cup diced lean ham, all visible fat removed*

*1 cup fat-free, lowfat, or a mixture of regular and fat-free Cheddar cheese*

*Chopped fresh parsley or chives for garnish*

### Omelet

*1* Prepare the omelet according to the Basic Fluffy Omelet recipe at the beginning of this section.

*2* When the omelet is ready to fold, loosen the bottom with a rubber spatula, place the ham and cheese on one side of each omelet, and fold over. Briefly cover to melt the cheese. The cheese should slightly run out.

*3* Garnish with chopped parsley or chives.

### Egg Scramble

*1* Prepare the egg scramble according to the Basic Egg Scramble recipe at the beginning of this section.

*2* When you pour the eggs into the skillet, stir in the ham and cheese.

*3* Garnish with chopped parsley or chives.

*Nutrition at a glance (per serving):* Total fat 2.5 g; Saturated fat 1 g; Protein 27 g; Dietary fiber 1 g; Carbohydrate 4 g; Cholesterol 21 mg; Sodium 1,020 mg; % of calories from fat 16; Calories 162.

## Jelly Omelet or Egg Scramble with Jelly

*$^1/_2$ cup grape or cherry jelly (or 2 tablespoons for each individual omelet)*

*Chopped fresh parsley for garnish*

*(continued)*

### Omelet

**1** Prepare the omelet according to the Basic Fluffy Omelet recipe at the beginning of this section.

**2** When the omelet is ready to fold, loosen the bottom with a rubber spatula, place 2 tablespoons grape or cherry jelly on one side, and fold over with the jelly trickling out. Garnish with chopped parsley.

### Egg Scramble

**1** Prepare the egg scramble according to the Basic Egg Scramble recipe at the beginning of this section.

**2** Place a few tablespoons of grape or cherry jelly on top of each serving of the egg scramble. Garnish with chopped parsley.

***Nutrition at a glance (per serving):*** *Total fat 1 g; Saturated fat 0.5 g; Protein 12 g; Dietary fiber 0 g; Carbohydrate 27 g; Cholesterol 3 mg; Sodium 252 mg; % of calories from fat 5; Calories 164.*

## Onion Omelet or Egg Scramble with Onions

*2 medium onions, peeled and chopped, or 6 to 8 shallots, chopped, or 2 leeks, thinly sliced, or 6 scallions, thinly sliced, or a mixture*

*Chopped fresh parsley for garnish*

**1** Prepare the omelet or the egg scramble according to the Basic Fluffy Omelet or Egg Scramble recipe at this beginning of the section.

**2** Lightly coat a large nonstick skillet with no-stick vegetable oil spray. Add the onions, shallots, leeks, or scallions, or a mixture of any of them. Lightly coat the vegetables with no-stick spray and heat until cooked, stirring, about 6 minutes. (They don't have to be fully cooked.)

**3** Pour over the egg scramble or place inside and over the omelet. Garnish with chopped parsley.

***Nutrition at a glance (per serving):*** *Total fat 1 g; Saturated fat 0.5 g; Protein 12 g; Dietary fiber 1 g; Carbohydrate 7 g; Cholesterol 3 mg; Sodium 241 mg; % of calories from fat 11; Calories 87.*

## Western Omelet or Huevos Rancheros (or Egg Scramble with Salsa)

*1 medium onion, peeled and chopped*

*3 medium tomatoes, chopped, or 1 16-ounce can tomatoes*

*1 8-ounce can tomato sauce*

*1 medium green bell pepper, chopped*

*1 tablespoon chili powder*

*1/2 teaspoon cumin*

*1/2 teaspoon dried basil*

*1/2 teaspoon dried oregano*

*2 tablespoons chopped dried cilantro*

*1 teaspoon finely diced jalapeño*

*4 fat-free corn tortillas*

*Chopped fresh parsley, cilantro, or scallions for omelet garnish*

*Diced avocado, lime, and cilantro for egg scramble garnish (optional)*

### Omelet

*1* Prepare the omelet according to the Basic Fluffy Omelet recipe at the beginning of this section.

*2* Lightly coat a large nonstick skillet with no-stick vegetable oil spray. Combine the onion, tomatoes, tomato sauce, green pepper, chili powder, cumin, basil, oregano, cilantro, and jalapeño. Cook over low heat for 15 minutes.

Or heat 1¹/₂ cups of commercial or homemade salsa.

*3* When the omelet is ready to fold, loosen the bottom with a rubber spatula. Place several tablespoons of the filling inside the omelet and several on top of the omelet. Serve on a fat-free corn tortilla. Garnish with chopped parsley, cilantro, or scallions.

### Egg Scramble

*1* Prepare the egg scramble according to the Basic Egg Scramble recipe at the beginning of this section.

*2* Prepare the vegetable filling as directed in Step 2 of the omelet portion of this recipe. After the eggs are scrambled, place the vegetable mixture on top of the eggs.

Or pour 1¹/₂ cups heated salsa freshened with cilantro and scallions on top of the eggs.

*3* Serve on a fat-free corn tortilla. Garnish with a few tablespoons of diced avocado, lime, and cilantro (if desired).

***Nutrition at a glance (per serving):*** *Total fat 2 g; Saturated fat 0.5 g; Protein 14 g; Dietary fiber 3 g; Carbohydrate 25 g; Cholesterol 3 mg; Sodium 645 mg; % of calories from fat 11; Calories 173.*

# *Other Lowfat Breakfast Recipes*

You feel better and perform more effectively if you've had a good breakfast. The following recipes are varied, interesting, and easy to prepare; they offer a good incentive to begin eating a healthful breakfast every day.

## *Baked Apples*

Hot and homey country apples, baked sweet and luscious, are perfect on a cold weekend morning. When you core them, leave half an inch of apple on the bottom to hold the brown sugar filling. This method allows the filling to soak through but not run out of the apples as they bake. Serve baked apples hot or cold, with fat-free or lowfat yogurt or vanilla ice cream or liquid fat-free non-dairy creamer.

**Tools:** *8-inch glass baking pan*

**Preparation time:** *3 (most of it baking time)*

**Yield:** *4 servings*

*4 large tart apples (such as Gravenstein, Granny Smith, or Rome), cored*

*$^1/_4$ cup fresh lemon juice*

*$^1/_4$ cup brown sugar*

*$^1/_4$ cup chopped walnuts or pecans (optional)*

*$^1/_4$ cup currants or raisins*

*$^1/_4$ cup maple syrup*

*Cinnamon (about $^1/_4$ teaspoon)*

*Nutmeg (slightly less than the cinnamon)*

*1* Preheat the oven to 350°.

*2* Place the cored apples in an 8-inch glass baking pan.

*3* In a small bowl, combine the lemon juice, brown sugar, walnuts or pecans (if desired), and currants or raisins. Mix well.

*4* Divide the mixture into four equal parts and stuff into the cored apples. If you have extra, just sprinkle the remaining filling on top. Pour the syrup over the apples. Dust the apples with cinnamon and a smaller amount of nutmeg. (See Figure 7-2.)

*5* Bake in the oven, uncovered, for 1 hour.

**Nutrition at a glance (per serving):** *Total fat 1 g; Saturated fat 0 g; Protein 1 g; Dietary fiber 5 g; Carbohydrate 62 g; Cholesterol 0 mg; Sodium 7 mg; % of calories from fat 3; Calories 237.*

*(continued)*

*Lynn's apple tips:* Smell the apples at the market to see which ones are tart and flavorful. The produce person will cut one for you. Many new varieties are available. You never want to bake with Red Delicious apples; they have little flavor, and they fall apart.

**Figure 7-2:**
Stuffing
cored
apples is
a cinch.

## Stuffing Cored Apples

Divide the mixture into 4 equal parts... ...and stuff into the cored apples. Pour the syrup over the apples. Dust the apples with cinnamon and a smaller amount of nutmeg.

## Blueberry Pancakes

These thick and fluffy pancakes filled with a gazillion plump blueberries aren't dainty, polite pancakes. These pancakes are lush and sensuous, and they're my personal favorite. Add extra berries on top.

**Tools:** *Large nonstick skillet, small saucepan*

**Preparation time:** *2*

**Yield:** *6 servings*

| | |
|---|---|
| *1 cup whole wheat or all-purpose flour* | *1 tablespoon canola or safflower oil* |
| *$^1/_2$ teaspoon baking powder* | *$^1/_2$ teaspoon vanilla* |
| *$^1/_2$ teaspoon baking soda* | *1 pint fresh blueberries, washed, drained, and arranged on a plate* |
| *1 teaspoon sugar* | |
| *1 cup skim milk or skim buttermilk* | *1 cup blueberries* |
| *$^1/_4$ cup substitute eggs* | *1 cup maple or pancake syrup* |

**1** In a large bowl, combine the flour, baking powder, baking soda, and sugar.

**2** In another bowl, combine the milk or buttermilk, substitute eggs, oil, and vanilla. Pour the liquid ingredients into the dry ingredients and blend with a whisk.

*(continued)*

**3** Lightly coat a large nonstick skillet with no-stick vegetable oil spray. When the pan is very hot, pour in enough batter to make a 1-, 3-, or 4-inch pancake. Immediately add enough blueberries to cover 80 percent of the top. Do the same with the other 3 pancakes. Cook until the bubbling on the batter stops. Turn each pancake and cook for another minute or two.

**4** In a small saucepan, heat 1 cup blueberries and syrup, but don't boil. Pour the heated berries and syrup over the pancakes and serve.

***Nutrition at a glance (per serving):*** *Total fat 3 g; Saturated fat 0.5 g; Protein 6 g; Dietary fiber 4 g; Carbohydrate 64 g; Cholesterol 1 mg; Sodium 193 mg; % of calories from fat 9; Calories 291.*

***Lynn's easier-to-make lowfat pancake tip:*** *Look for reduced-fat Bisquick and lowfat Pioneer biscuit mix at your market. Follow the mix directions and just add the berries for easy blueberry pancakes.*

## French Toast

Good country bread soaked in eggs, toasted hot and crusty golden in a skillet, covered with maple syrup, and sprinkled with blueberries or raspberries is such an easy crowd pleaser. Serve with lean slices of Canadian bacon, add some orange juice and coffee or decaf, and you have my idea of pure pleasure.

***Tools:*** *Large nonstick skillet*

***Preparation time:*** *2*

***Yield:*** *4 servings*

*³/₄ cup substitute eggs*

*1 egg white*

*2 tablespoons liquid fat-free non-dairy creamer or evaporated skimmed milk*

*Dash of nutmeg*

*¹/₂ teaspoon vanilla*

*8 slices day-old white or whole grain bread*

*1 cup maple or pancake syrup*

*1 cup blueberries or raspberries*

*(continued)*

*1* In a large shallow dish or bowl, combine the substitute eggs, egg white, creamer or evaporated skimmed milk, nutmeg, and vanilla and whisk until blended.

*2* Place the bread in the egg liquid and let soak, turning once, for a minute or two.

*3* Lightly coat a large nonstick skillet with no-stick vegetable oil spray and heat on medium-high.

*4* Pan-fry the egg-soaked bread until lightly browned, turning once, until both sides are fully cooked. Cut diagonally or in fingers. Serve with the syrup and berries.

***Nutrition at a glance (per serving):*** *Total fat 3 g; Saturated fat 1 g; Protein 12 g; Dietary fiber 2 g; Carbohydrate 96 g; Cholesterol 3 mg; Sodium 437 mg; % of calories from fat 6; Calories 452.*

***Lynn's french toast tips:*** *You don't know what to do with French bread that's a day or two old? Slice it diagonally and make real French toast. French bread contains almost no fat.*

## Hash Browns or Potato Pancakes

Crispy, potatoey good are these hash browns with onions and peppers. If you have a cup or so of leftover lean roast beef or ham (all visible fat removed), add that, too. The meat adds about 2 grams of fat per serving.

***Tools:*** *Large nonstick skillet with lid*

***Preparation time:*** *2*

***Yield:*** *4 servings*

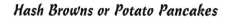

*1 large Spanish onion, peeled and shredded*

*2 large russet potatoes, shredded, peeled or unpeeled*

*1 green bell pepper, shredded (optional)*

*2 tablespoons flour*

*1 egg white*

*Salt (optional) and freshly ground black pepper*

*(continued)*

*1* Place in a colander the shredded onions, potatoes, and green pepper (if desired). Press lightly with a clean paper towel to drain out the liquid. Place the vegetables in a large bowl and add the flour, egg white, and salt (if desired) and mix well.

*2* Lightly coat a large nonstick skillet with no-stick vegetable oil spray. Make several potato patties the size of small hamburgers. Place in the skillet and lightly spray again. Cook over medium-high heat for about 20 minutes, covered part of the time, turning often to keep the patties from becoming too dark. Season with pepper.

*Nutrition at a glance (per serving):* Total fat 0 g; Saturated fat 0 g; Protein 4 g; Dietary fiber 2 g; Carbohydrate 26 g; Cholesterol 0 mg; Sodium 33 mg; % of calories from fat 2; Calories 117.

*Lynn's potato pancake additions:* Serve with Apple Sauce (see Chapter 16) and lowfat or fat-free sour cream.

## Hearty Roast Beef Hash

Hearty Roast Beef Hash isn't just breakfast food; it's good for brunch, lunch, or an easy dinner, too. Use leftover well-done roast beef. To spice up this dish, add several shakes of crushed red pepper.

*Tools:* Large nonstick skillet

*Preparation time:* 2

*Yield:* 4 servings

2 large potatoes, cooked and diced

$^1/_2$ to 1 cup chopped onion

1 green bell pepper, diced

1 scallion, finely chopped

1 cup diced, cooked, well-done lean roast beef, all visible fat removed

Salt (optional) and freshly ground black pepper

*1* Lightly coat a large nonstick skilet with no-stick vegetable oil spray. Sauté the potatoes, onions, and pepper over medium heat, lightly spraying the vegetables if necessary, tossing often, until the vegetables are golden brown (about 10 minutes).

*2* Add the scallion, roast beef, and salt (if desired) and pepper and heat thoroughly. Turn up the heat until the ingredients sizzle. Toss for about 2 minutes, making sure not to scorch them.

*(continued)*

*Nutrition at a glance (per serving):* Total fat 1 g; Saturated fat 0.5 g; Protein 11 g; Dietary fiber 2 g; Carbohydrate 19 g; Cholesterol 23 mg; Sodium 23 mg; % of calories from fat 8; Calories 128.

*Lynn's lowfat hash heaven ideas:* You can add other vegetables (such as chopped or diced celery, peas, carrots, tomatoes, green beans, or mushrooms), lean ham, skinless turkey, or lowfat or fat-free gravy. You can also add any of the following flavorings: 1 teaspoon vinegar, 1 teaspoon Worcestershire sauce, a bouillon cube or granules, or 1 tablespoon of any of these flavorings: chili powder, chopped basil, chopped thyme, chopped parsley, or olives. Hash can be heated in the oven, but cover it to keep the ingredients from drying out.

## Oat Bran Muffins

Besides making your tummy feel good, golden brown oat bran muffins may help to lower your cholesterol. Top them with honey or preserves.

**Tools:** *Muffin cups*

**Preparation time:** *2*

**Yield:** *12 servings*

| | |
|---|---|
| *¹/₂ cup all-purpose flour* | *2 teaspoons baking soda* |
| *¹/₂ cup wheat bran* | *1 cup skim milk* |
| *¹/₂ cup oat bran* | *¹/₂ cup substitute eggs* |
| *1¹/₂ cups 5-minute rolled oats* | *5 teaspoons canola oil* |
| *²/₃ cup packed dark brown sugar* | *¹/₄ teaspoon almond extract* |

*1* Preheat the oven to 375°.

*2* In a large bowl, combine the flour, wheat bran, oat bran, oats, brown sugar, and baking soda.

*3* In a small bowl, combine the milk, substitute eggs, oil, and almond extract.

*4* Add the liquid mixture to the dry flour mixture. Mix just until moistened.

*5* Spoon into muffin cups lightly coated with no-stick vegetable oil spray, filling each cup half full. Bake for 18 minutes or until light brown (a toothpick inserted into the center of the muffin should come out clean).

*(continued)*

***Nutrition at a glance (per serving):*** *Total fat 3 g; Saturated fat 0.5 g; Protein 5 g; Dietary fiber 2 g; Carbohydrate 27 g; Cholesterol 0 mg; Sodium 242 mg; % of calories from fat 18; Calories 143.*

***Lynn's muffin additions:*** *Try adding $^1/_4$ to $^1/_2$ cup raisins, currants, chopped dried dates, apricots, apples, or prunes or a small amount of nuts to your oat bran muffins.*

## Pineapple Upside Down Cake

This cake is sumptuous and golden-rich-looking with pineapple and brown sugar. Using the nuts adds 1 gram of fat, but nuts offer nutrients and a little fiber. (I encourage using natural fats more than added oils.)

***Tools:*** *9- or 10-inch ovenproof nonstick frying pan or glass, tin, or ceramic round cake pan*

***Preparation time:*** *3*

***Yield:*** *10 servings*

| | |
|---|---|
| *1$^1/_3$ cups all-purpose flour* | *$^1/_4$ teaspoon coconut flavoring or extract* |
| *$^2/_3$ cup sugar* | |
| *2 teaspoons baking powder* | *1 16-ounce can pineapple slices, drained, 2 tablespoons juice reserved* |
| *$^2/_3$ cup fat-free or lowfat buttermilk* | *12 to 20 pecan halves (optional)* |
| *$^1/_4$ cup liquid diet margarine* | *1$^1/_2$ tablespoons liquid diet margarine, melted* |
| *$^1/_2$ cup substitute eggs* | |
| *1$^1/_2$ teaspoons vanilla* | *1 cup dark brown sugar, loosely packed* |

*1* Preheat the oven to 375°.

*2* Over a large bowl, sift together the flour, sugar, and baking powder. Shake them into the bowl, discarding or pressing through any hard pieces of sugar or flour left. With a rubber spatula, mix the sifted dry ingredients thoroughly.

*3* In another bowl, combine the buttermilk, $^1/_4$ cup liquid margarine, substitute eggs, vanilla, and coconut flavoring or extract and mix well. Add the liquid ingredients to the dry ingredients and whisk hard for 2 minutes, breaking up any lumps and beating the batter well.

*(continued)*

**4** Coat a 9- to 10-inch ovenproof nonstick frying pan or round cake pan (glass, tin, or ceramic) with no-stick vegetable oil spray, covering all sides and the bottom.

**5** In the bottom of the pan, place the pineapple slices in any design you want. In the center of each ring, in between the rings, and at the edges of the rings, place an unbroken pecan half (use from 12 to 20 if desired) with the "good" side down. Sprinkle the pineapple juice and brown sugar evenly over the pineapple. Drizzle 1¹/₂ tablespoons liquid margarine over the sugar.

**6** Slowly and carefully pour the batter over the rings, making sure that all the nuts, brown sugar, and pineapple are covered.

**7** Reduce the heat to 350° and bake for 40 to 50 minutes. When the cake is done (a toothpick inserted in the center comes out clean), cool for 10 minutes.

**8** Slide a flat rubber spatula around the edges. Using hot pads (and if possible, a helper), place a plate that is larger than the cake pan on top of the pan and quickly invert the cake onto the plate. Remove any pineapple rings, nuts, or brown sugar that stuck to the cake pan and put them back on the cake.

***Nutrition at a glance (per serving):*** *Total fat 3 g; Saturated fat 0.5 g; Protein 4 g; Dietary fiber 1 g; Carbohydrate 56 g; Cholesterol 0 mg; Sodium 217 mg; % of calories from fat 11; Calories 262.*

***Lynn's nut substitutions:*** *If you don't want to use nuts, use currants, raisins, dates, or Grape-Nuts.*

# Chapter 8

# Appetizers and Snacks

*In This Chapter*

▶ Delighting your guests with lowfat appetizers

▶ Choosing appetizers and snacks that are usually low in fat, saturated fat, and cholesterol

*W*hen party food is at its best, it is colorful, tasty, and low in fat. At home, you can control the fat content in the food you serve. When eating out, however, monitoring your fat intake isn't as easy. Still, eating appetizers can be great fun and offers built-in encouragement for self-restraint.

If a waiter serves the appetizers at a cocktail party, the food keeps moving. If the people are really interesting, you become engrossed in the conversation and don't concentrate on eating. If food is placed on trays on a table and the room is crowded, you have to keep moving to give others a chance. If the room isn't crowded, everyone knows who's making a pig of herself! So cocktail parties help you keep your intake down — sometimes.

I love party food, and you probably do, too. But what do you do at parties when nothing is low in fat, when all you see are deep-fat-fried brown stuff and piles of diced cheese squares, and you're very hungry?

I always tell folks to eat the bread and the garnishes. Eating rose radishes, chrysanthemum tomatoes, and a lattice-work of carrots is quite a luxury. If the garnish is just fruit, such as bananas, apples, oranges, mangoes, papayas, pears, grapes, and kiwis, make sure to find a knife; a waiter can find one for you. I grab a plate and cut off mango slices. Soon, people begin asking me, "Where did you get that?"

If you don't want *your* guests searching the appetizer table for garnishes, this chapter gives you techniques for making lowfat appetizers a specialty. I tell you how to make easy, quick, special-looking, and delicious-tasting lowfat appetizers and snacks for a few people or many, for a formal gathering or a football game on television. The chapter gives you a list of quickie appetizer assemblies. I also include a list of high-fat appetizers and snacks and a list of lowfat alternatives, because many people don't know that cold shrimp cocktail contains a miniscule amount of fat and that hot garlic shrimp in butter is loaded with it.

## Delighting Your Guests with Lowfat Appetizers

You can control the fat content in food when giving your own party. Just having friends over for drinks, let alone dinner, is hard work, so appetizers should be simple. I tell hosts and hostesses to forget the Brie en croute, diced Swiss, Cheddar cheese nut balls, fried Camembert, wedges of Roquefort, and dips made of high-fat mayonnaise and cream cheese. For the knowledgeable and health-conscious, these foods are not welcoming or fun; they're tempting and can be dangerous.

I went to a recent gathering where no one ate a very expensive, already cut, huge wheel of Brie. Although some Brie is now made lower in fat, lower-fat versions are hard to find, and some cheese store managers know little and care less about ordering them. In addition, most lowfat cheeses aren't good enough to stand on their own. You can make dozens of other good appetizers, including dips, instead.

Do you need an easy dip? Dips are convenient, expected, and can be used with vegetable crudités, fruits, crackers, pita wedges, and all styles of breads. Many commercially prepared dips are lowfat or fat-free. You can freshen and enhance these dips by adding more of the main ingredient, such as shrimp or clams, and especially by adding fresh chopped vegetables and herbs, such as onions, peppers, chives, parsley, mustard, or extra-fresh horseradish. Just look on the label, see what's in the dip, and add more of the same. A lowfat or fat-free store-bought dip makes a good start for your healthful appetizer menu.

You can make your own dips, too, with the new lowfat and fat-free sour creams (which are impossible to tell from the traditional dairy kind), lowfat and fat-free mayonnaises and yogurts (drain the liquid from yogurt for a few hours first), and even fat-free or 1 percent cottage cheese. Puree the cottage cheese for about 4 minutes until very smooth, and you have a great base for a dip.

Fat-free cream cheese admittedly isn't very good by itself, but when you add a little sherry, fresh crab, horseradish, white wine, hot sauce, lemon juice, and a few herbs and spices, shake on some paprika, and tuck in a sprig of parsley it looks elegant and tastes great to a hungry crowd. And this dip is low in fat.

Other help is available, too. On a recent trip to both regular and fancy food markets, I found several lowfat, ready-made items that looked quite delicious and could supplement what you make at home. I saw jars of eggplant dip, caponata, baba ghanoush, vegetable pâté, ratatouille, tinned mussels, spicy shrimp, smoked oysters, lobster bits, calamari, and several varieties of canned fish, plus the usual marinated mushrooms, artichoke hearts, hearts of palm, and all manner of sardines in sauces ranging from tomato to hot and spicy to mustard. You can always find interesting pickles, from okra to string beans to watermelon. Take a look at the fat content, but almost all these foods qualify for lowfat appetizer assistance and can be kept on your shelf almost indefinitely to use when you need them.

***Note:*** I include avocados, nuts, seeds, olives, and hearts of palm (which some people think are high-fat) on a lowfat appetizer menu because I like to see people eat a wide variety of foods, and some natural fat, I think, is fine. Nuts contain a little fiber and different nutrients than you get in a tomato, plus they are hard and crunchy, so chewing these foods is good for your teeth and jaws. They also contain natural fat, not processed, added fat. Even an avocado contains less fat than the leanest cut of meat, but eat avocados sparingly.

When purchasing avocados, buy the smooth-skinned Florida variety called a Fuerte. This type has about half the fat of the smaller, black, pebbly-skinned Hass. (See Figure 8-1.) Avocado fat is mainly a monounsaturated fat. However, avocado fat contains the same number of calories as any other type of fat. Hearts of palm, unlike coconut, contain virtually no fat. Eat a heart of palm as you would a stick of celery (except the heart of palm is more expensive!). Olives are varied in color, size, and flavor, with hundreds of varieties. Although olives contain some fat, most of it isn't saturated.

**Figure 8-1:**
Contrary to what you may think, you *can* enjoy avocados on a lowfat eating plan.

Avocados

Hass

Fuerte

Like all vegetables, none of these foods contains cholesterol, unlike pigs-in-a-blanket or bacon-covered chicken livers, which contain enormous amounts of fat and saturated fat and are laden with cholesterol.

If the food is attractively presented and the guests are hungry, most will not be disappointed that you are serving colorful vegetables with tasty dips, hummus and pita, and stuffed grape leaves rather than the usual cheese balls and fried chicken wings — as long as the food is delicious. Those who don't care about their health won't know that you made your food low in fat, and those who do care will appreciate your efforts and really enjoy your party.

# Ten quick and easy lowfat appetizers

These dips and spreads are easy to prepare, and you can use the same ideas for creating your own favorite mixtures. For example, the ham spread recipe includes the same basic ingredients as a clam or shrimp spread.

✔ **Bean dip:** Puree a drained can of black, pinto, or white beans with 1/4 cup chopped onion, 1 clove garlic, 1/2 jalapeño pepper, 2 tablespoons fresh lemon or lime juice, and 1/2 teaspoon cumin. Serve with lowfat or fat-free toasted tortillas, tortilla chips, pitas, or vegetables.

✔ **Chutney and cream cheese spread:** Mix an 8-ounce block of reduced-fat or fat-free cream cheese (or form tub cream cheese into a block) with half a bottle of hot and spicy chutney. Sprinkle with chopped scallions or onions. Serve with lowfat crackers, carrot sticks, baby carrots, and celery.

✔ **Crab or clam dip:** To 8 ounces reduced-fat or fat-free cream cheese, stir in 1 chopped onion, 1 clove minced garlic, a few

tablespoons white wine or sherry, a little fresh lemon juice, a little hot sauce, 1/2 to 1 teaspoon horseradish, and seasoning salt or Beau Monde spice mixture. Mix in 6 ounces fresh or canned crab meat, sprinkle with paprika and chopped fresh parsley, and serve cold or hot.

✔ **Curry dip:** To 2 cups lowfat or fat-free sour cream or mayonnaise (or a mixture of the two), add 1 tablespoon curry powder, 2 tablespoons onion juice, and 1/2 teaspoon Worcestershire sauce. Serve with carrots, celery, sugar snaps, green beans, and other vegetables.

✔ **Dill dip:** To 1 cup of lowfat or fat-free sour cream and 1 cup of mayonnaise, add 3 tablespoons chopped fresh dill and 1/2 teaspoon each fresh lemon juice, garlic, and onion powder. Garnish with a dill sprig.

✔ **Ham spread:** In a food processor, combine 8 ounces very lean Smithfield, country, or plain baked ham (with all visible fat removed), 1 cup reduced-fat or fat-free cream cheese or 1 cup lowfat or fat-free mayonnaise, 2 tablespoons Dijon mustard, and ¼ teaspoon cayenne pepper.

✔ **Herb and veggie dip:** To 2 cups lowfat or fat-free mayonnaise or sour cream or a mixture of both, add 1 coarsely chopped small red bell pepper, 1 coarsely chopped green bell pepper, 1 chopped onion, 2 minced garlic cloves, 5 sprigs parsley, and ½ teaspoon each of chopped thyme, basil, chives, and marjoram. Serve with vegetables and lowfat crackers.

✔ **Marinated mushrooms, artichoke hearts, baby corn, green or red peppers, and string beans:** Place fresh or canned, drained vegetables in a jar and cover with a favorite lowfat or fat-free Italian dressing, several tablespoons each of vinegar and chopped onions, a sprinkle of allspice and cracked pepper, and a dash of hot sauce. Refrigerate for at least 24 hours before serving.

✔ **Stuffed celery, Belgian endive, or cherry tomatoes:** Fill celery, Belgian endive, or cherry tomatoes (scoop tomatoes with a melon baller) with reduced-fat or fat-free cream cheese, top with a small slice of olive (green with pimento), and sprinkle on paprika. Or stuff with chicken or tuna salad made with lowfat or fat-free mayonnaise. Cut celery in bite-sized pieces or, for picnics and casual gatherings, leave long and whole with leaves.

✔ **Tuna spread:** To 2 6-ounce cans drained, water-packed tuna, add 8 ounces reduced-fat or fat-free cream cheese or mayonnaise, the juice of half a lemon, a small chopped onion, and ¼ cup sweet pickle relish.

# *Choosing the Right Appetizers to Snack On*

Appetizers can be detrimental to a lowfat eating plan, but they don't have to be. Knowing which tasty morsels to try — and which to steer clear of — makes all the difference. This section should give you a good idea of which appetizers are "safe" and which should be avoided.

Appetizers and snacks that are usually low in total fat, saturated fat, and cholesterol include the following:

- Baked tortilla or potato chips

- Bean or chili dip (without lard, oil, or regular cream cheese)

- Beef jerky (check the label)

- Calamari (steamed, roasted, or broiled instead of batter fried)

- Canadian bacon (under 2 ounces)

- Chestnuts (7 or fewer)

- Clam dip (with lowfat or fat-free mayonnaise or sour cream)

- Crudités (with lowfat or fat-free Ranch dressing or dip)

- Cucumber sandwiches

- Dried or fresh fruit

- Ham (if lean and baked)

- Hard-cooked egg whites

- Herring (1 ounce without sour cream)

- Hummus (with limited tahini and olive oil)

- Marinated mushrooms or artichokes, drained and rinsed

- Mock (eggplant) caviar

- Mushrooms stuffed with bread or onions

- Oysters (not fried)

- Pepperoni and salami (labeled lean or lowfat)

- Pizza (with vegetables and lowfat or small amounts of cheese)

- Popcorn (air-popped and without butter)

- Potted turkey spread (without mayonnaise or extra fat)

- Pretzels

- Prosciutto and melon (with lean Prosciutto)

- Ratatouille

- Salmon mousse (with lowfat or fat-free sour cream, cream cheese, or mayonnaise)

- Salsa

- Sardines (without oil)

- Scallops (broiled or grilled)

- Shrimp, crab, or lobster cocktail with cocktail sauce (under 3 ounces)

- Smoked oysters or salmon

- Sour cream dips made with lowfat or fat-free sour cream

- Steamed clams or mussels

- Tuna (packed in water)

- Yogurt dips made with lowfat or fat-free yogurt

The following appetizers and snacks are usually high in fat, saturated fat, and cholesterol:

- Artichoke dip (with regular mayonnaise or sour cream)

- Beef roll-ups

- Bourbon balls

- Broccoli cheese dip

- Canapés with eggs or cream cheese

- Caviar

- Cheese

- Cheese twists

- Chicken livers or wings

- Chinese, Vietnamese, or Thai fried egg rolls
- Clam dip
- Corn chips
- Cottage cheese dip
- Crab Louis
- Cream cheese-stuffed celery, cherry tomatoes, or snow peas
- Creamed shrimp, lobster, or crab
- Deep-fat-fried calamari, oysters, cheese, or vegetables in batter
- Deviled eggs
- Fried shrimp balls
- Lunch meat (unless lowfat or fat-free)
- Mayonnaise dips
- Meatballs
- Mushrooms in butter or cream sauce
- Nachos
- Nuts
- Pâté
- Pickled eggs
- Pigs-in-a-blanket
- Potato chips
- Potato skins with cheese, sour cream, or bacon
- Quiche
- Ribs
- Salmon mousse (with regular cream, sour cream, or cream cheese)
- Sausage and sausage dishes
- Sour cream dips
- Stuffed celery
- Tacos
- Whipped cream dips
- Yogurt dips

# Appealing Appetizer Recipes

The following appetizers and snacks are easy to prepare, and you won't need to spend an afternoon searching the specialty shops for the ingredients. Don't wait for your next big party to try these delectables; your family and friends will appreciate these treats on any occasion.

### Baked Cod

I enjoyed this appetizer in a cozy country inn in damp, cold England, when chilled to the bone, and I never forgot the warm satisfaction of the taste that came from my individual little pot of this hot, creamy mixture. You can substitute mackerel, which I like, but it is slightly higher in fat. Garnish with fresh parsley if desired.

*(continued)*

**Tools:** *Four 3-x-3-inch baking dishes with lids*

**Preparation time:** *2*

**Yield:** *4 servings*

4 ounces smoked black cod (sable) or mackerel

1 large onion, peeled and sliced

2 large tomatoes, sliced

1 cup liquid fat-free non-dairy creamer

$^1/_4$ cup flour

$^1/_2$ cup white wine or beer (optional)

1 teaspoon Worcestershire sauce

$^1/_2$ cup shredded fat-free or lowfat mozzarella cheese

4 teaspoons fat-free Parmesan topping or grated Parmesan cheese

*1* Preheat oven to 400°.

*2* Lightly coat with no-stick vegetable oil spray four 3-x-3-inch baking dishes with lids (or cover with foil). Divide the fish into fourths. Place one piece of fish in the bottom of each pot, and place a 1-inch slice of onion and a 1-inch slice of tomato on the fish.

*3* In a small bowl, whisk together the creamer, flour, wine or beer (if desired), and Worcestershire sauce until smooth. Divide and pour over the vegetables and fish. Divide the mozzarella and Parmesan cheese and sprinkle across the top. Cover each pot, bake for 10 minutes, lower the heat to 375°, and bake for 15 additional minutes.

**Nutrition at a glance (per serving):** *Total fat 0.5 g; Saturated fat 0 g; Protein 14 g; Dietary fiber 2 g; Carbohydrate 40 g; Cholesterol 24 mg; Sodium 367 mg; % of calories from fat 3; Calories 224.*

**Lynn's lowfat cheese tips:** *In my own recent taste test of several brands of packaged, shredded fat-free and lowfat mozzarella and other cheeses, I found that the more well-known the brand, the better the taste and melting properties.*

## Baked Portobello Mushrooms

These large, flavorful, meaty, and elegant mushrooms can serve as an entree. You can omit or vary the wine, using sherry, white wine, port, or Madeira instead. Garnish with chopped fresh parsley and leeks.

**Tools:** *Large nonstick frying pan*

**Preparation time:** *2*

**Yield:** *4 servings*

*(continued)*

*4 portobello mushrooms (see Figure 8-2)*

*1 to 2 medium onions or 1 leek or 4 shallots, finely chopped*

*1 clove garlic, peeled and minced*

*2 tablespoons chopped fresh parsley*

*2 tablespoons Marsala (optional)*

*$^1/_2$ cup herbed dried bread crumbs*

*2 tablespoons fat-free Parmesan topping or grated Parmesan cheese*

*Salt (optional) and freshly ground black pepper*

*1* Preheat the oven to 350°. Wash the mushrooms, remove the mushroom stems, and chop the stems.

*2* Lightly coat a large nonstick frying pan with no-stick olive oil spray. In the frying pan, combine the chopped stems, onions (or leek or shallots), garlic, parsley, Marsala (if desired), and bread crumbs. Lightly spray the vegetables and crumbs again and cook over medium heat for 5 minutes or until nearly cooked, stirring often, covering between stirrings. Add a teaspoon or two of water for moisture if necessary.

*3* Lightly coat a baking sheet with no-stick spray. Place the mushroom caps on the sheet, stem side up, and lightly spray. Divide the filling and spoon some into the gill area of each mushroom, patting down lightly. Sprinkle with Parmesan cheese and salt (if desired) and pepper. Lightly cover with foil, bending down the foil edges, and bake for 25 minutes.

***Nutrition at a glance (per serving):*** *Total fat 0.5 g; Saturated fat 0 g; Protein 8 g; Dietary fiber 0 g; Carbohydrate 19 g; Cholesterol 0 mg; Sodium 448 mg; % of calories from fat 4; Calories 86.*

***Lynn's lowfat cheese tip:*** *To extend taste but keep the fat low with fat-free Parmesan topping, purchase the best Parmesan cheese or the one with the strongest flavor and mix half and half with fat-free Parmesan topping.*

**Figure 8-2:**
A portobello mushroom.

## Eggplant Caviar

This Middle Eastern-style dip is slightly sweet, yet tangy and savory, and has a rich reddish color flecked with green peppers. You can serve it at room temperature or make it a day ahead and chill it. You can even mold it, because eggplant is slightly gelatinous when chilled. Vary the amount of lemon and vinegar to taste. Serve with crackers, crudités, or toasted pita triangles and garnish with sprigs of fresh parsley or lemon wedges.

**Tools:** *Microwaveable dish or baking sheet, large nonstick skillet*

**Preparation time:** *3*

**Yield:** *About 4 cups, or 16 servings*

*1 large eggplant*

*1 cup finely chopped onion*

*1/2 cup finely chopped green bell pepper*

*1/2 cup finely chopped red bell pepper*

*2 cloves garlic, peeled and minced*

*1/4 cup finely chopped fresh parsley*

*1 tablespoon fresh lemon juice*

*1 to 2 tablespoons balsamic or cider vinegar*

*1/2 teaspoon sugar*

*1 tablespoon tomato paste*

*1 15 1/2-ounce can crushed tomatoes, undrained*

*1 teaspoon dried basil*

*Salt (optional)*

*2 teaspoons drained capers (optional)*

*1* Pierce the eggplant several times with a fork. Microwave in a microwaveable dish for 15 minutes, turning once or twice, or bake on foil on a baking sheet in a 400° oven for 45 minutes or until tender, turning over once. Cut in half and let cool slightly.

*2* Coat a large nonstick skillet with no-stick vegetable oil spray. Lightly spray the onion, green and red peppers, and garlic and sauté for 5 minutes over medium-low heat until the vegetables begin to soften, adding a tablespoon or two of water for moisture if needed.

*3* With a spoon, scrape the pulp from the eggplant and add the pulp to the mixture in the skillet. Discard the skin.

*4* Add the parsley, lemon juice, vinegar, sugar, tomato paste, crushed tomatoes, basil, and salt (if desired). Cook for 3 minutes, crushing the eggplant with the back of a spoon to break it up, mashing but not pureeing it.

*5* Cover the skillet, reduce the heat to low, and simmer for 1 hour, stirring occasionally.

*(continued)*

*6* Transfer the eggplant caviar to a bowl and stir in the capers (if desired). Garnish and serve chilled or at room temperature.

**Nutrition at a glance (per serving):** *Total fat 0 g; Saturated fat 0 g; Protein 1 g; Dietary fiber 1 g; Carbohydrate 5 g; Cholesterol 0 mg; Sodium 55 mg; % of calories from fat 7; Calories 24.*

**Lynn's eggplant news:** *Hot and cold eggplant appetizers and side dishes seem to be present in every culture. Caponata is the Italian version of the French eggplant ratatouille. The Middle Eastern version is called baba ghanoush. With slight shifts in herbs and spices, a dozen other types exist, proving that eggplant is a worldwide favorite.*

## Hummus

Hummus is a delicious Middle Eastern specialty that has become popular in the United States. You can serve hummus with pita triangles, rye toast strips, pumpernickel mini breads, lowfat crackers, an assortment of cold vegetables, or stuffed into hard-cooked egg whites. If you like, garnish with chopped black olives and lemon slices.

**Tools:** *Blender or food processor*

**Preparation time:** *1*

**Yield:** *About 2 cups, or 8 servings*

*1 16-ounce can garbanzo beans (chickpeas), drained, or 1¹/₂ cups cooked garbanzo beans, well mashed or pureed*

*1 tablespoon tahini or olive oil*

*3 tablespoons chopped fresh parsley*

*3 tablespoons fresh lemon juice*

*3 cloves garlic, peeled and minced*

*¹/₄ teaspoon cayenne pepper (optional)*

*Salt (optional)*

In a blender or food processor (or mash by hand), puree the beans, tahini or olive oil, parsley, lemon juice, garlic, cayenne pepper (if desired), and salt (if desired).

*(continued)*

*Nutrition at a glance (per serving): Total fat 2 g; Saturated fat 0 g; Protein 3 g; Dietary fiber 2 g; Carbohydrate 9 g; Cholesterol 0 mg; Sodium 76 mg; % of calories from fat 25; Calories 64.*

*Lynn's lowfat tahini tip: Tahini is a paste made from sesame seeds. You can slightly lower the fat and intensify the flavor by pouring off all the oil and using only the thick, mashed seeds.*

## Potato Skins

Potato skins are fun to make and eat. Serve with several lowfat toppings, such as salsa mixed with fat-free or lowfat sour cream, chives or chopped scallions, fat-free or lowfat cheese (which can be melted on the skins), bacon pieces (cooked meat part only), and hot sauce.

*Preparation time:* 3

*Yield:* 4 servings

| | |
|---|---|
| *4 medium russet baking potatoes* | *3 tablespoons shredded Cheddar cheese* |
| *2 to 4 teaspoons liquid diet margarine* | *1 cup fat-free or lowfat sour cream* |
| *¹/₄ cup skim milk* | *¹/₂ cup chopped scallions* |
| *Salt (optional) and freshly ground black pepper* | |

*1* Preheat the oven to 350°.

*2* Wash the potatoes and place wet in the oven, but not touching each other, directly on the rack (which crisps them). Bake for 1 hour and 10 minutes.

*3* Remove and cut in half lengthwise. Scoop out the filling, leaving some potato (at least ¹/₄ inch), being careful to keep the skins intact. Reserve the filling for another use.

*4* Using scissors, cut the skins in half again and, if very large potatoes, in fourths. Drizzle margarine in a line from one end of the potato to the other and then do the same with the milk. With a fork, mash some of the white on the skins to slightly flatten them.

*5* Season with salt (if desired) and pepper, add the cheese, and place under the broiler for 1 to 2 minutes until crisp and golden. Garnish with the sour cream and scallions.

*(continued)*

*Nutrition at a glance (per serving):* *Total fat 3 g; Saturated fat 1.5 g; Protein 8 g; Dietary fiber 3 g; Carbohydrate 39 g; Cholesterol 6 mg; Sodium 118 mg; % of calories from fat 13; Calories 218.*

*Lynn's potato tips:* *The best and sweetest potatoes are a type of stone-smooth, dark brown russet (many russet varieties exist). They have no eyes, are smaller than most russets, and are sold only in the fall.*

Salsas deserve their own corner. Nearly everyone enjoys them. Always make two versions: one hot, one not. These are easy to tell apart. The hottest is red (decorate with jalapeños), the less-hot one is yellow, and the mild version is green for go.

At least 8 percent of all Americans, including the late actor W.C. Fields, have a skin condition called *rosacea.* They can't tolerate capsicums or hot peppers and the spices made from their seeds. Plus, many children and seniors find heavily spiced foods unpalatable.

## Salsa: Green for Go Cilantro

This salsa is good with baked tortilla chips, vegetables, tacos, or beans. Use it to spice up a hot or cold soup (as they do in South America). Place it on grilled fish or poultry or roll it in soft tortillas. You can use a food processor or chop the ingredients by hand. Garnish with diced avocados, cilantro sprigs, and lime wedges.

**Tools:** *Blender or food processor*

**Preparation time:** *1*

**Yield:** *About 2$^1$/$_2$ cups, or 10 servings*

*$^1$/$_2$ cup chopped scallions, green part only*

*1 cup chopped cucumber*

*1 cup chopped mild Vidalia, Maui, or other sweet onion*

*$^1$/$_2$ cup chopped fresh cilantro*

*2 stalks celery*

*$^1$/$_2$ green bell pepper*

*1 tablespoon cider vinegar*

*2 tablespoons fresh lime juice*

*$^1$/$_2$ teaspoon sugar*

*Salt (optional)*

*3 yellow tomatoes*

*(continued)*

In a blender or food processor, place the scallions, cucumber, onion, cilantro, celery, green pepper, vinegar, lime juice, sugar, and salt to taste (if desired) and coarsely chop. Add the tomatoes and coarsely chop.

**Nutrition at a glance (per serving):** *Total fat 0 g; Saturated fat 0 g; Protein 1 g; Dietary fiber 1 g; Carbohydrate 5 g; Cholesterol 0 mg; Sodium 11 mg; % of calories from fat 8; Calories 20.*

**Lynn's cilantro suggestions:** *You can use cilantro as a leafy garnish. Stuff little yellow tomatoes with cilantro, cook it in soups with a chicken or pork base, or chop it in cooked rice.*

## Salsa: Moderately Spicy Yellow

Made with the sweeter yellow tomatoes, this salsa is semi-mild and does not contain cilantro. Serve it with lowfat or fat-free yellow tortilla chips of different sizes and shapes, yellow peppers, and celery for dippers. Garnish with fresh parsley. You can use a blender or food processor or chop everything by hand.

**Tools:** *Blender or food processor*

**Preparation time:** *1*

**Yield:** *About 3$^{1}/_{2}$ cups, or 14 servings*

$^{1}/_{2}$ stalk celery

4 scallions, white part only

$^{1}/_{4}$ Spanish onion

2 large cloves garlic, peeled and minced

1 yellow bell pepper, cut in fourths

$^{1}/_{4}$ red bell pepper

3 large yellow tomatoes, or 3 cups yellow cherry tomatoes

1 4-ounce can chopped mild green chilies

$^{1}/_{4}$ cup fresh lime juice

1 tablespoon vinegar

$^{1}/_{2}$ teaspoon finely chopped jalapeño pepper

Salt (optional)

In a blender or food processor, place the celery, scallions, onion, garlic, and yellow and red peppers and coarsely chop. Add the tomatoes, chilies, lime juice, vinegar, jalapeño, and salt to taste (if desired) and coarsely chop.

*(continued)*

**Nutrition at a glance (per serving):** *Total fat 0 g; Saturated fat 0 g; Protein 1 g; Dietary fiber 1 g; Carbohydrate 4 g; Cholesterol 0 mg; Sodium 101 mg; % of calories from fat 8; Calories 19.*

**Lynn's pepper seed pointers:** *You don't have to discard bell pepper seeds. Reserve them every time you use peppers and sprinkle them on top or add them to the food while cooking. They are sweet and contain fiber and nutrients, so why waste them?*

## Salsa: Some Like It Red Hot

Hot and spicy salsa with a smoky base is especially satisfying. Surround the salsa with a few hot peppers to give guests a tip as to the heat. Make the dish ahead of time to incorporate the flavors. You can use a food processor or chop everything by hand.

**Tools:** *Blender or food processor*

**Preparation time:** *2*

**Yield:** *About 3 cups, or 12 ¹/₄-cup servings*

| | |
|---|---|
| *1 chipotle pepper, soaked for 30 minutes* | *3 to 4 very ripe tomatoes* |
| *1 small jalapeño pepper, seeds, vein, and stem removed (see Figure 8-3 for seeding instructions)* | *1 tablespoon cider vinegar* |
| | *3 tablespoons fresh lime juice* |
| *1 red onion, peeled* | *¹/₂ teaspoon sugar* |
| *¹/₄ cup chopped fresh cilantro (optional)* | *Salt (optional)* |

In a blender or food processor, place the chipotle and jalapeño and finely chop or nearly puree. Add the onion and cilantro (if desired) and very coarsely chop. Add the tomatoes, vinegar, lime juice, sugar, and salt to taste (if desired) and pulse just a few times.

**Nutrition at a glance (per serving):** *Total fat 0 g; Saturated fat 0 g; Protein 0 g; Dietary fiber 1 g; Carbohydrate 3 g; Cholesterol 0 mg; Sodium 4 mg; % of calories from fat 7; Calories 15.*

**Lynn's sweet and sour tips:** *Using both vinegar or lime or lemon juice and sugar creates a sweet and sour taste. You can vary the amounts of each ingredient and get the exact flavor you like. Salt heightens both flavors.*

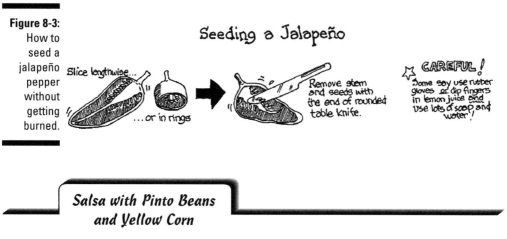

**Figure 8-3:**
How to seed a jalapeño pepper without getting burned.

## Salsa with Pinto Beans and Yellow Corn

Salsa with beans and corn is thick and hardy. Use it as a dip for celery or soft tortillas. Use cherry tomatoes for a slightly sweeter flavor. You can use a food processor or chop ingredients by hand. Garnish with steamed, chilled shrimp.

**Tools:** *Blender or food processor*

**Preparation time:** *2*

**Yield:** *About 4 cups, or 16 $^1/_4$-cup servings*

$^1/_4$ cup chopped fresh cilantro, including stems

2 tablespoons chopped fresh parsley

1 large Spanish onion, peeled and cut into fourths

2 cloves garlic, peeled and minced

$^1/_2$ green bell pepper

1 jalapeño pepper

3 tablespoons fresh lemon juice

1 tablespoon vinegar

Several drops hot pepper sauce

Salt (optional)

20 cherry tomatoes (or more if small), cut into fourths

$1^1/_2$ cups cooked and drained pinto beans, or 1 16-ounce can pinto beans, drained

$1^1/_2$ cups cooked fresh or frozen corn kernels

In a food processor, place the cilantro, parsley, onion, garlic, green pepper, jalapeño pepper, lemon juice, vinegar, hot sauce, and salt to taste (if desired) and coarsely chop. Add the tomatoes, beans, and corn and mix well.

**Nutrition at a glance (per serving):** *Total fat 0.5 g; Saturated fat 0 g; Protein 2 g; Dietary fiber 2 g; Carbohydrate 10 g; Cholesterol 0 mg; Sodium 44 mg; % of calories from fat 6; Calories 50.*

**Lynn's flavor facts:** *Use the cilantro stems, too, because they have more flavor. Let all salsas sit for several hours so that the flavors can become more intense. If you don't like cilantro, substitute watercress or parsley.*

## Stuffed Grape Leaves

*Dolmas* or *dolmathes,* which can be Arabic, Greek, Lebanese, or Turkish, to name a few, are small and flavorful rice pillows wrapped in grape leaves. They don't have a strong flavor but are slightly lemony, distinctive, and refreshing. Grape leaves are easy to find bottled in most large markets. You can make dolmas days ahead of time. They are served chilled. The following recipe calls for an optional small amount of lamb. Grind it in your food processor.

**Tools:** *Large nonstick saucepan, large baking dish, ovenproof plate or heavy lid and foil*

**Preparation time:** *3*

**Yield:** *8 servings*

*4 cloves garlic, peeled and minced*

*2 teaspoons olive oil*

*2 ounces lean lamb, all visible fat removed, ground (optional)*

*$1/2$ cup finely chopped onion*

*$1/4$ cup finely chopped fennel*

*$1/4$ cup chopped fresh parsley*

*$3/4$ cup dry white or brown rice*

*Salt (optional)*

*1 tablespoon plus $1/3$ cup fresh lemon juice*

*$1^1/2$ cups water*

*2 tablespoons raisins or currants*

*$1/4$ teaspoon ground nutmeg*

*20 to 30 grape leaves (if fresh, parboiled and dried, center stem removed if large and fibrous)*

*2 cloves garlic, peeled and slivered*

*1* Preheat the oven to 350°.

*2* In a small dish or bottle, combine the garlic and olive oil and set aside. In a large nonstick saucepan, heat the lamb (if desired), onion, fennel, and parsley for about 5 minutes, tossing, until the lamb is no longer pink. Drain any oil.

*3* To the onion mixture, add the rice, salt (if desired), and 1 tablespoon lemon juice and heat until the rice is hot, about 2 minutes. Add the water, stir, cover, and cook for 20 minutes.

*4* Remove from the heat. Mix in the raisins (or currants) and nutmeg.

*5* Place the leaves opened and flat on a board and drop about 1 tablespoon of the rice mixture onto each leaf. Wrap the leaves around the mixture, rolling and folding in the ends. Don't wrap tightly. (See Figure 8-4 for wrapping instructions.)

*6* In a large baking dish lightly coated with no-stick vegetable oil spray, place the leaves wrapped side down and close to one another so that the wrapping stays neat.

*(continued)*

**7** Pour the olive oil and garlic over the leaves, weight down with an ovenproof plate or foil and a heavy lid, and bake for 15 to 20 minutes.

**8** Transfer to a serving dish, pour the remaining ¹/₃ cup lemon juice and the slivered garlic cloves over the mixture, and chill, covered, for several hours.

*Nutrition at a glance (per serving):* Total fat 1.5 g; Saturated fat 0 g; Protein 3 g; Dietary fiber 1 g; Carbohydrate 23 g; Cholesterol 0 mg; Sodium 9 mg; % of calories from fat 12; Calories 115.

*Lynn's lowfat meat tips:* Although most store meat cutters let you purchase any amount of meat you want, purchase a pound even if you need only a few ounces. Remove all the fat, dice or slice, and divide the extra meat into 2- or 4-ounce portions (or whatever you serve four people). Place in zippered bags, mark well, and freeze so that it's all ready for use later. Small amounts of sliced and diced meats defrost quickly or, for a stir-fry, cook right from the freezer.

**Figure 8-4:**
Making stuffed grape leaves involves wrapping a leaf around some filling mixture.

Wrapping Stuffed Grape Leaves

Place the leaves on a board.

and drop about 2 teaspoons of the rice on each leaf.

Wrap the leaves around the mixture,

rolling and folding the ends.

DON'T WRAP TOO TIGHTLY!

I'm stuffed!

# Chapter 9
# Salads and Salad Dressings

## In This Chapter

▶ Salad history: All cultures love salads

▶ Salads that are usually low or high in total fat, saturated fat, and cholesterol

▶ Lowfat salad substitutions

▶ Vinegars and other flavorings

▶ Twelve quick lowfat salads

*"B y choosing romaine, red leaf lettuce, or spinach instead of iceberg lettuce in salads or on sandwiches, you get six times the amount of vitamin C and eight times the amount of vitamin A."*

— The George Washington University Health Plan

Salads are great additions to a lowfat menu plan. This chapter gives a historical, psychological, and physiological perspective as to why every culture loves salads — raw vegetables with a dressing — and has for thousands of years. It emphasizes how healthful and satisfying salads can be and encourages our natural yen for them. I also include ten quick salad "assemblies" (open a can or two, add a few fresh items, and you've assembled a great lowfat salad).

I offer 12 delicious salad recipes in this chapter. Salad dressing can be a major high-fat culprit and good-tasting lowfat dressings are elusive. So I also include 7 delicious lowfat dressing recipes. I provide a handy list of lower-fat salad substitutions and a list of salads that naturally contain less fat, as well as those salads that usually contain more fat. Because vinegar is fat-free, I tell you how to flavor your own.

# Salads: Past and Present

Salads are totally satisfying when you're very hungry or when you only want a light meal. Salads are naturally low in fat because most fruits and vegetables are the foods with the least fat and the most nutrition — if you don't mess them up with fatty dressings and other high-fat foods.

Americans eat salads voraciously but always before the main dish, much like an appetizer. Europeans eat salads as a cleansing and satisfying end to their meal, followed by cheese, fruit, and occasionally dessert. But no matter what part of the world you're from, the global love affair with salads is here to stay. You spot a good salad, and your mouth waters. Salads with romaine or spinach and brightly colored vegetables just look healthful, so follow that urge to eat more of them. You know from experience that you feel good when you eat them, and you feel good afterward.

ANECDOTE

## A little know-how goes a long way

I know that Caesar salad is high in fat and can even be dangerous if made with raw egg products, which are in every fancy restaurant recipe. I now order a Caesar only after asking the restaurant staff to omit fresh eggs (because of the potential for salmonella bacteria contamination) and to put the now-eggless dressing on the side. Regardless of the salad, I order all my salads with the dressing on the side, which has been quite successful. Sometimes I stab and dip, stabbing a chunk of lettuce or tomato and dipping it about 1/8 inch into the dressing (you use less dressing but still get the flavor in every bite). I often request cruets of oil and vinegar (they come together) and mix a teaspoon or two of the restaurant dressing with some vinegar or lemon juice to increase the quantity of liquid. I let the oil sit.

The "side" request doesn't work with slaw, which is always made with the fattiest mayonnaise, and restaurants seem to use a gallon for each quart of cabbage. To reduce the amount of dressing, I tip the dish and empty the usual 1/2 cup of extra liquid into an empty water glass and put it on the bussing tray. Messy, but it works.

When at a banquet, I use the tipped-plate trick, as shown in the following figure. If the salad contains an abundance of prepared dressing, I unobtrusively place a knife under the edge of the plate so that the oily stuff slides to one side, and I eat from the other side.

Tipped plate trick!

Long before scientists proclaimed how nutritious salads are, some humans instinctively knew that salads were good food — making our salad communion historic. In 14th-century Europe, for example, the wealthy ate salads called *sallets, salets, salds, salatas,* and *salates,* named after salt (which was the common salad dressing in about the 11th century). The ingredients in those medieval salads were similar to the ingredients we love today. A typical cold salad of the wealthy may have consisted of cooked artichoke hearts, chilled asparagus spears, bright pickled beets, onions, marinated mushrooms, hard-cooked eggs, radishes, pieces of meat such as duck or salmon, and even a sprinkle of nuts. It was all topped with the finest imported Italian cold-pressed virgin olive oil and a wine vinegar and sprinkled with fine spices and herbs.

In the Middle Ages, warring noblemen soon learned the practical and healthful value of fresh produce. A smart observer noticed that when soldiers and sailors were sent off to wars in the winter and spring, many died before even getting to battle. But if they were sent during the fall, after a summer of eating healthful fresh fruits and vegetables, the combatants lasted long enough to fight. Among the savvy, wars were waged and naval forays advanced only in late summer and fall. Humankind discovered the scientific need for salads and other nutritious fresh foods.

In the southern parts of the Western Hemisphere, people have been eating fresh avocado salads for thousands of years. The fruit of the avocado tree was mixed with onions, tomatoes, and hot peppers, and was served on a corn tortilla. The lemon juice came later.

Early Asians regularly ate their own variety of fresh raw vegetables, including bean sprouts and lettuce (which originated in China), often topped with spicy vinegars and fermented bean sauces (similar to the soy sauce we enjoy today).

Salads have only recently become a problem to healthful eating, largely because of dressings and other additions. Now salads can contain copious amounts of high-fat shredded cheese, bacon, duck with the skin, hard-cooked eggs, and the ubiquitous fat-filled dressings of mayonnaise, sour cream, and all manner of oils.

The ratio of oil to vinegar in dressings changes according to what is currently in vogue. In the late 1940s after World War II, when previously rationed goods became more plentiful, rich foods, such as cream, sour cream, egg yolks, sugar, and mayonnaise, were often used in such salad dressings as Indian, Waltham, Thousand Island, horseradish cream (containing an amazing amount of heavy cream), Suzette (made from both cream cheese and whipped cream), and the standard French, which was then 3 parts of oil to 1 part of vinegar. In California, warm bacon grease gained a toe-hold as a favorite dressing for spinach salad. Health was not yet an issue.

Today, that situation is changing. People are beginning to understand what makes them fat and what doesn't help their hearts and arteries. Salads can be deceptive, but thousands of healthful ingredients are available to substitute for the fatty ones. Consumers can choose from a dozen varieties of lettuce and half a dozen types of cabbage, with a half dozen more if you count Asian cabbages. Hundreds of fruits and vegetables are available. And the oil-to-vinegar ratio has been reversed to 3 parts vinegar and 1 part oil.

Modern salads can be an eclectic mixture of good lowfat foods. Everything from quinoa, the only grain with all eight amino acids, to kamut, a type of wheat, plus barley, lentils, beans, raisins, and a small amount of nuts can go in salads. You could eat a different, utterly delicious, lowfat, and healthful salad every day of your life, at every meal, with never a duplication. But people do have favorites that they like to enjoy regularly. For example, the Caesar Salad recipe in this chapter is a favorite of my friends. You can omit nearly all the fat and whole eggs and still barely notice the difference in taste.

# Recognizing Lowfat and High-Fat Salads

People aren't always sure about the exact ingredients and fat content of the salads and dressings they eat. The lists in this section tell you which salads and dressings are generally low in fat and which are usually high in fat (based on traditional recipes).

The following salads are usually low in total fat, saturated fat, and cholesterol when prepared without excessive oil, cheese, eggs, meat, poultry, or mayonnaise:

- ✔ Artichoke hearts and hearts of palm
- ✔ Artichokes with vinegar dip
- ✔ Aspic
- ✔ Bean or lentil salad
- ✔ Bean sprout salad
- ✔ Cranberry salad
- ✔ Cucumber salad
- ✔ Fruit salad
- ✔ Gelatin salads
- ✔ Greek salad (with a small amount of feta cheese and lowfat dressing)

- Raisin and carrot salad
- Rice or wild rice salad
- Roasted red pepper salad
- Salad Niçoise (without egg yolks)
- Shrimp, crab, and lobster salads
- Stuffed tomatoes (depending on the stuffing)
- Tomato, basil, and mozzarella salad (made with small amounts of fat-free or lowfat mozzarella)
- Tuna salad
- Waldorf salad

If made with little or no oil, the following salad dressings are usually low in total fat, saturated fat, and cholesterol:

- Buttermilk dressing (some varieties)
- Celery seed dressing
- Chutney
- Cooked salad dressings
- Diet and fat-free dressings
- French dressing (some varieties)
- Greek dressing
- Honey dressing
- Italian dressing (some varieties)
- Lemon and lime dressing
- Lorenzo dressing
- Poppy seed dressing
- Rouille dressing
- Russian dressing (some varieties)
- Soy sauce dressing
- Tofu dressing
- Vinaigrette dressing (some varieties)
- Watercress dressing

Because they contain fatty meats or cheese or are coated with a dressing made with mayonnaise, eggs, or bacon grease, the following salads are usually high in total fat, saturated fat, and cholesterol:

- Antipasto
- Caesar salad
- Chicken salad
- Cobb salad
- Coconut and fruit salads
- Cottage cheese
- Crab Louis
- Egg salad
- German potato salad
- Ham salad
- Pasta salad
- Salads with cheese
- Shrimp, lobster, or crab salad with mayonnaise or whipped cream dressing
- Spinach salad
- Tuna salad
- Turkey salad

Mayonnaise, oil, eggs, cheese, and sour cream make these salad dressings usually high in total fat, saturated fat, and cholesterol:

- Andalouse dressing
- Bacon and bacon grease dressing
- Buttermilk dressing (unless it's made with skim buttermilk)
- Caesar salad dressing
- Chantilly dressing
- Cheese dressing (including blue, bleu, Roquefort, and Cheddar)
- Cream cheese dressing
- Creamy garlic dressing
- Creamy Italian dressing
- Egg dressing

✔ Green goddess dressing

✔ Mayonnaise (unless it's fat-free or lowfat)

✔ Restaurant dressings

✔ Sour cream dressing

✔ Thousand Island dressing

✔ Whipped cream dressing

# Lowfat Salad Substitutions

The lower-fat substitutions in Table 9-1 can save from 100 to 600 calories per serving, depending upon the item. Changing from cheese to beans makes a significant difference in calories and fat, but even changing the ratio of oil to vinegar in your favorite homemade dressing helps to reduce fat and calories. (So does lessening the amount of meat and poultry in a salad recipe.)

| Table 9-1 | Lowfat Salad Substitutions |
|---|---|
| *Try This* | *Instead of This* |
| Anchovy paste | Anchovies |
| Bottled lowfat or fat-free dressing | Bottled regular dressing |
| Cannellini or other beans | Cheese |
| Chopped hard-cooked egg whites | Chopped hard-cooked eggs with yolks |
| Chunks of lean skinned chicken breast | Chunks of unskinned chicken thighs |
| Diced lean Canadian bacon | Bacon pieces |
| Fat-free or lowfat mozzarella or other lowfat cheese | Mozzarella or other cheese |
| Fat-free Parmesan topping | Parmesan cheese |
| Homemade lowfat dressing | Homemade high-fat dressing |
| Lean baked ham slices | Spam or fatty ham slices |
| Lean beef, flank, or London broil slices | Prime rib slices |
| Less oil, more vinegar | More oil, less vinegar |
| Lobster, shrimp, crab, or clams | Beef or lamb |
| Seasoned toast cubes or stuffing cubes | Croutons made with fat |
| Skinless lean cooked turkey or chicken breast | Lunch meat like bologna or salami |
| Water-packed tuna | Oil-packed tuna |

# Using Flavored Vinegars

Reducing the amount of oil in salads makes good health sense. One way to do so is to add interesting, attractive, and delicious herbs and spices to different kinds of vinegar. (See Chapter 4 for more information about vinegars.) You can find many pretty and inexpensive bottles available for homemade vinegars to keep or to give away as gifts.

For each recipe, add a scant quart of cider or distilled white vinegar to a 1-quart bottle. Slip in the herbs and spices or fruits, such as raspberries or blueberries, and then cork or cap the bottle, as shown in Figure 9-1. Let the contents sit for a week before use. You can use spiced, herbed, fruited, and flavored vinegars with or without oil and on foods other than salads.

**Figure 9-1:**
Flavored
vinegars
add zip to
any salad.

- ✔ **Basil vinegar:** Add 2 tablespoons chopped dried basil, a pinch of sugar, $^1/_2$ teaspoon minced garlic, 1 bay leaf, 2 sprigs of oregano, and several leaves or sprigs of basil.

- ✔ **Blueberry tarragon vinegar:** Add $^1/_4$ cup frozen blueberries, pureed and sweetened with 1 tablespoon sugar, if necessary; $^1/_4$ teaspoon pickled peppercorns; a pinch of celery seed; at least 10 fresh blueberries; and a sprig of fresh tarragon.

- ✔ **Caper vinegar:** Add 2 teaspoons finely chopped onion, 2 tablespoons lemon juice, $^1/_2$ teaspoon Worcestershire sauce, 2 tablespoons drained capers, 2 tablespoons caper juice, and $^1/_4$ teaspoon celery seed. You can use capers with long stems or add some long, uncut chives.

- ✔ **Celery vinegar:** Add 2 tablespoons chopped celery, 1 teaspoon celery seed, $^1/_4$ teaspoon dry mustard, $^1/_4$ teaspoon sugar, a small stalk of celery with the leaves, and 1 bay leaf.

- ✔ **French vinegar:** Add 1 clove minced garlic, $^1/_2$ cup finely chopped tomatoes, 1 teaspoon sugar, 2 teaspoons chopped fresh parsley, a sprig of rosemary, and a sprig of thyme.

- ✔ **Garlic vinegar:** Add 3 cloves garlic, minced; 2 cloves garlic, sliced wafer thin lengthwise; 5 small, whole garlic cloves, peeled; and 5 to 10 whole cloves.

- ✔ **Hot pepper vinegar:** Add 2 teaspoons chopped jalapeño pepper plus all the seeds from the pepper. Add 2 or more very small hot red, green, or jalapeño peppers (depending upon your taste); several long, thin hot red peppers; and several slices of sun-dried tomato.

- ✔ **Italian vinegar:** Add 2 cloves minced garlic, 1 teaspoon dried or 2 teaspoons chopped fresh sweet basil, 1 teaspoon dried oregano or $1^1/_2$ teaspoons chopped fresh oregano, $^1/_2$ teaspoon dry mustard, $^1/_2$ teaspoon sugar, salt (if desired), and 2 tablespoons fresh lemon juice. If you want leaves in the bottle, omit the dried or chopped oregano or basil and use a small leafy sprig of either.

- ✔ **Onion vinegar:** Add $^1/_4$ cup finely chopped onion, 2 teaspoons chopped chives, 1 chopped scallion, whole scallions, and several long chives.

- ✔ **Raspberry vinegar:** Add $^1/_2$ cup mashed, frozen, sweetened, raspberries; $^1/_4$ teaspoon pickled peppercorns; a pinch of celery seeds; and 10 to 15 whole fresh raspberries to sit in the bottom of the bottle.

- ✔ **Tarragon vinegar:** Add 2 tablespoons dried tarragon, 1 clove minced garlic, a pinch of sugar, $^1/_2$ teaspoon fresh lemon juice and a large sprig of fresh tarragon.

Be careful about adding dried black pepper or red pepper flakes to vinegar, unless you want a hot, hot, hot pepper vinegar. Pepper tends to become stronger with time and can overpower the vinegar.

# Other Salad Flavorings

Those who don't like or can't tolerate vinegar can use lemon, lime, carrot, celery, or tomato juice or buttermilk, along with herbs and spices and perhaps a small amount of olive or canola oil. Lemon juice is already the basis for many popular salads, such as Caesar salad, and predominates in fruit salad dressings.

Salad herbs and spices, including dry and prepared mustard, mustard seed, poppy seed, celery seed, garlic or onion powder, dried or fresh sweet basil, dried oregano, thyme, tarragon, sage, cilantro, curry, and cumin, give dressings a different flavor. For an Asian-style salad, try slivered fresh ginger or ground dry ginger added to low-sodium soy sauce and lemon juice or plain vinegar along with a pinch of sugar — good for sliced cucumbers, sprouts, greens, and wilted spinach. Other salad additions can include bottled peppers, sun-dried tomatoes, pickles, horseradish, and red pepper flakes. When experimenting with herbs and spices on salads or in dressings, try several in a small amount of dressing, but only one at a time to see whether you like them. Some mixtures just don't work.

To make a good bottle of commercial diet dressing better, add some of your own ingredients, such as balsamic vinegar, mustard, curry, fresh minced garlic, onions, chives, oregano, basil, or other herbs and spices.

To use less oil but still have delicious olive or canola oil on every bite of lettuce, purchase a spray bottle and put your own oil mixture in the bottle to spray the leaves. You can also use a commercial olive oil spray.

# Ten Quickie Lowfat Salads

The following are ten quickie lowfat salads that I call "fast assemblies." Suppose you want a salad for one or two, you have a few cans or jars of this and that, and you have 5 minutes to throw it all together; this list does ya just fine. Not only do these salads taste good, but they look good, too. Most don't require a recipe. You just need to know what to add to some leftover potatoes, pasta, or a can of beans. Directions vary; some are for a single plate of salad, and others are for four servings.

- **Avocado salad:** Line a plate with lettuce leaves; a few avocado slices; capers; many radishes; cherry tomatoes; 4 or 5 canned, sliced, and drained beets; several baby corn or bamboo shoots; and carrot slices. Sprinkle on balsamic or cider vinegar. Add salt (if desired) and coarsely ground black pepper.

- **Bean salad:** To a drained can of any type of bean (such as kidney, pinto, field pea, navy, or cannellini), add 2 to 3 tablespoons diced onion; 5 baby carrots, sliced; 1 red or green pepper, sliced; $1/2$ stalk celery, chopped; 1 teaspoon olive oil; about 3 tablespoons vinegar; a pinch of sugar; and a sprinkle of garlic salt or garlic pepper (or 1 minced clove). Toss and serve.

✔ **Celery salad:** To half a head of romaine, add 1 cup diced or sliced celery or fennel (including some leaves or ferns); 6 drained baby corn cobs; 2 chopped scallions or half a small onion, chopped; and half a red and half a green pepper, sliced. Make a dressing of the juice of $^1/_2$ lemon, 1 clove minced garlic, 2 tablespoons cider vinegar, 1 teaspoon olive oil, a sprinkle of Parmesan, salt (if desired), and coarsely ground black pepper.

✔ **Marinated mushrooms and artichoke salad:** To a small jar of drained marinated mushrooms and another of drained marinated artichokes, add 1 diced tomato or several red or yellow cherry tomatoes or 1 can drained tomato wedges; 1 stalk celery or half an onion, chopped; $^1/_4$ cup frozen peas (they defrost in 2 minutes); 1 teaspoon drained capers; and 1 to 2 tablespoons diced reduced-fat feta or Swiss cheese. Place the mixture on a bed of curly lettuce sprinkled with cider or balsamic vinegar and coarsely ground black pepper.

✔ **Pasta or potato salad:** To 1 cup of cooked pasta or diced cooked potatoes, add any combination of drained canned or fresh green beans (about 10 if fresh), sliced; 2 chopped scallions or 6 chives; 1 stalk celery, chopped; $^1/_4$ cup diced canned or bottled roasted red peppers or pimentos; 4 or 5 sliced olives (green or ripe); 3 or 4 cherry tomatoes; and $^1/_4$ cup chopped fresh parsley. Top with a dressing of several tablespoons of cider vinegar mixed with a clove of minced garlic, fat-free or lowfat sour cream or mayonnaise, and coarsely ground black pepper.

✔ **Shrimp salad:** To $^1/_4$ cup each of chilled, lightly steamed (or canned and drained) shrimp, add $^1/_4$ cup finely diced or chopped celery, shallots, onions, or chives; a pinch of chopped fresh or dried tarragon; and 2 tablespoons finely diced red pepper. Mix with $^1/_4$ cup dressing of half fat-free or lowfat mayonnaise and half fat-free or lowfat sour cream, plus some hot sauce, 1 teaspoon horseradish, and a few teaspoons lemon juice. Top with paprika and white pepper.

✔ **Slaw:** To 3 cups of store-bought prechopped cabbage/carrot slaw mix, add $^1/_2$ cup each chopped onion, celery, golden raisins, and sliced radishes. Make a dressing of $^1/_2$ cup fat-free or lowfat mayonnaise, 1 teaspoon sugar, 2 tablespoons each vinegar and skim milk, and $^1/_2$ teaspoon celery seed or poppy seed.

✔ **Tomato mozzarella salad:** To 1 sliced, very ripe tomato, add 2 tablespoons chopped fresh sweet basil, 1 tablespoon chopped lowfat mozzarella, and 2 tablespoons cider vinegar. Add a healthy sprinkle of dried oregano and coarsely ground black pepper.

✔ **Tropical fruit cocktail salad:** To an 8-ounce can of drained fruit cocktail, add 1 cup diced fresh fruit of any kind, such as pears, apples, bing cherry halves, melon, mango, or sliced bananas. Sprinkle with lemon juice mixed with some honey, 1 teaspoon chopped fresh mint, and 1 tablespoon shredded coconut and lightly toss.

> ✔ **Tuna salad:** To a 6-ounce can of drained, water-packed tuna, add $^1/_2$ cup chopped celery, $^1/_2$ cup chopped onion, and a dressing of a few tablespoons fat-free mayonnaise, $^1/_2$ teaspoon dry mustard, 2 tablespoons fresh lemon juice, 2 tablespoons pickle relish, and some pepper.

# Favorite Lowfat Salad Recipes

The following salad recipes are lowfat versions of traditional favorites. The ingredients are readily available; you can probably find most of the items in your pantry or refrigerator right now.

## Asparagus and Shrimp Salad

Asparagus and Shrimp Salad is formal and arranged, unlike the tossed salad. Meant to impress, Asparagus and Shrimp Salad is very satisfying and quite luxurious with a large fat shrimp sitting on the cold asparagus waiting to be plucked. Garnish just the shrimp with a squirt of lemon, a dollop of cocktail or hot sauce, and a tiny sprig of parsley. Garnish the rest of the salad with a teaspoon of slivered Parmesan cheese.

*Preparation time: 2*

*Yield: 4 servings*

**Salad:**

*Mache, arugula, or spinach leaves to lightly line plates*

*1 pound asparagus (about 24), lightly steamed and chilled*

*8 strips bottled pimento or red pepper, drained, or fresh red bell pepper, each 3 inches long*

*4 extra-large shrimp, lightly steamed*

*1 cup finely diced celery*

**Salad Dressing:**

*$^1/_2$ cup white wine or white vinegar*

*2 tablespoons finely chopped tarragon*

*1 clove garlic, peeled and minced*

*1 tablespoon olive oil*

*$^1/_2$ teaspoon dry mustard*

*2 teaspoons fresh lemon juice*

*Freshly ground black pepper*

*Parmesan cheese*

*1* On each of four medium salad plates, arrange a bed of greens. Place a neat bundle of five to eight asparagus spears across the center of each plate. Criss-cross two strips of pimento or red pepper across the top of the asparagus or place the strips 1 to 2 inches apart. Place a shrimp in the center of the pepper strips. (See Figure 9-2 for an illustration of the finished salad.)

*(continued)*

**Figure 9-2:**
Arranged salads are both attractive and tasty.

**2** In a small bowl, mix together the vinegar, tarragon, garlic, olive oil, dry mustard, and lemon juice.

**3** Sprinkle on the celery, drizzle on the dressing, sprinkle liberally with black pepper, and garnish with Parmesan cheese.

***Nutrition at a glance (per serving):*** *Total fat 2.5 g; Saturated fat 0.5 g; Protein 8 g; Dietary fiber 2 g; Carbohydrate 4 g; Cholesterol 55 mg; Sodium 100 mg; % of calories from fat 30; Calories 66.*

***Lynn's perfect shrimp steaming tip:*** *For perfectly steamed shrimp, peel shrimp to the tail. (To keep the tail meat, peel to the tail, crack the unshelled tail to one side, and pull the shell off the tiny tail meat.) Place about an inch of water in a pot. Bring to a boil and add the shrimp. Steam, covered, for 1 to 3 minutes or just until pink. If serving chilled, remove with a slotted spoon and immerse immediately in a large pot of cold water with several dozen ice cubes. Drain the shrimp and then chill. If you want to spice the shrimp, don't peel them before steaming. Add a tablespoon of Old Bay Seasoning, cayenne pepper (to taste), and 1 cup of beer or white wine to the water used for steaming.*

## Black and White Bean Salad with Tomatoes and Olives

A colorful salad of beans, bright tomatoes, black olives, and several other vegetables, this salad is one of my personal favorites. I vary the ingredients slightly depending upon what I have on hand and feel like eating that day. Although I seldom use garlic salt or pepper, in certain food combinations those flavors do work. You can add a clove or two of minced fresh garlic to the dressing.

***Preparation time:*** *1*

***Yield:*** *6 servings*

*(continued)*

*¹/₂ cup cider or spiced vinegar*

*1 tablespoon olive oil*

*¹/₄ teaspoon sugar*

*1 teaspoon garlic pepper*

*¹/₂ teaspoon garlic salt*

*1 16-ounce can black beans, drained*

*1 16-ounce can cannellini beans, drained*

*2 large tomatoes or 15 to 20 small cherry tomatoes*

*1 medium onion*

*1 medium green or red bell pepper*

*2 stalks celery, including tops*

*2 large carrots, or 10 baby carrots*

*¹/₂ cup coarsely chopped fresh parsley*

*12 pitted ripe olives (optional)*

*¹/₂ teaspoon crushed red pepper (flakes)*

*Coarsely ground black pepper*

*1* In a large bowl, combine the vinegar, olive oil, sugar, garlic pepper, garlic salt, and both cans of drained beans and toss. Let the mixture sit while you prepare the other vegetables.

*2* Dice the tomatoes and add them to the mixture in the large bowl, tossing lightly. Coarsely chop the onion, dice the pepper, slice the celery and carrots, and add to the salad along with the parsley and olives (if desired), and then toss. Sprinkle with red pepper flakes and black pepper to taste.

*Nutrition at a glance (per serving):* Total fat 3 g; Saturated fat 0.5 g; Protein 8 g; Dietary fiber 9 g; Carbohydrate 29 g; Cholesterol 0 mg; Sodium 409 mg; % of calories from fat 16; Calories 169.

*Lynn's lower-fat salad tip:* Because some vegetables, such as canned beans, are already starchy and have a thick liquid, making bean salads with the right texture without using any oil is easy. Drain the beans, reserving a tablespoon or two of the liquid. Add vinegar, herbs, and spices to the bean liquid and pour over the beans. You get all the flavor and texture you want with no added fat. (The liquid does contain sodium, however.)

## Caesar Salad

Dark, cold, crispy lettuce with garlic and lemon and a sprinkle of Parmesan cheese is always refreshing. This combination is far lower in fat than any restaurant Caesar salad. The egg substitutes you use are 99 percent egg and are pasteurized. (Never eat raw egg products in any food because of the dangers of salmonella contamination.) Add skinned chicken or turkey chunks, all visible fat removed, or shrimp for a heartier or whole-meal version.

*(continued)*

*Preparation time: 1*

*Yield: 4 servings*

*1 large head romaine lettuce*

*Olive oil spray or 1 teaspoon olive oil*

*2 large garlic cloves, peeled and minced*

*1 teaspoon Worcestershire sauce*

*$^1/_2$ teaspoon anchovy paste, or 4 anchovies, patted dry (optional)*

*$^1/_4$ cup fresh lemon juice*

*$^1/_4$ cup substitute egg*

*2 tablespoons each freshly grated Parmesan cheese and fat-free Parmesan cheese topping*

*Coarsely ground black pepper*

*1 cup garlic croutons (optional)*

**1** Wash and shake dry or spin the romaine in a large cloth to remove all the water. Spray the leaves with olive oil spray or toss them in the olive oil. Leave them whole, cut them, or break them into pieces, depending on the look of the salad you want, and place them in a large salad bowl.

**2** In a small bowl, mix the garlic, Worcestershire sauce, anchovy paste (if desired), lemon juice, and substitute egg with a whisk. Pour on the salad and toss. Sprinkle with Parmesan cheese, pepper, and croutons (if desired).

*Nutrition at a glance (per serving): Total fat 2.5 g; Saturated fat 1 g; Protein 7 g; Dietary fiber 2 g; Carbohydrate 8 g; Cholesterol 2 mg; Sodium 160 mg; % of calories from fat 26; Calories 77.*

*Lynn's Caesar salad tip: To make a special effect for the cheese, slice four 2-inch x 2-inch wafer-thin pieces of Parmesan and heat on a tray for 2 to 3 minutes, until crisp but not melted. Add one to the top of each salad.*

## Croutons (optional)

Here's an easy way to make terrific croutons. You can make them pungent with garlic or with just a light whiff. Or use herbed stuffing croutons, which are tasty and usually low in fat.

*Preparation time: 2*

*Yield: About 4 servings*

*4 small French bread slices, toasted*

*2 large cloves garlic, peeled and cut in half*

*Salt (optional)*

*Olive oil spray*

*2 tablespoons dried parsley*

*(continued)*

*1* Preheat the oven to 350°.

*2* Place the toast on a cutting board. For a light coating, rub the cut side of the garlic halves onto both sides of the toast. For a heavier coating, mince the garlic and rub the garlic into the toast on both sides. Lightly salt (if desired).

*3* Rub the parsley into the palms of your hands to break it up and release the flavor. Dice the toast. Lightly spray the toast with olive oil and toss with the parsley.

*4* Place the coated toast on a baking sheet and bake for 3 to 10 minutes or until golden and crunchy.

*Nutrition at a glance (per serving): Total fat 0.5 g; Saturated fat 0 g; Protein 1 g; Dietary fiber 1 g; Carbohydrate 8 g; Cholesterol 0 mg; Sodium 90 mg; % of calories from fat 10; Calories 43.*

## Chicken Salad

This chicken salad is chunky and makes a hearty but casual chicken sandwich stuffed in pita with lettuce. This recipe is also fancy enough for a brunch or a wedding, where I serve it mounded on a bed of watercress with small bunches of grapes, kumquats, and walnut halves. Good chicken salad means cooking your own chicken, which takes about 5 minutes. To find out how, see "Lynn's lowfat chicken tip" at the end of this recipe.

**Preparation time:** *1 (or more if you have to cook the chicken)*

**Yield:** *4 servings*

*¹/₂ cup fat-free or lowfat sour cream or mayonnaise*

*2 tablespoons orange juice*

*¹/₂ teaspoon orange zest*

*1 tablespoon skim milk*

*¹/₄ teaspoon Worcestershire sauce*

*2 cups cooked, diced, skinned chicken breast (8 or 9 ounces), all visible fat removed*

*1 cup finely chopped celery*

*¹/₄ cup finely chopped onions, shallots, or scallions*

*3 tablespoons chopped fresh parsley*

*¹/₂ cup ¹/₂-inch fresh pineapple chunks*

*¹/₄ cup chopped walnuts (optional)*

*Enough watercress or lettuce to make 4 beds*

*(continued)*

_1_ In a large bowl, combine the sour cream or mayonnaise, orange juice, orange zest, skim milk, and Worcestershire sauce and mix well with a whisk.

_2_ Add the chicken, celery, onions (or shallots or scallions), parsley, pineapple, and walnuts (if desired) and toss to coat.

_3_ Place the watercress or lettuce on each plate, add a mound of chicken salad, and garnish.

_**Nutrition at a glance (per serving):**_ _Total fat 2 g; Saturated fat 0.5 g; Protein 20 g; Dietary fiber 1 g; Carbohydrate 11 g; Cholesterol 48 mg; Sodium 105 mg; % of calories from fat 14; Calories 151._

_**Lynn's lowfat chicken tip:**_ _To cook your own chicken for this salad, coat 1 whole, unfrozen, chicken breast (2 halves) with seasoning salt [or a light spray of olive oil, white wine, a small sprinkle of chopped thyme, salt (optional), pepper, and rosemary], place in an oven bag, and microwave for 5 minutes, turning once or twice, or bake, covered, in a 350° oven for 15 minutes or until no longer pink._

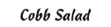

### Cobb Salad

Cobb salad is always different, depending upon your part of the country. You can add anything you like; just cut the ingredients into small pieces.

_**Preparation time:**_ _1_

_**Yield:**_ _4 servings_

| _Salad:_ | _Dressing:_ |
|---|---|
| _1 medium head iceberg lettuce_ | _$^1/_2$ tablespoon olive oil_ |
| _1 cup diced avocado (optional)_ | _$1^1/_2$ tablespoons cider vinegar_ |
| _$^1/_2$ cup grapes_ | _$1^1/_2$ tablespoons balsamic vinegar_ |
| _2 carrots, chopped_ | _1 tablespoon water_ |
| _12 small cherry tomatoes, cut in half_ | _Salt (optional) and coarsely ground black pepper_ |
| _4 ounces fat-free or lean ham, diced_ | |

_1_ Cut the iceberg lettuce into $^1/_4$-inch pieces, making crosswise rows. Either toss the avocados (if desired), grapes, carrots, tomatoes, and ham in a salad bowl or arrange them in separate wedges on individual plates.

_(continued)_

**2** In a small bowl, combine the olive oil, vinegars, water, and salt (if desired) and pepper. Mix together and either toss the salad with the dressing or drizzle the dressing on the plates.

*Nutrition at a glance (per serving): Total fat 2.5 g; Saturated fat 0.5 g; Protein 7 g; Dietary fiber 3 g; Carbohydrate 15 g; Cholesterol 9 mg; Sodium 363 mg; % of calories from fat 20; Calories 100.*

## Five-Bean Salad

Different varieties of beans go well together. You can use several types of canned beans, or stick with only one kind. The recipe can be doubled easily, and you can add or substitute cooked barley, lentils, corn, or wild rice. Although you can lightly steam the yellow and green beans, steaming isn't necessary. Garnish with a pepperoncini or hot (spicy) okra pickle.

*Preparation time: 2*

*Yield: 6 servings*

**Salad:**

*¹/₂ cup canned or cooked lentils, drained*

*¹/₂ cup canned dark kidney beans, drained*

*¹/₂ cup canned navy beans, drained*

*1 cup wax beans (5 to 6 ounces), cut into 1-inch lengths*

*1 cup green beans (5 to 6 ounces), cut into 1-inch lengths*

*1 small stalk celery, chopped*

*1 small onion, peeled and coarsely chopped*

*1 red bell pepper, finely chopped*

*¹/₂ cup pitted green salad olives with pimentos*

**Salad Dressing:**

*¹/₂ cup cider vinegar*

*¹/₂ teaspoon sugar*

*¹/₂ to 1 teaspoon chopped basil*

*¹/₂ teaspoon crushed red pepper (flakes)*

*2 cloves garlic, peeled and minced*

*Coarsely ground black pepper*

In a large bowl, combine the lentils, canned beans, fresh beans, celery, onion, pepper, olives, vinegar, sugar, basil, red pepper flakes, and garlic, and toss to mix well. When serving, sprinkle on the black pepper.

*Nutrition at a glance (per serving): Total fat 1.5 g; Saturated fat 0 g; Protein 5 g; Dietary fiber 5 g; Carbohydrate 17 g; Cholesterol 0 mg; Sodium 370 mg; % of calories from fat 15; Calories 98.*

*(continued)*

***Lynn's garlic tip:*** *To quickly break up garlic bulbs and remove the peel, lightly rap the bulb with the bottom of a small, strong skillet. The cloves pull apart easily. Then give each clove a good rap, and the peel should fall off.*

## Greek Salad

Feta has a strong flavor, but it is not low in fat. Ask for the lowest-fat brand. Use Greek feta cheese sparingly, because a little goes a long way. Garnish this salad with one or more sardines or a teaspoon of canned tuna.

***Preparation time:*** *1*

***Yield:*** *4 servings*

$^1/_3$ *cup red wine vinegar*

*2 teaspoons fresh lemon juice*

*1 tablespoon dried oregano*

*1 teaspoon fresh chopped basil, or $^1/_2$ teaspoon dried*

*2 tablespoons finely chopped fresh parsley*

*1 teaspoon sugar*

*1 medium head lettuce, or a mixture of lettuce and spinach (about 8 cups chopped)*

*Olive oil spray or 1 tablespoon olive oil*

*12 Greek or Kalamata olives, pitted (optional)*

*1 medium ripe tomato, cut into 12 pieces*

*1 medium red onion, slivered*

$^1/_2$ *cup whole pepperoncinis*

*2 ounces reduced-fat feta cheese, crumbled*

*Freshly ground black pepper*

**1** In a salad bowl, combine the vinegar, lemon juice, oregano, basil, parsley, and sugar. Mix well.

**2** Chop or break the lettuce (and spinach, if desired). While the leaves are on a tray or cutting board, lightly spray the lettuce with olive oil spray or toss in the olive oil. Add to the salad and toss. Add the olives (if desired), tomatoes, onions, and pepperoncinis.

**3** Plate the salad and crumble the feta cheese on top. Sprinkle with freshly ground black pepper.

***Nutrition at a glance (per serving):*** *Total fat 2.5 g; Saturated fat 1.5 g; Protein 5 g; Dietary fiber 3 g; Carbohydrate 10 g; Cholesterol 5 mg; Sodium 388 mg; % of calories from fat 28; Calories 78.*

## Italian Fennel, Beet, Mushroom, and Carrot Salad

Italian Fennel, Beet, Mushroom, and Carrot Salad is a refreshing composed salad. (*Composed* means that the salad isn't tossed; the ingredients are arranged in small mounds, in this case a mound of julienned fennel, one of carrots, and another of beets.) This salad can be a complete meal. Use smaller amounts for a dinner salad or side salad. Garnish with some of the fern tops of the fennel, slivers of onion, a teaspoon of grated Parmesan cheese, or chopped scallions.

**Preparation time:** *1*

**Yield:** *4 servings*

**Salad:**

*Arugula or spinach to line plates*

*2 cups thinly sliced raw fennel or celery*

*1¹/₂ cups julienned fresh carrots, very lightly steamed, if desired, and then chilled*

*4 medium beets, cooked and thinly sliced*

*1 6-ounce jar marinated mushrooms, drained*

**Salad Dressing:**

*1 tablespoon olive oil*

*¹/₂ cup balsamic, red wine, or cider vinegar*

*Salt (optional) and coarsely ground black pepper*

**1** On each salad plate, make a bed of greens. Place a mound of fennel or celery, a mound of carrots, and a mound of beets. In the center, divide and place the mushrooms.

**2** In a small bowl, whisk together the olive oil and vinegar. Drizzle on the salad. Lightly salt (if desired) and grind pepper over the top.

**Nutrition at a glance (per serving):** *Total fat 2 g; Saturated fat 0.5 g; Protein 3 g; Dietary fiber 5 g; Carbohydrate 18 g; Cholesterol 0 mg; Sodium 262 mg; % of calories from fat 19; Calories 94.*

**Lynn's fennel tips:** *Increase your vegetable repertoire and enjoyment with fennel, shown in Figure 9-3. It looks like a fat celery bulb, has a slightly sweet and mild licorice flavor, and is absolutely delicious when lightly steamed, served raw, or baked with potatoes.*

**Figure 9-3:**
Fennel is terrific prepared a variety of ways, and it goes great in salads.

fennel

## Niçoise Salad

Niçoise salad is a large salad, composed rather than tossed, that originally came from the south of France. This dish is suitable for a formal occasion or a very informal one, because the ingredients have a good country feel. This salad is especially attractive. You also can use the tiny French string beans called haricots verts.

***Preparation time:*** *2*

***Yield:*** *4 servings*

***Salad:***

*1 small head Boston or Bibb lettuce*

*$^1/_2$ pound small red or white potatoes, cooked and chilled, cut into $1^1/_2$-inch pieces*

*1 pound string beans, lightly steamed and then chilled*

*2 hard-cooked eggs, cut in half, yolks discarded*

*$^1/_2$ cup bottled ratatouille or pickled red and green peppers, drained*

*1 $6^1/_2$-ounce can water-packed tuna, drained*

*2 large ripe tomatoes, cut into wedges*

*4 anchovy fillets, patted dry (optional)*

*12 black olives (optional)*

***Salad Dressing:***

*$^1/_2$ cup white wine or white vinegar*

*1 tablespoon olive oil*

*$^1/_2$ teaspoon prepared mustard*

*1 tablespoon water*

*2 tablespoons small capers, drained*

*1 small onion, slivered or thinly sliced*

*Salt (optional) and coarsely ground black pepper*

*(continued)*

**1** On 4 large plates lined with lettuce, place the potatoes near the edge of the plate. Next to the potatoes, place a neat bundle of beans, and then a hard-cooked egg half. Fill each egg half full with ratatouille or pickled red and green peppers. Place the tuna next to the egg, the tomato wedges in the center, and top with an anchovy (if desired). Place 3 black olives on each plate (if desired). (See Figure 9-4.)

**2** For the dressing, in a small bowl, combine the vinegar, olive oil, mustard, and water. Pour over the salads. Sprinkle with capers, slivered onion, and salt (if desired) and pepper to taste.

***Nutrition at a glance (per serving):*** *Total fat 2.5 g; Saturated fat 0.5 g; Protein 17 g; Dietary fiber 7 g; Carbohydrate 30 g; Cholesterol 12 mg; Sodium 387 mg; % of calories from fat 12; Calories 199.*

***Lynn's pepper pointer:*** *Tellicherry pepper is the best black pepper. It's more expensive, but a little goes a long way. Ask for it in any fancy food market and grind it in your own pepper mill for an extra-fresh pepper taste.*

**Figure 9-4:**
An assembled Niçoise salad.

Niçoise Salad

## *Pinto Bean Salad with Tomatoes, Basil, and Mozzarella Cheese*

The following recipe is a slightly different take on the traditional Italian tomato, fresh basil, and mozzarella salad. Traditional recipes call for too much mozzarella to keep fat intake low, and not enough of the other ingredients. Served on a bed of black beans, this salad is a tasty change. Add the mozzarella just before eating, because the beans discolor it. Garnish the tray or each plate with a sprig of fresh sweet basil. This salad can serve as a whole meal. Reduce the amount of ingredients for a smaller yield.

***Preparation time:*** *1*

***Yield:*** *4 servings*

*1 16-ounce can pinto, navy, or black beans, drained*

*$^1/_2$ cup chiffonaded basil (see the tip following the recipe)*

*1 tablespoon olive oil*

*$^1/_2$ teaspoon minced garlic*

*3 to 4 tablespoons fresh lemon or lime juice*

*$^1/_2$ cup red wine or cider vinegar*

*2 ripe tomatoes*

*1 small red onion*

*2 or 3 lettuce leaves*

*Salt (optional)*

*2 tablespoons oregano*

*$^1/_2$ cup diced fat-free or lowfat mozzarella cheese*

*Coarsely ground black pepper*

*1* In a large mixing bowl, place the beans, half the basil, olive oil, garlic, lemon juice, and half the vinegar. Lightly toss and let the mixture sit until the rest of the salad is prepared.

*2* Slice the tomatoes and onion thinly.

*3* On a round or rectangular platter, place the lettuce leaves in the center, the beans on the leaves, and the tomato slices around the beans. Add the sliced onions on top and sprinkle on some salt (if desired). Pour the remaining vinegar over the tomatoes, sprinkle on the remaining basil and oregano. Just before serving, add the diced mozzarella and some black pepper.

***Nutrition at a glance (per serving):*** *Total fat 3 g; Saturated fat 0.5 g; Protein 12 g; Dietary fiber 8 g; Carbohydrate 28 g; Cholesterol 2 mg; Sodium 287 mg; % of calories from fat 15; Calories 179.*

*(continued)*

*Lynn's chiffonade tip:* To chiffonade, roll several basil leaves together tightly and slice narrow ($^1/_8$-inch) strips sideways across the stems. This action makes ribbons of the leaves called chiffonades.

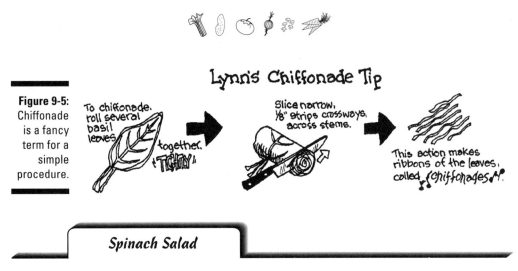

**Figure 9-5:** Chiffonade is a fancy term for a simple procedure.

## Spinach Salad

I use real bacon in spinach salad, but no bacon fat. Large croutons and chopped egg whites add interest and color. You can also add chopped or sliced radishes. If you're using olive oil and want the oil to have a bacon flavor, soak the cooked bacon pieces in the olive oil for several hours before serving.

*Preparation time: 1*

*Yield: 4 servings*

1 pound spinach, cleaned and drained, cut or torn into bite-sized pieces

Olive oil spray or 1 tablespoon olive oil

12 slices bacon, cooked, drained, patted dry, all visible fat removed, the remaining meat portion cut into 1-inch long pieces or chopped

$^1/_2$ cup slivered red onion

$^1/_2$ cup cider vinegar

$^3/_4$ teaspoon sugar

$^1/_4$ teaspoon dry mustard

Coarsely ground black pepper

**1** In a large salad bowl, place the spinach and lightly coat with olive oil spray or toss in olive oil.

**2** In a small bowl, combine the bacon, onion, vinegar, sugar, mustard, and black pepper to taste. Add to the spinach and toss to coat.

*(continued)*

*Nutrition at a glance (per serving):* *Total fat 2.5 g; Saturated fat 0.5 g; Protein 6 g; Dietary fiber 3 g; Carbohydrate 9 g; Cholesterol 7 mg; Sodium 290 mg; % of calories from fat 28; Calories 73.*

*Lynn's mustard musing:* *Mustard is one of the few spices grown and exported by the United States. Several kinds are available, from black to almost white.*

## Waldorf Salad

Try making Waldorf salads with more than one variety of fresh apples, such as Winesap, Stayman, Jonathan, or McIntosh. Garnish with a small bunch of grapes, mandarin orange slices, and watercress.

*Preparation time:* *1*

*Yield:* *4 servings*

**Salad Dressing:**

*1 tablespoon fresh lemon juice*

*1 tablespoon orange juice*

*$^1/_2$ teaspoon sugar*

*2 tablespoons skim milk*

*$^1/_4$ cup fat-free or lowfat mayonnaise*

**Salad:**

*4 large romaine or lettuce leaves*

*2 large apples, cored and coarsely chopped*

*2 stalks celery, including leaves, coarsely chopped*

*$^1/_2$ cup coarsely chopped dried or fresh figs*

*$^1/_4$ cup coarsely chopped walnuts (optional), plus 4 walnut halves*

*1* In a large bowl, combine the lemon juice, orange juice, and sugar. Mix with the skim milk and mayonnaise.

*2* Place a large lettuce leaf on each of 4 salad plates. Toss the apples, celery, figs, and chopped walnuts (if desired) with the dressing and spoon onto the lettuce. Top each plate with a walnut half.

*Nutrition at a glance (per serving):* *Total fat 2 g; Saturated fat 0.5 g; Protein 2 g; Dietary fiber 5 g; Carbohydrate 35 g; Cholesterol 0 mg; Sodium 118 mg; % of calories from fat 11; Calories 152.*

*Nutty information:* *Nuts, although not low in fat, have a little fiber and some nutrients. The fat is natural fat, and most of it isn't saturated.*

# Easy Lowfat Salad Dressing Recipes

Most low-cholesterol, gourmet salad dressings are made without oil, but you can add oil by the teaspoonful, or spray on olive oil (olive oil spray is available in most grocery stores), canola oil, or corn oil. You can make your own spray with any spray bottle. An additional benefit to using low-saturated-fat oils is that they are the most liquid when cold. The vegetable oil section (see Chapter 4) gives you the saturated fat contents of the most popular salad oils, including olive, canola, safflower, corn, and walnut.

If you want to try your hand at making your own lowfat dressings, try the following recipes. If you eat 2 tablespoons or less per serving, most of these dressings qualify as lowfat. However, 2 tablespoons of blue cheese or French dressing contains too much oil to be considered low in fat. For these dressings, limit use to 1 tablespoon.

## Blue Cheese or Roquefort Dressing

This blue cheese or Roquefort dressing will become your favorite cheese dressing. A 1-tablespoon serving qualifies as lowfat.

**Preparation time:** 1

**Yield:** About 1$^1$/$_2$ cups

| | |
|---|---|
| 1 cup white wine vinegar | $^1$/$_4$ teaspoon dried rosemary |
| 3 tablespoons fresh lemon juice | $^1$/$_2$ teaspoon paprika |
| 2 tablespoons olive oil | 1 teaspoon finely chopped fresh parsley |
| 1 clove garlic, peeled and minced | $^1$/$_4$ pound blue or Roquefort cheese, crumbled |
| $^1$/$_2$ teaspoon sugar | |
| $^1$/$_2$ teaspoon dry mustard | |

**1** Mix together the vinegar, lemon juice, and oil in a small bowl.

**2** Add the garlic, sugar, mustard, rosemary, paprika, parsley, and cheese. Use immediately if you want the parsley to retain its fresh green color.

*Nutrition at a glance (per tablespoon): Total fat 2.5 g; Saturated fat 1 g; Protein 1 g; Dietary fiber 0 g; Carbohydrate 0 g; Cholesterol 4 mg; Sodium 67 mg; % of calories from fat 79; Calories 28.*

## Creamy Italian Garlic Dressing

**Tools:** *Blender*

**Preparation time:** *1*

**Yield:** *About 2 cups*

*1 cup fat-free cottage cheese*

*1 cup skim milk*

*2 tablespoons fresh lemon juice*

*3 cloves garlic, peeled and minced*

*1 small onion, sliced in half*

*Salt (optional)*

In a blender, puree the cottage cheese and the skim milk (which takes about 4 minutes). Mix in the lemon juice, garlic, onion, and salt to taste (if desired).

**Nutrition at a glance (per tablespoon):** *Total fat 0 g; Saturated fat 0 g; Protein 1 g; Dietary fiber 0 g; Carbohydrate 1 g; Cholesterol 1 mg; Sodium 24 mg; % of calories from fat 2; Calories 8.*

**Lynn's Italian dressing tip:** *Make this dressing more colorful by adding a teaspoon each of chopped fresh oregano and sweet basil, plus a tablespoon each of finely chopped green and red bell pepper. To add some heat or a more peppery flavor, add $^1/_4$ teaspoon of crushed red pepper (flakes).*

## French Dressing

Authentic French dressing is just fine olive oil, wine vinegar, and salt, but American versions incorporate tomatoes, and this variation is great. A 1-tablespoon serving qualifies as lowfat.

**Tools:** *Blender*

**Preparation time:** *1*

**Yield:** *About 1 cup*

$^1/_2$ *cup red wine vinegar*

$^1/_4$ *cup vegetable juice or tomato juice*

*3 tablespoons olive or canola oil*

*2 tablespoons fresh lemon or lime juice*

*1 clove garlic, peeled and minced*

$^1/_4$ *teaspoon sugar*

$^1/_2$ *teaspoon paprika*

*(continued)*

Mix together in a blender the vinegar, vegetable or tomato juice, oil, lemon or lime juice, garlic, sugar, and paprika.

*__Nutrition at a glance (per tablespoon):__ Total fat 2.5 g; Saturated fat 0.5 g; Protein 0 g; Dietary fiber 0 g; Carbohydrate 1 g; Cholesterol 0 mg; Sodium 15 mg; % of calories from fat 90; Calories 25.*

### Fruit Salad Dressing

Fruit salads always benefit from a drizzle of just a bit of sweet flavor.

*__Preparation time:__ 1*

*__Yield:__ About 1¹/₂ cups*

| | |
|---|---|
| *¹/₂ cup honey* | *2 tablespoons walnut oil* |
| *¹/₄ cup fresh lemon juice* | *¹/₂ teaspoon lemon zest* |
| *¹/₄ cup water* | *¹/₄ cup frozen raspberries* |

Mix together the honey, lemon juice, water, walnut oil, zest, and raspberries in a small bowl.

*__Nutrition at a glance (per tablespoon):__ Total fat 1 g; Saturated fat 0 g; Protein 0 g; Dietary fiber 0 g; Carbohydrate 7 g; Cholesterol 0 mg; Sodium 0 mg; % of calories from fat 28; Calories 35.*

### Green Goddess Tarragon Dressing

Green goddess dressing is an old standby, with the taste of tarragon prevailing.

*__Preparation time:__ 1*

*__Yield:__ About 1¹/₂ cups*

*(continued)*

2 tablespoons fat-free or lowfat mayonnaise

1 cup fat-free or lowfat plain yogurt

2 teaspoons fresh lemon juice

1 teaspoon vinegar

1 clove garlic, peeled and minced

2 tablespoons chopped fresh parsley

$^1/_2$ teaspoon prepared mustard

1 teaspoon chopped fresh tarragon, or $^1/_2$ teaspoon dried

Mix together the mayonnaise, yogurt, lemon juice, vinegar, garlic, parsley, mustard, and tarragon in a small bowl.

**Nutrition at a glance (per tablespoon):** *Total fat 0 g; Saturated fat 0 g; Protein 1 g; Dietary fiber 0 g; Carbohydrate 1 g; Cholesterol 0 mg; Sodium 17 mg; % of calories from fat 4; Calories 7.*

## Raspberry Vinegar Dressing

Raspberry vinegar dressing originally came from Scotland Yard, an authentic Scottish restaurant in Alexandria, Virginia. The lowfat ingredients go well on a combination of greens with perhaps some slivers of cooked, cold, lean, skinless poultry.

**Preparation time:** *1*

**Yield:** *About 1$^1/_2$ cups*

1 cup cider vinegar

$^1/_4$ teaspoon dried savory

$^1/_4$ teaspoon dried thyme

$^1/_4$ teaspoon dried tarragon

1 teaspoon chopped fresh chives

1 teaspoon chopped fresh parsley

$^1/_4$ cup frozen sweetened raspberries (add $^1/_4$ teaspoon sugar if you use fresh raspberries)

2 inches of the white part of a leek, sliced wafer thin

2 tablespoons canola oil

In a small bowl, mix together the vinegar, savory, thyme, tarragon, chives, parsley, and raspberries, mashing the raspberries. Stir in the leeks and canola oil.

**Nutrition at a glance (per tablespoon):** *Total fat 1 g; Saturated fat 0 g; Protein 0 g; Dietary fiber 0 g; Carbohydrate 1 g; Cholesterol 0 mg; Sodium 0 mg; % of calories from fat 64; Calories 15.*

## Thousand Island Dressing

Thousand Island dressing is an old-time favorite. Men and boys seem to prefer this thick dressing over all others.

***Preparation time:*** *2*

***Yield:*** *About 2¹/₂ cups*

| | |
|---|---|
| *1¹/₂ cups fat-free or lowfat mayonnaise* | *2 tablespoons chopped fresh parsley* |
| *¹/₄ cup skim milk* | *2 tablespoons chopped green olives* |
| *¹/₃ cup chunky chili sauce* | *3 tablespoons chopped onion* |
| *2 tablespoons vinegar* | *¹/₂ teaspoon crushed red pepper (flakes)* |
| *¹/₄ cup sweet pickle relish* | *1 teaspoon paprika* |
| *3 hard-cooked eggs, yolks discarded, finely chopped* | |

In a small bowl, mix together the mayonnaise, skim milk, chili sauce, vinegar, and pickle relish. Add the hard-cooked egg whites, parsley, olives, onion, red pepper flakes, and paprika.

***Nutrition at a glance (per tablespoon):*** *Total fat 0 g; Saturated fat 0 g; Protein 0 g; Dietary fiber 0 g; Carbohydrate 2 g; Cholesterol 0 mg; Sodium 117 mg; % of calories from fat 6; Calories 13.*

# Chapter 10
# One-Pot Soups and Casseroles

## In This Chapter

▶ Making lowfat soups and casseroles the easy way
▶ Soup and casserole recipes that are usually low or high in fat

*B*ack in merry olde England, this 13th-century nursery rhyme was about a one-dish meal of muddled peas that never died. (Pease were dried peas.) Each day, a little more fresh food was added. Doctors in 15th-century England, in one noteworthy account, kissed and thanked the cooks because everyone in the household was always sick, making the doctors very rich.

*Pease porridge hot,*
*Pease porridge cold.*
*Pease porridge in the pot,*
*Nine days old.*

The reasons that soups and casseroles are so popular today are simple. Soups and casseroles are easy to make, and there's something primordial and deeply satisfying about your good food baking or simmering over a hot stove, ready for family or friends to dip into. The problem today is making soups and casseroles healthful because so much meat and poultry is filled with fat, and meat, cheese, and cream have somehow become the casserole's best friends. But these ingredients are really its worst enemies.

This chapter explains why soups and casseroles can be a boon to a lowfat eating plan. I explain easy ways to make soups low in fat while still using any fat-filled meat, bones, chicken fat, and skin for flavor. I give tips on making casseroles very low in fat, and show you how to adapt your own soup and casserole recipes to lowfat versions by defatting the meat base. I include a list of soup thickeners because flour mixed with fat and oil is no longer a "safe" option. You can also find handy lists of soup and casserole dishes that are usually the highest in fat, saturated fat, and cholesterol, and those that are the lowest.

## Soups and casseroles in history

As soon as humans figured out how to fashion a cooking pot, they began making soups and casseroles. Someone combined all the stuff she had gathered: meat, vegetables, leaves, mushrooms, nuts, seeds, honey, bone marrow, and fruits like dried figs and dates (depending upon which part of the world she lived in). By 25,000 BC, evidence indicates that humans were placing these mixtures over a fire to simmer into a sumptuous feast. Mixtures of foods were cooked together in hollowed wood or rocks. Some were slow-cooked in animal stomach pouches suspended on poles and slung over fires. For seasoning, our early ancestors knew to use olives, butter, seaweed, salt, pepper, beer, wine, vinegar, coriander, caraway seeds, and aromatic leaves.

As America was being settled by Europeans in the 17th and 18th centuries, households had few pots, so much of the food was cooked together for soups and casseroles for practical reasons.

Today, with pressure cookers, microwaves, slow cookers, large pots, small pots, baking and casserole dishes in iron, aluminum, clay, glass, and steel, and incredibly reliable stoves and ovens, soups and casseroles are still a favorite, and they're easier than ever to make.

# Making Lowfat Soups from Meat and Poultry

Making soups lowfat from fatty meat and poultry is pretty easy if you know how. Even on the most extreme lowfat eating plan, you can make lowfat soups with chicken fat and skin, seasoning pork, salt pork, bacon, marrow bones, fat-encased beef knuckles, fatty ham bones, and tallow (beef fat), or any kind of meat for that meaty flavor.

To defat a soup made with a meat base, you need to make it in two stages.

1. **Prepare the soup base.**

   In a large pot, boil 2 or 3 quarts of water and add beef bones, bacon or fat back, skin, fat, or poultry (for chicken soup), along with any herbs and spices you choose. You can also add vegetables to flavor the liquid. Simmer, covered or uncovered, for at least 1$^1/_2$ hours. Remove from the heat.

   Remove the fat, bones, or meat with a slotted spoon and discard, along with the vegetables and any herb sprigs, which are soaked with fat. Set aside any lean meat so that you can add it back to the soup later. (Meat is more dense and can be rinsed.)

**2. Defat the soup or stock base.**

You can do so in several ways:

- Chill it and then pick off the fat that rises and congeals at the top. This method takes a few hours and, usually, refrigeration.

- For more immediate results, spoon off every bit of fat. This method takes considerable time, but it's worth it.

- Or do as I usually do when I'm in a hurry. I use a large glass defatting pitcher, the one with a spout on the bottom (available in most kitchen stores). I defat with it several times to make sure that I remove all the fat.

Don't worry that your meat is going to cook too long because it's being twice cooked with this defatting method. Long-cooking methods bring out the flavor of meats and poultry. I always cook chicken, beef, bone, or ham-based soups for at least $1^1/2$ hours. If you like a stronger meat or poultry flavor, add a bouillon cube or meat flavor granules, especially to casseroles in which you aren't using that much meat but don't want the whole dish to cook for very long. The salty cubes are pretty diluted, so don't be concerned about adding too much sodium.

If you're worried about overcooking vegetables, you can cook them in several degrees, giving layers of flavors. For example, cook some onions with the fatty meat for hours (if you are just going to use the stock or soup base after defatting) and then discard them, leaving just the flavor in the broth. You can add more onions and cook those for 20 to 40 minutes with the rest of the soup ingredients, and even sprinkle some raw ones on top as a garnish.

When using the meat or poultry that was cooking in the broth, remove it, cut off all visible fat, and discard the fat. Cut the meat into pieces, rinse it well in a colander under hot running water to remove excess fat residue, and return the meat pieces to the broth. Wash the meat- and fat-cooking pot with hot, soapy water, rinse, and place the defatted broth and meat back in the same pot.

# Using beans in soups

Soaking beans for bean soup isn't necessary, though some people say that it helps to reduce flatulence. Cooking them from scratch gives them slightly more texture and takes only an additional hour or two of cooking time to make them tender and flavorful. Usually I just let a pot of beans simmer all afternoon and add some vegetables 30 minutes before serving, so I always cook beans from scratch without presoaking. Simmering to perfection the longest-cooking dried garbanzo, kidney, lima, or pisole (a type of corn) takes about 3 hours total.

Now you're ready to make your soup. Instead of water, you have highly flavored and fat-free stock. Add whatever dried or soaked beans, onions, tomatoes, carrots, celery, and herbs and spices your recipe calls for and simmer over low heat for the necessary time — perhaps hours for beans, or just a few minutes for vegetables. You now have a fat-free soup in any meat or poultry flavor you want.

# *Making Lowfat Casseroles*

Casseroles were born of necessity. They're a time and energy saver, and they don't have to contain fat to be special. Knowing how to flavor them without fat can keep meat-based casseroles in your lowfat menu plan. The best part is, when you make a casserole, you only need to add a salad, bread, and a fruit dessert, and you have everything that's necessary for a nutritious and sumptuous dinner, ready and hot when you come home.

Not all foods are casserole-friendly. A few vegetables, such as asparagus, broccoli, and spinach, aren't the best suited for long cooking methods, although people seem to have endured Turkey Divan, made by baking forever that leftover turkey, cheese, and broccoli. Some green vegetables are better bright green and snappy, not brown and gooey.

Peas and green beans are two green vegetables, though delicious barely cooked, that can also be baked and gain a different deeper flavor. Starchy fresh vegetables, such as corn and lima beans, plus onions, leeks, garlic, mushrooms, carrots, parsnips, celery, fennel bulbs, potatoes, some squash, artichoke hearts, rutabagas, and turnips, also fare well with longer cooking.

Fresh, soft pasta is too fragile to use in baked casseroles. Use barely cooked, dried pasta, which is hardier, instead.

## Using dried beans or uncooked pasta or rice in casseroles

Using dried, unsoaked beans or uncooked pasta or rice in a casserole is tricky because you have to add exactly the right amount of liquid or your casserole can easily become too dry (with the beans, rice, or pasta remaining hard) or too watery (with the ingredients becoming mushy or even disintegrating). It's safer to use cooked beans or canned and drained beans and nearly cooked pasta and rice for casseroles.

# Using Meat and Poultry in Lowfat Casseroles

The trick to making lowfat casseroles and stock pot dishes with meat and poultry is to reduce the amount meat or poultry to 2 ounces or less per person (remember that the casserole should contain an abundance of additional foods, such as carrots and onions).

Partially freeze the meat or poultry (doing so takes about 20 minutes) and cut it into ½-inch to 1½-inch cubes. You can see and remove every bit of fat on these smaller pieces of meat more easily — even those almond-sized fatty pieces in the flavorful chicken or turkey thigh — making it lower in fat. Plus, because lowfat cooking uses less meat, dicing rather than grinding gives people a real meat feel.

In a casserole, you don't need fat because the liquid and slow cooking method keep even dry meat moist. For especially good flavoring, brown meat or poultry pieces first, with or without flour, not only for extra flavor but also to enable you to pour off more excess fat. (The browning skillet is not the casserole dish, and some fat drips out in precooking.)

# Making Lowfat Cream Soups and Casseroles

You can make creamed soups and casseroles lowfat and nearly fat-free easily, thanks to all the new lower-fat dairy and nondairy products. For cream or milk, substitute liquid fat-free non-dairy creamer, evaporated skimmed milk, a mixture of nonfat dry milk powder and skim milk, or another lowfat or fat-free dairy product, such as lowfat or fat-free ricotta or cottage cheese (whipped velvety smooth in your food processor). Liquid fat-free non-dairy creamer, in case you have never used it, boils without curdling and keeps its flavor when baked. It doesn't have as pretty a color as cream or milk, and when cooked a long time, it goes back to its slightly gray or brown vegetable color, so be prepared to use bright, attractive garnishes like diced tomatoes and parsley — a small price to pay for so little fat and so much flavor.

You can sometimes substitute reduced-fat or fat-free cream cheese for regular cream cheese in a casserole. Numerous other lower-fat dairy products, such as lowfat or fat-free cheeses, including Parmesan, Swiss, Cheddar, American, feta, and many others, are being offered in new and improved versions every day. Although producers are continually improving lowfat and fat-free cheeses, these products do not match the high-fat versions in flavor and texture. Be aware that substituting $1/2$ cup of lowfat or fat-free Cheddar may not bring you the same results as the high-fat cheese. You may have to abandon a few recipes that require high-fat cheeses.

## Great lowfat ways to thicken soups

Because thickening can't rely on flour and fat, you have to try other methods. If what you want to thicken is clear, such as bouillon or chicken broth, use cornstarch or arrowroot, which becomes clear and shiny when heated. For opaque soups or casseroles, such as those with potatoes or creamy mixtures, use flour, mashed or pureed cooked potatoes, or rice. For vegetable soup, use red lentils, which disintegrate after 20 minutes when cooked. You can also mix together cornstarch and flour.

For thickening, a whisk works better than a spoon because it distributes the thickening agent, such as flour, which tends to lump. If your dish to be thickened contains vegetables, beans, pasta, or rice, and they are soft, a whisk may break them up, which you may not want. You can either strain the soup, thicken, and add the strained foods back; or, an easier method, whisk the thickening agent in a cup or two of cooled strained broth, getting out all the lumps, and then add it back to the pot, stirring well. You almost always need to dilute cornstarch or flour in a cool liquid (unless you're very experienced and can whisk at 90 mph).

Thicken with any of the following ingredients:

✔ **Bread cubes and bread crumbs:** Add $1/3$ cup of day-old bread cubes or herbed or plain bread crumbs for each quart of hot liquid. Stir over medium-high heat for at least 3 minutes or until thick. The cubes may not disintegrate completely, but the bread crumbs will.

✔ **Cornstarch or arrowroot:** For each quart of liquid, dissolve 2 tablespoons cornstarch or arrowroot into $1/2$ cup of cool liquid. Add the cornstarch liquid to the soup, stirring over medium-high heat until thick, about 1 minute. Neither cornstarch nor the more fragile arrowroot stays thick upon reheating. Unlike flour, you can add more cornstarch with little change in taste.

✔ **Flour:** Whisk 2 to 3 tablespoons of flour into each quart of preferably cool liquid. Heat flour-thickened liquids to a boil, lower the heat, and stir for at least 3 or 4 minutes to get rid of flour's uncooked or doughy taste. If you're bravely adding flour to a hot liquid, constantly whisk like crazy. If other foods are in the liquid, such as vegetables or noodles, you may never get all the lumps out. For best results, whisk the flour into 1 cup of cooled strained liquid; (chill with ice cubes); then add that to the larger amount, bring to a boil, lower to simmer, and stir and cook until thick. Flour-thickened liquids stay thick when reheated.

✔ **Mashed potatoes:** Add one medium cooked, mashed potato for each quart of liquid. Stir over medium heat for about 4 minutes or until thick.

✔ **Pureed cooked rice:** Add $1/2$ to 1 cup of pureed, cooked white, brown, or wild rice (puree in a food processor with a little liquid) per quart, and stir or whisk into the soup over medium heat, about 4 minutes or until thick. Thickening continues as the liquid cools.

✔ **Pureed or whole pasta:** Add 1 cup of pureed, cooked orzo or couscous to each quart of hot liquid. Thickening continues as the liquid cools.

✔ **Raw potatoes, carrots, or onions:** Stir in raw, grated, or shredded potatoes, carrots, or onions (about 1 cup for each quart of liquid), whisking or stirring occasionally, and cook over medium-low heat for at least 20 minutes (when the vegetables release their starches or natural thickening properties). Thickening is more subtle.

✔ **Red or orange lentils:** Stir about 1 cup of lentils per quart of liquid and cook over medium heat for 20 minutes, stirring occasionally. The lentils disintegrate, thickening the liquid.

✔ **Rice or potato flour:** Whisk 2 or more tablespoons of rice or potato flour (or even instant mashed potatoes) into a cool liquid. Add to the soup and stir or whisk over medium heat for about 4 minutes or until thick.

# Seasoning Soups

To season soups like a professional, get out three or four small bowls, add ¹/₄ cup of soup to each, add a pinch of the herb or spice you think you might like and a few drops of wine, write the differences on a piece of paper, place the paper upside down under each cup so that you can't see what you wrote, and taste. Some herbs and spices need cooking to expand properly, but you'll get the idea.

If your taste buds get dizzy, ask another person to help evaluate the results, or save the bowls for later, microwave to heat, and taste on a fresh palate. My trick is to taste the three or four variations when I'm hungry, go away, and completely change the subject. The one I want to just take another little taste of later is always the best.

A few basic combinations of soup ingredients are nearly foolproof:

✔ For a Southern bean soup, add carrots, onions, garlic, celery, and a Cajun spice mixture.

✔ Leeks and fennel go well with potatoes, rice, and beans. You can substitute scallions, pearl onions, cibolas, shallots, or onions for the leeks.

✔ Tomatoes work with most beans, meat, poultry, fish, shellfish, vegetables, and chilies.

✔ To beef, pork, chicken, or vegetable soups, you can add potatoes, pasta, rice, tomatoes, corn, dumplings, matzo balls, or gnocchi.

✔ If you get brave, try adding turnips, parsnips, or rutabagas to tomato, carrot, beet, or potato soups. Cabbage sweetens onions, corn, and potatoes and works well in most vegetable soups.

# Soups That Are Usually Low or High in Fat

These dishes can be and, like consommé, are often made lowfat. If they're prepared without meat, cream, sour cream, cream cheese, oil, butter, cheese, or egg yolks, and they have been defatted or are made without a meat or poultry base, they are usually low in fat.

- Barley soup (without pork, ham, or bacon)

- Bean soup (without pork, ham, or bacon)

- Borscht (without sour cream)

- Bouillabaisse (without butter)

- Cabbage soup

- Chili (without meat or cheese)

- Corn or okra chowder (without cream or butter)

- Cucumber soup

- Fish soup

- Fish, poultry, or meat stock (defatted)

- Fruit soup (without cream or milk products)

- Gazpacho

- Gumbo

- Leek or onion soup (without butter or cream)

- Lentil soup (without pork, ham, or bacon)

- Manhattan clam chowder (without bacon)

- Minestrone

- Miso soup

- Mulligatawny soup

- Mushroom soup (without cream or butter)

- Pepper pot soup

- Sweet and sour soup (without pork fat)

- Tomato soup

- Turtle and mock turtle soup

- Vegetable soup

- Wonton soup (without too many pork-filled wontons)

These traditional soup recipes are usually made without any fat removal. Often, they contain additional high-fat items, such as butter, cream cheese, sour cream, whole milk, cream, cheese, oil, and fatty meat.

- Beef and barley soup

- Bisque (with cream)

- Borscht (with sour cream)

- Cheese soup

- Chicken soup (with lots of chicken fat)

- Chili (with meat)

- Cream soups

- Cucumber soup (with cream, milk, or buttermilk)

- Egg drop soup

- French onion soup (with cheese and meat fat)

- Hot and sour soup (with fried pork or chicken and egg yolks)

- Manhattan clam chowder (with a bacon base)

- New England clam chowder (with cream or milk)

- Oxtail soup

- Oyster stew (with cream and butter)

- Pot-au-feu (with marrow)

- Potato soup (with cream or milk)

- Pumpkin soup (with cream or milk)

- Salt pork or seasoning meat-based soups

- Sausage soup

- Scotch broth or stock

- Soups made with fat-filled meat or poultry stock

- Split pea soup (with a ham bone base)

- Vegetable and beef soup (with excessive amounts of beef fat)

- Vichyssoise (with cream or milk)

# Casseroles That Are Usually Low or High in Fat

These casseroles, if not made with salt pork, bones, cream, cream cheese, butter, cheese, half and half, whole milk, or large amounts of meat, poultry, or egg yolks, can be low in fat.

✔ Baked beans

✔ Baked spaghetti marinara

✔ Chicken and rice casserole (if the chicken is skinless and small amounts are used)

  ✔ Chili casserole (if the meat is low in fat and small amounts are used)

  ✔ Danish meatball and noodle casserole (if the meat is low in fat and small amounts are used)

  ✔ Meatless chili casserole

  ✔ Seafood casserole (without cream or butter)

  ✔ Vegetable casserole (without cheese or butter)

These casseroles, if made the usual way with cream, cheese, cream cheese, butter, half and half, whole milk, sour cream, salt pork, bacon, meat or poultry fat, or egg yolks, are often very high in fat.

  ✔ Au gratin or cheese casserole

  ✔ Cassoulet with salt pork

  ✔ Chicken or turkey pot pie

  ✔ Creamed salmon casserole

  ✔ Hamburger casserole

  ✔ Macaroni and cheese bake

  ✔ Paella

  ✔ Quiche Lorraine

  ✔ Scalloped potatoes (with ham or cheese)

  ✔ Seafood casserole

  ✔ Steak and kidney pie

  ✔ Taco casserole

  ✔ Tuna noodle casserole

# Sumptuous Soup and Casserole Recipes

If you know how to prepare satisfying soups and casseroles, staying on a lowfat eating plan is easy. You can make several of these recipes in an afternoon and freeze them in small containers. Whenever you need a quick, lowfat meal, just heat up a frozen serving of one of these pleasing dishes.

## Beef and Vegetable Root Stew

This especially delicious stew, all cooked in one pot, richly deserves the accolades it gets. I have made it for 20 years, and it's always a favorite. I use an 8-quart pressure cooker, but you don't need to. The secret is in the browning and the lengthy cooking of the meat and bones. Sometimes I add a teaspoon of herbs de Provence or a bouquet garni (premixed dried spices and herbs found in most markets). This is good company food because it can cook for an additional hour. One friend adds corn on the cob chunks and green beans. You can leave out many items (such as tomatoes, garlic, parsnip, and rutabaga), and the stew is still wonderful.

**Tools:** *8-quart soup pot or pressure cooker*

**Preparation time:** *3*

**Yield:** *8 servings*

*1 cup flour*

*Salt (optional) and freshly ground black pepper*

*¹/₂ teaspoon sugar*

*1 pound bones, all visible fat removed*

*¹/₂ pound lean top round, all visible fat removed, cut into ³/₄-inch cubes*

*1 large onion, cut into eighths*

*2 teaspoons olive oil*

*15 pearl onions, peeled, or 1 large onion, peeled and cut into chunks*

*2 to 4 large cloves garlic, peeled and cut in fourths*

*3 carrots, sliced in thirds, or 10 baby carrots*

*3 stalks celery, including tops, sliced in fourths*

*2 parsnips, sliced into 2-inch rounds*

*1 turnip or rutabaga, peeled and cut in large chunks*

*2 potatoes, cut into large cubes*

*2 ripe tomatoes, diced*

*2 15-ounce cans tomatoes, tomatoes cut in fourths, juice reserved*

*2 12-ounce cans tomato sauce*

*2 bay leaves*

*4 beef bouillon cubes*

*1 cup chopped fresh parsley*

*1 teaspoon dried thyme*

*2 quarts low-sodium vegetable stock, defatted beef stock, or water*

**1** Fill a sealable bag with the flour, salt to taste (if desired), a small amount of pepper, and sugar. Place the bones, cubed meat, and onion in the bag, seal, and shake until all are coated.

**2** In an 8-quart soup pot or pressure cooker over medium heat, place the olive oil, bones, meat, and onion. Reserve the flour mixture left in the bag. Brown the bones, meat, and onions over medium heat for about 25 minutes, turning often.

*(continued)*

**3** Add the pearl onions, garlic, carrots, celery, parsnips, turnip or rutabaga, potatoes, fresh and canned tomatoes with juice, tomato sauce, bay leaves, bouillon cubes, parsley, thyme, and 1¹/₂ quarts of the stock.

**4** Pour the remaining 2 cups stock into a bowl and add the reserved flour mixture. Whisk until blended and then pour into the soup pot.

**5** Bring the stew to a boil (being careful not to burn it), lower the heat, and pressure-cook for 40 minutes; or cook, covered, for 1 hour and 15 minutes. Remove the bay leaves, mash the garlic, add additional salt (if desired) and pepper, and stir to incorporate.

*Nutrition at a glance (per serving): Total fat 3 g; Saturated fat 0.5 g; Protein 15 g; Dietary fiber 7 g; Carbohydrate 54 g; Cholesterol 18 mg; Sodium 1844 mg; % of calories from fat 9; Calories 293.*

*Lynn's oregano tips: If you're an oregano lover and want to put half a teaspoon in a long-cooking root stew (which would be good), don't add dried oregano until the last 15 or 20 minutes of cooking. Oregano can get bitter with long cooking.*

## Chicken Soup, Asian Style

Chicken soup cooked in the Asian manner — lemony, clear yet thick, and filled with vegetables, topped with a nest of crinkly, crunchy threads — is a delicious treat. You'll want at least an extra hour, perhaps overnight, to marinate the chicken. Canned straw mushrooms (available in most grocery stores and Asian markets) make the soup more authentic, but the salt content increases slightly.

**Tools:** *Large Dutch oven or nonstick soup pot*

**Preparation time:** *2*

**Yield:** *8 servings*

**Meat and Marinade:**

*8 ounces skinless chicken breast, all visible fat removed, cut into ¹/₄-inch x 1-inch strips*

*2 tablespoons hoisin sauce*

*1 teaspoon sesame oil*

*2 teaspoons fresh lemon juice*

*1 clove garlic, peeled and minced*

*(continued)*

***Garnish of Hoisin Strings:***

2 8-inch flour tortillas

2 teaspoons hoisin sauce

***Soup:***

2 cups shredded carrots

3 cups shredded cabbage

1¹/₄ cups fresh shiitake mushrooms, stemmed and sliced, or 1 15-ounce can straw mushrooms, drained

1¹/₂ quarts (or 6 cups) homemade or canned, defatted low-sodium chicken stock

3 tablespoons cornstarch

¹/₄ cup low-sodium soy sauce

2 tablespoons grated ginger

2 tablespoons fresh lemon juice

¹/₂ cup diced red bell pepper

4 chopped scallions, plus 2 tablespoons chopped scallions for garnish

**1** In a small bowl or sealable plastic bag, toss the chicken with 2 tablespoons hoisin sauce, the sesame oil, and 2 teaspoons lemon juice. Add garlic and marinate overnight or for at least 1 hour in the refrigerator.

**2** Preheat the oven to 300°.

**3** Spread each tortilla with 1 teaspoon hoisin sauce. Cut the tortillas in half and each half into ¹/₈-inch-wide strips. Separate, place on a baking sheet, and bake for 30 minutes or until crispy. Set aside.

**4** Meanwhile, lightly coat a large Dutch oven or nonstick soup pot with no-stick vegetable oil spray. With the burner on medium-high, place the chicken strips in the Dutch oven or soup pot and sauté for about 5 minutes, tossing. Remove the chicken and reserve.

**5** Place the carrots, cabbage, and mushrooms in the Dutch oven or soup pot. Lightly spray the vegetables and sauté for 5 minutes, tossing, adding a few teaspoons of water for moisture if needed.

**6** Into 1 cup of cool chicken stock, whisk the cornstarch. Add to the soup. Add the soy sauce, ginger, lemon juice, red pepper, and the rest of the chicken stock. Bring to a boil, stirring until thickened, about 10 minutes.

**7** Add the reserved chicken and the scallions to the soup. Cook over low heat for 5 minutes. To serve, sprinkle on the hoisin strings and the reserved chopped scallions.

***Nutrition at a glance (per serving):*** *Total fat 2 g; Saturated fat 0.5 g; Protein 14 g; Dietary fiber 2 g; Carbohydrate 21 g; Cholesterol 17 mg; Sodium 681 mg; % of calories from fat 12; Calories 153.*

***Lynn's substitution tips:*** *Anytime a recipe calls for chicken breast, you can substitute completely defatted pork, Canadian bacon, lean ham, turkey breast, firm fish, or even duck without the skin and with all visible fat removed, all with only minor increases or decreases in fat.*

## Chicken Soup with Vegetables

This is the easy, fragrant, wonderful chicken soup that your grandma made — but without all the fat. Use everything that she may have: all the giblets (but the liver), the bones, the neck, the fat, and the skin. You can garnish the soup with chopped fresh parsley, diced or julienned carrots, or diced red peppers. For a velvety rich bisque, puree the finished soup with a hand or immersion blender or food processor.

**Tools:** *Large soup pot*

**Preparation time:** *3*

**Yield:** *10 servings*

*1 tablespoon butter*

*1 whole chicken with skin and parts, except the liver, chicken cut or uncut*

*2 large onions, peeled*

*2 carrots*

*2 stalks celery, including leaves*

*2 leeks or 6 shallots*

*4 cloves garlic, peeled*

*1 bay leaf*

*¹/₂ cup chopped fresh parsley*

*2 sprigs fresh thyme, or 2 teaspoons finely chopped dried*

*1 sprig fresh rosemary, or 1 teaspoon dried, finely chopped*

*Salt (optional) and freshly ground black pepper*

*2 tablespoons sherry, white wine, or sherry extract (optional)*

*1¹/₂ tablespoons flour (optional for thickening)*

*1¹/₂ tablespoons cornstarch (optional for thickening)*

*1* In a large soup pot, place the butter. Brown the chicken in the butter over medium heat, turning several times, being careful not to burn or scorch the chicken.

*2* Add 1 onion cut into eighths, 1 carrot cut into fourths, 1 stalk celery cut into fourths, 1 leek or 3 shallots cut into fourths, 2 cloves garlic (putting them in a tea strainer makes them easier to remove), and the bay leaf. Toss the vegetables in the pan and cook them over medium-low heat until the onions begin to soften, about 5 minutes.

*3* Add enough water to cover the chicken (4 to 5 quarts), ¹/₄ cup parsley, the thyme and rosemary, and some salt (if desired). Over high heat, cook to boiling. Reduce the heat to low, cover, and cook, simmering, for 1 hour and 15 minutes.

*(continued)*

**4** Remove the chicken with a slotted spoon or tongs and set aside, and remove the garlic. Discard the cooked vegetables and the bay leaf. Defat the stock completely with a defatting cup or by chilling it and removing the congealed fat that rises to the top. Reserve the defatted stock. (You can strain the stock if you want.) Add the garlic back to the stock, mashing it.

**5** Remove all the skin and fat from the chicken and discard. Remove the meat from the bones, discard the bones, and cut the meat into chunks, again removing all visible fat.

**6** In a clean soup pot, place the defatted stock. Add 1 onion, coarsely chopped; 1 carrot, sliced; 1 stalk celery, sliced; 1 leek, sliced; 1 clove garlic, minced; and ¼ cup parsley. Simmer for 25 minutes, covered. Add the sherry or white wine (if desired) and simmer for 5 minutes.

**7** If you want a thick soup, in a small bowl, blend the flour and cornstarch with 1 cup of cooled stock (an ice cube works well). Whisk together, add to the soup, and turn up the heat to medium-high, stirring for at least 5 minutes so that the flour cooks. Adjust the seasoning as needed.

***Nutrition at a glance (per serving):*** *Total fat 3.5 g; Saturated fat 1.5 g; Protein 15 g; Dietary fiber 2 g; Carbohydrate 7 g; Cholesterol 49 mg; Sodium 80 mg; % of calories from fat 26; Calories 119.*

***Lynn's tips for adding noodles or rice:*** *To add noodles or rice, cook them separately, drain them, place ¹/₂ cup on the bottom of the individual soup bowl, and pour soup over them. Don't store soup with rice or noodles in it unless you don't mind the rice or noodles getting mushy.*

## Chili

Chili is a most satisfying dish that takes little effort, whether baked or cooked on the stovetop. Make it with ground turkey, beef, or pork, or leave out the meat entirely. You can also add more peppers of different colors. The carrot gives the chili a nice sweetness, but you can omit it if you like. For garnish, sprinkle on some shredded lowfat cheese, finely chopped onions, and a dollop of fat-free sour cream.

***Tools:*** *Large nonstick skillet, large soup pot or casserole dish*

***Preparation time:*** *3*

***Yield:*** *6 servings*

*(continued)*

6 ounces skinless turkey breast, top round, or lean pork, all visible fat removed, coarsely ground

1 large onion, peeled and coarsely chopped

2 cloves garlic, peeled and chopped

1 green bell pepper, cut into 1-inch pieces

1 carrot, finely shredded

1 6-ounce can tomato paste

2 cups plus 1 quart water

1 15-ounce can whole or chopped tomatoes

1 15-ounce can dark kidney beans, drained

2 to 4 tablespoons chili powder

1 teaspoon cumin

Salt (optional)

Several shakes crushed red pepper (optional; for heat)

**1** If baking, preheat the oven to 350°.

**2** Lightly coat a large nonstick skillet with no-stick vegetable oil spray. Place the meat, onion, and garlic in the skillet, lightly spray, and sauté over medium heat, stirring, for about 5 minutes, browning the meat and making sure not to scorch the garlic. Add the green pepper and carrot, stir, and turn down the heat to medium-low.

**3** In a large soup pot (or casserole dish, if baking), whisk the tomato paste with 2 cups water. Add the meat mixture, tomatoes, kidney beans, chili powder, cumin, salt (if desired), and 1 quart water. If baking, cover and bake for 40 minutes. If cooking on the stovetop, bring the mixture to a boil, stir, lower the heat to a simmer, cover, and simmer for 40 minutes. Add the crushed red pepper (if desired).

*Nutrition at a glance (per serving): Total fat 1.5 g; Saturated fat 0.5 g; Protein 14 g; Dietary fiber 7 g; Carbohydrate 24 g; Cholesterol 20 mg; Sodium 481 mg; % of calories from fat 8; Calories 152.*

*Lynn's chili tips: Chili lends itself to many additions, including corn, diced tomatoes, red or yellow bell peppers, and even poured over cooked macaroni, rice, or a baked potato. I often add a teaspoon of sugar and a tablespoon of vinegar to bring out more flavor.*

## Fisherman's Casserole

There's nothing better than a good fish casserole — it's easy to make, it's all baked in one pot, and it's a fish-lover's delight. A few cooked mussels add a colorful touch. You can also add diced tomatoes, peas, or other seafood, because casseroles should be a practical surprise of good-tasting dishes using the foods you have on hand. Other fish or shellfish such crab, lobster, cod, and scallops can be added, too. Garnish with chopped fresh parsley. Corn on the cob, bread, and a salad round out the meal nicely.

*(continued)*

**Tools:** *5-quart Dutch oven or large high-sided skillet*

**Preparation time:** *2*

**Yield:** *8 servings*

*2 stalks celery, chopped*

*2 carrots, chopped*

*6 ounces mushrooms, sliced*

*1 green bell pepper, chopped*

*1 red bell pepper, chopped*

*1 medium onion, peeled and chopped*

*1$^1$/$_2$ cups skim milk*

*$^1$/$_4$ cup dry sherry (preferred) or Worcestershire sauce*

*1$^1$/$_2$ teaspoons Dijon mustard*

*$^1$/$_2$ cup water*

*$^1$/$_3$ cup all-purpose flour*

*$^1$/$_2$ teaspoon Old Bay Seasoning*

*$^1$/$_4$ to $^1$/$_2$ teaspoon hot sauce*

*Salt (optional) and freshly ground black pepper*

*8 mussels (optional)*

*8 ounces flounder or catfish fillets, cut into 2-inch chunks*

*6 ounces medium shrimp*

*2 tablespoons grated Parmesan cheese*

*1* Lightly coat a 5-quart Dutch oven or large, high-sided skillet with no-stick vegetable oil spray. In the Dutch oven or skillet, place the celery, mushrooms, green and red peppers, and onions and lightly spray the vegetables.

*2* Sauté over medium-high heat for 15 minutes or until golden brown, stirring frequently, adding a tablespoon or two of water if needed for moisture.

*3* In a small bowl, place the milk, sherry or Worcestershire sauce, Dijon mustard, water, and flour and whisk until smooth.

*4* Pour the mixture into the Dutch oven or skillet along with the Old Bay Seasoning. Add the hot sauce and some salt (if desired) and pepper. Stir well. Bring the mixture to a boil, stirring, and immediately reduce the heat to low.

*5* Add the mussels (if desired). Simmer on low, uncovered, for 15 minutes.

*6* Add the fish and shrimp and cook, covered, on low heat for an additional 5 minutes. Sprinkle with the remaining Parmesan cheese and garnish with chopped parsley if you like.

**Nutrition at a glance (per serving):** *Total fat 1.5 g; Saturated fat 0.5 g; Protein 13 g; Dietary fiber 2 g; Carbohydrate 12 g; Cholesterol 47 mg; Sodium 197 mg; % of calories from fat 11; Calories 116.*

**Lynn's fish and shellfish casserole tip:** *The secret to making good fish and shellfish casseroles is to not let the fish and shellfish overcook. You may want to cook or steam them to perfection separately and add them just before serving.*

## Lentil Soup

Oh, you wise lentil lovers! All that taste and valuable nutrition and fiber are in this homey, fragrant soup. More often than not, I make this soup without the ham or bone, adding 2$^1$/$_2$ quarts defatted chicken stock, vegetable stock, or water. To give the soup a New Orleans twist, add $^1$/$_2$ teaspoon of Cajun spice instead of the crushed red pepper.

**Tools:** Large soup pot

**Preparation time:** 3

**Yield:** 6 servings

Ham bone with about $^1$/$_2$ cup ham on the bone

3 cloves garlic, peeled

1 cup diced celery, with leaves

1 large onion, peeled and diced

1$^1$/$_2$ cups diced carrots

1 cup brown lentils, rinsed

1 cup yellow lentils, rinsed

$^1$/$_2$ cup orange or red lentils, rinsed

1 teaspoon thyme

Salt (optional) and freshly ground black pepper

Crushed red pepper (flakes)

$^1$/$_2$ cup crumbled feta cheese (optional)

$^1$/$_2$ cup diced tomatoes

*1* In a large soup pot, place the bone and 3 quarts water. Simmer, covered, for 1$^1$/$_2$ hours.

*2* Remove the bone from the broth. Let it cool enough to pick off all the meat. Cut off all fat from the meat and discard the fat. Reserve the meat. Defat the stock by using a defatting cup or by letting the broth chill in the refrigerator and then picking off the congealed fat.

*3* Lightly coat a clean soup pot with no-stick vegetable oil spray and heat over medium-high heat. Add the garlic, celery, onions, and carrots, lightly spray the vegetables, and, if needed, add a few teaspoons of water for moisture. Sauté for about 6 minutes, stirring.

*4* Add the lentils, defatted stock, meat, and thyme and bring to a boil. Reduce the heat and simmer for 45 minutes or until the lentils are soft (the red lentils will have disintegrated). Season with salt (if desired), black pepper, and crushed red pepper for heat. Top each serving with a sprinkling of feta cheese (if desired) and diced tomatoes.

*(continued)*

***Nutrition at a glance (per serving):*** *Total fat 1.5 g; Saturated fat 0.5 g; Protein 22 g; Dietary fiber 11 g; Carbohydrate 49 g; Cholesterol 4 mg; Sodium 167 mg; % of calories from fat 4; Calories 285.*

***Lynn's tips on substituting beans for lentils:*** *This also serves as a basic bean soup recipe and can be made with dried beans or barley instead of lentils. Use dried navy, brown, lima, kidney, pinto, black, or any bean you choose. If the beans are very large, such as kidneys, limas, or garbanzos, simmer the soup for 3 hours, covered. You can also use a mixture of several kinds of beans, cooking them all for 3 hours. For a change, serve the beans Puerto Rican style along with a bowl of rice, a small dish of raw, chopped onions, lime wedges, and hot sauce. If you presoak the beans, cook them an hour less. Adding salt during cooking makes for a very firm bean (which I like).*

## Pork and Garbanzo Bean Stew

This flavorful mixture of sweet pork and garbanzo beans has been a favorite of mine for many years. You're probably familiar with all the ingredients; they're just used in a slightly different way. In Mexico, a similar soup is served over a whole, barely heated, peeled tomato or half an avocado. Here, the parsley or scallions are used as a garnish.

***Tools:*** *Large nonstick Dutch oven or large soup pot, defatting cup*

***Preparation time:*** *3*

***Yield:*** *8 servings*

*10 ounces lean pork (pork tenderloin), all visible fat removed, cut into 1-inch cubes*

*3 tablespoons flour*

*Salt (optional) and freshly ground black pepper*

*2 medium Spanish onions, peeled and diced (about 3 cups)*

*4 cloves garlic, peeled and minced*

*6 medium plum tomatoes, diced*

*3 cups homemade or canned, defatted, low-sodium chicken stock*

*²/₃ cup Madeira (optional)*

*2 16-ounce cans garbanzo beans (chickpeas)*

*¹/₂ cup green stuffed olives, coarsely chopped (optional)*

*1 teaspoon dried basil*

*³/₄ cup golden or dark raisins*

*¹/₂ cup finely chopped pimentos or red bell peppers*

*2 tablespoons capers, drained*

*¹/₂ teaspoon dried oregano*

*¹/₄ cup chopped fresh parsley or scallions*

*(continued)*

*1* On a cutting board or in a plastic bag, toss the pork cubes with flour. Lightly coat a large nonstick Dutch oven or soup pot with no-stick vegetable oil spray and brown the pork cubes well over medium-high heat. Season the pork with salt (if desired) and pepper. Remove the pork cubes and wipe out the pot.

*2* Lower the heat to medium, add the onions and garlic, lift the pan off the burner, and lightly coat them for 1 or 2 seconds with no-stick vegetable oil spray. Sauté for 5 to 8 minutes or until softened, adding a teaspoon of water if needed for moisture.

*3* Add the cooked pork, plum tomatoes, stock, Madeira (if desired), garbanzos, olives (if desired), and basil. Bring to a boil. Lower the heat and simmer for 45 minutes, covered, stirring occasionally. Pour the liquid into a defatting cup and then pour the defatted liquid back into the pot.

*4* Add the raisins, pimentos, capers, oregano, and parsley or scallions and simmer, uncovered, for 15 minutes.

*Nutrition at a glance (per serving):* Total fat 3.5 g; Saturated fat 0.5 g; Protein 18 g; Dietary fiber 5 g; Carbohydrate 39 g; Cholesterol 21 mg; Sodium 172 mg; % of calories from fat 12; Calories 247.

*Lynn's wine-flavoring tip:* If you're cooking a soup or casserole with red wine, add a small pinch (about $1/16$ teaspoon) of dried cloves to bring out the flavor of the wine. This tip comes from Ann Wilder of Vann's Spices.

# Chapter 11

# Fish and Shellfish

## In This Chapter

▶ Why fish are an important part of a lowfat eating plan

▶ Fish and fish dishes that are low and high in fat

▶ Ten quick lowfat methods for cooking fish

*W*ith lots of protein, but generally little fat, fish and shellfish can be a significant element of a lowfat menu plan. This chapter explains why omega-3 fatty acids may benefit people, but it also reminds you of some of the many other reasons to eat fish and shellfish. I also tell you how to choose fish based on freshness and taste.

I also include handy lists of fish dishes that are usually high in fat and those that are lower in fat so that menus and fish dish names don't surprise you fat-wise. And, for when you cook fish at home, I show you how to cook lean fish so that it doesn't become dry and how to cook fattier fish so that it retains its natural moisture, all the while making sure that whatever you serve ends up being tasty.

The 10 versatile recipes, from casual spiced shrimp to elegant ten-minute Sole Meunière, give you a wide range of taste choices. And each recipe can be made with one of several types of fish or shellfish, not just the type that I name.

## Go Fish!

Fresh fish and shellfish are basic food items; ideal foods that are naturally low in fat and high in protein. Although fish and shellfish generally have the same amount of cholesterol as meat and poultry, unlike fish and shellfish, which are naturally lowfat, people have to struggle to breed, raise, and prepare meat and poultry in lowfat ways. Fish and shellfish can be delicious with a simple salsa or cocktail sauce or with a few carefully selected herbs and spices. Just be careful not to overcook them.

Outside of cereals, fish is the world's most important category of food. Worldwide, people eat 100 million tons of fish every year. Fish and shellfish are abundant, easy to catch, and good to eat. Good fresh fish is nearly odor free and has a clear, clean taste. No wonder every world culture loves it.

Fish and shellfish aren't measured by the terms *fat* and *lowfat* — only *lean* and *extra lean,* the same as meat (see Chapter 5 for more information). Lean fish and shellfish have less than 10 grams of fat, less than 4.5 grams of saturated fat, and less than 95 milligrams of cholesterol per RACC and per 100 grams. Fish and shellfish that qualify as extra lean by government definition have less than 5 grams of fat, less than 2 grams of saturated fat, and less than 95 milligrams of cholesterol per RACC and per 100 grams.

Shrimp, lobster, crab, clams, mussels, and oysters have almost no fat, and scallops have even less fat than that group. In the fish family, cod is extremely low in fat, similar to scallops. These fish and shellfish are some of the foods that helped us humans get our start. Fish and shellfish are thought to be (besides insects) one of the first animal proteins eaten, long before fowl or red meat. (See the sidebar "A short history of fish consumption" for interesting tidbits about fish eating throughout history.)

How often you should eat fish is a matter of opinion. The omega-3 fatty acids that are present in fattier fish may be beneficial for some people. The best advice is to eat a wide variety of all kinds of foods, including many different kinds of fish and shellfish. Try a new species often — you have 30,000 varieties to choose from.

## Freshness

Fish needs to be as fresh-caught as possible. Most fish today are frozen within hours right on the trawler that netted them. When a market says that its fish is fresh and not frozen, in most cases it means that the fish hasn't been *re*frozen.

In a few restaurants and grocery markets, you know that the fish isn't frozen because you pick out your own swimming around in a tank. That's why live lobsters and crabs are sought after; you know that they're fresh. Freezing slightly changes the consistency and texture of all animal proteins, causing toughening and fragmenting.

## A short history of fish consumption

Succulent lobster risotto, the most tender portion of fresh shad served with its firm roe, Dover sole butter-sautéed with a dash of white wine and a sprinkling of parsley, shrimp and crab gumbo — these are foods you may dream about. And if you don't eat too much of them (shad, for example, is high in fat) and don't add copious amounts of butter to the sole or the risotto, they all can be lowfat by government definition. And they are all definitely delicious by anyone's standards.

In 2300 B.C., the Assyrians knew and prepared 50 different species of fish. The Egyptians hand-raised their own favorite fish in ponds to have them readily available. Pliny considered oysters and sea urchins to be aphrodisiacs (he was probably right), eating them as often as possible, and Apicius wrote that he enjoyed his heavily salted, sun-dried anchovies each day.

The early Chinese set pots between stones, boiled soybeans and fermented wheat, and added various kinds of fish, depending on the season and the desired taste. Then they let this mixture ferment to a malodorous broth, which they used for seasoning. Asians do the same today, with each culture having its own fermented fish sauce: nuoc nam in Vietnam, shottsuru in Japan, and man pla in Thailand and all of Asia.

The 15th century Europeans loved their fish and kept trout and many other fish in those famous moats to eat when they desired. A few hundred years later, South Americans "cooked" raw fish (without really cooking it) in acidic juices after the Asians brought them limes and lemons. All these techniques have contributed to the huge number of ways in which fish is prepared and enjoyed today.

Health-wise, farmed fish contains (by law) as many as eight therapeutic drugs and some 30 other chemicals, so it is hardly "pure." But fresh products aren't pure, either. Fresh fish and shellfish can contain mercury, pesticides, sewage waste, and other chemical contaminants. The Food and Drug Administration says that of all food-borne illnesses, those related to seafood comprise only one-quarter of 1 percent of the total, so seafood is a relatively safe product. Just make sure that you buy fish from a trusted purveyor who has certain freshness standards — probably not a roadside stand where you have no recourse if the fish you buy is tainted, old, or diseased.

## *Taste*

Studies show that people are more likely to eat seafood in restaurants than at home because preparation can be tricky. But you can learn, and it isn't difficult. Nothing is easier to cook than fish. Here's a taste primer to help you choose a variety you like:

✔ Saltwater fish, such as salmon, are generally thought to be tastier than freshwater fish, such as pike.

> ✔ Fish from swiftly moving waters — black bass, for example — are thought to have a finer flavor than those from slow-moving waters, like catfish. (However, catfish has seen a dramatic upsurge in popularity because of fish farming and marketing, and this tender, sweet fish is now far more popular than bass.)

# Cooking Fish in Lowfat Ways

The method you use to cook fish or shellfish really affects the fat content of the finished dish. Instead of drowning that healthful piece of broiled fish in fat-filled cream sauce or butter, try one of the following lower-fat methods.

## Baking and roasting

Plain fish and shellfish can be baked covered or uncovered, wrapped in foil or ovenproof plastic wrap, usually in a very hot oven. You can bake fish such as mackerel and snapper in a sauce of wine, mushrooms, onions, carrots, or other vegetables. Baking fish makes it tender because the fish absorbs the flavor of the other ingredients, and baking is a good way to cook small pieces of fish. Wrapping fish in corn husks, leek leaves, cabbage, spinach, grape or lettuce leaves, polenta, pastry dough, filo, nori (seaweed), oven bags, or parchment paper is an easy way to get tender fish. Bread crumbs and baking make a crispy fish without frying.

## Boiling

Boil fish and shellfish in chowders, soups, and stews with many other foods, stirring carefully so as not to break the more tender fish. Firm fish that you can use for boiling are John Dory, skate, shrimp, lobster, blackfish, catfish, shark, swordfish, sturgeon, eel, and yellowtail, plus scallops, mussels, and clams.

## Braising and poaching

Good for dry fish, braising and poaching mean that the fish is cooked while partially or totally submerged in liquid. The liquid gets a concentrated fish flavoring as it cooks down, good for a quick sauce. Braise or poach whole fish or fillets in the oven, covered, or on the stovetop, covered or uncovered. Cover the fish with a liquid, such as vegetable, chicken, or fish broth, water, wine, or juice, and flavor with herbs and spices, such as a sprig of thyme. Take the skin off (while hot) after poaching, because poaching can make the skin rubbery.

## Letting nature take its natural lowfat course

It's important for people who are beginning to eat lowfat to know that when you change the way you eat, you're not going against tradition or history. You aren't going from what is normal to some stringent, restrictive method — in fact, quite the contrary. Eating lowfat isn't new; it's the natural way to eat. People ate that way for thousands of years. Food didn't always have added oils, butter, cream, or cheese — and some cultures still don't add those things. Meat wasn't always from over-fatted domesticated animals but was wild game. To know this may help you feel confident that eating lowfat is customary.

Few early cultures ate the large amounts of added fat that we do today because the fat wasn't readily available. Most animals and poultry were wild and, therefore, naturally lean. Fish are still lean. If you cook fish and shellfish simply and deliciously, they are, unlike most of today's meat and poultry, the ideal animal protein.

## Broiling

In broiling, the heat or flame is over the fish. Broil whole fish, boned fish, fish steaks, or thick fillets lightly sprayed with olive oil (if desired), rubbed with spices and herbs, and placed 4 inches from the broiler. Broil for about 2 minutes on each side, depending on the thickness of the fish.

## Marinating and grilling

Marinating and grilling, where the heat comes from under the fish, are good for oily fish such as salmon. Fish can be grilled in foil (this method really steams the fish), in a vegetable wrap, or whole, by itself. If pieces are small, grill them on lettuce leaves. Kebabs of shrimp, scallops, oysters, and firm fish cut into 1-inch square chunks, marinated or spice-rubbed first and then threaded on skewers, can be grilled. Marinate shrimp overnight, most fish for just a few hours. When grilling, you can also brush on a tasty sauce.

## Microwaving

Microwaves don't heat evenly, so be sure to use a turntable or turn often, and be aware that a large fish may cook unevenly. Aside from that, microwaving is good for fillets, seafood soup, shrimp, or small pieces of fish. Microwave the fish covered or in a microwaveable bag.

My 91-year-old dad quite effectively microwaves his favorite meal of 4 ounces of frozen catfish for 5 minutes.

## Pan-searing, dry-frying, or pan-frying

Lightly spray or rub fish with olive or canola oil and cook over high heat in a lightly coated nonstick skillet. A teaspoon of lemon, lime, or tangerine juice, Worcestershire sauce, wine, sherry, Marsala, or soy sauce, along with some chopped parsley, shallots, and herbs, can give lowfat pan-fried fish a whole new taste appeal.

## Smoking

Smoked fish has a special flavor that you can achieve no other way. You usually use equipment that is specially designed for smoking. Almost any fish, including salmon, and some shellfish, such as oysters, can be smoked.

## Steaming

Steaming is good for dry fish such as cod, halibut, and scallops. Use a fish steamer or poacher with a pierced rack, or even a vegetable steamer if the pieces of fish are small enough. Steam in $1/2$ to 1 inch of water, bouillon, defatted stock, skim milk, lemon or lime juice, or wine, and flavor the liquid with spices and herbs if you like.

## Serving fish in lowfat ways

**For breakfast or brunch:** Do as the English do and serve 2 ounces of pan-seared trout, kippers, lox and bagels, or shrimp omelets.

**As an appetizer:** Not only does shrimp make a great appetizer, but try lobster pieces, clams casino, or oysters Rockefeller — made lowfat. Serve fish pieces on a bed of leeks, a bed of chopped sun-dried tomatoes, or with capers and a few chopped olives.

**In salads:** Adding cold cooked shrimp, lobster, mussels, or pieces of cooked, cold fish to any salad — especially a Caesar — dresses it up.

**In soups:** Using chicken stock as a base, add shrimp and finely diced vegetables for an Asian-style soup. To a potato and corn soup base, add crab or clams or garnish with them.

**As an entree:** Serve plain fish with a lowfat or fat-free tartar sauce (you can find a recipe later in this chapter), chili sauce, a mild tomato cilantro salsa, or sweet, tangy, tropical salsa (also in this chapter). Shrimp and lobster can be part of various dishes or can go on their own, lightly steamed.

**In rice and pasta dishes:** To your favorite pasta marinara recipe, add pieces of halibut, shrimp, lobster, clams, or calamari. To a cream sauce, add pieces of fish, shrimp, clams, or lobster. To risotto, add shrimp, clams, or mussels.

**In salsa or gazpacho:** Garnish your favorite salsa or gazpacho with hot sauce, lemon or lime juice, chopped cilantro or onions, and pieces of crab or shrimp.

**In sauces:** Julia Child once directed people to grind up shrimp shells with a mortar and pestle for a marvelous shrimp sauce. Most people don't want to go to that much trouble today, but clam sauce, small shrimp in tomato sauce, or pieces of lobster in a lowfat or fat-free cream sauce can top a shell-style pasta, rice, couscous, quinoa, kamut, bulgur wheat, vegetables, or fish.

**For snacks:** Coat your favorite white fish with egg whites and roll in bread or cracker crumbs and bake for 10 minutes or until the fish is opaque when you cut the center lightly with the tip of a sharp knife.

**For drinks:** Make your favorite Bloody Mary with a base of clam juice and V8 or tomato juice, or Clamato (clam and tomato juice); plus fresh lemon juice, gin or vodka (optional), hot sauce, Worcestershire sauce, lots of pepper, and a stalk of leafy celery, a long green bean, or a stalk of cold steamed asparagus.

# Identifying Lowfat and High-Fat Fish Dishes

Color can be a clue to the fat content of the fish itself. Light-colored flesh usually indicates leaner fish. White-fleshed halibut, tuna, cod, scallops, and sole, for example, are low in fat. Darker mackerel, eel, shad, and salmon contain more fat. (Chapter 5 provides more information about the fat content of various types of fish.)

In general, fish dishes that are usually low in fat are baked (with little butter, cream, or cheese), broiled, dry-fried (with just a spritz of olive oil or less than $1/4$ teaspoon butter), foil-wrapped, grilled, sautéed or poached (with liquids other than oil), or steamed (without clarified butter). Canned fish and shellfish packed in water are generally lowfat, too.

You don't always have control over what goes into the fish dishes you eat, so it's good to know which dishes are generally lower in fat and which generally are higher in fat. You can review these lists before you go out to dinner or to a party so that you're better prepared to make a smart choice. Remember, you can always get sauce on the side.

The following fish and shellfish dishes, and some other recipes if prepared without added fat, are naturally low in total fat, saturated fat, and cholesterol (note that shrimp and lobster are higher in cholesterol):

✔ Bouillabaisse

✔ Crab, shrimp, lobster, or clam cocktail

- ✔ Curried shrimp
- ✔ Deviled crab
- ✔ Dover sole, lightly sautéed
- ✔ Fish in aspic
- ✔ Fish boulangère
- ✔ Fish cakes (not batter fried)
- ✔ Fish or shrimp kebabs
- ✔ Fish sandwich (if the fish isn't fried)
- ✔ Flounder stuffed with crab (with little butter, cream, or cheese)
- ✔ Frog legs (steamed, poached, broiled, baked, or grilled)
- ✔ Gefilte fish
- ✔ Lobster tails (without butter)
- ✔ Manhattan clam chowder (without bacon)
- ✔ Marinated herring (without sour cream)
- ✔ Oyster stew (with skim milk and little butter)
- ✔ Pike dishes
- ✔ Poached fish
- ✔ Salmon loaf
- ✔ Sardines in mustard or hot sauce
- ✔ Seviche
- ✔ Shrimp teriyaki (with little oil)
- ✔ Smoked fish or oysters
- ✔ Soft-shell crabs (baked without cream, cheese, or butter)
- ✔ Sole Duglère
- ✔ Sole Florentine
- ✔ Sole Véronique (with grapes but very little butter)
- ✔ Sweet and sour fish or shellfish (with little oil)

Cooks and chefs do countless things to make extremely fatty dishes from healthful lowfat fish. For example, watch out for fish in cream or cheese sauce, batter-fried fish and shellfish, butter-sautéed fish and shellfish, and fish or shellfish with butter dips. The following fish and shellfish dishes, many of which are made and served in some of these ways, are usually high in total fat, saturated fat, and cholesterol:

- Batter-fried calamari, oysters, or shrimp
- Brandade de Morue
- Codfish balls, fried
- Crab or fish cakes, fried
- Deep-fat-fried soft-shell crabs
- Fast-food fish sandwiches
- Fish au gratin
- Fish marguery
- Fish mousse
- Flounder stuffed with crab (can be lowfat)
- Lobster Newburg
- Lobster Thermidor
- Marinated herring in sour cream
- New England clam chowder (cream- or milk-based)
- Oyster stew
- Shrimp tempura
- Escargot (snails)
- Sole Ambassadeur
- Sole Meunière
- Sole Véronique (with grapes and a lot of butter)
- Stuffed lobster (with butter, cream, or cheese)
- Tuna fish sandwich

# Fabulous Fish Concoctions

These recipes give you an idea of the wide variety of flavors that you can add to fish. As I mentioned earlier, you can substitute another type of fish for the type listed in many of the recipes, such as any of the mild-tasting fish: pollack, whitefish, catfish, and monkfish.

## Cod with Ginger-Orange Sauce

Lightly sweet ginger and orange go well with cod, scrod, flounder, orange roughy, or any other mild white fish, as well as shrimp or scallops. Serve this dish with rice, orzo, angel hair pasta, or cellophane noodles. Garnish with a thin scallion or chives or several mandarin orange pieces.

**Tools:** *Large nonstick skillet*

**Preparation time:** *1*

**Yield:** *4 servings*

| | |
|---|---|
| *2 tablespoons minced fresh ginger* | *1¹/₂ cups fresh orange juice* |
| *2 tablespoons finely chopped onion* | *¹/₂ teaspoon sugar* |
| *2 tablespoons fresh lemon juice* | *4 5-ounce scrod fillets* |
| *2 tablespoons sherry (optional)* | *2 tablespoons cornstarch* |
| *1 teaspoon Dijon mustard* | *1 cup orange pieces (can use canned, drained mandarin oranges)* |
| *1 tablespoon regular or low-sodium soy sauce* | *4 scallions, chopped* |

*1* Lightly coat a large nonstick skillet with no-stick vegetable oil spray. Place the ginger and onion in the skillet and cook over medium-high heat, stirring for 2 minutes or until lightly browned.

*2* Add the lemon juice, sherry (if desired), mustard, soy sauce, 1 cup of the orange juice, and sugar, and stir to mix well. Add the fish, cover, and cook over low heat for 6 to 8 minutes or until the fish is opaque.

*3* Meanwhile, in a small bowl, place the remaining ¹/₂ cup of orange juice and the cornstarch and stir to dissolve. When the fillets are cooked, remove them to a plate and cover loosely with foil to keep warm.

*4* Put the cornstarch mixture in the skillet and cook, stirring constantly, for 1 minute or until the sauce thickens. Stir in the oranges and chopped scallions. Pour the sauce over the fish.

**Nutrition at a glance (per serving):** *Total fat 1.5 g; Saturated fat 0.5 g; Protein 29 g; Dietary fiber 2 g; Carbohydrate 22 g; Cholesterol 67 g; Sodium 368 mg; % of calories from fat 6; Calories 221.*

**Lynn's orange info:** *Oranges are a good source of vitamin C and folate. Temple oranges or clementines (little tangerines) have a better, stronger taste and keep their flavor in cooking.*

## Halibut with Cajun Sauce

This slightly spicy fish goes well with rice, slightly steamed okra, or, for those of you who aren't sure of okra, green beans or asparagus. You can substitute orange roughy, pollack, or other white fish, or shrimp or scallops. If you don't have Cajun spice blend, use cayenne pepper instead.

**Tools:** *Food processor or blender, large nonstick skillet*

**Preparation time:** *2*

**Yield:** *4 servings*

*2 cups V8 or tomato juice*

*1 medium onion, peeled and quartered*

*1 stalk celery, cut in half*

*1 red bell pepper, quartered*

*4 cloves garlic, peeled and minced*

*1 teaspoon dried basil leaves*

*$^1/_2$ to 1 teaspoon dried oregano*

*$^1/_2$ teaspoon cumin*

*$^1/_4$ to $^1/_2$ teaspoon Cajun spice blend or cayenne pepper*

*4 4-ounce halibut fillets*

*Salt (optional)*

*$^1/_4$ cup chopped fresh parsley*

*1* In a food processor (or a blender that can puree), place the tomato juice, onion, celery, red pepper, garlic, basil, oregano, and cumin. Process until pureed. Pour into a large nonstick skillet. Stir in the Cajun spice blend.

*2* Bring to a boil over medium-high heat. Reduce the heat to medium-low and cook, stirring occasionally, for 10 minutes or until the mixture thickens.

*3* Add the fish. Cover and cook for 6 to 7 minutes or until the fish is opaque. Spoon the sauce onto dinner plates and place the fish on top of the sauce, sprinkling with salt (if desired) and parsley.

**Nutrition at a glance (per serving):** *Total fat 2.5 g; Saturated fat 0.5 g; Protein 23 g; Dietary fiber 2 g; Carbohydrate 11 g; Cholesterol 33 g; Sodium 539 mg; % of calories from fat 15; Calories 161.*

**Lynn's Cajun spice tips:** *Cajun spice can add lots of flavor and spicy heat to any dish. Zatarine's is one brand from New Orleans that's available almost anywhere, but you can find many varieties. Use Cajun spice to flavor marinara sauce, chili, beef, Western Oven Fries (see Chapter 15), and chicken.*

## Herbed Mahi Mahi

This mahi mahi is tender and flavorful in a simple coating of bread crumbs. Serve it with several green vegetables and rice. You can substitute flounder, halibut, red snapper, or almost any other fish if you prefer.

**Tools:** *13-x-9-inch baking dish*

**Preparation time:** *2*

**Yield:** *4 servings*

*¹/₂ cup fat-free or lowfat mayonnaise*

*¹/₄ cup fat-free Parmesan topping or grated Parmesan cheese*

*1 teaspoon dried basil*

*1 teaspoon dried oregano*

*1 tablespoon fresh lemon juice*

*2 cloves garlic, peeled and minced*

*¹/₂ cup herbed bread crumbs*

*4 4-ounce mahi mahi fillets*

*Freshly ground black pepper*

*2 tablespoons chopped fresh parsley*

*1* Preheat the oven to 350°.

*2* In a small bowl, place the mayonnaise, Parmesan cheese, basil, oregano, lemon juice, and garlic. Mix well.

*3* Place the bread crumbs on a flat plate. With your hands, rub both sides of the fish with the mayonnaise mixture, and then coat each fillet with the bread crumbs. Place the fillets in a 13-x-9-inch baking dish. Season with pepper to taste.

*4* Bake for 20 to 25 minutes or until the fish is opaque in the center. Sprinkle with the parsley and serve.

**Nutrition at a glance (per serving):** *Total fat 1.5 g; Saturated fat 0.5 g; Protein 26 g; Dietary fiber 0 g; Carbohydrate 19 g; Cholesterol 84 mg; Sodium 783 mg; % of calories from fat 6; Calories 198.*

**Lynn's bread crumb hint:** *Making herbed bread crumbs instantly with a hand blender is easy. You can use stale bread, bagels, or even pretzels — just add a pinch of dried basil, oregano, thyme, and parsley. Place one or two slices of bread in a plastic bag with the mouth of the bag wide open. Lift a hand blender up and down in the open bag to process the bread. In a few seconds, you have crumbs. (See Figure 11-1.)*

**Figure 11-1:**
Using a hand blender, making your own bread crumbs is easy.

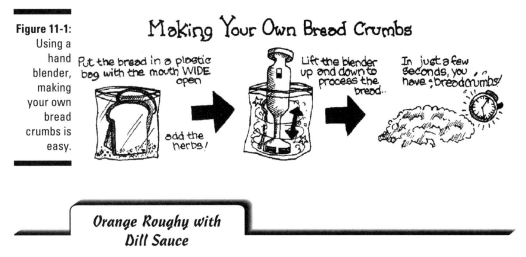

Making Your Own Bread Crumbs

Put the bread in a plastic bag with the mouth WIDE open

add the herbs!

Lift the blender up and down to process the bread..

In just a few seconds, you have bread crumbs!

## Orange Roughy with Dill Sauce

Dill and fish were meant to go together. You can substitute snapper, whitefish, pollack, cod, scrod, catfish, halibut, flounder, or scallops for the orange roughy if you prefer. Garnish with a sprig of dill.

**Tools:** *Large nonstick skillet with lid, small saucepan, whisk*

**Preparation time:** *1*

**Yield:** *4 servings*

*$^1/_2$ teaspoon freshly ground black pepper*

*4 3-ounce orange roughy fillets*

*Salt (optional)*

*1 cup liquid fat-free non-dairy creamer*

*1 cup skim milk*

*$2^1/_2$ tablespoons flour*

*1 tablespoon white wine or white Worcestershire sauce (optional)*

*3 tablespoons chopped fresh dill*

*1 tablespoon capers, drained (optional)*

**1** Rub $^1/_4$ teaspoon of the pepper into the flesh of the fillets and lightly sprinkle with salt (if desired). Lightly coat a large nonstick skillet with no-stick vegetable oil spray. Warm the skillet over medium-high heat.

**2** Put the fish in the skillet and cook for 1 minute on each side or until golden. Partially cover the skillet and cook for 10 minutes or until the fish is cooked. (Check by lightly pulling apart the center with a fork to see whether it's opaque.)

**3** While the fish is cooking, place the creamer, milk, flour, and wine or Worcestershire sauce (if desired) in a small saucepan off the heat. Whisk until smooth.

**4** Turn the heat on medium, put the saucepan on the heat, and whisk for about 4 minutes, cooking until thick. Add the dill.

*(continued)*

**5** Turn the heat as low as possible, cover, and heat for 1 minute (or more if necessary). Add more salt (if desired) and the remaining pepper.

**6** Place the fish on warmed dinner plates. Pour sauce across the middle of each fillet and sprinkle with the capers (if desired).

*Nutrition at a glance (per serving):* *Total fat 1 g; Saturated fat 0 g; Protein 16 g; Dietary fiber 0 g; Carbohydrate 31 g; Cholesterol 20 mg; Sodium 89 mg; % of calories from fat 4; Calories 203.*

*Lynn's fish facts:* *Wash each fish and pat it dry before cooking. Many folks and other fish have rubbed against your fish.*

## Potato Chip Crispy Whitefish with Tartar Sauce

Kids and kids at heart (meaning everyone!) enjoy crispy whitefish. To vary the tartar sauce, you can substitute chopped dill pickle relish, eggplant relish, or even chowchow for the sweet pickles. You can also substitute halibut, pollack, or any firm white fish. If you use regular potato chips instead of lowfat ones, you add 1 gram of fat to each serving.

*Tools:* *Baking sheet*

*Preparation time: 2*

*Yield: 4 servings*

*12 ounces halibut, cut into 4 fillets*

*Salt (optional)*

*2 egg whites*

*¹/₄ cup grated onion*

*¹/₂ cup herbed bread crumbs*

*¹/₃ to ¹/₂ cup finely ground lowfat or regular potato chips (about 10 to 12 chips)*

**1** Preheat the oven to 400°.

**2** Lightly salt the fish (if desired). Place the egg whites in a wide, shallow bowl and beat lightly with a fork until frothy. Add the onion and mix well. Place the bread crumbs and potato chips on a flat plate and mix well with a fork.

**3** Dip the fish in the egg mixture and then in the crumbs to coat it evenly on both sides.

*(continued)*

**4** Place the fish on a baking sheet and put it in the oven. Reduce the heat to 375°. Bake for 10 minutes or until the fish is opaque in the center when pulled apart slightly with a fork or the tip of a sharp knife.

*Nutrition at a glance (per serving): Total fat 3 g; Saturated fat 0.5 g; Protein 20 g; Dietary fiber 0 g; Carbohydrate 15 g; Cholesterol 25 mg; Sodium 517 mg; % of calories from fat 17; Calories 175.*

*Lynn's fish tips: You can also cut these fillets into 3-x-1-inch pieces for fish fingers. Bake the fish fingers for only 6 minutes. You can make your own bread crumbs in a food processor or hand blender in the blender cup. One and one-half to two slices make ¹/₂ cup crumbs.*

## Tartar Sauce

*Yield: 1¹/₄ cups, or 10 2-tablespoon servings*

| | |
|---|---|
| *1 cup fat-free or lowfat mayonnaise* | *2 teaspoons fresh lemon juice* |
| *1 teaspoon vinegar* | *1 teaspoon French or Dijon mustard* |
| *2 tablespoons chopped sweet pickles* | *1 tablespoon chopped fresh parsley* |
| *2 tablespoons chopped onion* | |

As the fish bakes, combine the mayonnaise, vinegar, pickles, onion, lemon juice, mustard, and parsley in a small mixing bowl and mix well. Serve with the fish.

*Nutrition at a glance (per serving): Total fat 0 g; Saturated fat 0 g; Protein 0 g; Dietary fiber 0 g; Carbohydrate 4 g; Cholesterol 0 mg; Sodium 187 mg; % of calories from fat 3; Calories 20.*

## Rockfish in a Packet

This fish recipe is flashy but simple. The flavor will surprise and delight you. You can bake it in parchment paper for a fancy presentation, or in foil — the flavor is the same. If you do it in foil, you can cook it on the grill. Substitute orange roughy, flounder, snapper, catfish, halibut, or any mild white fish that you like. You can chop all the vegetables together in a food processor to save time.

*Tools: Parchment paper (sold for baking) or foil, large roasting pan or sheet*

*Preparation time: 2*

*Yield: 4 servings*

*(continued)*

1 teaspoon butter

4 shallots or ¹/₄ cup sweet onion, finely slivered

4 4-ounce rockfish fillets

1 cup julienned carrots (matchstick size)

1 cup julienned leeks

1 cup julienned celery

8 thin slices lemon, peel and seeds removed

Salt (optional) and white or black pepper

¹/₄ cup white wine, vermouth, or white Worcestershire sauce

¹/₄ cup chopped fresh parsley

**1** Preheat the oven to 350°.

**2** Cut four sheets of baking paper or foil, each approximately 24 x 12 inches. Place the papers or foil sheets in front of you horizontally. Fold each sheet in half. With scissors, cut out half a large, fat heart. Open to reveal the heart shape. (See Figure 11-2.)

**3** Rub a slick of butter on the hearts (but leave ¹/₂ inch around the edge unbuttered). Divide the shallots or onion slivers and sprinkle them only on the right side of the four paper or foil hearts. Place a fish fillet on each pile of shallots.

**4** Sprinkle on the carrots, leeks, and celery. Add 2 slices lemon to each packet. Add salt (if desired) and pepper to taste, and 1 tablespoon wine, vermouth, or white Worcestershire sauce. Fold over the empty side of the heart half, carefully crimp the edges, and bake for about 6 minutes in a large roasting pan or on a baking sheet. Garnish with chopped fresh parsley.

***Nutrition at a glance (per serving):*** *Total fat 3 g; Saturated fat 1 g; Protein 22 g; Dietary fiber 2 g; Carbohydrate 10 g; Cholesterol 40 mg; Sodium 120 mg; % of calories from fat 16; Calories 162.*

***Lynn's fish tip:*** *Don't overcook fish. As soon as it flakes and is opaque, it's done.*

## Making a Packet

**Figure 11-2:** Elegant-looking Rockfish in a Packet isn't difficult to put together.

**1.** Fold the 4 pieces of foil in half, cut out a half a large heart and open to reveal the whole heart shape.

**2.** Rub a slick of butter on each heart. Divide the shallots and sprinkle on all 4 hearts. Place a fillet on each pile of shallots.

**3.** Sprinkle on the vegetables, add 2 lemon slices and seasoning to each packet.

**4.** Fold over the empty side of the heart, carefully crimp the edges and bake for about 6 minutes. Garnish with chopped parsley.

## Shrimp and Crab Gumbo

A rich stew, this New Orleans dish came directly from Dixie Gillette, a New Orleans belle who knows her Creole. Serve gumbo with cooked white or brown rice, a green vegetable or two, and a fruit salad. It's great for company because you can double the recipe or make it in advance. If making in advance, don't stir in the shrimp and crab after reheating or they'll toughen. You can add other vegetables, such as green beans, carrots, and peas, too.

***Tools:*** *Large nonstick soup pot*

***Preparation time:*** *3*

***Yield:*** *6 servings*

*3 strips bacon, all visible fat removed, cut into 1-inch pieces (about 1 ounce meat)*

*1 medium onion, peeled and chopped*

*1 clove garlic, peeled and minced*

*¹/₂ green bell pepper, chopped*

*¹/₂ celery stalk, chopped*

*1 bay leaf*

*6 medium tomatoes, chopped (juice reserved), or 1 28-ounce can chopped tomatoes (juice reserved)*

*¹/₂ pound okra (about 12 to 15 okras), finely sliced*

*2 cups defatted chicken stock or oyster liquor*

*2 teaspoons chopped fresh thyme, or 1 teaspoon dried*

*2 tablespoons chopped fresh parsley*

*1 teaspoon brown sugar*

*¹/₄ cup herbed bread crumbs*

*1 teaspoon hot pepper sauce (optional)*

*8 ounces shelled medium shrimp (about 12), cut in half lengthwise*

*6 ounces back fin crab meat*

*Salt (optional) and freshly ground black pepper*

*2 tablespoons filé powder (optional)*

**1** Lightly coat a large nonstick soup pot with no-stick vegetable oil spray. Place over medium heat, add the bacon, and stir, heating for about 2 minutes.

**2** Add the onions, garlic, green pepper, and celery and sauté, stirring for about 5 minutes or until the onions are translucent. (Add a teaspoon of water if necessary to prevent scorching.)

**3** Add the bay leaf, the juice of the tomatoes, and the okra. Cook, stirring occasionally, for about 4 minutes or until golden.

*(continued)*

**4** Add the chicken stock or oyster liquor and bring to a boil over medium-high heat. Reduce the heat to medium.

**5** Add the tomatoes, thyme, parsley, brown sugar, bread crumbs, and hot pepper sauce (if desired) and bring to a boil. Reduce the heat to medium-low and simmer, covered, for 1 hour.

**6** When nearly ready to serve, remove the bay leaf and add the shrimp and crab. Cook for 2 to 3 minutes or until the shrimp turn pink. Taste and add additional hot pepper sauce, salt (if desired) and pepper, and filé powder (if desired).

*Nutrition at a glance (per serving): Total fat 1.5 g; Saturated fat 0.5 g; Protein 18 g; Dietary fiber 3 g; Carbohydrate 16 g; Cholesterol 76 mg; Sodium 435 mg; % of calories from fat 10; Calories 145.*

*Lynn's Creole history: Creole and Cajun are similar — a riotous blend of many cultures, including French, French Canadian, Spanish, African American, and African, with a smidgen of Italian, Hispanic, and Native American. Both cuisines build on the trinity of green peppers, onions, and celery, and both use filé powder, a spice derived from the sassafras tree and available in most fancy food stores. Filé is never cooked but is stirred into the dish just before serving.*

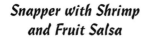

### Snapper with Shrimp and Fruit Salsa

This dish is colorful and tastes glorious — perfect for a summer dinner party or when you want a sparkly taste. You can substitute mahi mahi, swordfish, bonito, or other fish, and you can broil, pan-fry, or grill the seafood instead. Serve the dish with snow peas and black beans, which the salsa complements.

*Tools: Large nonstick skillet*

*Preparation time: 1*

*Yield: 4 servings*

### Snapper with Shrimp

*4 4-ounce snapper fillets*

*2 teaspoons fresh lime or lemon juice*

*4 ounces medium shelled shrimp (about 6 to 8), cut in half lengthwise*

**1** Coat both sides of the snapper fillets with no-stick vegetable oil spray, and lightly spray a large nonstick skillet. Warm the skillet over medium-high heat. Put the snapper in the skillet and sear for 1 minute on each side or until brown.

*(continued)*

**2** Add the lime or lemon juice. Reduce the heat to medium, cover, and cook for 4 minutes. Add the shrimp, cover, and cook for 2 to 3 minutes or until the shrimp are pink.

*Nutrition at a glance (per serving): Total fat 2 g; Saturated fat 0.5 g; Protein 21 g; Dietary fiber 3 g; Carbohydrate 21 g; Cholesterol 68 mg; Sodium 88 mg; % of calories from fat 9; Calories 179.*

## Fruit Salsa

You'll have some of this salsa left over for a bean dish.

*1 cup fresh pineapple chunks*

*1 cup diced mangoes or peaches*

*¹/₂ cup white seedless grapes, halved*

*4 scallions, sliced*

*¹/₂ teaspoon finely diced jalapeño pepper*

*1 small clove garlic, peeled and minced*

*1 red bell pepper, finely diced*

*¹/₂ cup fresh lime or lemon juice*

*¹/₄ cup chopped fresh cilantro*

*1 tablespoon chopped fresh mint*

While the fish is cooking, combine the pineapple, mangoes or peaches, grapes, garlic, red pepper, lime or lemon juice, cilantro, mint, scallions, and jalapeño pepper in a medium bowl and mix well to blend. Serve with the fish and shrimp.

*Lynn's mango-cutting tip: To dice a fresh mango, cut it in half lengthwise, slightly off center, just touching the large, flat oval pit with your knife. Cut crosswise with a sharp knife, making ¹/₂-inch slits on the flesh side, not cutting through the skin. Then score in the other direction ¹/₂ inch apart. Turn the flesh inside out, and the cubes pop forward, ready to be removed or eaten off the skin. Do the same with the remaining half of the fruit. (See Figure 11-3.)*

**Figure 11-3:**
Avoid a lot of hassle by using this mango-cutting method.

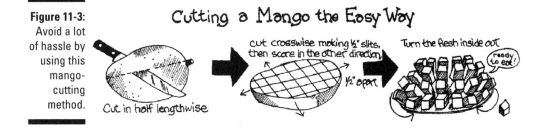

Cutting a Mango the Easy Way

Cut in half lengthwise

cut crosswise making ½" slits, then score in the other direction, ½" apart

Turn the flesh inside out

ready to eat!

## Sole Meunière

Serve the following celebrated and classic dish with new potatoes, green vegetables such as asparagus, broccoli, or green beans, a salad with tomatoes, and cheesecake (see Chapter 17) for dessert, and you have an elegant repast. This fish is particularly simple to make. You can substitute scrod, monkfish, shrimp, or any white fish.

**Tools:** *Large nonstick skillet, whisk*

**Preparation time:** *1*

**Yield:** *4 servings*

| | |
|---|---|
| *1 16-ounce can fat-free chicken broth* | *¹/₂ cup water* |
| *¹/₂ cup white wine* | *¹/₃ cup chopped fresh parsley* |
| *4 4-ounce Dover sole or flounder fillets* | *1 tablespoon fresh lemon juice* |
| *¹/₄ cup flour* | *2 teaspoons butter* |

**1** In a large nonstick skillet over medium-high heat, place the chicken broth and wine. Heat so that the liquid simmers but doesn't boil.

**2** Place the fish in the simmering liquid and cook for 7 to 8 minutes or until the fish flakes easily. Remove the fish to a heated plate and cover loosely with foil to keep it warm.

**3** Keep the poaching liquid lightly simmering and make the sauce very quickly. Whisk the flour with ¹/₂ cup water in a small bowl. To the simmering stock in the skillet, add the parsley, lemon juice, and butter and stir. Slowly pour the flour mixture into the skillet, constantly stirring with a whisk, until the mixture has thickened and cooked for about 3 minutes. Serve the sauce over the fish.

*Nutrition at a glance (per serving):* Total fat 3 g; Saturated fat 1.5 g; Protein 23 g; Dietary fiber 0 g; Carbohydrate 7 g; Cholesterol 58 mg; Sodium 186 mg; % of calories from fat 17; Calories 174.

*Lynn's fresh tips:* Using fresh lemon juice, fresh parsley, and fresh fish makes an enormous difference in the good taste of lowfat dishes like this one.

## Spiced Shrimp

Spiced shrimp are a family favorite. Serve these shrimp cold or hot, with or without the shells, letting people peel their own and dip them in cocktail sauce or Spicy Dipping Sauce. Serve with Western Oven Fries (see Chapter 15).

**Tools:** *2-quart saucepan*

**Preparation time:** *1*

**Yield:** *4 servings*

*12 ounces light beer, or 1 cup water*

*6 fresh basil leaves, or 1 teaspoon dried basil*

*$^1/_2$ to 1 teaspoon crushed red pepper (flakes) (optional)*

*$^1/_2$ teaspoon dried oregano*

*$^1/_2$ teaspoon dried thyme*

*$^1/_4$ teaspoon hot pepper sauce (optional)*

*$^1/_2$ teaspoon onion salt*

*2 tablespoons chili powder*

*12 ounces medium shrimp in the shell (about 15)*

**1** In a 2-quart saucepan, place the beer or water, basil, red pepper (if desired), oregano, thyme, hot pepper sauce (if desired), onion salt, and chili powder. Whisk to combine.

**2** Bring the mixture to a boil over medium-high heat. Add the shrimp.

**3** Reduce the heat to medium, cover, and cook for 1 to 2 minutes or until the shrimp are opaque and bright pink. Remove from the heat and drain. If serving chilled, place the shrimp in an ice bath and drain again to both stop the cooking and chill quickly.

### Spicy Dipping Sauce

*$^1/_2$ cup ketchup*

*1 tablespoon grated horseradish (optional)*

*1 tablespoon brown sugar*

*$^1/_4$ teaspoon hot pepper sauce*

*$^1/_2$ teaspoon prepared mustard*

*$^1/_2$ teaspoon soy sauce*

In a small bowl, combine the ketchup, horseradish (if desired), brown sugar, hot pepper sauce, mustard, and soy sauce and mix well. Serve with the shrimp.

**Nutrition at a glance (per serving):** *Total fat 1 g; Saturated fat 0.5 g; Protein 12 g; Dietary fiber 1 g; Carbohydrate 14 g; Cholesterol 101 mg; Sodium 716 mg; % of calories from fat 8; Calories 117.*

**Lynn's shrimp note:** *To spice shrimp only lightly, add 1 tablespoon Old Bay Seasoning to 1 inch white wine or beer. Steam for 3 minutes or until opaque and bright pink.*

# Chapter 12

# Meat and Poultry

. . . . . . . . . . . . . . . . . . . . . . . . . . . . .

## In This Chapter

▶ Including meat and poultry in a lowfat eating plan

▶ Cooking meat and poultry in lowfat ways

▶ Identifying meat and poultry dishes that are usually low or high in total fat, saturated fat, and cholesterol

. . . . . . . . . . . . . . . . . . . . . . . . . . . . .

*"**B**eef is a good meate for an Englisshe man, so be it the beest be yonge, & that it be not cowe fleshe. . . . Veal is good and easily digested, Brawn [boar] is an usual meate in winter."*

— Andrew Boorde, monk, physician, and writer, from *A Dyetary of health,* 1542

For most people, eating healthfully is a struggle. Fast-paced lifestyles, and the foods that supermarkets and restaurants offer, don't make eating lowfat easy. That bacon-cheeseburger that you grabbed from a fast-food joint, for example, can easily contain more fat than you should consume in a day.

Three major problems exist with meat and poultry:

✔ An overabundance of fatty cuts

✔ High-fat preparation methods

✔ Too-large portions

The bottom line is that if you like red meat, lamb, pork, chicken, turkey, and duck, you can still enjoy them. You need to buy them wisely, selecting lean or skinless, keep the serving sizes reasonable (about 3 ounces), and keep the preparation method sensible to keep the fat low. (You can find many more details about various cuts of meat and poultry and appropriate servings sizes in Chapter 5.) This chapter gives you complete directions for preparing meat and poultry in lowfat, easy, and tasty ways. You'll find lists of the fattiest meat and poultry dishes and lists of the leanest, and also seven recipes: two each of beef and chicken, and one each of lamb, pork, and turkey. All meat recipes, like all the recipes in the book, qualify as lowfat, according to government definitions.

# Cooking Beef, Pork, Lamb, Chicken, or Turkey in Lowfat Ways

The way you prepare even lean or skinless meat or poultry trimmed of all visible fat can have a huge impact on the fat content of the finished dish. Many cuts are naturally low in fat if you remove the skin (for poultry) and trim off all the visible fat (for meat and poultry), but your efforts are wasted if you then fry the meat or poultry coated in batter, oil, or butter and serve it with a high-fat sauce. The following sections talk about some of the lowest-fat cooking methods to try so that you can keep meat and poultry in your lowfat eating plan.

## Baking and roasting

All meat and poultry can be baked successfully in ovenproof plastic wrap, roasted on a rotisserie or a V-shaped roasting rack, roasted alone with herbs and spices, or roasted with vegetables. Roasting produces a moist interior and toughened exterior and helps to drip away exterior and interior fat. If you're making a gravy, make sure to defat the juices first.

## Boiling

Boiling beef or chicken removes fat by releasing some of the fat into the water. This method is good for several dishes, such as boiled beef and cabbage, boiled chicken, and especially boiled chicken wings. You can also boil beef or pork ribs before grilling to remove some of the fat.

## Broiling

Broiling reduces the amount of fat in meat and poultry. You do most broiling with smaller meat pieces, such as chops, steaks, ham slices, and chicken legs and breasts (you can remove the skin from poultry before broiling). Small quail and dove can be broiled, too.

Rub the meat or poultry to be broiled with a sauce, spices, and herbs if you like. Place it 4 inches from the broiler and, depending on the meat, broil it for 5 to 10 minutes per inch of thickness, being careful not to burn the meat. Broiling can also be done on a tipped or elevated-on-one-end countertop grill, from which the fat runs out, or in a toaster oven.

# Grilling

This method is good for all meat and poultry. Meat can be marinated first and then grilled or barbecued over coals, wood, or an electric grill. Grill whole cuts, such as a butterflied leg of lamb (lamb that has the bone removed and is split open with all visible fat removed), a London broil, Cornish game hens, chicken or turkey parts (skinned and all visible fat removed), or quail. Grilling can also be done on a stovetop grill.

*Note:* Grilling in foil actually steams the meat or poultry.

When grilling, you can brush on a tasty sauce, but don't use the same basting sauce for the cooked meat or poultry as you do for the raw. Doing so can cross-contaminate the cooked meat or poultry with bacteria from the raw meat or poultry.

# Microwaving

Microwaves can cook small pieces of meat and poultry in 5 minutes or so on high. Most meats cooked in microwaves don't brown, so spicing helps the look as well as the taste. Microwave whole skinned chickens placed in an ovenproof bag, turkey fillets in a sauce, or beef, lamb, or pork in sauces or stews.

# Pan-frying (also known as pan-searing or dry-frying)

Lightly coat beef, lamb, pork, skinned chicken or turkey fillets with no-stick vegetable oil spray. Heat on high in a nonstick skillet also lightly coated with no-stick spray to sear and brown. Then lower the heat and cook until well done. Meats can also be lightly dredged in flour, shaken to remove excess flour, lightly coated with no-stick spray, and dry-fried.

Well-done meat has less fat. The longer the meat cooks, the more fat drips out.

## Poaching and braising

To poach or braise is to cook a food in liquid. Poached or braised beef, pork, lamb, chicken, or turkey — whole or fillets — are usually browned first and then covered or partially covered with a liquid such as vegetable broth, defatted stock, water, or wine and cooked some more. Poaching or braising is done over very low heat, in the oven or on the stovetop, in a pan covered with a tight lid. This method allows tough cuts of meat like stew meat to become tender.

You can remove the fat from the liquid in which the meat or poultry was cooked. Use a defatting cup (or chill until the fat congeals) so that you can use the flavorful liquid as a sauce base.

## Pressure-cooking

This method is especially good for cooking meat and poultry fast, and for infusing moisture into tougher cuts of meat, such as stewing beef. (A pressure cooker is a cooking pan with a tight lid and a steam release.)

## Smoking and drying

Smoked turkey and other cuts of meat, such as pork and ham, have a special, sweet flavor that is achieved no other way. Electric and charcoal briquette smokers are available just for smoking. Because smoking can take several hours, it allows fats to drip away from the meat as the meat cooks.

Beef jerky used to be made by flavoring and drying meat in the sun. Some people still make beef jerky this way, but most people buy the commercially made product.

## Stir-frying (also known as strip-frying)

To stir-fry or strip-fry, remove all visible fat from a cut of beef, pork, lamb, turkey, or chicken. Then cut it into thin strips (using small pieces of meat allows you to remove more fat), lightly coat it with no-stick vegetable oil spray, and quickly cook and sear it over high heat, tossing and stirring at the same time. You can dredge the meat in flour first if you want to.

When cutting small pieces and removing all the visible fat, it helps if the meat is partially frozen.

# Lowfat Cuts of Meat and Poultry and the Best Ways to Cook Them

These cuts and meats are listed in order from least to most fat. Remember, using your eyes is the best way to judge how much fat is in the particular cut you want to purchase.

- ✔ **Turkey, whole or pieces:** The meat or poultry with the least fat is a turkey breast cutlet or fillet without skin and visible fat. In 4 or 5 minutes, these can be pan-seared (browned) plain, with a spice or herb rub, or with fat-free or lowfat mayonnaise, soy sauce, Worcestershire sauce, or lowfat or fat-free Italian or other salad dressing. Fillets can be microwaved, stir-fried, or braised, too. And they can be cooked by these methods without the skin. Roast or bake all turkey breast with skin and remove the skin before eating.

- ✔ **Canadian bacon:** The meat with the next lowest amount of fat can be baked, pan-fried in no-stick vegetable oil spray or maple syrup, grilled, or microwaved.

- ✔ **Ham, whole or slices:** Ham, a meat that's low in fat if it's lean and all visible fat is removed, can be baked, pan-fried in no-stick vegetable oil spray or maple syrup, grilled, or microwaved.

- ✔ **Chicken, whole or pieces:** Pan-sear (brown) a breast in 4 or 5 minutes with or without spice or herb rubs, soy sauce, Worcestershire sauce, or lowfat or fat-free Italian or other salad dressing. You can also Southern-fry chicken by skinning it, dredging it in flour, lightly spraying it with no-stick vegetable oil spray, and dry-frying it. Or dip it in lowfat batter and oven-bake it.

  Chicken can also be pan-seared, stir-fried, roasted or microwaved, baked stuffed whole, pressure-cooked, poached, boiled, or added to soups and stews. Because chicken is fattier than turkey, you can remove its skin before baking.

- ✔ **Beef tenderloin, round or sirloin steaks, or strips:** Beef can be relatively low in fat when it is lean and all visible fat is removed. Stir-fry, grill, broil, microwave, pressure-cook, or bake pieces or strips in stews.

- ✔ **Pork tenderloin, chops or pieces:** Pork pieces or chops can be low in fat if it is zero-trimmed, meaning that no fat is left on the edges. Stir-fry pieces or strips; or remove all visible fat from chops and then grill, broil, or pan-fry without added fat.

- ✔ **Beef roasts (filet, top round, or London broil):** Cut away all the fat and then roast a top round or broil or grill a London broil or filet to medium well so that internal fats can drip away.

- ✔ **Pork roasts:** Cut away all the visible fat and then roast, broil, or grill until well done so that internal fats can drip away.

- ✔ **Lamb, pieces or whole leg:** You can broil or pan-fry lamb without extra fat (except a small amount of no-stick vegetable oil spray). When lamb is cooked in a stew, you can't remove the fat (unless you chill it first and skim the congealed fat from the surface), but trim the lamb well before cooking. Or grill a whole butterflied leg, removing all visible fat first (which takes a long time).

- ✔ **Beef, turkey, or pork hot dogs or hamburgers:** Hot dogs can have no fat, have little fat, or be high in fat. Grill, microwave, pan-fry without extra fat, or boil fat-free or lowfat dogs. When hamburgers have little fat, the meat doesn't hold together. One solution is to select your hamburger meat from an exceptionally lean top round, have the meat cutter grind it, and add cooked bulgur wheat, moistened TVP (textured vegetable protein), egg whites, or bread crumbs.

# Finding the Fat in Red Meat Recipes

These dishes, if made with lean meat to start and with little added fat, can be lower in fat than other red meat dishes. Chili, for example, can have almost no fat, depending on the fat content of the meat, the type of meat (pork or beef versus turkey), and how much meat you use.

- ✔ Beef Stroganoff (with a small portion of lean meat and fat-free or lowfat sour cream)
- ✔ Beef stew (with a small portion of lean meat)
- ✔ Châteaubriand (if the meat portion isn't too large and it is well done)
- ✔ Chili (with a small portion of lean meat)
- ✔ Chinese firepot
- ✔ Fajitas (with a small portion of lean meat)
- ✔ Lamb ragout
- ✔ Lamb kebabs (with a small portion of lean meat)
- ✔ Pork chow mein (if lean)
- ✔ Rabbit stew
- ✔ Saurbraten
- ✔ Sukiyaki (if lean)
- ✔ Sweet and sour pork (if lean, not breaded and fried, and with a small portion of pork)

✔ Swiss steak (if lean and no more than 3 ounces)

✔ Tripe

✔ Venison pot roast

These dishes are usually high in total fat, saturated fat, and cholesterol:

✔ Beef bourguignonne

✔ Beef stew

✔ Beef stroganoff

✔ Beef Wellington

✔ Breaded pork chops

✔ Chili (with meat)

✔ Chicken or veal cordon bleu

✔ Corned beef and cabbage

✔ Fajitas

✔ Fried pork chops

✔ Goulash

✔ Hamburger or cheeseburger pie

✔ Ham loaf

✔ Hash (corned beef)

✔ Irish stew

✔ Lasagna with lots of meat, sausage, or cheese

✔ Leg or rack of lamb (with no fat removed)

✔ Liver and onions (can be made lowfat but not low in cholesterol)

✔ Meat loaf

✔ Meatballs

✔ Oxtail ragout

✔ Pan-fried steak

✔ Pasta or macaroni Bolognese with sausage

✔ Pork barbecue

✔ Pork pie

✔ Pork roast

✔ Pork sausage

- Pot roast
- Salisbury steak
- Southern short ribs
- Steak and kidney pie
- Steak au poivre (can be moderately low in fat if the portion isn't large)
- Steak Diane (can be moderately low in fat if the portion isn't large)
- Stuffed crown roast
- Sweetbreads (also high in cholesterol)
- Tournedos (depending on the sauce; can be lowfat if the portion isn't large and the meat is lean)
- Veal Oscar
- Veal Parmesan
- Veal scaloppini

The trick to eating meat on a lowfat eating plan is to serve small portions (3 ounces) of lean cuts prepared with little fat and enjoy them to the max.

## The ten leanest cuts of beef

These cuts tend to be lower in total fat and saturated fat than other cuts of meat, but one filet mignon can differ widely from another, so this list is a general guide only. Cut off all visible or edge fat to keep these cuts as lean as possible.

- Filet mignon
- Top round
- Round steak
- Round tip
- Top sirloin
- Shank crosscut
- Rump roast
- Top loin
- Bottom round
- Tenderloin

# Picking Out the Fat in Poultry Dishes

These dishes often can be lower in fat, depending on how they are prepared and whether they are made with skinless breast meat, all visible fat removed, and the poultry is in small amounts.

- ✔ Baked, boiled, broiled, grilled, or poached skinless chicken or skinned turkey breast, all visible fat removed
- ✔ Brunswick stew
- ✔ Chicken or turkey in aspic
- ✔ Chicken or turkey cacciatore
- ✔ Chicken or turkey Creole
- ✔ Chicken or turkey fricassee (without pan gravy, unless it's defatted)
- ✔ Chicken or turkey kebabs, or turkey breast fillets (skinned and trimmed of all visible fat)
- ✔ Chicken or turkey loaf
- ✔ Chicken or turkey salad (without excess mayonnaise)
- ✔ Chicken or turkey stew
- ✔ Chicken or turkey stir-fry
- ✔ Chicken or turkey teriyaki
- ✔ Oven-fried chicken or turkey
- ✔ Paella (without sausage or butter)

These dishes are usually very high in fat, although some can be made lower in fat.

- ✔ Batter-fried chicken or turkey
- ✔ Chicken liver mousse
- ✔ Chicken and biscuits or dumplings with gravy
- ✔ Chicken or turkey à la king
- ✔ Chicken or turkey croquettes
- ✔ Chicken or turkey divan (depending on how it's made)
- ✔ Chicken or turkey hash (depending on how it's made)
- ✔ Chicken or turkey Kiev
- ✔ Chicken or turkey paprikash (depending on how it's made)
- ✔ Chicken or turkey pot pie

✔ Chopped, fried chicken livers (depending on how they're made)

✔ Coq au vin (depending on how it's made)

✔ Creamed chicken or turkey

✔ Crispy duck

✔ Curried chicken or turkey (depending on how it's made)

✔ Duck, chicken, or turkey à l'orange

✔ Goose, chicken, or duck pâté

✔ Peking duck

✔ Roast goose

# Magnificent Meat and Poultry Recipes

Just because you're watching your fat intake doesn't mean that you have to subsist on bland, boring foods. These zippy dishes will make you a believer that lowfat is a healthy, natural, and tasty way to eat. In fact, lowfat is the healthiest way to eat meat.

## Two great and easy beef recipes

In this section, I rework two common beef recipes that every cook should have in his or her repertoire.

### Beef Fajitas

With fragrant hot strips of green, red, and yellow bell peppers, onion slices, and spicy beef all wrapped in a warm tortilla, fajitas are a favorite. Garnish with fat-free or lowfat sour cream, fat-free or lowfat shredded Cheddar cheese, salsa or diced tomatoes, and a sprig or two of cilantro. For a beverage, serve lemonade, Mexican beer, or sangria. Make sure to allow time to marinate the meat for several hours.

**Tools:** *Nonstick skillet, broiler*

**Preparation time:** *3*

**Yield:** *4 servings*

*(continued)*

$^1/_4$ cup salsa

1 teaspoon sugar

$^1/_2$ teaspoon salt (optional)

1 teaspoon chili powder

2 cloves garlic, peeled and minced

1 teaspoon dried oregano

12 ounces lean top round or skirt steak, cut in 1-inch-wide, $^1/_4$-inch-thick x 3-inches-long strips, all visible fat removed

4 fat-free flour tortillas

1 large Spanish onion, peeled and sliced

1 small green bell pepper, cut lengthwise into $^1/_2$-inch wide strips

1 small red bell pepper, cut lengthwise into $^1/_2$-inch wide strips

1 small yellow bell pepper, cut lengthwise into $^1/_2$-inch wide strips

*1* In a sealable plastic bag, put the salsa, sugar, salt (if desired), chili powder, garlic, and oregano. Add the meat strips, seal the bag, make sure that the sauce is well mixed and that all the meat gets sauce on it, and let marinate in the refrigerator for at least 2 hours, or even overnight, turning once or twice.

*2* Wrap the flat tortillas in aluminum foil and heat in a 350° oven for about 15 minutes. Remove and keep warm. Or microwave the tortillas wrapped flat in damp paper towels for 1 minute.

*3* Lightly coat a nonstick skillet with no-stick vegetable oil spray. Remove the meat from the marinade and set aside. Add the marinade to the skillet and let cook for several minutes. Add the onion and peppers, stirring and cooking over medium heat for 2 to 3 minutes. Turn off the heat and cover.

*4* Place the broiler tray 4 inches from the flame or coils and heat the broiler.

*5* Place the beef strips on aluminum foil and place the foil on the broiler tray. Broil for 3 to 4 minutes or until lightly browned. Turn over and brown for another 3 minutes.

*6* Remove the beef. Add it to the cooked onion and peppers and cook on high for 1 minute, tossing to blend the flavors. Wrap the beef, pepper, and onion mixture in the warm tortillas and garnish as desired.

***Nutrition at a glance (per serving):*** *Total fat 2.5 g; Saturated fat 1 g; Protein 25 g; Dietary fiber 3 g; Carbohydrate 25 g; Cholesterol 54 mg; Sodium 393 mg; % of calories from fat 11; Calories 230.*

***Lynn's meat tips:*** *If you cut beef into small enough strips, it almost doesn't matter how tough it is. You can use lean raw or cooked lamb, raw or cooked pork, or skinned chicken instead of beef if you prefer. Fajitas can also be made vegetarian by using more peppers and onions.*

## Meat Loaf

A flavorful slice of meat loaf is a family favorite, but meat loaf is usually very high in fat. This is a good time to try TVP (textured vegetable protein), available in many chains and health food stores. TVP can stretch your meat dollars and cut down on fat. Many meals, such as chili, tacos, and stuffed peppers, can benefit. It tastes good, and its texture is similar to beef even though it is a vegetable product. If you can't find TVP, try the same amount of cooked and well-drained bulgur wheat or rice.

**Tools:** *8-inch loaf pan*

**Preparation time:** *3*

**Yield:** *8 servings*

*10 ounces lean ground top round (have the meat cutter grind your lean round selection), all visible fat removed*

*1 carrot, shredded*

*2 stalks celery, sliced*

*1 large onion, peeled and chopped*

*3 tablespoons Worcestershire sauce*

*2 egg whites, or ¹/₂ cup substitute eggs*

*1 cup TVP, with the water amount called for on the package, or add 1 cup boiling water and let sit for 15 minutes to reconstitute (You can substitute cooked white or brown rice or bulgur wheat.)*

*3 tablespoons herbed bread crumbs*

*Salt (optional)*

*¹/₂ cup ketchup*

*1* Preheat the oven to 375°.

*2* In a large bowl, mix the ground round, carrot, celery, onion, Worcestershire sauce, egg whites or substitute eggs, TVP, bread crumbs, and salt (if desired).

*3* Place the meat loaf in an 8-inch loaf pan. Spread the ketchup on top and bake for 1 hour. Slice carefully.

**Nutrition at a glance (per serving):** *Total fat 2.5 g; Saturated fat 1 g; Protein 17 g; Dietary fiber 4 g; Carbohydrate 15 g; Cholesterol 20 mg; Sodium 356 mg; % of calories from fat 15; Calories 139.*

**Lynn's meat loaf layering tips:** *You can make this dish with optional layers of 1 cup each of julienned carrots; julienned yellow, red, or green bell peppers; 6 hard-cooked egg whites, slivered; 1 pound chopped spinach, parboiled and well drained (or chopped frozen and thawed, water pressed out); and sliced mushrooms. To make layers, place 1 inch of the meat loaf in the pan, add 1 or more layers, cover with 1 inch of meat loaf and the topping, and bake as usual.*

# *A great and easy pork recipe*

Pork is a very versatile meat, as you can see from the following recipe.

## Sweet and Sour Pork

This dish is considered Chinese in origin, but it has become an American favorite. For spicy heat, sprinkle on crushed red pepper. Garnish with chopped scallions and serve with rice to maintain the Chinese theme.

**Tools:** *Large nonstick skillet*

**Preparation time:** *2*

**Yield:** *4 servings*

*1 clove garlic, peeled and minced*

*1 large onion, peeled and coarsely chopped*

*1 green bell pepper, cut into 1-inch pieces, seeds reserved*

*1 carrot, julienned*

*10 ounces lean pork tenderloin, all visible fat removed, cut into ³/₄-inch cubes*

*1 tablespoon cornstarch*

*¹/₄ cup brown sugar*

*2 tablespoons rice wine (mirin) or vinegar or cider vinegar*

*2 tablespoons low-sodium soy sauce*

*1 8-ounce can pineapple chunks, juice reserved*

*¹/₄ cup chopped scallions*

*1* Lightly coat a large nonstick skillet with no-stick vegetable oil spray. Add the garlic, onion, pepper, and carrot and lightly spray the vegetables.

*2* Over medium heat, cook the vegetables for about 10 minutes, tossing and stirring frequently (add a few tablespoons of water for moisture if necessary). Remove the vegetables to a bowl and lightly cover with foil.

*3* Increase the heat to medium-high. Add the pork cubes and cook for about 6 minutes or until the pork cubes are no longer pink in the center, stirring occasionally.

*4* In a small bowl, combine the cornstarch, brown sugar, vinegar, soy sauce, pineapple juice, and enough water to total ³/₄ cup.

*5* Add the cornstarch mixture to the skillet with the meat, stirring until it begins to thicken, about 1 minute. Stir in the pineapple chunks and cooked vegetables, cooking on high for about 1 minute. Garnish with the chopped scallions.

*(continued)*

*Nutrition at a glance (per serving):* Total fat 3 g; Saturated fat 1 g; Protein 17 g;
Dietary fiber 2 g; Carbohydrate 32 g; Cholesterol 42 mg; Sodium 349 mg; % of calories
from fat 11; Calories 215.

*Lynn's pork additions:* You can add other foods, such as a red bell peppers, snow
peas, water chestnuts, and mandarin oranges, to sweet and sour pork.

# A great and easy lamb recipe

Don't be afraid to try lamb instead of pork or beef for a delightfully different
taste — especially if you like spicy and flavorful cuisines such as Mediterranean and Spanish. The cooking techniques you use are similar to those for
beef and pork. Just be sure to select lean lamb and remove all visible fat.

## Lamb and Eggplant with Rice and Tomatoes

A mound of fluffy rice topped with pan-fried lamb, eggplant, and onions, with bright
red tomatoes on top, is not only pretty but also absolutely delicious. The lamb,
eggplant, and onions are better when marinated. Tuck in some parsley sprigs around
the edges for a delightfully attractive dish.

*Tools:* Large saucepan, large nonstick skillet

*Preparation time:* 3

*Yield:* 6 servings

3 tablespoons low-sodium soy sauce

3 tablespoons Worcestershire sauce

1 tablespoon minced garlic

Salt (optional) and freshly ground black
pepper

9 ounces lean lamb, all visible fat
removed, cut into 1-inch cubes

1 pound eggplant, cut into 1-inch cubes

4 medium onions, peeled and cut into
quarters

5 cups water

2¹/₂ cups dry white or brown rice

5 summer-ripe tomatoes, stem remnant
removed, very coarsely chopped

*(continued)*

**1** In a gallon-sized plastic zipper bag, place the soy sauce, Worcestershire sauce, garlic, and salt (if desired) and pepper. Add the lamb, seal, and move the marinade around with your fingers, covering every part of the meat.

**2** Add the cubed eggplant and onion quarters, seal the bag, and turn once or twice to cover the vegetables. Place on a dish in the refrigerator from 6 hours to overnight.

**3** When ready to prepare the meal, remove the lamb from the marinade and reserve the marinade. In a large saucepan over high heat, bring 5 cups water to a boil.

**4** Stir in the rice. Wait for the water to reboil. Cover, immediately lower the heat to a simmer, and steam for 30 to 35 minutes. When the rice is finished, take it off the burner and keep the lid on for 5 minutes to continue steaming. Remove the lid, fluff the rice with a fork, and replace the lid until ready to serve.

**5** At the same time the rice is cooking, cook the meat and vegetables. Lightly coat a large nonstick skillet with no-stick vegetable oil spray. Add the eggplant and onions with 2 tablespoons of the reserved marinade. Lightly spray the vegetables and sauté on medium-high, tossing often, for about 5 minutes, adding a tablespoon of water if needed for moisture.

**6** Add the lamb and the remaining marinade. Sauté the meat over medium-high heat until cooked, about 10 minutes. Add the chopped tomatoes and toss until hot, about 2 minutes.

**7** To serve: On 4 large flat plates, slightly mound the rice in the center. Place the meat and tomatoes on top and garnish with parsley sprigs.

*Nutrition at a glance (per serving): Total fat 3 g; Saturated fat 1 g; Protein 17 g; Dietary fiber 5 g; Carbohydrate 86 g; Cholesterol 25 mg; Sodium 418 mg; % of calories from fat 7; Calories 442.*

*Lynn's lamb-grilling tips: You can also make this recipe with grilled or broiled lamb. Cut the lamb pieces slightly larger and broil for about 10 minutes, 4 inches from the broiler, watching continually to make sure that they don't burn. If grilling, place the lamb pieces on a small rack or on perforated, heavy-duty foil on the grill. Grill all lamb to well done to release as much fat as possible.*

# A great and easy turkey recipe

Turkey isn't just for Thanksgiving or other holiday dinners. You can purchase cuts of turkey that are very low in fat and prepare them with a variety of sauces.

## Turkey Cutlets with Tarragon

Flavorful, easily seasoned, quickly cooked turkey fillets fit the bill for an attractive dish that takes only about 10 minutes. Serve this dish with several vegetables and rice, potatoes, or pasta. Garnish the turkey with chopped fresh parsley if you like.

**Tools:** *Pie plate, nonstick skillet*

**Preparation time:** *1 (plus optional marinating time)*

**Yield:** *4 servings*

*¹/₄ cup fat-free or lowfat mayonnaise*

*1 tablespoon Dijon mustard*

*1¹/₂ tablespoons chopped dried tarragon, rolled in your palms to release oils*

*Salt (optional) and freshly ground black pepper*

*4 4-ounce skinless turkey cutlets or fillets, washed and patted dry*

*1* In a pie plate, mix the mayonnaise, Dijon mustard, tarragon, and salt (if desired) and pepper. Coat the turkey cutlets with the mayonnaise mixture. (If you have time, marinate the turkey in this mixture in a sealable plastic bag in the refrigerator for 1 hour.)

*2* Lightly coat a nonstick skillet with no-stick vegetable oil spray. Heat the skillet on medium-high. Cook the turkey for about 5 minutes, turning once, until the cutlets or fillets are no longer pink in the thickest part.

**Nutrition at a glance (per serving):** *Total fat 1.5 g; Saturated fat 0.5 g; Protein 28 g; Dietary fiber 0 g; Carbohydrate 3 g; Cholesterol 77 mg; Sodium 239 mg; % of calories from fat 10; Calories 144.*

**Lynn's turkey-seasoning tips:** *Instead of a mixture of mayonnaise and mustard, you can use Hellman's Dijonnaise, a fat-free spread that is a tasty mustard sauce, to cover the turkey fillets.*

# *Two great and easy chicken recipes*

Every cook needs a great quick and easy chicken recipe or two. Following are a slightly unusual recipe and a very basic one.

## Chicken and Apricots

Tender, sweet, and a little savory, this simple recipe of chicken breasts with apricots receives raves every time I make it. You can add other vegetables, too, such as mushrooms, snow peas, broccoli, or green bell peppers. If you don't have preserves, use the heavy syrup from the canned apricots.

***Tools:*** *Large nonstick skillet*

***Preparation time:*** *2*

***Yield:*** *6 servings*

| | |
|---|---|
| 1 8-ounce chicken breast, skinned, boned, and completely defatted, pounded flat, cut into 6 serving-sized pieces | $^1/_2$ cup dried cranberries or tart cherries |
| | 2 tablespoons fresh lemon juice |
| 1 small onion, peeled and coarsely chopped | $^1/_4$ teaspoon cinnamon |
| | $^1/_2$ teaspoon turmeric (optional; gives the dish a yellowish color) |
| $^1/_2$ cup white wine or water | |
| $^1/_2$ cup apricot preserves or apple jelly | Salt (optional) |
| | 3 tablespoons chopped fresh parsley |
| 1 17-ounce can pitted apricot halves in heavy syrup, drained | |

*1* Lightly coat a large nonstick skillet with no-stick vegetable oil spray. Add the chicken pieces and onion and brown the chicken over medium heat for 3 to 4 minutes, turning often, being careful not to scorch the chicken or onion. Remove the chicken and set it aside.

*2* Add the wine or water, preserves or jelly, apricots, cranberries or cherries, lemon juice, cinnamon, turmeric (if desired), and salt (if desired). Cover and cook over medium-low heat, stirring occasionally, for 15 minutes.

*3* Add the chicken back to the skillet and continue cooking for 5 minutes over low heat, covered, stirring the sauce over the chicken.

*4* Garnish with chopped parsley.

*(continued)*

*Nutrition at a glance (per serving): Total fat 1 g; Saturated fat 0.5 g; Protein 8 g; Dietary fiber 2 g; Carbohydrate 44 g; Cholesterol 21 mg; Sodium 35 mg; % of calories from fat 5; Calories 222.*

*Lynn's chicken tips: For moister, more flavorful chicken (although it's more trouble), purchase your chicken breast with the skin intact. If the plastic enclosing the package of skinless chicken breast isn't thick (some is), the chicken can lose flavor and become dry within hours. Cut off the skin or bones at home and make soup with them (see Chapter 10). Just defat the broth by using a defatting cup, and you have a fat-free chicken soup base.*

## Roast Chicken

This dish is tender, crusty, flecked with herbs and spices, and as juicy as a chicken can be. I often use this extremely simple recipe on television and in classes when I demonstrate. It's always a delicious hit and takes only 15 to 20 minutes from counter to table if you use a microwave. The real test is that I also make it at home for myself *and* for guests. Use paper towels and scissors to remove all the fat from the chicken.

**Tools:** *Oven roasting bag or foil, ovenproof pie plate or dish*

**Preparation time:** *2*

**Yield:** *6 servings*

*1 whole broiler-fryer chicken (about 1 pound), completely skinned and trimmed of all visible fat, wing ends and tail removed*

*Spice mixture such as Mrs. Dash or Spike, or Cajun-style spices*

*3 sprigs fresh rosemary*

*2 sprigs fresh thyme*

**1** If using the oven, preheat to 350°.

**2** Make sure that every bit of fat is removed from the chicken. Shake the spices on both the outside and the inside of the chicken, coating every part. Stuff the rosemary and thyme into the chicken.

**3** Place the chicken in an oven roasting bag, tie to seal, and pierce the bag at the top. (If you're baking and you don't have an oven bag, wrap foil loosely around the chicken, sealing tightly at the top.) Place the chicken in the bag or foil in an ovenproof pie plate or dish.

*(continued)*

**4** If using the oven, bake the chicken for 35 to 45 minutes. Remove the herbs before serving.

If microwaving, place the chicken in the bag in the microwave and cook on high for 12 to 18 minutes, turning once after 7 minutes if your microwave doesn't have a turntable. Remove the herbs before serving.

***Nutrition at a glance (per serving):*** *Total fat 3 g; Saturated fat 1 g; Protein 7 g; Dietary fiber 0 g; Carbohydrate 1 g; Cholesterol 20 mg; Sodium 20 mg; % of calories from fat 45; Calories 62.*

***Lynn's chicken gravy tips:*** *The juice from the bag in which the chicken cooks can be drained into a defatting cup, one of those cups with a spout at the bottom. Even a fat-trimmed and skinned chicken produces plenty of fat, which rises immediately. Pour off the flavorful liquid into a saucepan and make gravy by whisking in a tablespoon or two of flour and cooking over low heat, whisking constantly, for 4 to 5 minutes. (See Figure 12-1.)*

**Figure 12-1:** A defatting cup helps you make lowfat but delicious chicken gravy.

# Lynn's Chicken Gravy Tips

**1.** Microwave the chicken in a bag.

**2.** Remove the chicken from the bag....

**3.** Snip the end of the bag and drain into a defatting cup.

**4.** Pour off the liquid into a saucepan. Whisk in a tablespoon or two of flour and cook over low heat for 5 minutes.

**5.** Chicken, potatoes and fat-free gravy...with peas and carrots.... -yum- -yum-

# Chapter 13
# Pasta, Grains, Beans, and Rice

● ● ● ● ● ● ● ● ● ● ● ● ● ● ● ● ● ● ● ● ● ● ● ● ● ● ● ● ● ● ● ● ●

## In This Chapter

▶ Pasta, grains, and rice: the bottom of the food pyramid

▶ Ways to cook rice, grains, and beans (you know how to cook pasta)

▶ Ten quick sauces for pasta, grains, beans, and rice

▶ Pasta, grain, bean, and rice recipes that are usually low or high in total fat, saturated fat, and cholesterol

● ● ● ● ● ● ● ● ● ● ● ● ● ● ● ● ● ● ● ● ● ● ● ● ● ● ● ● ● ● ● ● ●

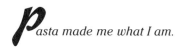*asta made me what I am.*

— Sophia Loren

*Rats fed a diet of beans did not develop colon or breast cancer.*

— Anne Kennedy, researcher at the
Harvard School of Public Health

**Recipes in This Chapter**

▶ Barley with Ham and Vegetables

▶ Boston Four-Bean Bake

▶ Field Peas and Rice

▶ Fresh Herb Risotto

▶ Hopping John

▶ Mac and Chili

▶ Paella

▶ Softly Curried Easy Lentils

▶ Straw and Hay (or Pasta Carbonara)

▶ 20-Minute Pasta and Asparagus

Ah! Pasta! This chapter talks about how easy and simple pasta is to make. Grains, beans, and rice are the staff of life, and I include directions for preparing many of them — from basmati to bulgur, quinoa to corn, pisolas to pintos. Beans, historically humankind's first food, have a starring role. I offer suggestions on how much you should eat and how often. I also discuss why pasta, grains, and rice form the base and beans, another layer of the U.S. Department of Agriculture Food Guide Pyramid. I also discuss beans as a meat alternative. I include lowfat recipes for pasta, grains, rice, and beans individually, and recipes that combine them. The sidebar "Ten quick fat-free sauces or flavor enhancers for rice, grains, beans, and pasta" gives you ten quick and easy sauces for these foods when you don't want a lot of fuss. You can also find handy lists of dishes that are usually high in total fat, saturated fat, and cholesterol, and those that are low.

Understanding a few techniques for preparing beans, grains, rice, and pasta so that you don't undo their healthful qualities means unlearning a few habits. These techniques are important because if you don't like these foods, you won't eat them, and these foods are important.

You can eat beans and grains every day. Most people already do in the form of breads, cereals, doughnuts, and pastries. With better recipes and easier cooking methods, these nutritious foods are gaining favor. Grains, beans, rice, and pasta contain no cholesterol and almost no fat, and they feel good in your stomach. Most important, instead of being energy robbers like fatty foods, they are energy producers. These foods, along with fruits and vegetables, are what our bodies are meant to eat to stay strong and healthy.

# Pasta

Pasta is usually made from wheat grains, although you can find pasta made from rice, quinoa, and vegetables. It can be made from the flour of different kinds of wheat, some sturdier, some softer. Commercial dried pasta, the kind you get in boxes and bags at the market, is usually made without fat or eggs and doesn't need them. The cooking directions may say to add oil to the water, which isn't necessary.

A few pasta types are very low in fat, with 0.5 grams per 2-ounce dry uncooked serving, but most pasta contains double that amount of fat. Without sauce, though, nearly all dried pasta is still very low in fat. Look at the label to see whether your pasta is slightly higher or lower in fat. Some pasta is labeled yolk-free, usually making it a lower-fat variety. Other dried pastas, such as egg noodles and some fettuccine, contain eggs, making them a little higher in fat. Adding eggs may make the pasta, especially if thick, more tender.

Commercial fresh pasta is, however, most often made with eggs and oil. Fresh pasta is found in the refrigerator case rather than on the shelf. Some fresh pasta has very little fat, but most contains up to 5 grams of fat per serving, without any sauce. If you add a "heart-attack-on-a-plate" Alfredo sauce (which is what the Center for Science in the Public Interest calls it), the fettuccine dish can contain 97 grams of total fat and 48 grams of saturated fat (compared to 5 grams when you top the dish with a lowfat marinara sauce at home).

Neither fresh nor dried pasta, if made without oil or yolks, is better than the other, because each type serves a different purpose. Dried pasta is firmer and, when cooked, is usually better for baked dishes and soups and under chunky sauces. Silkier fresh pasta is better for folding, stuffing, or making a softer pasta with a delicate sauce. Making fresh pasta at home is a great activity to do with friends for a small dinner party. Both hand-cranked and electric pasta-making machines are available in kitchen stores and many catalogs.

One pound of dried pasta, when cooked, usually feeds four people, with 1 cup cooked per person. For cooking each pound of fresh or dried pasta, use 4 to 6 quarts of boiling water. Salting the water is optional. Table 13-1 gives cooking times for various types of pasta, which are illustrated in Figure 13-1. Pasta generally doubles in size from dried to cooked.

| Table 13-1 | Preparing Pasta |
|---|---|
| **Type** | **Cooking Time** |
| **Fresh (commercial or homemade)** | |
| Small pasta | 3 to 4 minutes |
| Stuffed pasta | 6 to 10 minutes |
| **Dried** | |
| Orzo (rice size) and stars | 7 minutes |
| Spaghetti | 12 to 14 minutes |
| Linguine | 12 to 20 minutes |
| Angel hair pasta | 10 minutes |
| Rigatoni or manicotti (large tubes) | 15 to 20 minutes |
| Macaroni | 12 to 20 minutes |

**Figure 13-1:**
Pasta comes in a wide variety of shapes.

# Grains

The most popular grains, except corn, are always sold dried. These grains are rice (which I discuss separately later in this chapter), wheat (such as bulgur, cracked, or wheat berries), corn, hominy (lye-treated corn), oats, barley, and rye. Grains used less often are kamut (pronounced "ka-MOUT"), a form of wheat that looks like long brown rice, and quinoa (pronounced "KEEN-wa"), a tiny, round, white grain that is the only complete food of the group (meaning that this grain contains all eight essential amino acids, making it a complete protein food). Both kamut and quinoa are ancient grains, enjoyed thousands of years ago. Both are gaining in popularity today and are found in fancy food markets.

When Columbus' forays brought back maize (corn), the Italians didn't take long to discover interesting ways to cook it. They dried it, ground it, cooked it with water or broth, made it into cakes, fried it, covered it with sauce, or incorporated other foods with it and called it *polenta*. Maize quickly became an Italian staple.

Other old grains, such as millet (a tiny, light tan seed), can be high in protein. Millet is a staple for one-third of the world but is not widely used in the United States; nor is sorghum or triticale, two other grains used for centuries. Grains contain protein, fiber, almost no fat, and, like all plant foods, no cholesterol. Grains (and some beans) are a good source of complex carbohydrates.

Grains are easy to cook in water, defatted stock, or stock or water flavored with herbs and spices, onions, celery, mushrooms, carrots, garlic, bones, meat, and many other foods. They make a good-tasting side or base for a main dish.

Some grains, such as cooked bulgur or cracked wheat, can be used to extend hamburger meat for burgers, meat loaf, sloppy Joes, and other hamburger dishes. Adding grains can keep the fat and calories down with little loss in taste or texture. To extend your ground meat, try adding $^1/_4$ cup cooked, drained bulgur, rice, or barley to $^3/_4$ cup lean ground sirloin. I personally use $^3/_4$ cup of grains to $^1/_4$ cup of lean hamburger for meat loaf; plus I add many vegetables. I use a higher meat ratio for hamburgers.

Different grains require different cooking times — from 5 minutes to a few hours. The following list can help you choose the right grain for the amount of time you have to prepare your meal. Because cooking grains is so easy, I hope this list encourages you to cook grains more often and experiment with different types.

- ✔ **5 minutes:** Couscous: Tiny granules made of wheat, much like itty bitty pasta. Mild flavor. Cover 1 cup couscous with 2 cups boiling water and place a plate over the dish (or steam in a couscoussière). Steam for 5 minutes if you're using the usual precooked variety. Serve like pasta or with eastern Mediterranean foods.

- ✔ **5 to 10 minutes:** Oats: Mild flavor. Cooking times vary depending on whether you're using the quick or the long-cooking variety. Double the recommended amount of liquid and simmer, covered, usually for 5 minutes. Some varieties cook instantly and tend to be mushy, and others, such as Irish oatmeal, are more textural and must cook for as long as 45 minutes. Use oats as a cereal, as an ingredient in bread, meat loaf, or cookies, or as a topping on a fruit crisp or casserole.

✔ **15 minutes:** Bulgur or cracked wheat: Mild flavor. To each cup, add 2 cups defatted broth or water and simmer for 15 minutes, covered. Wheat berries, another form of wheat, must cook for $1^1/2$ hours before either eating or baking in bread or muffins. Use bulgur or cracked wheat in soups, in salads, as a side dish, in casseroles, or to extend hamburger meat.

✔ **20 minutes:** Quinoa: Very mild flavor. To each cup of quinoa, add 2 cups defatted broth or water and simmer for 20 minutes, covered. Use like rice in soups, in salads, in casseroles, or as a side dish.

✔ **25 minutes:** Rice: Very mild flavor. To each cup of white rice, add 2 cups of defatted broth or water and simmer 18 to 25 minutes, covered. (See the more complete rice-cooking instructions in the next section.) Use rice in soups, in salads, in casseroles, or as a side dish.

✔ **30 minutes:** Barley: Deep flavor. To each cup of barley, add $2^1/2$ cups defatted broth or water and simmer for 30 minutes, covered. Use in soups, in salads, as a side dish, in casseroles or other entrees, or to extend hamburger meat.

✔ **35 minutes:** Millet: Mild flavor. To each cup of millet, add 3 cups of defatted broth or water and simmer for 35 minutes, covered. Use in soups, in salads, in casseroles and other entrees, or as a side dish.

✔ **45 minutes:** Polenta, grits, and corn meal mush (all are a form of ground corn): Bland flavor. To each cup of ground corn, add 3 to 4 cups water or defatted broth and simmer, covered. Different brands of polenta give different directions on the package and some varieties may be precooked. Polenta and mush are often fried after cooking. Use for breakfast with syrup or salt and pepper, as a main dish with a sauce, or as a side dish.

✔ **1 hour:** Kamut (a type of wheat): Deep flavor. To each cup of kamut, add 6 cups defatted broth or water and simmer for 1 hour, covered. Use in soups, in salads, in casseroles and other entrees, as a side dish, or to extend hamburger meat.

✔ **3 to 6 hours:** Dried corn (such as pisole or dried whole or cracked corn): Mild flavor. To each cup of dried corn, add 3 to 6 cups defatted broth or water. If the dried corn is unsoaked, simmer for 3 to 6 hours (cracked corn takes less time, whole corn requires more time), covered, to soften the corn kernels sufficiently but retain a chewy texture. Use in soups, in salads, as a side dish, or in casseroles.

# *Rice*

Rice is a cinch to make, and it's the grain with the least amount of fat. However, white rice contains little fiber. Rice can be baked, boiled, fried, steamed, microwaved, or cooked in a rice cooker, and almost every method produces a good result.

Like pasta, rice can be overcooked or undercooked, but it's generally pretty foolproof. You can cook plain rice covered in boiling water, pouring off the excess liquid after the rice is finished cooking, or you can steam or bake it with more exact amounts of liquid. Some recipes call for toasting the rice first in a small amount of butter, margarine, or olive oil, and some call for adding butter or olive oil after cooking. Both methods add fat, however. If you're doing your own cooking, you can use smaller quantities of oil and butter to reduce the fat content.

Rice is incredibly inexpensive, especially if bought in bulk. A 10-pound bag in an Asian store costs the same as a 1-pound box in a chain market. A 25-pound bag is really economical.

Dried grains stored in bulk can interest bugs, however. You can freeze dried foods or store them in glass containers with airtight lids. Most bugs can easily chomp through even the toughest plastic bags, any cardboard, and even some soft, thin plastic containers. Protecting these fat-free and healthful foods from little predators keeps them appetizing and more enticing when you're trying to decide between an entree of pasta, grains, beans, or rice and a high-fat food.

## Types of rice

Thousands of kinds of rice exist, so you're sure to find a rice you like. Figure 13-2 shows just a few types you can try:

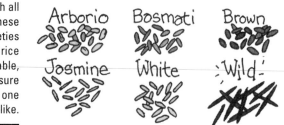

**Figure 13-2:** With all these varieties of rice available, you're sure to find one you like.

My current favorite is basmati, a long-grained, aromatic rice that is easy to cook. Basmati can be stored or aged almost indefinitely (unlike short-grained rice) and, in India, aged basmati is given as a cherished wedding gift if it's suitably old, about 25 years.

Another popular "rice" is wild rice. Actually an aquatic grass, wild rice also comes in numerous forms and colors. Because I love it and have many leftover bags squirreled away, I was amazed to see that my own wild rice ranged in color from nearly white to shiny black and all shades of brown. Plus, it came in sizes from $1/4$ inch long to over an inch long. Some were as slender as pencil leads, others as thick as a straw. I cooked them all together with a few onions, carrots, celery, herbs, spices, and a bouillon cube, and the result was great.

Brown rice, which is white rice still in its natural coating (before refinement where the bran is removed), has a nutty flavor and takes 5 or 10 minutes longer than white rice to cook, depending on the amount and variety. Arborio rice, an Italian variety of white rice, is used in a creamy dish called *risotto.* This short-grain rice is starchy and needs to be heated slowly, with liquid added a little at a time, continually stirring to incorporate it. Some cooks say that they microwave Arborio rice quite successfully.

I personally don't recommend quick-cooking white rice because the savings in time (overall, about 10 or 15 minutes) isn't worth the loss of taste, texture, appearance, and aroma. Two exceptions are quick-cooking wild rice and quick-cooking brown rice. The loss in taste and texture is less with the quick-cooking varieties of these hardier forms of rice.

## Cooking rice

Cooking rice is really easy if you have a rice cooker, and nearly as easy if you have a pot with a lid. Following are instructions for cooking 1 cup of rice in a pot with a lid in a variety of lowfat ways:

- To steam rice, bring $1^1/2$ cups of water to a boil, add 1 cup of rice, turn the heat to very low, cover, and simmer for 20 minutes. If you're cooking brown rice, add slightly more water and simmer for 25 minutes. If you're cooking wild rice, add $3/4$ cup additional water and steam for 35 to 45 minutes.

- To boil 1 cup of rice like you boil pasta, use four to six times as much water as rice, boil uncovered for about 25 minutes or until the rice is cooked, pour off the excess water, and drain the rice in a fine mesh colander.

- To cook Arborio rice (such as for paella or risotto), put 1 cup of rice in a large skillet or pan, add the liquid $1/4$ cup at a time, stirring, for 10 minutes at each addition, with the heat on medium-low so that the liquid gets incorporated and doesn't evaporate. (Arborio can also be microwaved in 4-minute batches.)

- To bake any white or brown rice, place 1 cup of rice in 2 cups of hot or boiling water or other liquid (use twice as much liquid as rice). Bake, covered, at 350° for 40 to 50 minutes. Wild rice requires $1/3$ cup more liquid and 10 more minutes.

> ✔ To microwave rice, place 1 cup of rice in 2 cups of boiling water or other liquid, heat on high, lightly covered (or covered with plastic wrap that has been punctured so that steam can escape), for 5 minutes, stir, and then decrease the temperature by 50 percent and heat, lightly covered, for 15 minutes. For wild rice, stir after the 15 minutes, re-cover, and heat for another 5 minutes.

> ✔ For pilaf, lightly coat 1 cup of dry rice or saucepan with no-stick vegetable oil spray or coat with $1/2$ teaspoon of olive oil, butter, margarine, or corn oil and toss over high heat. Add 2 cups of water or defatted chicken stock, bring to a boil, cover, and simmer for 25 minutes.

About halfway through cooking, you can look at the rice. If you find that you have too much water, you can pour some off, but you don't have to. If not enough liquid remains, add some and stir. If rice doesn't look done after the designated cooking time, cook it some more. If you forget and put the rice in the cold water before it boils, never mind; it'll be good anyway.

Rice expands during cooking. Experts recommend that you let rice stand for a few minutes after cooking, covered and undisturbed, so that the rice kernels can swell to their fullest. Then toss the rice with a fork to fluff it, or fluff the rice as you transfer it to a platter or plates.

# Beans

Beans are every bit as versatile as pasta, grains, and rice, and a surprising number of varieties of beans are available. They are a good alternative to meat, contain almost no fat, and are a good source of fiber and protein. The difference in taste, size, texture, and color of beans is enormous. Even in a single bean family such as the kidney bean, vast differences exist. The almost-mushy, muted-tasting white kidney or cannellini is very different from my chili and salad favorite, the darkest red, firm-textured kidney bean.

Canned beans of all kinds make adding beans to dishes fast and easy. Although canned beans usually contain a large amount of sodium, you can remove some by draining and rinsing. Canned beans can also contain fat, lard, sugar, pork or beef, spices, and vegetables. (The label tells you what has been added, and the Nutrition Facts panel tells you how much fat is in the product.) Canned beans lose flavor, color, and texture, so cooking dried beans from scratch offers some extra taste and health benefits (you don't need to use as much salt).

Unfortunately, very few types of fresh beans are available; some exceptions are lima beans, fava beans, soybeans, and black-eyed peas. One of my favorite bean dishes is fresh, bright green soybeans boiled and served in their furry shells as a salty appetizer — available in Japanese restaurants.

## Ten quick lowfat canned bean recipes

- **Hummus:** Mash drained garbanzo beans and add small amounts of lemon juice, garlic, tahini (sesame paste), and salt, and serve with pita bread.

- **Pinto bean salsa:** Add canned, drained pinto beans to bottled salsa and serve with lowfat tortilla chips or crudités.

- **Pinto bean dip:** Mash canned, drained beans and add small amounts of chopped red onions, vinegar, lemon juice, cumin, salt, and pepper.

- **Three-bean salad:** Combine drained garbanzo beans, kidney beans, and green beans, and add small amounts of vinegar, garlic, onions, oregano, and sugar.

- **Soybean salad:** Combine drained soybeans with small amounts of chopped celery, tomatoes, carrots, cucumbers, vinegar, Dijon mustard, and minced garlic.

- **Black bean or kidney bean chili:** Combine drained beans with small amounts of cubed lean beef or pork trimmed of all visible fat, onions, garlic, corn, red or green bell peppers, tomato sauce, chili powder, cumin, and crushed red pepper flakes. Heat for 20 minutes, covered.

- **Baked beans:** Combine drained navy beans, molasses, mustard, onions, garlic, green peppers, and tomato sauce and bake, covered, for 1 hour.

- **Lentil soup:** Combine dried lentils, onions, garlic, carrots, celery, mushrooms, water, and defatted stock and cook, covered, for 1 hour.

- **Kidney bean, navy bean, pinto bean, and adzuki bean salad:** Combine canned, drained beans with small amounts of onions, garlic, carrots, celery or fennel, tomatoes, lettuce, and Italian dressing.

- **Red beans and rice:** Combine drained beans, cooked rice, a bouillon cube, and small amounts of diced lean ham, onions, and garlic. Cook for 15 minutes.

Occasionally, you see long fava bean pods in a grocery store bin. If you break one open, you find a large, plump, greenish, lima-like bean, more wrinkly than limas, and a favorite among many, although I find them slightly bitter.

## Common dried bean varieties

Beans are low in fat and can be prepared in myriad ways, and all have different flavors and textures. Enjoy them often and get to know the different types. Here are some names of common bean varieties with notations as to whether they are sweet, tender, mushy, firm, flavorful, or bitter.

- Adzuki or azuki (firm sweet)
- Appaloosa (firm and mild)

- ✔ Black bean or black turtle bean (flavorful and firm, slightly sweet)
- ✔ Black-eyed pea or bean (flavorful and tender)
- ✔ Calico (firm and mild)
- ✔ Cargamento (flavorful)
- ✔ Cranberry or scarlet runner (flavorful and firm)
- ✔ European soldier (firm)
- ✔ Fava (often available fresh) and fava rattlesnake (bitter or flavorful and firm)
- ✔ Flageolet (sweet, tender, and sometimes mushy)
- ✔ Garbanzo (flavorful and firm)
- ✔ Great northern (firm and mild)
- ✔ Indian woman yellows (flavorful)
- ✔ Jacob's cattle (firm)
- ✔ Kidney bean: Comes in many colors, including dark maroon (firm), pale red (semi-firm), or white (called cannellini). The pale red and white are more tender or mushy than the darker kidney. All are flavorful.
- ✔ Lentil: Miniature, red (red and orange are tender and mushy), yellow, brown (firm), black (firm), green (firm). All are flavorful.
- ✔ Lima: Christmas, cranberry (firm and flavorful)
- ✔ Lupini (firm and bitter): Needs 12 days of soaking and water changing to remove the bitter taste.
- ✔ Maine yellow eye (sweet)
- ✔ Mung or moong dal (firm and flavorful)
- ✔ Navy (semi-sweet and bland)
- ✔ Persian (tender and mushy)
- ✔ Pink (firm and mild)
- ✔ Pinto (sweet)
- ✔ Red (sweet)
- ✔ Roman (firm and lusty)
- ✔ Small white (semi-sweet)
- ✔ Soybean (firm and slightly sweet)
- ✔ Spanish tolosana (sweet)
- ✔ Split golden graham (mushy and sweet)
- ✔ Split pea (flavorful, tender, or mushy)
- ✔ Stuben golden or yellow eye (sweet)

✔ White bean (semi-sweet and bland)

✔ Yellow-eyed pea (mushy and sweet)

## To soak or not to soak?

Presoaking beans is not necessary. It's less time-consuming if you don't presoak. Unsoaked beans have more texture, but soaked beans are reputed to cause less flatulence.

To soak, cover beans with 3 inches of water and let sit, uncovered, overnight or for at least 8 hours. They don't need refrigeration while soaking, but refrigerating doesn't hurt them, either. Discard the soaking water. If beans end up soaking for longer than 10 hours, change the water, cover, and refrigerate to keep them from spoiling.

For a quicker soak, microwave 1 cup of dried beans covered in water for 15 minutes, discard the water, cover the beans with water again, and soak for 4 hours.

Small beans, such as lentils (not really a bean), don't need soaking, and 1 cup of most varieties cooks in 20 to 25 minutes, but some larger lentils require longer cooking. To 1 cup dried lentils, add 3 cups water or defatted stock and simmer. The small green French lentil stays firm and takes 20 minutes to cook. The largest brown lentils take 35 minutes. Cooking time and amount of liquid also depend on how dry the beans are.

## Cooking dried beans and legumes

To cook 1 cup of beans, follow these directions:

1. **Rinse the beans carefully in a colander and remove any dirt or pebbles that may be left from the harvesting and packaging process (you'll almost always find a few tooth-chippers).**

2. **Place the beans in a 4-quart pot with 8 to 12 cups of cold, fresh water.**

3. **Bring to a boil, reduce the heat, cover, and simmer for the time listed in Table 13-2 or until tender.**

4. **Just before the end of the cooking time, add salt. Waiting until the end of the cooking time to add salt is important; salting while cooking makes the beans slightly tough.**

All times and amounts in the following table are for 1 pound, and all are approximate. Beans can be very dry and very old (age won't hurt them), and they may need more liquid or more cooking time. Beans can cook longer than recommended. Most freeze well.

| Table 13-2 | Cooking Dried Beans | |
|---|---|---|
| *Type* | *Cooking Time* | *Yield in Cups* |
| Black beans | 2 hours | 6 |
| Black-eyed peas | 45 minutes to 1 hour | 7 |
| Butter beans | 2 hours | $6^{1}/_{4}$ |
| Calico beans | 2 hours | 6 |
| Cannellini or kidney beans (white) | 2 hours | 7 |
| Fava beans | 2 hours | 7 |
| Garbanzo beans (chickpeas) | 3 hours | $6^{1}/_{4}$ |
| Great northern beans | 2 hours | $6^{2}/_{3}$ |
| Kidney beans (red) | 3 hours | 6 |
| Lentils (brown) | 30 minutes to $1^{1}/_{2}$ hours | 5 |
| Lentils (red) | 20 to 30 minutes | 5 |
| Lima beans (baby) | $1^{1}/_{2}$ hours | $6^{1}/_{2}$ |
| Lima beans (large) | 2 to 3 hours | $6^{1}/_{4}$ |
| Mung beans | 45 minutes to 1 hour | 6 |
| Navy beans | 2 hours | 7 |
| Pinto beans | $2^{1}/_{2}$ hours | $6^{1}/_{2}$ |
| Red beans | $1^{1}/_{2}$ hours | 6 |
| Soybeans | 3 hours | 7 |
| Split peas | 50 minutes | 6 |

In addition to simmering beans on the stovetop, you can cook beans in any of the following ways:

✔ **Pressure-cooking beans:** To 1 cup soaked or unsoaked dry beans (don't pressure-cook canned beans, or they may fall apart), add $1^{1}/_{2}$ quarts water or defatted broth. Pressure-cook unsoaked or dry beans for 50 minutes, soaked beans for 30 minutes.

✔ **Microwaving dry, unsoaked beans:** Place 1 cup beans in 2 cups water or defatted stock (use twice as much water as beans) and heat on high, covered, for 15 minutes. Let rest for 5 minutes and add 2 to 4 cups more water and microwave for 35 to 55 minutes, depending upon the size of the beans. (You can always add more water.)

✔ **Microwaving soaked beans:** Place 1 cup beans in 2 cups water or defatted stock (use twice as much water as beans), microwave for 30 minutes, let rest for 5 minutes, double the water again, and microwave for 15 minutes (1 cup beans, 2 cups liquid, rest, 2 cups more liquid).

✔ **Baking unsoaked, dry beans or soaked beans:** As long as you keep checking to be sure that enough water or defatted broth remains, beans can bake covered or uncovered for many hours, even overnight, usually in a 275° to 350° oven. Long cooking improves the flavor. Covering may be advisable for holding in the moisture.

✔ **Baking drained, canned beans:** Empty the beans in a colander and rinse with cool water if you want to remove more salt. Season with raw or precooked vegetables and lean meat and bake for ¹/₂ to 1¹/₂ hours in a 350° oven, depending upon the amount and sizes of the added vegetables. (The beans need only to get hot.)

# Pasta, Rice, Grain, and Bean Dishes That Are Usually Low or High in Fat

Because so many lowfat pasta, rice, grain, and bean dishes exist, I mention only a few here, but they give you an idea of which dishes are generally low in fat. I'm assuming that these dishes are made without large amounts of fat, oil, cream, meat, or cheese.

✔ Hummus

✔ Pasta marinara

✔ Pasta or rice primavera (without cream, cheese, or butter)

✔ Pasta or rice with red or white clam sauce (without cream or butter)

✔ Rice cooked Asian style (without sauce or oil)

✔ Rice pilaf (if it isn't made with excessive amounts of oil or butter)

✔ Rice salad (with a small amount of salad dressing or oil)

✔ Spanish rice (if little fat is used)

✔ Vegetarian baked beans

Of the thousands of high-fat, high-cholesterol pasta, rice, grain, and bean dishes, this list gives you an idea of some dishes that are usually fatty, assuming that they are made with the usual amounts of butter, oil, cream, cheese, or egg yolks. Most, but not all, restaurant pasta, grain, bean, and rice dishes are high in fat.

- Almond rice mold
- Bacon-sauced dishes
- Baked rice (with cheese or meat)
- Boston baked beans with pork or bacon
- Butter-sauced dishes
- Pasta carbonara (with cream)
- Cheese-sauced dishes
- Cream-sauced dishes
- Fettuccine Alfredo
- Meat-sauced dishes
- Fried polenta or rice
- Italian rice (with cheese or meat)
- Lasagna (with high-fat cheese and meat)
- Macaroni and cheese
- Paella
- Pasta or rice sauce with sausage
- Rice or grain croquettes or fritters
- Risotto (with cheese)
- Spaetzle (with butter)
- Stuffed pasta (with high-fat cheese, fatty meat or shellfish, and butter)

## Ten quick fat-free sauces or flavor enhancers for rice, grains, beans, and pasta

Some of the following suggestions may work better with one food than another, but the list gives you ideas for quick and easy rice, grain, bean, and pasta sauces:

- Instead of plain water, boil rice, grains, beans, or pasta in canned beef bouillon, or in water with beef or chicken flavor granules, or in defatted chicken stock (canned versions are slightly higher in sodium).

- Instead of plain water, boil rice, grains, beans, or pasta in water with onions, vegetables, herbs, and spices (such as tarragon or cumin, or jalapeño peppers).

- Boil rice, grains, beans, or pasta in plain water, but make a quick sauce from defatted chicken stock or beef broth and a small can of drained mushrooms. Thicken the sauce with cornstarch or flour and sprinkle with a chopped fresh herb.

✔ Top cooked rice, grains, beans, or pasta with heated lowfat mushroom soup, mushroom sauce, corn chowder, tomato soup, or clam or lobster bisque (mix the bisque with liquid fat-free non-dairy creamer).

✔ Add a lowfat white sauce seasoned with chopped dill or other chopped fresh herbs, such as rosemary, parsley, or thyme.

✔ Cover cooked rice, grains, beans, or pasta with bottled lowfat or fat-free chicken or beef gravy heated with diced lean giblets, chicken, turkey, beef, or pork with all visible fat removed.

✔ Top cooked rice, grains, beans, or pasta with heated, lowfat canned chili or a tablespoon or two of tomato paste (mix the paste into the rice), shredded lowfat cheese, a spoonful of lowfat or fat-free sour cream, and chopped onions and jalapeño peppers.

✔ Top cooked rice, grains, beans, or pasta with a mild, heated salsa or barbecue sauce and diced lean beef or chicken, diced fresh tomatoes, and a small amount of diced avocados sprinkled with dried oregano and lemon juice or vinegar.

✔ Toss rice, grains, beans, or pasta with a small amount of olive oil, chunks of canned, drained water-packed tuna or salmon, lowfat or fat-free cheese, Parmesan cheese, and chopped parsley and basil.

✔ Toss rice, grains, beans, or pasta with roasted garlic and chopped sun-dried tomatoes sprinkled with parsley and finely chopped scallions and garnish with a few black olives.

Canned beans and cold cooked grains like barley and lentils need only vinegar and a few drops of olive oil or lowfat salad dressing and chopped vegetables (such as celery, onions, tomatoes, carrots, and lettuce) for a quick, lowfat salad. The bottom line is that pasta, grains, beans, and rice are easy to fix.

# Pasta, Bean, Rice, and Grain Recipes

These pasta, bean, rice, and grain recipes offer one great advantage: You can make large quantities and freeze the surplus. When you're in a hurry, instead of turning to high-fat fast food, just pop the leftovers in the microwave.

## Barley with Ham and Vegetables

Smoky, substantial, and warming, this simple and flavorful barley dish (you can substitute lentils or beans for the barley) can be served over white rice for an entree, as a side, or even cold as a salad. The recipe takes time to prepare, but most of that time is unattended. If you don't like okra, use green beans. Garnish with chopped yellow bell peppers, lemon or mandarin orange slices, or hot sauce.

*(continued)*

**Tools:** *Large saucepan, large skillet*

**Preparation time:** *3*

**Yield:** *4 servings*

*1 ham hock (can be smoked) with a small amount of meat (about 2 ounces, or the size of a lemon)*

*1 cup dried barley or lentils*

*¹/₂ cup chopped onion*

*1 clove garlic, peeled and minced*

*¹/₂ cup chopped celery*

*¹/₂ cup chopped carrot*

*¹/₂ pound okra, sliced*

*1 14¹/₂-ounce can stewed tomatoes*

*Salt (optional) and freshly ground black pepper*

**1** In a large saucepan, place the ham hock and enough water to cover the hock by 2 inches, or about 6 to 8 cups. Bring to a boil, reduce the heat to low, and simmer, uncovered, for 1 hour and 45 minutes.

**2** With a slotted spoon, remove the ham hock with the meat on it and set aside. Defat the broth with a defatting cup, or chill and skim off all visible fat. Wash the pot with soapy water and rinse well. Place the defatted broth back in the clean pot and add the barley. Bring to a boil, lower the heat to low, and cook the barley, covered, for 45 minutes or until tender.

**3** When the barley is cooked, drain the cooking liquid (save it for another use, such as for cooking rice or vegetables), but reserve ¹/₂ cup for this recipe. Cut the ham from the hock, remove all visible fat, dice the ham, and discard the bone. Reserve the ham.

**4** Lightly coat a large skillet with no-stick vegetable oil spray. Combine the onion, garlic, celery, and carrot, lightly spray the vegetables, and sauté over medium heat for 10 minutes or until they begin to soften.

**5** Add to the skillet the ¹/₂ cup of reserved defatted ham broth, okra, stewed tomatoes, and salt (if desired) and pepper. Bring to a boil, reduce the heat to medium-low, and cook the vegetables, stirring frequently, for 5 minutes.

**6** Add the barley and diced ham. Reduce the heat to low and simmer for 5 to 10 minutes, covered.

**Nutrition at a glance (per serving):** *Total fat 2.5 g; Saturated fat 0.5 g; Protein 13 g; Dietary fiber 12 g; Carbohydrate 49 g; Cholesterol 5 mg; Sodium 350 mg; % of calories from fat 8; Calories 254.*

**Lynn's bone-cooking tips:** *Bones, whether from poultry or meat, don't really begin to give up their great flavor until they have cooked for at least 1¹/₂ to 2 hours. Bones can also be baked separately for an hour, lightly covered with foil so that they don't become too dry, and then added to water or broth and simmered for another hour.*

## Boston Four-Bean Bake

Put several kinds of beans in a pot, and with a few good but simple additions, you have this delicious, easy, and very pretty dish, which takes little time because you use canned beans. Pancetta or Italian bacon adds a slightly different flavor, but, as with any bacon, you have to cut off every bit of fat with scissors. Why eat fat when the meat contains just as much flavor?

**Tools:** *Large nonstick skillet, 3-quart casserole dish*

**Preparation time:** *2*

**Yield:** *8 servings*

*2 pieces thick center-cut bacon slices (about 2 ounces), all visible fat removed*

*3 stalks celery, chopped*

*1 medium onion, peeled and chopped*

*2 cloves garlic, peeled and minced*

*1 16-ounce can fat-free vegetarian baked beans in tomato sauce*

*1 15-ounce can butter beans or lima beans, rinsed and drained*

*2 10$^1$/$_2$-ounce cans dark kidney beans, rinsed and drained*

*1 19-ounce can cannellini beans, rinsed and drained*

*1 8-ounce can tomato sauce*

*4 teaspoons dry mustard*

*2 tablespoons brown sugar*

*2 tablespoons cider or white wine vinegar*

*$^1$/$_4$ teaspoon hot pepper sauce*

*1* Coat a large nonstick skillet with no-stick vegetable oil spray and place over medium-high heat. Cook the bacon, celery, onion, and garlic in the skillet, stirring occasionally, for 7 or 8 minutes or until the vegetables soften.

*2* Add to the mixture in the skillet the baked beans, butter or lima beans, kidney beans, cannellini beans, tomato sauce, dry mustard, brown sugar, vinegar, and hot pepper sauce and toss to combine.

*3* Lightly coat a 3-quart casserole dish with no-stick spray. Pour in the bean mixture and place in a 400° oven. Bake for 45 minutes until hot and bubbly.

**Nutrition at a glance (per serving):** *Total fat 1.5 g; Saturated fat 0 g; Protein 15 g; Dietary fiber 12 g; Carbohydrate 46 g; Cholesterol 2 mg; Sodium 815 mg; % of calories from fat 5; Calories 253.*

**Lynn's vegetable-sautéing tip:** *Vegetables sautéed just with no-stick vegetable oil spray get a caramel-like flavor, imparting a depth that simply putting all the vegetables in raw with the beans doesn't provide. The dish is still good without precooking the vegetables, and I do it that way when in a pinch for time (or energy).*

## Field Peas and Rice

This attractive stew is a favorite. The garnish — limes and hot sauce — adds immeasurably. You can buy seasoned, canned field peas in most large markets. I could tell you numerous stories about how people from masons to moguls love this dish, but the bottom line is that it's quite remarkable for its simplicity and delicious flavor.

**Tools:** *Large soup pot*

**Preparation time:** *3*

**Yield:** *8 servings*

*1¹/₂ cups fresh English peas, or 1 10-ounce package frozen peas*

*2 cups dry rice (brown or a mixture of white, brown, and wild)*

*6 cups water*

*8 ounces baby carrots, or 6 medium carrots, quartered*

*3 stalks celery, cut into 4-inch lengths*

*2 large cloves garlic, peeled and sliced*

*12 pearl onions, peeled, or 1 large onion, peeled and chopped*

*2 medium tomatoes, quartered*

*3 tablespoons dried parsley*

*2 teaspoons chicken-flavored bouillon granules, or 2 bouillon cubes*

*1 15-ounce can seasoned field peas, drained*

*1 large ripe lime, quartered*

*Salt (optional)*

*Hot pepper sauce (optional)*

*1* Shuck the peas or bang the frozen peas on the counter to loosen and separate them. Set aside.

*2* In a large soup pot, combine the rice, water, carrots, celery, garlic, onions, tomatoes, parsley, and bouillon granules. Bring to a boil, cover, lower the heat, and simmer on low for 1 hour, stirring occasionally.

*3* Stir in the field peas and fresh or defrosted peas and cook for 2 or 3 minutes or until hot. Serve with lime wedges, salt (if desired), and hot sauce (if desired).

**Nutrition at a glance (per serving):** *Total fat 2 g; Saturated fat 0.5 g; Protein 9 g; Dietary fiber 8 g; Carbohydrate 52 g; Cholesterol 0 mg; Sodium 473 mg; % of calories from fat 7; Calories 258.*

**Lynn's rice cooking tips:** *To prepare rice pilaf, place 1 cup uncooked white rice in a saucepan, add ¹/₂ teaspoon butter or olive oil, and heat while stirring constantly. Add 2 cups water or defatted broth, cover, and cook for 25 minutes.*

## Fresh Herb Risotto

Here's an herb recipe that deliciously flavors risotto, a creamy, delicious rice dish. Use any two herbs you like, such as basil and parsley or rosemary and thyme. Go light on tarragon, oregano, marjoram, and rosemary; use heavier amounts of parsley and basil. This versatile dish can serve as an entree or an appetizer. Garnish with lemon wedges and sprigs of fresh herbs. You can add cooked shrimp or scallops or defatted and skinless turkey or chicken during the last stages of cooking.

**Tools:** *Large saucepan; large, attractive, serving-type nonstick skillet*

**Preparation time:** *2*

**Yield:** *4 servings*

5 cups defatted chicken broth, or
3 14$^1$/$_2$-ounce cans fat-free chicken broth

$^1$/$_3$ cup minced onion

2 tablespoons minced celery

1$^1$/$_2$ cups Arborio rice

$^1$/$_2$ cup white wine or additional chicken broth

1 cup finely chopped fresh herbs, such as basil, parsley, oregano, marjoram, rosemary, or thyme

$^1$/$_4$ cup grated Parmesan cheese

Freshly ground black pepper

Lime wedges for garnish

**1** Place the broth in a large saucepan and bring to a boil. Reduce the heat to low and simmer, covered.

**2** In a large, attractive, serving-type nonstick skillet lightly coated with no-stick vegetable oil spray, cook the onion and celery over medium heat, tossing, for 2 minutes.

**3** Add the rice to the onion and celery in the skillet, lightly coat all the food with no-stick vegetable oil spray, and continue to stir for 1 minute.

**4** Add the wine or broth to the mixture in the skillet and stir until it is completely absorbed, which takes several minutes.

**5** Add the simmering broth to the skillet, $^1$/$_4$ to $^1$/$_2$ cup at a time, stirring frequently. Wait until each addition is almost completely absorbed before adding the next $^1$/$_2$ cup, reserving $^1$/$_2$ cup at the end. Stir frequently to prevent sticking. If the liquid seems to evaporate without being incorporated into the food, turn the heat down slightly. This step takes about 18 minutes.

**6** When the rice is nearly cooked, very tender but still slightly firm, stir in the herbs and the remaining $^1$/$_2$ cup broth. Allow the broth to be absorbed before adding the Parmesan cheese. Turn off the stove, continuing to stir until the cheese is incorporated and the risotto is creamy. Add pepper and garnish with lime wedges and herb sprigs.

*(continued)*

*Nutrition at a glance (per serving):* Total fat 2.5 g; Saturated fat 1 g; Protein 18 g; Dietary fiber 2 g; Carbohydrate 71 g; Cholesterol 5 mg; Sodium 337 mg; % of calories from fat 5; Calories 419.

*Lynn's rice tip:* By boiling the liquid before adding it to the risotto, you coax the rice to expand more quickly, a little like making risotto in a microwave, but with better results.

## Hopping John

Hopping John (or Hoppin' John), or any dish with black-eyed peas, is said to bring good luck if eaten on New Year's Day. If you aren't a green bean lover, substitute okra, fresh English peas, sugar snaps, snow peas, or even artichoke hearts. White rice takes 20 minutes to steam, but Asian restaurants sell it for about $1 per large serving, so I buy several when I dine out. You can also pour the Hopping John over the rice instead of adding the rice to it.

**Tools:** *Small nonstick skillet, saucepan, large nonstick skillet*

**Preparation time:** *2*

**Yield:** *4 servings*

| | |
|---|---|
| *4 slices center-cut bacon (4 ounces)* | *1 10¹/₂-ounce can black-eyed peas* |
| *1¹/₂ cups frozen sliced green beans* | *2 cups cooked white rice* |
| *3 celery stalks, chopped* | *¹/₈ teaspoon cayenne pepper* |
| *1 large onion, peeled and chopped* | *2 teaspoons Worcestershire sauce* |
| *1 clove garlic, peeled and minced* | *Salt (optional)* |
| *1 15¹/₂-ounce can diced tomatoes in juice* | *Louisiana hot sauce* |

*1* With scissors, remove all visible fat from the bacon and discard (or see "Lynn's bacon fat tip" at the end of this recipe).

*2* In a small nonstick skillet, cook the bacon over medium-low heat for 5 to 7 minutes, turning until the bacon is cooked. Drain on paper towels and chop or break into small pieces.

*3* In a saucepan, place the green beans in 1 inch of water and steam over high heat, covered, for 3 to 4 minutes. Drain and add ice and cold water to quickly stop the cooking. Drain and set aside.

*(continued)*

**4** In a large nonstick skillet lightly coated with no-stick vegetable oil spray, cook the celery, onions, and garlic over medium heat, stirring frequently, for about 5 minutes or until the vegetables begin to soften.

**5** To the mixture in the skillet, add the tomatoes with juice, black-eyed peas, rice, green beans, and bacon. Reduce the heat to low and simmer for 5 minutes or until most of the liquid is absorbed. Add the red pepper and Worcestershire sauce and season to taste with salt (if desired). For extra heat, sprinkle on a few drops of Louisiana-style hot sauce.

*Nutrition at a glance (per serving): Total fat 2 g; Saturated fat 0.5 g; Protein 12 g; Dietary fiber 7 g; Carbohydrate 53 g; Cholesterol 7 mg; Sodium 677 mg; % of calories from fat 7; Calories 275.*

*Lynn's bacon fat tip: Instead of discarding the bacon fat, boil it, uncovered, in a quart of water for 30 minutes. Defat the liquid with a defatting cup or by chilling and picking the fat off. For Southern-style green beans, heat the beans in the bacon-flavored broth.*

## Mac and Chili

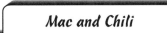

Mac and Chili aren't two characters out of a movie; they are best friends in an easy-to-fix pot of good food. Additions or substitutions include corn, peppers, and, of course, beans; you can add all kinds of foods to this dish. The turkey gives it a sweet flavor and a great texture. Canned foods never had so much taste!

*Tools: Large soup pot, large nonstick skillet*

*Preparation time: 2*

*Yield: 8 servings*

*1 cup uncooked elbow macaroni (or pasta of similar size)*

*1/2 pound ground skinless turkey breast, all visible fat removed*

*1 medium onion, peeled and chopped*

*1 small green bell pepper, chopped*

*2 cloves garlic, peeled and minced*

*1 15-ounce can kidney beans, rinsed and drained*

*1 15$^1$/$_2$-ounce can diced tomatoes, juice reserved*

*1 11-ounce can corn, drained*

*1 8-ounce can tomato sauce*

*1 6-ounce can tomato paste*

*1$^1$/$_2$ tablespoons Mexican chili powder, or chili powder with a pinch of oregano, garlic powder, sugar, and cayenne*

*2 teaspoons ground cumin*

*(continued)*

**1** In a large pot of boiling water, cook the pasta until al dente. Drain the pasta and set aside.

**2** While the pasta is cooking, lightly coat a large nonstick skillet with no-stick vegetable oil spray. Place the turkey, onion, bell pepper, and garlic in the skillet and cook over medium-high heat, stirring frequently, for 10 minutes. Make sure that the turkey is cooked through, breaking it up as needed with the back of a wooden spoon.

**3** Add the macaroni, kidney beans, diced tomatoes and juice, corn, tomato sauce, tomato paste, chili powder, and cumin, and stir to combine.

**4** Raise the heat to high and cook until the mixture begins to boil. Reduce the heat to low and simmer, uncovered, for 20 minutes, stirring occasionally.

*Nutrition at a glance (per serving): Total fat 1.5 g; Saturated fat 0.5 g; Protein 14 g; Dietary fiber 6 g; Carbohydrate 34 g; Cholesterol 19 mg; Sodium 629 mg; % of calories from fat 7; Calories 197.*

*Lynn's turkey tip: For a more meaty feel to this dish, partially freeze a turkey fillet (a $^{1}/_{4}$-inch slice of turkey breast). Cut the meat into $^{1}/_{4}$-inch pieces and toss them into the chili in place of the ground turkey.*

## Paella

Paella is a Spanish creation that can include all manner of foods, such as saffron rice, shrimp, lobster, clams, chicken, pork, and a variety of vegetables. You can create your own version and improvise with foods you particularly like. This version is exceptional and so simple. The shrimp act as a garnish, but you can add additional garnishes, such as sprigs of dill, rosemary, long chives, diced tomatoes, or lemon slices. If you're making the artichoke hearts from scratch, cook them ahead of time. (See "Lynn's artichoke tip" at the end of this recipe.)

*Tools:* Two-handled paella pan, Dutch oven, or large skillet

*Preparation time:* 2

*Yield:* 6 servings

*(continued)*

2 cloves garlic, peeled and minced

1 cup chopped onion

2 medium tomatoes, coarsely chopped

8 small clams in shells, shells scrubbed

3 cups defatted chicken broth

6 ounces large shrimp (about 6 shrimp), shelled and deveined

1¹/₂ cups uncooked white rice, preferably short-grain

¹/₄ cup chopped fresh parsley

¹/₄ teaspoon saffron threads

¹/₂ teaspoon dried oregano

1 cup fresh or frozen green peas

6 artichoke hearts, fresh or canned

¹/₄ to ¹/₂ teaspoon hot sauce

4 ounces Canadian bacon or lean ham, all visible fat removed, diced

*1* Coat either a stovetop two-handled paella pan, a Dutch oven, or a large skillet with no-stick vegetable oil spray. Place the garlic and onion in the skillet and sauté over medium heat for 5 minutes, stirring often so that the garlic doesn't burn. Add a few tablespoons of water for moisture if necessary.

*2* Add the tomatoes, clams, and ¹/₂ cup of the broth. Cover and cook for 3 minutes. Add the shrimp and cook for another 2 minutes. The clam shells should open. Remove the clams and shrimp and lightly cover them with foil to keep them warm.

*3* Add the rice, remaining broth, parsley, saffron, and oregano. Raise the heat to high and bring the mixture to a boil. Cover and reduce the heat to low. Simmer the rice mixture on low for 20 minutes. Stir once or twice near the end.

*4* Add the peas and artichoke hearts. Cook, covered, for another 5 minutes.

*5* Mix in the Canadian bacon or ham, shrimp, and reserved clams. Cook for 1 minute or until heated through. Serve in the paella pan or transfer to a large platter.

**Nutrition at a glance (per serving):** *Total fat 2.5 g; Saturated fat 0.5 g; Protein 18 g; Dietary fiber 4 g; Carbohydrate 40 g; Cholesterol 54 mg; Sodium 425 mg; % of calories from fat 8; Calories 256.*

**Lynn's artichoke tip:** *Making your own artichoke hearts is easy. They are so much better and less salty than the metallic-tasting canned variety. Cut off the bottom stem of the artichoke even with the leaves. Hold it upside-down on a counter. With your palm, push down hard against the stem end to open the leaves. Rinse the inside leaves well under cold running water. Invert, place in a large saucepan, cover with water, and boil the artichokes (with a slice of lemon if you like) for 50 minutes. Or microwave in a microwaveable bowl with 1 inch of water for 30 minutes. Or pressure-cook 4 to 6 artichokes for 25 minutes. Pull off the leaves and cut out the choke, and the delicious hearts are left. (See Figure 13-3.)*

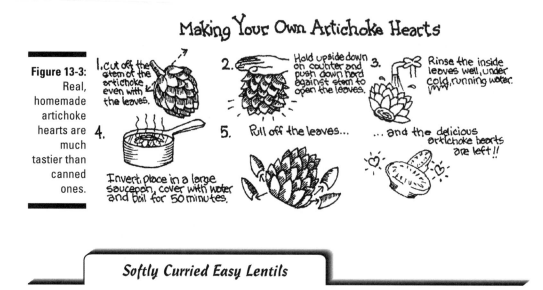

**Figure 13-3:**
Real, homemade artichoke hearts are much tastier than canned ones.

## Softly Curried Easy Lentils

This recipe is a lightly spiced, natural dish of lentils, onions, and tomatoes. You essentially make your own curry, which any East Indian cook will tell you is much better than ready-made. You can substitute dried peas, barley, or even small dried beans. Serve with plain (drained) fat-free yogurt or fat-free or lowfat sour cream for a cooling contrast. For a salad, sliced cucumbers mixed with a little sugar and a few tablespoons of vinegar go nicely.

**Tools:** *Small saucepan, small nonstick skillet*

**Preparation time:** *2*

**Yield:** *4 servings*

| | |
|---|---|
| *1 cup dried lentils, beans, or a mixture* | *$1/4$ teaspoon ground coriander* |
| *1 bay leaf* | *$1/8$ teaspoon cayenne pepper* |
| *3 cups water* | *$1/8$ teaspoon turmeric* |
| *$1/2$ cup chopped onion* | *$1/16$ teaspoon ground cloves* |
| *1 large tomato, chopped* | *1 tablespoon minced fresh cilantro* |
| *$1/2$ teaspoon ground cumin* | *1 teaspoon salt (optional)* |
| *$1/4$ teaspoon cinnamon* | *Freshly ground black pepper* |
| *$1/2$ teaspoon minced fresh ginger root, or $1/4$ teaspoon dried, ground ginger* | |

*(continued)*

*1* In a small saucepan, combine the lentils, bay leaf, and water and place over medium-high heat. Bring to a boil, reduce the heat to low, and simmer for 35 minutes, stirring occasionally, until the lentils are tender. Set the lentils aside and discard the bay leaf.

*2* Coat a small nonstick skillet with no-stick vegetable oil spray. Place the onion in the skillet and sauté over medium heat for 5 minutes, stirring, until it begins to soften. Add the tomato, cumin, cinnamon, ginger, coriander, cayenne pepper, turmeric, and cloves. Cook for 10 minutes, stirring occasionally.

*3* Add the lentils, the ¹/₂ to ³/₄ cup remaining liquid, and the cilantro. Add the salt (if desired) and pepper to taste.

*4* Reduce the heat to low and simmer for 5 minutes.

> **Nutrition at a glance (per serving):** *Total fat 0.5 g; Saturated fat 0 g; Protein 12 g; Dietary fiber 7 g; Carbohydrate 29 g; Cholesterol 0 mg; Sodium 13 mg; % of calories from fat 4; Calories 163.*

> **Lynn's curry tip:** *Serving currylike dishes with small custard cups of "pass-arounds" is great fun. Fill them separately with raisins, chopped chutney, chopped peanuts, chopped coconut, hot sauce or crushed red pepper flakes, sesame seeds, or chopped dates.*

## Straw and Hay (or Pasta Carbonara)

Creamy-textured with peas and ham, this pasta is thick, delicious, and rich-tasting. Make sure that the cottage cheese is completely pureed. (Pureeing takes about 4 minutes in a blender or food processor.)

**Tools:** *Large pot, blender or food processor, large nonstick skillet*

**Preparation time:** *2*

**Yield:** *4 servings*

8 ounces lowfat fettuccine or pasta of your choice

¹/₂ cup skim milk

¹/₄ cup fat-free sour cream

¹/₂ cup fat-free cottage cheese

¹/₄ cup fat-free Parmesan cheese topping or grated Parmesan cheese

¹/₈ teaspoon ground nutmeg

¹/₈ teaspoon salt (optional)

¹/₈ teaspoon freshly ground black pepper

4 ounces cooked lean ham, all visible fat removed, diced

2 cloves garlic, peeled and minced

¹/₂ cup frozen peas

Chopped fresh parsley for garnish

*(continued)*

*1* In a large pot of boiling water, cook the pasta until al dente. Drain and set aside.

*2* While the pasta is cooking, place the milk, sour cream, cottage cheese, Parmesan cheese, nutmeg, and salt (if desired) and pepper in a blender or food processor. Process until very smooth.

*3* Coat a large nonstick skillet with no-stick vegetable oil spray. Place the ham, garlic, and peas in the skillet and cook over medium heat, stirring often, for 2 minutes.

*4* Add the milk mixture to the ham and pea mixture and cook for 1 minute or until heated through. Add the pasta and toss to coat. Garnish with additional Parmesan cheese (if desired) and chopped parsley.

*Nutrition at a glance (per serving):* Total fat 2.5 g; Saturated fat 0.5 g; Protein 22 g; Dietary fiber 3 g; Carbohydrate 53 g; Cholesterol 16 mg; Sodium 627 mg; % of calories from fat 7; Calories 324.

*Lynn's cottage cheese tip:* You can make all kinds of creamy dishes without fat, but with a slightly different taste, using fat-free cottage cheese. Completely pureeing the fat-free cottage cheese takes about 4 minutes and a good processor or blender. Some equipment leaves tiny curds, which are unpleasant. You may have to try a hand or immersion blender or mini-chopper.

## 20-Minute Pasta and Asparagus

An Italian-style way of serving asparagus, this dish can be garnished with slivered prosciutto ham with all visible fat removed. For the pasta, go wild with Trio Italiano, a combination of rotini, mostaccioli, and shells, by San Giorgio. If you aren't an asparagus lover, substitute green beans or broccoli.

*Tools:* Large pot, large nonstick skillet

*Preparation time:* 2

*Yield:* 6 servings

1 pound dry penne or other noodle-type pasta

2 cloves garlic, peeled and minced

1 large onion, peeled and chopped

1 15$^1$/$_2$-ounce can Italian-style herb tomatoes

1 8-ounce can Italian-style tomato sauce

1 pound asparagus, ends trimmed, cut into 1$^1$/$_2$-inch pieces

Salt (optional) and freshly ground black pepper

$^1$/$_4$ teaspoon crushed red pepper (flakes)

$^1$/$_4$ cup fat-free or lowfat grated Parmesan cheese

*(continued)*

*1* In a large pot of boiling water, cook the pasta until al dente. Drain and set aside.

*2* While the pasta is cooking, coat a large nonstick skillet with no-stick vegetable oil spray. Cook the garlic and onions in the skillet over medium heat until the onions begin to soften.

*3* Add the tomatoes and tomato sauce, asparagus, salt (if desired) and pepper, and crushed red pepper to the garlic and onions. Reduce the heat to medium-low and cook, uncovered, for 10 minutes or until the sauce thickens slightly, breaking up the tomatoes with the back of a spoon or a knife and stirring occasionally. Cook until the asparagus is tender but still al dente.

*4* Add the cooked penne and Parmesan cheese and cook for 2 to 3 minutes or until heated through. Season with salt (if desired) and pepper to taste.

**Nutrition at a glance (per serving):** *Total fat 3 g; Saturated fat 0.5 g; Protein 15 g; Dietary fiber 5 g; Carbohydrate 70 g; Cholesterol 0 mg; Sodium 474 mg; % of calories from fat 7; Calories 362.*

**Lynn's asparagus tips:** *You can cook asparagus in many ways:*

- ✔ Steam pieces in a mesh colander right in the pasta water while the pasta is cooking. Lift the colander out after 2 or 3 minutes (the pasta keeps cooking).

- ✔ Steam whole asparagus spears directly in the pasta water while the pasta is cooking.

- ✔ In a tall asparagus-cooking pot, steam whole spears upright in an inch of water.

- ✔ Place whole spears on their side in $1/2$ inch of water in a skillet and steam, covered.

- ✔ Bake covered with grated Parmesan cheese.

- ✔ Microwave in a microwaveable bag with just the water that clings during rinsing.

# Chapter 14

# Sandwiches

*J*ohn Montagu, the fourth Earl of Sandwich, discovered in the 1700s that he didn't want to leave the gaming tables or get his fingers too soiled while he was eating greasy meat, so he put it between two slices of bread. Which is reportedly how the sandwich was named.

— *History of Food,* Maguelonne Toussaint-Samat

Sandwiches are a mainstay. This chapter shows you how to make plenty of them, from tacos to grilled cheese, chicken salad to subs, all low in fat. I include a list of hot dog variations and peanut butter sandwich variations that can be lowfat, and another list of fat-free condiments. I also provide handy lists of the fattiest and leanest sandwiches, plus the breads that usually contain the most fat, saturated fat, and cholesterol, and those that contain the least.

# Sandwiches Are Forever

Whether hot or cold, lowfat sandwiches are easy to prepare. With just a few, mostly minor changes to lessen the fat content, a wide variety of food choices are literally at your fingertips.

Sandwiches have continually changed as our society has become more affluent. From a meager slick of peanut butter and jelly on white bread in the

1940s and '50s, we have "advanced" to sandwiches with sometimes $1/4$ to $1/2$ pound of sliced meat, several layers of cheese, $1/4$ cup of mayonnaise, and double and triple bread or buns — and so big you can't get your mouth around them. The amount of calories and fat in these monsters is astronomical. Unfortunately, many people have gotten used to eating extremely large and extremely high-fat sandwiches.

On the other hand, a bacon, lettuce, and tomato sandwich prepared slightly differently, with an ounce or two of good, crisp bacon, all fat stripped off; many leaves of crisp, cold iceberg lettuce; slices of red, juicy tomatoes; lowfat or fat-free mayonnaise; and lots of pepper; all on toasted whole grain bread, gets only 20 percent of its calories from fat and is so good-tasting.

# The Elements of a Lowfat Sandwich

To create a lowfat or fat-free sandwich with meat or poultry, you need to be familiar with the new presliced deli-style fat-free ham, chicken, and turkey slices by Oscar Mayer and other companies. Keep the meat slices on a sandwich to a minimum or it won't stay fat-free or lowfat, and pack the sandwich with lettuce, tomatoes, shredded cabbage or carrots, sprouts, and lowfat or fat-free condiments and spreads.

Cheese on a sandwich is one of the hardest foods to duplicate in lowfat form; most lowfat and fat-free cheeses aren't very good yet. But some are better than others, and kids don't often care whether the American cheese slice on their sandwich is high or low in fat. You may as well go low if the cheese flavor doesn't have to be exact and you put many other items on the sandwich.

Vegetable sandwiches can be piled high with cole slaw or avocado slices, which, though higher in fat, aren't as high in fat as most meats, and the fat isn't saturated. Cold baked beans and other styles of beans, lightly mashed, can go on a sandwich, such as hummus in a pita with sprouts. Combinations such as chopped hard-cooked egg whites in lowfat mayonnaise, chopped or sliced onions, and grilled peppers, or sweet mustard with shredded romaine and sprouts on rye toast, make good sandwiches. You can try many other additions, such as a few chopped olives, shredded celery, and reduced-fat or fat-free cream cheese, to make interesting lowfat sandwiches. Figure 14-1 shows that a vegetable and cheese sandwich looks as tasty as it tastes — you shouldn't feel deprived at all!

Many breads are made without fat, making bread relatively low in calories, but bakers are beginning to add fat to formerly fat-free breads, such as French loaves, Italian loaves, crumpets, bagels, English muffins, and even plain white bread, so check the fat content on the label. Using a really good bread is one way to hide a reduction in high-fat meat and cheese.

**Figure 14-1:**
The trick to making lowfat sandwiches is to pile them high with veggies and fat-free condiments and limit the meat and cheese.

TIP

# The ten most important tips for making lowfat sandwiches

✔ Use a good, thick-sliced style of bread that is low in fat (not croissants, for example, which usually get over 40 percent of their calories from fat).

✔ Toast the bread for more crunch and texture.

✔ Use diet margarine or fat-free butter-type spray instead of stick butter or margarine, which has more fat than any other food except oil.

✔ Use fat-free or lowfat mayonnaise or other fat-free or lowfat spreads. Let the taste of the tomatoes, bread, lettuce, and meat take center stage, not the high-fat spread.

✔ Use lean and well-done beef, lean pork or ham with the edge fat cut off, lean lamb with no fat, and only skinless and lean poultry.

✔ Include smaller amounts of meat and poultry — only one or two thin slices.

✔ For high-fat cheese, use just one slice. Or use fat-free or lowfat cheeses, or one slice of regular Swiss cheese and one slice of lowfat.

✔ Use plenty of lettuce, sprouts, onions, roasted peppers, green pepper slices, mushrooms, tomatoes, and other vegetables.

✔ Use plenty of pickles, relishes, mustard, ketchup, and other lowfat and fat-free condiments.

✔ Slice sandwiches into four pieces endwise so that they look and feel like more food and take up more space on the plate. That way, you and the people you're cooking for don't feel deprived.

# Sandwiches and Sandwich Breads That Are Usually High or Low in Fat

These sandwiches can be very low in fat, especially if the mayonnaise or sandwich spread is lowfat or fat-free:

- Chicken breast sandwich (3 ounces of skinless chicken or about two thin, lean slices)
- Club sandwich (1 ounce of lean meat, lowfat or fat-free cheese, and fat-free extras)
- Cucumber sandwich
- Egg white salad sandwich (with lowfat spread)
- Ham sandwich (2 ounces of lean ham, or about two thin slices)
- Mushroom sandwich
- Roast beef sandwich (2 ounces, or about two thin, lean, well-done slices)
- Shrimp sandwich (without high-fat mayonnaise; not low in cholesterol)
- Sprout sandwich
- Tomato sandwich
- Turkey breast sandwich (3 ounces of skinless turkey, or about two thin, lean slices)
- Vegetarian sandwich (without cheese)
- Veggie burger

These sandwiches are, by tradition and with the usual recipe, exceptionally high in fat. The salad sandwiches can be made low in fat with lowfat or fat-free mayonnaise.

- Bacon, lettuce, and tomato sandwich
- Cheese or grilled cheese sandwich
- Deviled egg or ham sandwich
- Hamburger (with or without cheese or bacon)
- Lamb sandwich
- Meat loaf sandwich
- Peanut butter sandwich
- Pork sandwich

> ✔ Reuben or corned beef sandwich
>
> ✔ Roast beef sandwich
>
> ✔ Salad sandwich: chicken, turkey, egg, crab, ham, shrimp, or tuna
>
> ✔ Sandwich au jus or with gravy
>
> ✔ Submarine sandwich

With so many good, fat-free or lowfat breads available, you don't need to add fat to your sandwich in the bread. These breads are traditionally low in fat:

> ✔ Bagels
>
> ✔ Boston brown bread (canned)
>
> ✔ Bran bread
>
> ✔ English muffins
>
> ✔ French or Italian bread
>
> ✔ Hamburger and hot-dog buns
>
> ✔ Hard rolls
>
> ✔ Indian flat bread
>
> ✔ Kaiser rolls
>
> ✔ Lavache
>
> ✔ Matzoh
>
> ✔ Mountain or flat bread
>
> ✔ Oatmeal bread
>
> ✔ Potato bread
>
> ✔ Raisin bread
>
> ✔ Rye and other grain breads, such as pumpernickel
>
> ✔ Sourdough bread
>
> ✔ Tortillas (some varieties)
>
> ✔ White bread
>
> ✔ Whole wheat and cracked wheat breads

Fat can sneak up on you in the form of bread if you don't choose carefully. The following breads are usually high in fat:

> ✔ Biscuits
>
> ✔ Brioche

- ✔ Butter breads
- ✔ Challah
- ✔ Cheese breads
- ✔ Crescent rolls
- ✔ Croissants
- ✔ Egg breads
- ✔ Nut breads
- ✔ Sour cream breads

## Ten good lowfat or fat-free condiments to put on sandwiches

You're in luck. Many great-tasting condiments have no fat and few calories but a great deal of terrific flavor.

- ✔ **Capers:** The pickled flower buds of the caper bush are fat-free.

- ✔ **Chutney:** All kinds, from hot to mango, peach to pear, are fat-free.

- ✔ **Dijonnaise:** Hellman's creamy mustard blend is fat-free. You can find other fat-free and lowfat spreads, including butter types, too.

- ✔ **Horseradish:** Check the label, but most horseradishes, if they don't contain cream, are fat-free.

- ✔ **Hot sauce:** Hot sauce is fat-free.

- ✔ **Ketchup, chili sauce, and salsa:** These tomato-based products are fat-free.

- ✔ **Mayonnaise:** Mayo comes fat-free, lowfat, light, no egg, and with egg — all kinds of ways.

- ✔ **Mustard (prepared, not dried), including Dijon:** Look at labels; some have added fat and egg yolks, but most mustards are fat-free.

- ✔ **Pickles:** From fancy cornichons to plain dill, watermelon to okra, almost every pickle (except for egg pickles) is fat-free.

- ✔ **Relishes:** Try corn, pepper, tomato, cranberry, chow chow, pickle, cherry pepper, or onion; all are fat-free.

# *Sumptuous Sandwich Recipes*

Sandwiches are easy to make low in fat — just limit the amounts of meat, cheese, and high-fat spreads. Many of the recipes in this section are lowfat versions of traditional favorites.

## Bacon, Lettuce, and Tomato Sandwiches

A simple and traditional sandwich at its best. Regular rather than diet bread increases the fat content by only a fraction.

*Tools:* *Nonstick skillet or griddle*

*Preparation time:* *1*

*Yield:* *4 servings*

12 slices bacon, all fat removed

2 tablespoons fat-free or lowfat mayonnaise

8 slices low-calorie white or whole wheat bread, toasted

4 to 12 lettuce leaves

8 slices ripe tomato

*1* Judiciously cut all the fat off the bacon and discard. In a nonstick skillet or griddle, fry the bacon, or wrap it in paper towels and cook in a microwave, watching and turning it every 2 minutes. After the bacon is cooked, blot with paper towels.

*2* Spread $1/2$ tablespoon mayonnaise on each of 4 slices of toast. Add 1 to 4 lettuce leaves, 2 tomato slices, and 3 bacon slivers (the meat after you remove the fat), and cover with a second slice of toast.

***Nutrition at a glance (per serving):*** *Total fat 3 g; Saturated fat 1 g; Protein 10 g; Dietary fiber 5 g; Carbohydrate 23 g; Cholesterol 14 mg; Sodium 645 mg; % of calories from fat 18; Calories 148.*

***Lynn's BLT tip:*** *When ordering a BLT at a restaurant, I ask, "Light on mayonnaise, please, and the bacon on the side." I've found that I get better bacon, never burned, and often more lettuce and tomato, so the sandwich doesn't look skimpy. Although I have to take the time to pick off all the bacon fat and put the bacon slivers back on the sandwich, the result is worth the effort.*

## Chicken Salad Sandwiches

The secret to a good chicken salad sandwich is the chicken, which takes 10 minutes to cook from scratch in the microwave. Chicken salad sandwiches can be hefty and scrumptious and don't have to contain the usual $1/4$ cup of mayonnaise or 600 calories. I call for low-calorie bread here, but using regular bread doesn't significantly increase the fat content.

**Tools:** *Microwaveable bag, microwaveable bowl, small saucepan*

**Preparation time:** *2*

**Yield:** *4 servings*

| | |
|---|---|
| *1 whole 8-ounce chicken breast, skinless and boneless* | *1 tablespoon fresh lemon juice* |
| *$1/4$ teaspoon each dried thyme, rosemary, oregano, basil, and salt (salt optional)* | *$1/2$ to $3/4$ cup fat-free or lowfat mayonnaise* |
| *3 eggs* | *2 tablespoons crushed canned pineapple, drained (optional)* |
| *1 stalk celery, including tops, chopped* | *8 lettuce leaves* |
| *3 tablespoons chopped onion* | *8 slices low-calorie bread, toasted if desired* |
| *1 scallion, finely chopped* | *Freshly ground black pepper* |

**1** Place the chicken in a microwaveable bag, top pulled back to reveal the breasts. In a large bowl, combine the herbs. Rub the herbs on the chicken. Close and seal the bag. Place in a microwaveable bowl and slit the bag on top to let steam escape. Microwave for 8 to 10 minutes on high, turning once.

**2** Meanwhile, hard-cook the eggs, boiling them for 20 minutes (to keep the shells from cracking, place the eggs in cold water and then bring to a boil). In the herb bowl, combine the celery, onion, scallion, lemon juice, and mayonnaise and mix well. Add the pineapple (if desired), mixing well.

**3** After the chicken is done, remove and check it with the tip of a sharp knife, slicing through the thickest part to make sure that no pink color remains.

**4** Dice the chicken into $3/4$-inch pieces, add them to the mixture in the bowl, and mix well. Cover the mixture with plastic wrap and place it in the freezer for 5 minutes to chill.

**5** Run the eggs under cold water, peel, discard the yolks, chop the whites, and add them to the chilled mixture, tossing lightly.

**6** Place two lettuce leaves on each slice of bread or toast, spoon on the chicken salad, add pepper to taste, cover with a second slice of toast, cut diagonally, and skewer with colored, fringed toothpicks (so that they can be seen).

*(continued)*

*Nutrition at a glance (per serving):* *Total fat 2.5 g; Saturated fat 0.5 g; Protein 19 g; Dietary fiber 4 g; Carbohydrate 24 g; Cholesterol 34 mg; Sodium 486 mg; % of calories from fat 11; Calories 190.*

*Lynn's chicken-seasoning tips:* *I suggest the herb mixture in this chicken salad recipe, but you can always use $^1/_2$ teaspoon of a prepared spice mix, such as Spike or Mrs. Dash, Cajun spice for more heat, lemon salt or pepper, garlic powder, seasoning salt or pepper, or chopped fresh herbs.*

## Deviled Ham Sandwiches

Deviled ham doesn't have to come from that little can wrapped in paper that you never open. Try this tasty retro variety, and you'll be hooked. Add sprouts, watercress, sliced pepperoncini, and sliced cherry tomatoes to this easy-to-eat, tasty ham sandwich. I use low-calorie bread, but using regular bread doesn't significantly increase the fat content.

**Tools:** *Blender or food processor*

**Preparation time:** *1*

**Yield:** *4 servings*

| | |
|---|---|
| *6 ounces lean ham, all visible fat removed* | *1 teaspoon grated horseradish* |
| *1 tablespoon prepared mustard* | *2 tablespoons sweet pickle relish, drained* |
| *$^1/_4$ cup fat-free or lowfat mayonnaise* | *8 slices low-calorie white bread* |
| *$^1/_4$ teaspoon vinegar* | *8 to 12 lettuce leaves* |
| *$^1/_2$ small onion, peeled and finely chopped* | *Freshly ground black pepper* |

*1* In a blender or food processor, puree or process the ham, mustard, 2 tablespoons of the mayonnaise, and vinegar. Add the onion, horseradish, and pickle relish and stir with a spoon.

*2* Spread the remaining 2 tablespoons mayonnaise on 4 slices of bread. Then spread the deviled ham on the other 4 slices of bread. Place 2 or 3 lettuce leaves on each ham-filled side, sprinkle with several shakes of pepper, cover, and slice.

*Nutrition at a glance (per serving):* *Total fat 3.5 g; Saturated fat 1 g; Protein 13 g; Dietary fiber 4 g; Carbohydrate 24 g; Cholesterol 13 mg; Sodium 871 mg; % of calories from fat 17; Calories 170.*

*(continued)*

*Lynn's deviled ham tips: You can also use deviled ham on toasted wheat rounds as canapés, or stuff it into raw snow peas, tiny bliss potatoes, or grade B or small, hard-cooked egg white halves. For dinner, stuff a big spoonful of deviled ham into baked sweet potatoes or russet potatoes.*

### Egg Salad Sandwiches

Everyone always loves this nearly cholesterol-free sandwich. You can add slices of tomatoes, canned chopped and drained chilies, relish, or pickles if you like.

**Tools:** *Large nonstick skillet*

**Preparation time:** *2*

**Yield:** *6 servings*

| | |
|---|---|
| *1 cup substitute eggs, well beaten* | *1 medium onion, peeled and chopped* |
| *Salt (optional)* | *1 large stalk celery, chopped* |
| *$^{1}/_{2}$ cup fat-free or lowfat mayonnaise* | *2 tablespoons finely chopped fresh parsley* |
| *2 teaspoons cider vinegar* | |
| *1 tablespoon prepared mustard* | *$^{1}/_{4}$ teaspoon freshly ground black pepper* |
| *6 hard-cooked eggs, 5 yolks discarded, whites coarsely chopped* | *12 slices white or whole wheat bread* |
| | *12 lettuce leaves* |

*1* Lightly coat a large nonstick skillet with no-stick vegetable oil spray. Add the beaten eggs and salt (if desired) and cook, covered, on medium-low heat until firm, being careful not to burn them. Don't scramble them while they cook.

*2* Slide the eggs onto a cutting board. With a large knife, chop the egg pancake into $^{1}/_{4}$- to $^{1}/_{2}$-inch pieces. Crumble the hard-cooked egg yolk over the top of the chopped substitute eggs.

*3* In a large bowl, combine the mayonnaise, vinegar, and mustard, mixing well.

*4* Add the chopped eggs, chopped hard-cooked egg whites, onion, celery, parsley, and pepper and coat well with the dressing.

*5* Spread the mixture on half the bread slices, add the lettuce, and top with the remaining bread slices. Cut into halves or fourths.

*(continued)*

**Nutrition at a glance (per serving):** *Total fat 3.5 g; Saturated fat 1 g; Protein 15 g; Dietary fiber 2 g; Carbohydrate 40 g; Cholesterol 38 mg; Sodium 657 mg; % of calories from fat 13; Calories 255.*

**Lynn's egg tips:** *To easily extract hard-cooked eggs from the shell, place the eggs in cold water and bring to a boil. Simmer for 20 minutes and then immediately immerse them in ice water or run them under very cold water. Crack the shells on the counter and roll with your palms. Pick off one end and continue peeling. (See Figure 14-2.) Often, the whole peel comes off at once. If the eggs are old, the shell will stick to the eggs regardless of what method you use.*

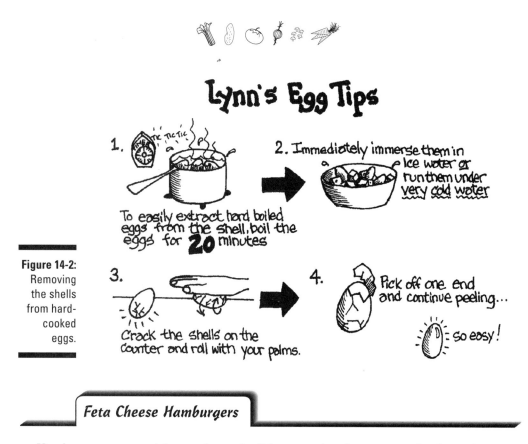

**Figure 14-2:** Removing the shells from hard-cooked eggs.

## Feta Cheese Hamburgers

Hamburgers are great fun, and you don't have to give them up on a lowfat eating plan. These thick, food-filled burgers don't look skimpy. Serve them with carrot sticks, radishes, and lowfat chips.

**Tools:** *Large nonstick skillet, grill, or broiler*

**Preparation time:** *2*

**Yield:** *4 servings*

*(continued)*

7 ounces lean top round, all visible fat removed, ground

2 tablespoons finely chopped green bell pepper

2 tablespoons finely chopped onion

4 ounces mushrooms (about 10 medium), finely chopped

1 clove garlic, peeled and minced

2 teaspoons Worcestershire sauce

2 teaspoons soy sauce

1 egg white

2 tablespoons bread crumbs

8 slices low-calorie bread or 4 hamburger buns, split

$^1/_4$ cup fat-free or lowfat ranch dressing

4 lettuce leaves

4 slices tomato

4 slices onion

4 teaspoons reduced-fat feta or blue cheese, crumbled

**1** In a large bowl, place the ground round, green pepper, onions, mushrooms, garlic, Worcestershire sauce, soy sauce, egg white, and bread crumbs and mix well with your hands. Make 4 patties and set aside. (Be sure to wash your hands before handling the buns.)

**2** Lightly coat a large nonstick skillet, grill, or broiler rack with no-stick vegetable oil spray and place over medium heat. When hot, place the burgers in the skillet and cook to well done, about 8 minutes, turning once.

**3** Toast the bread or buns, spread on the dressing, and place a lettuce leaf, tomato slice, and onion slice on each bun or on each of 4 slices of bread. Put a hamburger and 1 teaspoon crumbled feta or blue cheese on top. Cover with the other bun half or bread slice.

***Nutrition at a glance (per serving):*** *Total fat 3 g; Saturated fat 1 g; Protein 19 g; Dietary fiber 5 g; Carbohydrate 30 g; Cholesterol 33 mg; Sodium 658 mg; % of calories from fat 14; Calories 215.*

***Lynn's burger-flavoring tips:*** *You can use many different fat-free or lowfat salad dressings to sauté and season hamburgers as they cook. Try fat-free or lowfat Italian, French, Caesar, or mayonnaise.*

## Grilled Cheese Sandwiches

This recipe works well because it isn't just the cheese you're enjoying. All the ingredients need to be at room temperature. On the side, serve radishes, carrot sticks, and fat-free or lowfat pretzels or chips.

*(continued)*

**Tools:** *Extra-large nonstick skillet, or 2 smaller nonstick skillets*

**Preparation time:** *1*

**Yield:** *4 servings*

*8 slices white or whole wheat bread*

*4 1-ounce slices fat-free or lowfat Cheddar or Muenster cheese*

*12 thin slices avocado (optional)*

*8 thin slices ripe tomato*

*4 slices onion, rings separated*

*Salt (optional) and freshly ground black pepper*

*4 whole canned mild green chilies, cut in half; pepperoncinis, sliced; or jalapeño peppers, chopped*

**1** Lightly coat an extra-large skillet (large enough for 4 bread slices, or use 2 smaller skillets for 2 slices each) with no-stick vegetable oil spray. Begin heating on medium heat.

**2** Lightly coat one side of each piece of bread with I Can't Believe It's Not Butter! spray (not tub).

**3** Raise the heat to medium-high. Place 4 slices of bread, sprayed side down, in the skillet.

**4** On each slice in the skillet, layer 1 slice cheese, 3 thin slices avocado (if desired), 2 slices tomato, several onion rings, and 2 chili pepper halves (or several small rounds of chilies, depending on the type of peppers you use).

**5** Add the second bread slice to the top, sprayed side up.

**6** Cover the food with a smaller lid to melt the cheese, or, if you like a flatter sandwich, place a smaller, heavy, flat-bottomed frying pan on the top slices to flatten them. Check often to make sure that they aren't burning.

**7** When browned, turn and brown the other side.

*Nutrition at a glance (per serving): Total fat 2.5 g; Saturated fat 1 g; Protein 16 g; Dietary fiber 4 g; Carbohydrate 43 g; Cholesterol 7 mg; Sodium 1389 mg; % of calories from fat 9; Calories 259.*

*Lynn's skillet-heating tips: To heat items in a skillet more quickly, select a curved lid that is a few inches smaller in diameter than the skillet. Cover the items with the lid, letting the lid edges rest on the bottom of the skillet.*

## Ham and Egg Sandwiches with Tomatoes

Similar to a Denver sandwich, this ham and egg sandwich on toast can be a quick lunch, breakfast on the run, or a light dinner. I call for low-calorie bread, but using regular bread doesn't significantly increase the fat content.

**Tools:** *Large nonstick skillet or square griddle*

**Preparation time:** *1*

**Yield:** *4 servings*

$1^1/_2$ cups substitute eggs, beaten

Salt (optional)

8 slices low-calorie bread, toasted

$^1/_2$ cup fat-free or lowfat Russian or horseradish dressing

8 lettuce leaves

4 1-ounce slices Canadian bacon or lean ham, all visible fat removed

8 slices tomato

$^1/_4$ teaspoon freshly ground black pepper

*1* Lightly coat a large nonstick skillet or square griddle with no-stick vegetable oil spray. Add the beaten eggs and some salt (if desired) and cook, covered, on medium-low heat until firm, being careful not to burn the eggs. Don't scramble them while they cook.

*2* Remove the eggs and cut them into more or less sandwich-sized slices (not pie-shaped) and set aside.

*3* Spread dressing on one side of each piece of toast. Place the lettuce on the dressing, the eggs on the lettuce, the bacon on the eggs, and the tomato slices on the bacon. Pepper well. Cover with the remaining slice of toast. Cut each sandwich into four slices and secure with a fringed toothpick (so that you can see it).

**Nutrition at a glance (per serving):** *Total fat 3.5 g; Saturated fat 1 g; Protein 19 g; Dietary fiber 5 g; Carbohydrate 30 g; Cholesterol 34 mg; Sodium 749 mg; % of calories from fat 13; Calories 226.*

**Lynn's sandwich tips:** *A Denver sandwich is a mixture of sautéed onions and green peppers with lean ham and chopped hard-cooked eggs on toast. Make it low in fat by using a thin slice of lean ham, sautéing plenty of onions and green peppers in no-stick vegetable oil spray, and adding chopped hard-cooked egg whites and a good lowfat dressing.*

IMPROVISE

# Ten ways to serve hot dogs

All these methods are low in fat, including the bacon dogs if all the fat is removed from the bacon.

- **Chili dog:** Add heated lowfat bean chili to the dog in the bun. (You need to use lowfat or fat-free hot dogs and buns, of course.)

- **Sauerkraut dog:** Add heated and drained sauerkraut to the dog in the bun.

- **Cheese dog:** Add a couple of slices of fat-free or lowfat cheese, or if using a fat-free dog, a tablespoon of crumbled reduced-fat feta.

- **Barbecue sauce and cole slaw dog:** Heat the dog in a skillet in barbecue sauce. Put the dog in a bun and pour on the extra sauce. Add a couple tablespoons of slaw made with lowfat or fat-free mayonnaise.

- **Baked bean dog:** Add several tablespoons heated lowfat Boston baked beans to the dog in the bun.

- **Onion dog:** Sauté sliced onions in no-stick vegetable oil spray. When translucent, add them to the dog in the bun.

- **Bacon dog:** Add fat-free Dijonnaise and 2 slices coarsely chopped or crumbled cooked bacon, all fat removed (before or after cooking), to the dog in the bun.

- **Ketchup or steak sauce dog:** To ketchup or chili sauce, add chopped raw onions, olives, horseradish, and hot sauce. Add the sauce to the dog in the bun.

- **Pepper salsa dog:** Sauté the dogs with green bell peppers, finely diced jalapeño peppers, and chopped, canned, drained chilies. Serve with salsa and finely chopped lettuce.

- **Chilies rellenos dogs:** Stuff a whole canned, drained chili with a hot dog. Place on the opened bun, place several slices lowfat or fat-free cheese on top, and bake for 15 minutes in a 350° oven. Add another slice of cheese and chopped raw onions. Serve in a flour tortilla with salsa.

## Submarine Sandwiches

Easy to make and very filling. Use a good, crusty baguette.

*Preparation time: 1*

*Yield: 4 servings*

*(continued)*

*1 8-inch loaf French bread, cut in half lengthwise*

*¹/₂ cup fat-free or lowfat vinaigrette or Italian dressing*

*8 romaine lettuce leaves*

*¹/₄ cup sliced pepperoncini or jalapeño peppers*

*1 cup shredded iceberg lettuce*

*4 ounces fat-free or very lean deli-style boiled ham*

*4 ounces fat-free or very lean deli-style chicken or turkey slices*

*8 slices fat-free or lowfat Swiss cheese*

*8 slices tomato*

*8 slices green bell pepper*

*1 Bermuda onion, peeled and thinly sliced*

*4 scallions*

**1** Onto each half of the sliced baguette, spoon 2 tablespoons dressing. Add 1 lettuce leaf, 1 tablespoon pepperoncini or jalapeño, and ¹/₄ cup shredded lettuce.

**2** Overlap slices of the ham, chicken or turkey, cheese, tomatoes, peppers, and onions. Place the whole scallions lengthwise across the slices so that the ends stick out, place more lettuce on top, and cover with the top slice of the baguette. Slice into fourths.

***Nutrition at a glance (per serving):*** *Total fat 2 g; Saturated fat 0.5 g; Protein 24 g; Dietary fiber 3 g; Carbohydrate 44 g; Cholesterol 22 mg; Sodium 1953 mg; % of calories from fat 6; Calories 294.*

***Lynn's lowfat sub tricks:*** *Although salami is often on subs, no tasty, firm salami that is low in fat is available yet. You can substitute pepperoni slices, though. Hormel makes a good lower-fat pepperoni with only 4 grams of fat in 17 slices. It's made of turkey and tastes almost the same as regular pepperoni.*

## Tacos

Making great lowfat tacos from scratch is a cinch. The garnishes make all the difference.

***Tools:*** *Nonstick skillet*

***Preparation time:*** *2*

***Yield:*** *4 servings*

*(continued)*

*¹/₄ pound lean top round, all visible fat removed, ground*

*1 medium onion, peeled and coarsely chopped*

*1 clove garlic, peeled and minced*

*1 tablespoon chili powder*

*¹/₂ teaspoon ground cumin*

*Salt (optional) and freshly ground black pepper*

*1 4-ounce can tomato sauce*

*1 15-ounce can pinto or kidney beans, drained, rinsed, and mashed*

*8 fat-free corn tortillas, hard and folded, or soft*

**Garnishes:**

*1 head iceberg lettuce, finely shredded*

*1 very ripe medium tomato, diced*

*1 medium onion, peeled and finely chopped*

*¹/₂ cup salsa or taco sauce, or a few squirts hot pepper sauce*

*1 cup fat-free or lowfat sour cream*

*¹/₂ cup sliced ripe olives (optional)*

*¹/₂ cup shredded fat-free or lowfat Cheddar cheese (optional)*

**1** Preheat the oven to 375°.

**2** Lightly coat a nonstick skillet with no-stick vegetable oil spray. Brown the top round, onion, and garlic in the skillet over medium heat, tossing, for 5 minutes. Stir in the chili powder, cumin, and salt (if desired) and pepper and cook for 1 minute, tossing.

**3** Add the tomato sauce and beans. Cook for 5 minutes, stirring, until little liquid is left.

**4** Divide and fill the 8 tortillas with this mixture.

**5** Top each mixture with the garnishes, such as shredded lettuce first, chopped tomato, raw onion, and salsa or hot sauce and sour cream, topped with any of the optional garnish ingredients.

**Nutrition at a glance (per serving):** *Total fat 2.5 g; Saturated fat 0.5 g; Protein 23 g; Dietary fiber 9 g; Carbohydrate 62 g; Cholesterol 20 mg; Sodium 881 mg; % of calories from fat 7; Calories 368.*

**Lynn's taco tips:** *You can bake your own flat corn tortillas into fat-free taco-shaped shells yourself, as shown in Figure 14-3. Remove one oven rack. Pull out, but don't remove, the second rack, which should be in the center part of the oven. Drape the tortillas over the rack, ends hanging down, making a shell that can be filled. Depending on how close or far apart your rack tines are, you may have to drape over two rack tines. With the oven at 350°, bake the tortillas for 5 to 10 minutes.*

**Figure 14-3:** You can bake your own taco shells and avoid a great deal of fat.

# Ten peanut butter sandwich variations

Using reduced-fat peanut butter helps greatly, but peanut butter sandwiches are fairly high in fat no matter what products you buy, especially if you use more than 1 or 2 teaspoons of peanut butter per sandwich. Fortunately, most of the fat isn't saturated — in my philosophy, an "okay" or natural, not added, fat.

On bread or toast, the following favorites and are low in fat if you use 1 teaspoon of peanut butter per sandwich (use 1 tablespoon for moderate fat). Remember that the peanut butter is only flavor; the filling adds texture.

✔ **Jelly:** Spread any jelly on the sandwich.

✔ **Cheese:** Add two slices of fat-free or lowfat cheese.

✔ **Bananas:** Mash a banana and spread it on the sandwich, or slice it lengthwise and place it on the sandwich. You can also mix the peanut butter and bananas together.

✔ **Honey:** Add a tablespoon of honey to the optional tablespoon of peanut butter.

✔ **Bacon:** Cook one slice of bacon, cut off all the fat, crumble it, and place the meat part only on the peanut butter. (Doing so raises the fat content of the sandwich slightly.)

✔ **Berries:** Thinly slice three or four strawberries or lots of raspberries or blueberries and place them on the peanut butter.

✔ **Tomatoes:** Place a slice or two of tomato on the peanut butter.

✔ **Margarine and dried fruit:** Use fat-free or diet margarine on one slice of the bread and dot with raisins, dried cranberries, or tart cherries.

✔ **Diced or sliced apples:** Add three thin slices of cored apple.

✔ **Cream cheese:** Spread peanut butter on the bottom slice of bread and fat-free or reduced-fat cream cheese on the top half.

# Chapter 15

# Vegetables

## In This Chapter

▶ Discovering the allure of vegetables

▶ Trying out lowfat vegetable cooking methods

▶ Making smart choices of vegetables and vegetable dishes

*"W*e *ate supper, and upon my word, I needed it. She served me morels, (peas, carrots,) truffles and with a sauce of mushrooms . . . so we hastened straight from table to bed."*

— Mirabeau, *Le libertin de qualité*

Vegetables are the fastest fast lowfat food; you can just wash and eat most of them. The desire for fresh vegetables is booming, and no wonder; vegetables are inexpensive, nutritious, and versatile. No longer regarded merely as a side dish for meat, they have come into their own as entrees, soups, sides, snacks, salads, and appetizers. Low in fat and high in fiber, minerals, and vitamins, vegetables are one of the most important foods.

You can choose from many brand-new varieties, and you can rediscover old favorites. Produce departments in markets everywhere have expanded to meet the growing demand, and even chain grocery stores carry a wide selection of vegetables. For example, in addition to the traditional green bell peppers, you can purchase a rainbow of peppers — red, orange, yellow, and purple bells — at your local supermarket.

You'll even see several bins of different kinds of the lowly potato — from russets to Idahos, California longs to goldens, new reds to blues — which is not surprising when you realize that between 4,000 and 8,000 varieties exist (depending on which expert you talk to). Potatoes are a good vegetable choice. Like lima beans, they're good sources of complex carbohydrates, fiber, vitamins, and minerals; they're easy to cook; and you feel full and satisfied after eating them. (See Figure 15-1.)

**Figure 15-1:**
Even the common potato comes in thousands of varieties.

Because most vegetables, legumes, and fungi (mushrooms) are perfect foods on a lowfat eating plan, this chapter encourages you to cultivate the vegetable-eating habit. It explains vegetables' vitamin and fiber content and revisits old favorites prepared in new, lowfat ways. I include 14 vegetable recipes, and most of the ingredients are interchangeable with several types of vegetables. I also provide a handy list of vegetable dishes that are usually high in fat and a list of usually lowfat alternatives.

# The Healthy Alternative

Some experts say that vitamin supplements aren't necessary for most people if they eat a well-rounded diet, which means a wide variety of vegetables, lean meats, fruits, lowfat or fat-free dairy products, and grains. Many leafy green vegetables are good sources of calcium and important vitamins, such as A, C, and beta-carotene (a precursor of vitamin A). Be aware that vegetables lose some of their vitamins, especially C, in cooking.

Vegetables are low in calories, too. If you don't add oil during cooking, a medium potato has just 135 calories. But watch how toppings can add fat and calories *fast:*

- ✔ Top it with 2 tablespoons of fat-free sour cream and 1 tablespoon of chopped scallions, and the total is 166 calories with trace amounts of fat.

- ✔ If you use 2 tablespoons of lowfat sour cream and 1 tablespoon of chopped chives, the dish provides 170 calories and 2 grams of fat.

- ✔ If you use 1 tablespoon of butter or margarine and 2 tablespoons of regular sour cream, you rack up 296 calories and 18 grams of fat.

- ✔ If you fill the potato with 2 tablespoons of butter or margarine and $1/4$ cup of cheese, the result is 450 calories and a whopping 32 grams of fat (two-thirds of the fat is saturated)!

So go with the baked potato and fat-free sour cream. You can eat almost three whole potatoes with fat-free sour cream for the same amount of calories and fat as a potato with butter and cheese, and fat-free sour cream tastes good. Also keep in mind that 20 potato chips contain about 14 grams of fat and 214 calories — and you don't even feel full after eating 20 potato chips!

So beef up your vegetable repertoire and try new potato, pepper, onion, bean, and tomato varieties. What you try may be a gem or a dud, but the dud usually costs under a dollar — pretty cheap to sample what may become a lifelong favorite. Try new or unknown vegetables when you're very hungry; everything tastes better then.

In adding more vegetables to your diet, try not to make too rapid a dietary change; add more fresh produce gradually to let your body adjust slowly.

Vegetables are one of life's greatest bargains and greatest pleasures. Where else can you get so many interesting varieties, so little fat, so much fiber, and such great enjoyment for so little time, effort, and money?

# *Buying and Storing Vegetables*

When buying produce, be flexible. If the store doesn't have good-looking snow peas for your Chinese meal, be prepared to go Italian instead. Also, be aware that you can't always count on perfect-looking vegetables to taste great. Vegetables with no imperfections at all often taste like plastic. Many flawless vegetables are waxed, which probably isn't healthy, and they offer little flavor and a mealy texture. I'm always ready to change my whole menu after looking over the produce.

To keep produce as long as possible, don't store potatoes, tomatoes, onions, or garlic in plastic, whether refrigerated or not. Keep other refrigerated vegetables (such as leeks, scallions, celery, carrots, lettuce, parsley, and especially mushrooms) unwashed in their plastic bags until you're ready to use them. Too much moisture tends to cause rotting, and keeping unwashed vegetables in plastic bags tends to keep them fresher.

They say to put unripe tomatoes and avocados in a brown bag under the sink, but I always forget about them. So I just ripen this produce on the counter in a fruit and vegetable basket, or I refrigerate them to slow their ripening, but only for a day or two.

# Cooking Vegetables in Lowfat Ways

Vegetables readily lend themselves to being cooked in lowfat ways. You can exercise your culinary creativity: Decide which vegetable — or combination of vegetables — will satisfy your current craving and then choose from the cooking methods discussed in the following sections. The possibilities are endless. Don't just settle for your usual baked potato; try some unfamiliar vegetable combinations cooked in nontraditional ways.

## Baking

Bake garlic and onions (both wrapped in foil and lightly coated with no-stick spray), peppers, eggplant, carrots, turnips, parsnips, tomatoes, potatoes, squash, or almost any other hard and dense vegetable. Many vegetables can be baked in covered stews and casseroles. You can also bake cabbage-wrapped or pastry-covered vegetables.

## Boiling, parboiling, and blanching

Boiling cooks hard vegetables, such as potatoes, artichokes, carrots, turnips, squash, rutabagas, corn, and beets. The food is usually covered in water or stock. Vegetables can also be boiled in soups, stews, and chowders along with other foods.

*Parboiling* means to partially cook by boiling briefly. *Blanching* is the same as parboiling except that, after boiling briefly, you immediately stop the cooking process by immersing the vegetables in ice water for a few minutes. Parboiling and blanching can be used to firm the flesh, loosen the skin, set the color, or precook longer-cooking vegetables before combining them with other vegetables for further cooking (such as in stir-fries or kebabs).

# Braising

*Braising* means that the vegetables are cooked while partially submerged in liquid, such as stock or water. The method is similar to steaming, but vegetable braising is often done in the oven. After cooking, the liquid contains concentrated vegetable flavoring, good for a quick and tasty sauce. Braise whole or cut vegetables (such as carrots, beets, turnips, brussels sprouts, onions, and celery) in water, juice, or vegetable or defatted chicken stock.

# Broiling and grilling

During broiling, the direct heat comes from above; during grilling, the heat comes from below. Both methods are good (as long as the heat source isn't too close) for cooking many vegetables, especially those that hold their shape, such as peppers, onions, mushrooms, squash, eggplant, and zucchini. However, broiling and grilling are usually not advisable for broccoli, cauliflower, and peas unless they are cooked in closed foil packets. Foil packets are also recommended for cooking tomatoes with onions, herbs, and spices; whole onions with diced celery, herbs, and spices; and large mushrooms with carrots, onions, herbs, and spices.

# Microwaving

Microwaves don't heat foods evenly, so be sure to use a turntable or turn vegetables often. Be aware that large vegetables especially may cook unevenly. You can microwave large vegetables (such as squash, potatoes, and eggplant) whole, but pierce them several times with a knife, fork, or skewer first. Microwaving is good for both cut and baked potatoes, although microwaved baked potatoes are nicer if you microwave them first and then finish by baking in the oven. Microwave all other vegetables covered in a bowl or in a microwaveable bag with a teaspoon of water or other liquid, such as defatted chicken stock.

# Poaching

Poach vegetables such as carrots, celery, and cabbage- or leek-wrapped bundles. Cover in liquid, whether in the oven or on the stovetop, and lightly simmer. You can add herbs, parsley, or onions to the liquid if you like.

## Pressure-cooking

If you use a special stovetop cooking pot with an airtight lid and regulator or valve, food cooks twice as fast under the intense steam pressure because it cooks at a higher temperature. Pressure-cooking is good for dried beans, soups, stews, and long-cooking vegetables, such as artichokes, potatoes, and whole carrots.

## Roasting

To roast peppers, place them directly on an electric or gas burner or under the broiler, turning often, until much of the pepper is blackened. Then place in a paper or plastic bag, close the bag, let sit for half an hour, and then peel off the skin. To roast whole garlic bulbs or onions, spray the unpeeled bulb with olive oil, wrap foil loosely (but sealed) around the vegetable, bake for 40 minutes in a 350° oven, and then peel.

## Steaming

Steaming is a good method for preparing all types of vegetables, including onions, garlic, broccoli, asparagus, beans, okra, cauliflower, and peas. You can use a vegetable steamer, skillet, or saucepan with or without a perforated second pot. Boil ¼ to 1 inch of water, adding more if necessary but keeping as much of the vegetables out of the water as possible.

For extra flavor, steam vegetables in defatted stock, skim milk (for corn and peas), lemon or lime juice (for artichokes and asparagus), or plain water flavored with half a bouillon cube or spices and herbs.

## Stir-frying

Stir-frying is a great method for making a vegetable entree or side dish. Lightly coat a nonstick skillet with no-stick vegetable oil spray, add chopped vegetables, lightly spray the vegetables, and cook over high heat until browned, tossing often.

# Choosing Lowfat Vegetable Dishes

The following vegetables and vegetable dishes are low in total fat, saturated fat, and cholesterol if made without adding more than $^1/_2$ teaspoon of butter or margarine and without cream, cheese, sour cream, cream cheese, or other high-fat products:

✔ Butter beans (canned beans)

✔ Candied sweet potatoes (without butter or margarine)

✔ Crudités with fat-free or lowfat dressing or dip

✔ Fresh (plain), canned, or frozen vegetables (with lowfat or fat-free sauces)

✔ Parsleyed potatoes

✔ Poi

✔ Ratatouille

✔ Vegetable casseroles, soups, stews, or terrines

✔ Vegetable chutneys or relishes

✔ Vegetable croquettes (if baked and not batter-fried)

✔ Vegetable kebabs

✔ Vegetable pâté (without palm kernel oil)

✔ Vegetables en papillote

The following vegetables and vegetable dishes are usually high in total fat, saturated fat, and cholesterol:

✔ Chilies rellenos

✔ Chinese vegetables stir-fried in oil

✔ Creamed broccoli, corn, onions, or spinach

✔ Croquettes (deep-fried)

✔ Eggplant Parmesan

✔ Fajitas with peppers and onions

✔ Fried vegetables

✔ Guacamole

- ✔ Mirepoix
- ✔ Sautéed vegetables
- ✔ Scalloped potatoes
- ✔ Tostadas with vegetables and cheese
- ✔ Vegetables au gratin
- ✔ Vegetables and butter, cheese, cream, hollandaise sauce, or margarine
- ✔ Vegetables Lyonnaise
- ✔ Vegetables with meat sauce
- ✔ Vegetables Milanese
- ✔ Vegetables à la Polonaise
- ✔ Vol-au-vent with vegetables (vegetables with butter in puff pastry)

## Serving vegetables in lowfat ways

For proper nutrition, you should eat three to five servings of vegetables every day. However, you may have difficulty meeting that requirement if you eat vegetables only as a side dish. Following are some creative suggestions for incorporating vegetables into your diet.

**Appetizers:** Not only are crudités (raw vegetables) an appetizer must, but vegetables of all kinds, such as tiny bliss potatoes with a topping, are starring as appetizers. Vegetable appetizers are low in fat, but be aware that high-fat ingredients used in preparation, garnish, or accompanying dips can increase the fat content and calories.

**Breakfasts or brunches:** Hash-browned potatoes, Western fries, and huevos rancheros all can be made lowfat by baking instead of frying.

**Drinks:** V8 and tomato juice are perennial favorites, but you may love carrot juice with fresh lemon juice, celery juice with seasoning salt, or all the other vegetable juice possibilities that your probably-put-away juicer can

make. Get the juicer down from the top shelf and make some vegetable juice. It's low in fat. Using a blender rather than a juicer retains the fiber in the juice.

**Entrees or sides:** Mounds of easily cooked vegetables (diced eggplant, cooked dried beans, potatoes, squash, and mixed vegetables, for example) are perfect for entrees. Flavor with a lowfat sauce or salsa for a lowfat main dish or side. Tomato and fruit salsas also pair nicely with cooked dried beans. Roll your favorite vegetables (such as zucchini, okra, slices of sweet potato, and eggplant) in egg whites and herbed bread crumbs or lowfat cracker crumbs and bake for a crunchy, tasty lowfat entree or side dish.

**Grains and pastas:** Vegetables and pastas (which are grains) go well together in dishes like pasta primavera, pasta marinara, and pasta with garlic and onions. Rice, mushrooms, and vegetables blend favorably in risotto and paella. All these dishes can be made lowfat.

**Salads:** Vegetables make up the base of most salads. Vegetable salads are usually lowfat if the dressing is fat-free or low in fat and the preparer doesn't add an abundance of cheese, nuts, meats, or seeds. Use lots of vegetables in salads.

**Salsas, relishes, and pickles:** Top crab or shrimp with your favorite vegetable salsa (or gazpacho) or hot sauce, and the dish is still low in fat. Almost all pickles, chili sauce, ketchup, soy sauce, relishes, mustards, and other condiments contain no fat.

**Sauces:** Lowfat cream or curry sauce, dill or tomato sauce, pureed vegetables, soy or hoisin sauce, and dozens more make delicious lowfat sauces for vegetables.

**Snacks:** Vegetables such as carrots and celery come already cut for snacking. Snacking on vegetables has become so popular that the sales of baby carrots, sugar snaps, and cherry tomatoes have skyrocketed.

**Soups, stews, and chowders:** Soups, stews, and chowders have always been a base for many delicious lowfat dishes. You can add small amounts of lean meat and poultry (with all visible fat and skin removed) or almost any seafood to a healthful vegetable soup base, and the dish is still lowfat.

# Vivacious Vegetable Recipes

You can easily toss together a filling and pleasing vegetable dish that is inexpensive and takes advantage of all the great produce that's available. Ease into a lowfat, even vegetarian, lifestyle with the following recipes. Going vegetarian three or four times a week is a great idea.

## Beets and Beet Greens

This is my favorite beet recipe, developed because beets alone aren't quite enough, and I didn't want to waste the tasty and nutrient-filled greens. Chop and cook the red stems, too, if you wish. I use the juice of the sharper-flavored clementine rather than plain fresh or carton orange juice. Fresh beets and a few slices of good bread are often my lunch.

**Tools:** *Large saucepan*

**Preparation time:** *2*

**Yield:** *4 servings*

*6 medium-large beets (about 1 pound), greens removed and reserved*

*1 teaspoon fat-free spray (poured), margarine, or butter*

*1 tablespoon orange zest*

*$^1/_2$ cup clementine or orange juice*

*Salt (optional) and freshly ground black pepper*

*(continued)*

***1*** Cut the beets into eighths, roll the leaves, and chop every 2 inches, including the stems. (See Figure 15-2.)

***2*** Place the beets in a large saucepan with 3 inches water and boil for 20 minutes. Drain, peel the beets, and cut the chunks in half.

***3*** In the same saucepan, combine the spray, margarine, or butter; beets; orange zest; and clementine or orange juice. Place the chopped greens and stems on top, cover, and cook over medium-low heat for 3 to 4 minutes or until the greens are completely wilted. Stir several times to incorporate the flavors. Add salt (if desired) and pepper to taste.

***Nutrition at a glance (per serving):*** *Total fat 0.5 g; Saturated fat 0 g; Protein 2 g; Dietary fiber 2 g; Carbohydrate 11 g; Cholesterol 0 mg; Sodium 118 mg; % of calories from fat 11; Calories 53.*

***Lynn's beet suggestion:*** *You can "Harvardize" the cooked beets (not the leaves) by dissolving 1 tablespoon cornstarch with 2 tablespoons each vinegar and cooked beet liquid and 1 tablespoon sugar. Add back to the cooked, peeled, drained beets and heat for 1 minute, stirring, until the sauce is thick and shiny.*

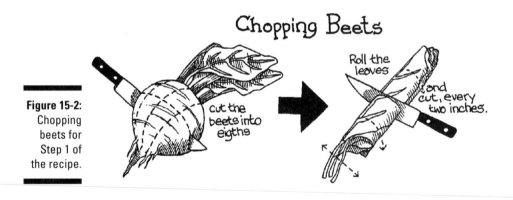

**Figure 15-2:** Chopping beets for Step 1 of the recipe.

Chopping Beets

Roll the leaves

cut the beets into eigths

and cut, every two inches.

## Brussels Sprouts with Apples and Walnuts

Brussels sprouts should be crunchy and bright green. I think that these little cabbages are great fun to eat. When tossed with apples and walnuts, this usually plebeian vegetable becomes very festive — good for holidays, Sundays, and luncheons. For more flavor, toast the walnuts first in a 350° oven for 5 to 6 minutes. If your brussels sprouts are different sizes or large, cut them in half and then steam.

**Tools:** *Large saucepan, nonstick skillet*

**Preparation time:** *1*

**Yield:** *4 servings*

| | |
|---|---|
| *1 pound brussels sprouts* | *¹/₄ cup currants or dark raisins* |
| *¹/₂ cup apple juice* | *1 teaspoon cornstarch* |
| *1 teaspoon butter* | *¹/₄ cup water* |
| *¹/₂ teaspoon dried or fresh rosemary, crushed or snipped very fine* | *1 tablespoon finely chopped walnuts* |
| *1 large tart apple, diced* | *Salt (optional) and freshly ground black pepper* |

*1* In a large saucepan with 1 inch water, steam the brussels sprouts, covered, for 8 minutes or until tender. Drain and return them to the pan.

*2* In a nonstick skillet, combine the apple juice, butter, and rosemary. Bring to a boil over medium-high heat. Add the apples and currants (or raisins).

*3* In a small bowl, mix the cornstarch with ¹/₄ cup water. Stir to dissolve the cornstarch and add it to the skillet mixture. Cook, stirring constantly, for about 1 minute or until the mixture thickens.

*4* Add the walnuts and brussels sprouts. Stir to combine the sauce and add salt (if desired) and pepper to taste.

**Nutrition at a glance (per serving):** *Total fat 3 g; Saturated fat 1 g; Protein 4 g; Dietary fiber 7 g; Carbohydrate 25 g; Cholesterol 3 mg; Sodium 37 mg; % of calories from fat 19; Calories 122.*

**Lynn's brussels sprouts tip:** *Try the petite frozen brussels sprouts for a bit of heaven.*

## Creamed Corn

This recipe is pure, sweet, golden delight — real creamed corn with all the taste but without the fat in cream. Serve as a side for holidays and family suppers. Garnish with a sprinkle of chopped, bottled pimentos or a sprig of parsley.

**Tools:** *Food processor, medium saucepan*

**Preparation time:** *1*

**Yield:** *4 servings*

*6 large ears yellow or white corn, husks removed and cleaned of silk*

*¹/₂ cup skim milk*

*¹/₃ cup liquid fat-free non-dairy creamer*

*Salt (optional)*

*¹/₈ teaspoon sugar (optional)*

*Freshly ground black pepper*

**1** On a large cutting board, cut off the kernels the corn close to the cob with long strokes of a large, sharp knife. Divide the kernels roughly in half. Don't discard the cobs yet.

**2** Place half the kernels in a food processor. Pulse a few times until the corn is coarsely chopped. With a rubber spatula, scrape the chopped corn into a medium saucepan.

**3** Add ¹/₄ cup of the skim milk to the corn in the saucepan, stir, and turn the heat on medium-low.

**4** Meanwhile, in a food processor, place the rest of the corn, the remaining ¹/₄ cup skim milk, creamer, salt to taste (if desired), and sugar (if desired); then puree (which takes several minutes).

**5** Add the pureed corn to the corn in the saucepan, stir several times to blend, and cook on medium heat for about 6 minutes, stirring occasionally, until thick. Add pepper at the table.

**Nutrition at a glance (per serving):** *Total fat 2.5 g; Saturated fat 0.5 g; Protein 7 g; Dietary fiber 5 g; Carbohydrate 56 g; Cholesterol 1 mg; Sodium 47 mg; % of calories from fat 8; Calories 243.*

**Lynn's suggestions for extra corn flavor:** *(1) Milk the corn whenever kernels are to be removed. To milk corn, cut off the kernels and then scrape the corn cobs closely with a sharp knife to release any sweet corn "milk" and buds. This extra effort makes creamed corn extra delicious. (2) Try microwaving corn in the corn husks. Pull back the husk halfway, remove the silk, moisten with water, pull up the husks, and microwave each ear for 4 to 6 minutes, or 10 minutes for four ears. (3) When making a corn-based soup, cook the scraped cobs with the chicken or vegetable broth, discarding them after 25 minutes.*

## Creamed Pearl Onions and Peas

For those of you who love pearl onions and peas, this is the flavorful, creamy combination of comfort foods that you've been craving. You can substitute sliced leeks, shallots, or Vidalia spring onions for the pearl onions and add corn kernels if you like. The peppers and pimentos are the bottled type, and scallions are part of the recipe, not just a garnish.

**Tools:** *Medium nonstick saucepan, colander*

**Preparation time:** *1*

**Yield:** *6 servings*

*1 pound pearl onions, peeled, or 1 16-ounce package frozen pearl onions*

*1 cup water*

*2 tablespoons dry sherry, or 1 teaspoon sherry extract*

*8 ounces fresh peas, or 1 8-ounce package frozen peas*

*1 teaspoon butter*

*2 cups liquid fat-free non-dairy creamer or skim milk*

*2 tablespoons flour*

*Salt (optional) and freshly ground black pepper*

*Pinch of ground nutmeg*

*1 tablespoon chopped fresh parsley*

*$^1/_4$ cup strips roasted red peppers or pimentos*

*$^1/_4$ cup chopped scallions*

*Paprika*

*1* Place the onions, water, and sherry or sherry extract in a medium nonstick saucepan. Cover and bring to a boil over medium-high heat. Reduce the heat to low and cook for 15 to 20 minutes.

*2* Add the peas and bring to a boil. Reduce the heat and cook for 4 to 5 minutes or until the onions are tender and the peas are bright green. Drain in a colander, lightly cover with foil, and set aside.

*3* In the same saucepan, combine the butter, creamer or skim milk, and flour, whisking continually over medium-high heat until you make a smooth mixture. After the butter melts, add the salt (if desired), pepper, and nutmeg. Cook the cream sauce over medium heat, whisking constantly, for 3 to 4 minutes.

*4* Add the onions and peas to the sauce and cook for 1 minute to reheat them. Sprinkle with the parsley, peppers or pimentos, scallions, and paprika.

**Nutrition at a glance (per serving):** *Total fat 1 g; Saturated fat 0.5 g; Protein 3 g; Dietary fiber 3 g; Carbohydrate 48 g; Cholesterol 2 mg; Sodium 191 mg; % of calories from fat 4; Calories 218.*

**Lynn's fat-free flavor:** *If your goal is to further reduce the fat in this recipe, substitute fat-free I Can't Believe It's Not Butter! spray (pouring it) for the butter.*

## Creamed Spinach and Mushrooms

Spinach that's all creamy and mushroomy is very satisfying. For the spinach, you can substitute other vegetables, such as broccoli, kale, collards, or asparagus. Garnish with a few tablespoons of diced lean baked ham and orange zest for color and extra flavor.

**Tools:** *Large nonstick skillet, large pot, colander*

**Preparation time:** *2*

**Yield:** *4 servings*

| | |
|---|---|
| *2 cloves garlic, peeled and minced* | *$^1/_2$ cup fat-free or lowfat sour cream* |
| *$^1/_3$ cup chopped onions, or 4 shallots, chopped* | *$^1/_4$ cup fat-free Parmesan topping or grated Parmesan cheese* |
| *$^1/_2$ cup sliced mushrooms* | *$^1/_8$ teaspoon ground nutmeg* |
| *1 teaspoon water* | *Salt (optional)* |
| *2 tablespoons flour* | *$1^1/_4$ pounds spinach, stems removed, coarsely chopped* |
| *$1^1/_2$ cups liquid fat-free non-dairy creamer* | *Freshly ground black pepper* |

*1* Lightly coat a large nonstick skillet with no-stick vegetable oil spray. Place the garlic and onions in the skillet, lightly spray them, and cook over medium heat for 2 to 3 minutes, stirring often.

*2* Add the mushrooms and water and cook, stirring, for about 5 minutes or until the mushrooms are cooked and the onions are translucent. Remove briefly from the heat and add the flour to the mixture in the skillet. Slowly add the creamer, whisking until smooth.

*3* Over medium heat, bring to a boil, stirring or whisking constantly for 4 minutes or until thickened. Stir in the sour cream, Parmesan cheese, nutmeg, and salt (if desired) and turn off the heat.

*4* Meanwhile, in a large pot, bring 1 inch of water to a boil over high heat. Add the spinach, cover, and steam for 6 to 7 minutes or until the spinach is wilted and tender. Drain well in a colander for 1 minute. Add the spinach to the cream sauce and stir to combine. Cook over low heat for 1 to 2 minutes to reheat the sauce. Add pepper to taste.

**Nutrition at a glance (per serving):** *Total fat 0.5 g; Saturated fat 0 g; Protein 9 g; Dietary fiber 3 g; Carbohydrate 53 g; Cholesterol 0 mg; Sodium 197 mg; % of calories from fat 1; Calories 252.*

**Lynn's creamed vegetable tip:** *If you don't have liquid fat-free non-dairy creamer, use skim milk, which makes a fine cream sauce when mixed with flour.*

## Elegant Peeled and Sliced Baked Potatoes

Rather fancy-looking but easy, this recipe requires a jar of sun-dried tomatoes packed in oil. This potato dish is the perfect food for any occasion because it is so easy to make.

**Tools:** *Baking sheet*

**Preparation time:** *3*

**Yield:** *4 servings*

*4 California long Yukon Gold potatoes, peeled*

*2¹/₂ teaspoons oil from the jar of sun-dried tomatoes*

*2 teaspoons chopped sun-dried tomatoes, plus extra slivers for garnish*

*Paprika*

*Salt (optional)*

*2 tablespoons chopped fresh chives or parsley (optional)*

*1* Preheat the oven to 350°.

*2* Place the peeled potatoes on the counter to see which side they rest on naturally. Make ¹/₄-inch slits, crosswise, across the top of the potato, leaving ¹/₄ inch of potato at the bottom to hold it together. (See Figure 15-3.)

*3* Pour the sun-dried tomato oil into a flat dish. Mix in the chopped sun-dried tomatoes. Dip each cut side of the potato in the oil, oiling it well using your hands. Drizzle some oil into the slits. Sprinkle with paprika and salt (if desired).

*4* Place the potatoes on a baking sheet and bake for 60 minutes or until tender and golden. Sprinkle with chopped chives or parsley (if desired) and more slivers of sun-dried tomatoes.

*Nutrition at a glance (per serving):* *Total fat 3 g; Saturated fat 0.5 g; Protein 3 g; Dietary fiber 2 g; Carbohydrate 34 g; Cholesterol 0 mg; Sodium 31 mg; % of calories from fat 15; Calories 173.*

*Lynn's potato pointers:* *You can also cook a baking potato in the microwave. The microwaved potato ends up with a softer skin, much like bread kept in plastic. A dual cooking method, using the microwave for speed and the oven for texture, gives you the best of both worlds. Cook in the microwave for 3 to 4 minutes, and finish cooking in a preheated 350° oven for 15 to 20 minutes.*

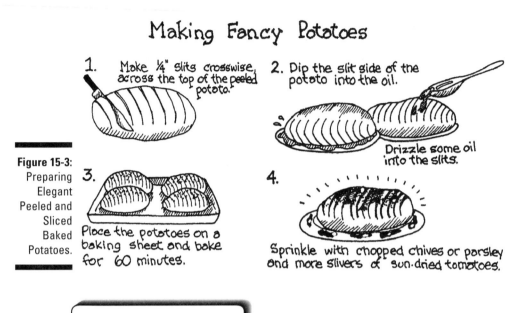

## Making Fancy Potatoes

1. Make ¼" slits crosswise, across the top of the peeled potato.

2. Dip the slit side of the potato into the oil.

Drizzle some oil into the slits.

**Figure 15-3:**
Preparing
Elegant
Peeled and
Sliced
Baked
Potatoes.

3. Place the potatoes on a baking sheet and bake for 60 minutes.

4. Sprinkle with chopped chives or parsley and more slivers of sun-dried tomatoes.

## Golden Mashed Potatoes

Christin Loudon, a registered dietitian who's worked with me for years, told me of this recipe, which is pure gold. Although the potatoes look amber in color, you can't taste the carrots — just an earthy sweetness. If you aren't sure about the carrots, just omit them and enjoy perfect mashed potatoes.

**Tools:** *Medium saucepan, small saucepan, potato masher or ricer*

**Preparation time:** *2*

**Yield:** *6 servings*

| | |
|---|---|
| *4 medium Yukon Gold or russet potatoes, peeled and diced* | *¹/₂ cup liquid fat-free non-dairy creamer* |
| *1¹/₂ cups diced carrots* | *Freshly ground black pepper* |
| *1 teaspoon salt (optional)* | *Chopped fresh parsley and freshly ground nutmeg for garnish* |
| *1 teaspoon butter* | |

**1** In a medium saucepan, place the potatoes, carrots, and salt (if desired) in enough water to cover. Bring to a boil over medium-high heat, reduce the heat to medium, and simmer, bubbling, for 25 minutes or until the carrots are tender.

**2** Drain the potatoes and carrots and return to the saucepan. Add the butter. After the butter melts, mash the vegetables with a potato masher or ricer, leaving some small lumps of carrots.

*(continued)*

*3* Warm the creamer in a small saucepan over medium heat. Add to the vegetables and stir to combine.

*4* Add some pepper and garnish with a sprinkle of chopped parsley and a whisper of freshly ground nutmeg.

**Nutrition at a glance (per serving):** *Total fat 1 g; Saturated fat 0.5 g; Protein 2 g; Dietary fiber 2 g; Carbohydrate 30 g; Cholesterol 2 mg; Sodium 36 mg; % of calories from fat 5; Calories 132.*

**Lynn's fat-free flavor:** *Making luscious fat-free or lowfat mashed potatoes is easy. I often bake rather than boil, using the peels for appetizers and snacks. After mashing, add one of the following lowfat or fat-free ingredients: a few tablespoons of skim milk, liquid fat-free non-dairy creamer, fat-free or lowfat buttermilk, pureed fat-free or lowfat cottage cheese, sour cream, yogurt, or ricotta (ricotta needs to be whipped in a food processor). You can also add butter-flavored spray or granules; chopped fresh scallions, chives, or fresh or roasted garlic; or a small amount of chopped dill, tarragon, thyme, rosemary, or basil.*

## Mediterranean Vegetables and Rice or Orzo

This lemony Mediterranean dish is particularly good with shrimp, scallops, or grilled fish. Garnish with fat-free Parmesan topping, grated Romano, or a dollop of plain yogurt and a sprinkle of lemon zest.

**Tools:** *Large nonstick saucepan*

**Preparation time:** *1*

**Yield:** *4 servings*

*1 medium onion, peeled and chopped*

*1 stalk celery, sliced*

*2 large cloves garlic, peeled and minced*

*1 teaspoon ground cumin*

*2 teaspoons chopped fresh or dried basil*

*2 teaspoons dried oregano*

*¹/₂ cup cooked rice or orzo*

*2 plum tomatoes, diced*

*1 cup cooked or canned, drained garbanzos (chickpeas)*

*8 ounces chopped kale or spinach*

*¹/₄ cup diced bottled roasted red peppers or pimentos*

*3 tablespoons fresh lemon juice*

*Salt (optional)*

*Crushed red pepper (flakes) (optional)*

*(continued)*

*1* In a large nonstick saucepan, combine the onions, celery, garlic, cumin, basil, and oregano. Cover and cook over medium-low heat, stirring occasionally, for 5 minutes or until the onions are translucent. If necessary, add 1 or 2 teaspoons of water to keep the mixture moist.

*2* Stir in the rice or orzo, tomatoes, and garbanzos. Cook for 2 to 3 minutes or until the tomatoes soften.

*3* Add the kale or spinach, peppers or pimentos, and lemon juice. Cook over medium-high heat, stirring, for 1 minute or until the kale or spinach wilts. Add the salt (if desired) and red pepper flakes (if desired).

***Nutrition at a glance (per serving):*** *Total fat 2 g; Saturated fat 0 g; Protein 7 g; Dietary fiber 5 g; Carbohydrate 29 g; Cholesterol 0 mg; Sodium 141 mg; % of calories from fat 10; Calories 152.*

***Lynn's nutrient tips:*** *The area around the outer edge of the seeds of a tomato contains the most nutrition, so it's best not to seed tomatoes. Another reason not to seed or even peel tomatoes: The seeds and peels are sources of fiber.*

## Scalloped Potatoes and Fennel

The rich flavor of baked potatoes and fennel is irresistible. Use golden potatoes or white California longs. Garnish with fennel fern. This dish is often better reheated. Because the fat content is so low, you can use regular Cheddar and Parmesan cheese.

***Tools:*** *10-inch ovenproof glass pie plate or 8-inch square baking dish*

***Preparation time:*** *3*

***Yield:*** *6 servings*

*3 large white- or yellow-fleshed potatoes, such as Yukon Gold, very thinly sliced*

*1 medium onion or leek, thinly sliced*

*1 fennel bulb, thinly sliced*

*4 tablespoons flour*

*2 tablespoons grated Cheddar cheese*

*Salt (optional) and freshly ground black pepper*

*$^1/_2$ cup vegetable or defatted chicken stock*

*1 cup liquid fat-free non-dairy creamer*

*2 tablespoons grated Parmesan cheese*

*Several shakes paprika*

*(continued)*

*1* Preheat the oven to 350°.

*2* Lightly coat a 10-inch ovenproof glass pie plate or 8-inch square baking dish with no-stick vegetable oil spray. Place half the potatoes in an even layer and lightly spray. Sprinkle on half the chopped onion or leek and half the fennel. Sprinkle with 2 tablespoons of the flour and a dusting of pepper and salt (if desired). Repeat with the remaining vegetables, flour, and pepper and salt (if desired).

*3* Combine the stock and creamer and pour over the potatoes. Sprinkle on the Cheddar cheese. Cover tightly with foil or a lid and bake for 60 to 70 minutes or until the potatoes are tender. Remove the cover and bake for 10 minutes more or until the cheese browns.

*4* Sprinkle the Parmesan cheese and paprika over the top and serve.

**Nutrition at a glance (per serving):** *Total fat 2.5 g; Saturated fat 1.5 g; Protein 7 g; Dietary fiber 6 g; Carbohydrate 72 g; Cholesterol 6 mg; Sodium 197 mg; % of calories from fat 7; Calories 340.*

**Lynn's potato pointer:** *Have you ever peeled a whole potato, briefly stepped away to answer a ringing phone, and returned to find the potato almost black after only 5 minutes? That's oxidation, and the process doesn't hurt the potato. Just put the potato under running water, and with a soft brush or clean washcloth, wash it off.*

## Spicy Green Beans and Mushrooms

The green beans are crunchy and bright green, the mushrooms tender and flavorful, the sauce spicy — perfect vegetables. If you don't want heat, omit the cayenne pepper. If you want a garnish or side for the beans, try canned and drained mandarin oranges, apricots, or peach.

**Tools:** *Large nonstick skillet*

**Preparation time:** *2*

**Yield:** *4 servings*

*2 cloves garlic, peeled and minced*

*1 cup finely slivered onions*

*8 ounces button mushrooms (about 8 to 10 large), sliced*

*3 tablespoons soy sauce*

*1 pound green beans, trimmed and cut into 1-inch pieces*

*1/4 red bell pepper, chopped*

*(continued)*

*¹/₂ teaspoon sugar*

*¹/₄ teaspoon cayenne pepper, or several drops Chinese hot oil*

*¹/₂ cup vegetable stock or defatted chicken stock*

*1 tablespoon cornstarch*

*Salt (optional) and freshly ground black pepper*

**1** Lightly coat a large nonstick skillet with no-stick vegetable oil spray. Place the garlic, onions, and mushrooms in the skillet and lightly spray the vegetables. Cook over medium-high heat for 8 to 10 minutes, stirring often, until the vegetables are golden.

**2** Add the soy sauce, beans, red pepper, sugar, cayenne, and ¹/₄ cup of the stock. Stir, cover, and cook for 6 minutes or until the beans are bright green.

**3** In a small bowl, dissolve the cornstarch in ¹/₄ cup stock. Tip the skillet so that the liquid pools in one end, add the cornstarch mixture to the liquid, and whisk rapidly. Set the pan down on the burner and toss the sauce throughout the vegetables. Sprinkle with salt (if desired) and pepper to taste.

**Nutrition at a glance (per serving):** *Total fat 0.5 g; Saturated fat 0 g; Protein 4 g; Dietary fiber 5 g; Carbohydrate 19 g; Cholesterol 0 mg; Sodium 852 mg; % of calories from fat 5; Calories 87.*

**Lynn's stock-defatting tip:** *To quickly defat canned stock, open the can and spoon off the fat that rises to the top, or chill the stock and pick off the fat, or use a defatting cup. Remove it all. A significant amount is saturated fat.*

## Sweet Baked Carrots

Sweet raisins play beautifully off the earthy flavor of carrots. This dish is easy to make and attractive to serve.

**Tools:** *Casserole or 8-inch square baking dish*

**Preparation time:** *2*

**Yield:** *4 servings*

*1 pound carrots (baby or long), cut into 2-inch lengths*

*1 teaspoon butter, melted*

*2 tablespoons currants or dark raisins*

*Salt (optional)*

*2 tablespoons thinly sliced fresh basil*

*2 tablespoons chopped fresh parsley*

*2 tablespoons brown sugar*

*(continued)*

*1* Preheat the oven to 350°.

*2* Place the carrots, butter, currants or dark raisins, salt (if desired), basil, parsley, and brown sugar in a casserole or 8-inch square baking dish and mix. Cover tightly with foil. Place in the oven and bake for 45 minutes.

**Nutrition at a glance (per serving):** *Total fat 1.5 g; Saturated fat 0.5 g; Protein 1 g; Dietary fiber 4 g; Carbohydrate 17 g; Cholesterol 3 mg; Sodium 53 mg; % of calories from fat 17; Calories 81.*

**Lynn's vegetable tips:** *Purchase several soft, card-sized plastic vegetable brushes. They are perfect for getting the grit out of the folds in carrots, celery, and potatoes; the soft ones even clean large portobello mushrooms well. Peeling vegetables isn't necessary in a long-cooking recipe; peeling is mainly for aesthetics.*

## Sweet and Sour Asian Stir-Fry

Everyone loves the flavor of sweet and sour because it gives a sprightly lift to tossed vegetables. You can add sprouts, water chestnuts, bamboo shoots, or other Asian foods, or even sliced shiitake mushrooms. If you like heat, add $1/2$ teaspoon crushed red pepper and garnish with chopped scallions. Serve with rice and hot tea to complete the Asian ambiance.

**Tools:** *Large nonstick skillet*

**Preparation time:** *2*

**Yield:** *6 servings*

*6 ounces dark or portobello mushrooms, thickly sliced*

*2 teaspoons soy sauce*

*1 teaspoon sugar*

*1 acorn squash or sweet potato*

*4 stalks bok choy, sliced*

*8 baby carrots, sliced*

*1 medium onion, peeled and coarsely chopped*

*2 cloves garlic, peeled and minced*

*1 teaspoon finely chopped fresh ginger, or $1/2$ teaspoon ground*

*2 tablespoons hoisin sauce*

*2 tablespoons rice or cider vinegar*

*1 teaspoon sugar*

*$1/4$ cup currants or raisins*

*$1/2$ pound sugar snaps or snow peas*

*(continued)*

*1* Place the mushroom slices in a sealable plastic bag with the soy sauce and sugar. Knead with your fingers to mix and set aside.

*2* Pierce the squash or sweet potato 2 inches deep a couple of times with a knife or fork. Microwave on high for 7 minutes, turning once or twice or using a turntable. The squash or potato should be just cooked but not mushy. Cool under water and cut into 1-inch chunks. Peel and remove the seeds, reserving them for another use if you wish or discarding them.

*3* Lightly coat a large nonstick skillet with no-stick vegetable oil spray. Lightly spray the bok choy, carrots, onion, garlic, and ginger and cook in the skillet over medium heat, stirring, until the vegetables are golden, about 7 minutes. Add the squash or sweet potato chunks, hoisin sauce, vinegar, sugar, and currants or raisins and stir over medium heat, tossing frequently, for 4 to 5 minutes. Add the sugar snaps or snow peas, cover, and cook for 2 minutes or until the snaps or peas turn bright green.

***Nutrition at a glance (per serving):*** *Total fat 0.5 g; Saturated fat 0 g; Protein 4 g; Dietary fiber 5 g; Carbohydrate 20 g; Cholesterol 0 mg; Sodium 311 mg; % of calories from fat 3; Calories 82.*

***Lynn's Asian tips:*** *People love Chinese food because it contains many layers of flavor: bitter, tangy, acrid, bland, crunchy, spicy, nutty, and sweet. Flavor layering takes several steps and several ingredients, such as vinegar, sugar, and crushed red pepper, all combined with bland vegetables. The preparations are very simple, and you can use any vegetables that are handy. Have vegetables cut and ready to use.*

## Vegetable-Filled Baked Potatoes

This colorful way to bake potatoes is a personal favorite. You can substitute many other vegetables, but none of the vegetable called for needs precooking, so this dish is quick and convenient. If microwaved, it's on the table in 15 minutes. If you're using other vegetables — such as broccoli florets, green beans, peas, or carrots — steam and drain the vegetables first.

**Preparation time:** *1 if microwaving, 2 if baking*

**Yield:** *4 servings*

*4 large russet potatoes*

*1¹/₂ cups diced fresh or canned (drained) tomatoes*

*1 cup chopped scallions*

*1 cup chopped fresh parsley or watercress*

*Salt (optional) and freshly ground black pepper*

*2 tablespoons crumbled feta cheese*

**1** If baking, preheat the oven to 350°. Place the potatoes wet in the oven for 50 minutes. If microwaving, place the wet potatoes in the microwave and heat on high for 10 minutes or until cooked.

**2** When cooked, cut the potatoes lengthwise, about 1 inch deep, and push the ends to open. Without removing the potato flesh, lightly mash or mix the top inch.

**3** In a medium microwaveable bowl, combine the diced tomatoes, scallions, parsley or watercress, and salt to taste (if desired). Microwave the filling on high for 3 minutes, stirring once. Divide into 4 parts and pile each potato with the mixture. Sprinkle with black pepper and feta cheese.

**Nutrition at a glance (per serving):** *Total fat 2 g; Saturated fat 1.5 g; Protein 7 g; Dietary fiber 6 g; Carbohydrate 53 g; Cholesterol 7 mg; Sodium 119 mg; % of calories from fat 8; Calories 248.*

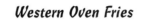
## Western Oven Fries

Great for breakfast, brunch, or dinner, these plump wedges are spicy and moist with crispy skins that warm your tummy. They disappear fast, so make plenty.

**Tools:** *Large baking sheet*

**Preparation time:** *2*

**Yield:** *4 servings*

| | |
|---|---|
| *4 large russet potatoes* | *1 teaspoon Cajun spice blend* |
| *Salt (optional)* | *1 teaspoon paprika* |
| *2 teaspoons chili powder* | |

**1** Preheat the oven to 400°. Lightly coat a large baking sheet with no-stick vegetable oil spray.

**2** Slice the potatoes in half lengthwise and cut each half into thirds or fourths lengthwise. Place the potatoes on a baking sheet.

**3** Lightly coat the potatoes with no-stick spray. Sprinkle evenly with salt (if desired), chili powder, and Cajun spice blend. Use your fingers to coat the potatoes evenly. Top with a sprinkle of paprika.

**4** Place the potatoes in the oven. Lower the heat to 350° and bake for 30 to 40 minutes or until the potatoes are crisp and golden brown on the outside and tender when pierced with a fork.

**Nutrition at a glance (per serving):** *Total fat 0.5 g; Saturated fat 0 g; Protein 5 g; Dietary fiber 5 g; Carbohydrate 48 g; Cholesterol 0 mg; Sodium 146 mg; % of calories from fat 2; Calories 208.*

**Lynn's Cajun spice recipe:** *To make your own Cajun spice mixture, combine 1 teaspoon salt; $^1/_2$ teaspoon each cayenne pepper and paprika; 1 teaspoon each onion salt (or powder), garlic salt (or powder), and chili powder; and $^1/_4$ teaspoon each freshly ground black pepper, dried sweet basil, marjoram, and oregano.*

# Chapter 16

# Sauces and Gravies

*I*n contrasting his native country, France, with England, Voltaire made this incorrect but funny witticism:

> *"France is a land of 42 sauces and one religion. Britain is a land of one sauce and 42 religions."*

And the infamous Archie Bunker said:

> *"Potatoes ain't no good without gravy."*

This chapter tells you, no matter what your station, why sauces and gravies are important on a lowfat menu plan, and it gives you recipes and tips for preparing them. I also include a list of ten quick white sauces and handy lists of which sauces are usually high or low in total fat, saturated fat, and cholesterol.

# Using Sauces and Gravies in a Lowfat Eating Plan

Sauces and gravies take on a new importance when you're cooking and eating lowfat. Because sauces and gravies traditionally are made with fat, that healthful turkey cutlet, fish fillet, pasta or rice dish, potato, or broccoli loses all its healthy properties when you pour a high-fat sauce or gravy on top. So knowing how to make sauces and gravies low in fat is really important.

Sauces and gravies are especially important because taste and moisture may be lacking in less-fatty meat or poultry. Sauces and gravies spreading luxuriously across the plate also help to keep you from feeling deprived by smaller portions of lean meat, poultry, and fish or plain beans, veggies, or a starch like potatoes or pasta.

Sauces are also important because they often complement a dish, adding something a food lacks or heightening a flavor. They make a dish look especially attractive, inviting, and even extravagant. A small piece of fish sitting naked on a plate doesn't look nearly as enticing as that same fillet plated with a dazzling sauce and a sprig of rosemary.

Changing a diet, whether by choice or by necessity, is always difficult, especially if you've had pretty much the same diet for most of your life. Making and eating delicious lowfat sauces and gravies makes that process easier. The following lists help you make smart sauce choices.

# Telling High-Fat Sauces and Gravies from Lowfat Ones

If these sauces are made without butter, cheese, cream, sour cream, oil, or fatty meat products, they are usually very low in fat:

- Apple sauce
- Barbecue sauce
- Chutney
- Clam sauce (tomato-based)
- Cocktail sauce
- Cranberry sauce
- Curry sauce (without coconut milk)
- Dijon or mustard sauce
- Dill sauce (with fat-free sour cream or cream cheese)
- Fruit sauces
- Honey mustard sauce
- Horseradish sauce
- Mushroom sauce

- Oyster sauce (Asian or American style, without cream, cheese, or milk)
- Red pepper sauce
- Rhubarb sauce
- Salsa
- Steak sauce
- Sweet and sour sauce
- Tartar sauce (some varieties)
- Tex-Mex sauce
- Tomato sauce
- Wasabe (Japanese horse-radish)
- White sauce (with skim milk and flour only)
- Wine sauce

When made the usual way, with butter, cream, cheese, egg yolks, and whole-milk dairy products, these sauces are high in fat:

- Béarnaise sauce
- Béchamel sauce
- Beurre blanc
- Bordelaise sauce
- Butter sauce
- Cheese sauce
- Clam sauce (with cream and butter)
- Cottage cheese sauce
- Cream sauce
- Custard sauce
- Gravy (meat, chicken, or turkey, unless completely defatted)
- Hard sauce (with butter or margarine)

- Hollandaise sauce
- Lemon butter
- Mayonnaise-based sauce
- Milk or half-and-half sauce
- Peanut sauce
- Rémoulade
- Roux
- Sour cream sauce
- Tartar sauce (some varieties)
- Velouté
- Whipped cream sauce
- White sauce (with whole milk, butter, or cream)
- Yogurt sauce

# Preparing Lowfat Sauces

Some of the lowfat sauces and gravies in this chapter are adaptations of old favorites. Others, because of the slightly different tastes of fat-free or lowfat mayonnaise and sour cream, are entirely different, but I think that you'll love them. My light tartar sauce and a refreshingly different cucumber sauce are perfect companions for a simple sautéed fish or a poached turkey breast fillet. The barbecue sauce in this chapter is especially good, traditional but without the fat, which barbecue sauce never needs anyway — fat just impedes the marinating process. The dill sauce is refreshing and attractive on fish.

Because they are technically sauces, I've included two basic pasta sauces, one tomato and one clam. Because I'm such a snob about how easy and how much better a good, fresh, fruit sauce is than the pale-in-comparison, canned variety, I include a plum sauce, an apple sauce, and a cranberry sauce. (Two extra fruit sauces, raspberry and honey lemon, are in Chapter 17.) My basic gravy recipe is tried and true and can be used for every type of meat; the principle is the same.

A light sauce doesn't mean a thin sauce; you can make any sauce as thick as you want it, either with thickeners (such as cornstarch, flour, mashed potatoes, or pureed rice) or by cooking it until most of the moisture evaporates and you're left with an intense, thick, rich sauce. (Look in Chapter 10 for thickening tips.) Keep in mind that the luxuriousness of a sauce or gravy isn't determined by the amount of fat, but by the amount of flavor.

So sauce away. Add almost all the gravy you want. These sauces and gravies are nearly fat-free, not just lowfat, and most are very easy to make. You won't feel heavy and lethargic when you get up from the table after eating mashed potatoes and lowfat gravy or asparagus with lowfat hollandaise sauce, either.

## Hot sauce recipes

The following hot sauce recipes offer many creative ways to add flavor, style, and variety to lowfat dishes.

### Clam and Mushroom Pasta Sauce

The following is an incredibly tasty sauce for pasta, bulgur wheat, couscous, polenta, or rice. If you love the taste of mushrooms, use a mixture of darker, wild mushrooms, such as portobellos, shiitakes, or cremini.

**Tools:** *Large, heavy, nonstick skillet*

**Preparation time:** *1*

**Yield:** *About 2 cups, or 8 servings*

| | |
|---|---|
| *1 6-ounce can baby clams* | *1$^1$/$_2$ cups defatted chicken stock* |
| *6 ounces mushrooms, chopped* | *1 tablespoon cornstarch* |
| *2 tablespoons finely chopped onion* | *$^1$/$_3$ cup chopped fresh parsley* |
| *2 large cloves garlic, peeled and minced* | *Salt (optional)* |

**1** Boil the clams, drain, and reserve the liquid.

**2** Lightly coat a large, heavy, nonstick skillet with no-stick vegetable oil spray. Cook the mushrooms, onion, and garlic in the skillet, stirring, for about 5 minutes over medium heat, covered for the first 1 or 2 minutes, until the onions are translucent.

*(continued)*

*3* Add the clam liquid, stir, and cook for about 6 minutes. Add the clams and heat for about 2 minutes.

*4* In a medium bowl, whisk the chicken stock and cornstarch to dissolve.

*5* Add the cornstarch mixture to the skillet with the clams. Add the parsley and some salt (if desired). Over medium heat, whisk for about 2 minutes or until thick.

*Nutrition at a glance (per serving):* Total fat 0.5 g; Saturated fat 0 g; Protein 5 g; Dietary fiber 1 g; Carbohydrate 3 g; Cholesterol 16 mg; Sodium 139 mg; % of calories from fat 12; Calories 35.

*Lynn's clam sauce tips:* If you have small amounts of shrimp or fish, or even lobster, mussels, or crab meat, cut them into same-sized pieces and add them. Adding lots of different kinds of seafood can make a sauce delicious. Clam sauce can take corn, peas, diced tomatoes, chopped fresh spinach, watercress, green beans, and finely diced carrots.

## Hollandaise Sauce

Thick and lemony good, this hollandaise goes over skinless chicken or turkey breasts, asparagus, broccoli, green beans, cauliflower, or fish. If the hollandaise is thicker than you want it to be, thin it with several tablespoons of defatted chicken stock.

*Tools:* Small saucepan, large glass pitcher with spout

*Preparation time:* 1

*Yield:* About 1$^1$/$_4$ cups, or 10 servings

2 tablespoons margarine, diet margarine, or butter

$^1$/$_4$ cup fresh lemon juice

$^1$/$_2$ teaspoon Worcestershire sauce

2 tablespoons flour

1 cup substitute eggs

Cayenne pepper (optional)

*1* In a small saucepan, whisk together the margarine or butter, lemon juice, Worcestershire sauce, and flour. Over medium-high heat, whisk constantly until thick, about 4 minutes, to make sure that the flour is cooked.

*2* Have the eggs ready in a large glass pitcher with a spout. Ladle 2 or 3 tablespoons of the margarine mixture into the eggs in the pitcher and whisk together.

*3* Turn down the heat to low. Pour the pitcher contents very slowly into the cooking stock, whisking continually.

*(continued)*

**4** Continue whisking vigorously and cook on low heat until the mixture thickens, about 2 minutes. Remove the saucepan from the heat as soon as the mixture is thick. Stir in some cayenne pepper if you like this sauce slightly spicy.

*Nutrition at a glance (per serving): Total fat 2.5 g; Saturated fat 0.5 g; Protein 3 g; Dietary fiber 0 g; Carbohydrate 2 g; Cholesterol 0 mg; Sodium 69 mg; % of calories from fat 52; Calories 40.*

*Lynn's hollandaise tips: Hollandaise should be made only with substitute eggs. (Substitute eggs are fat-free; a regular egg contains 5 grams of fat.) But it isn't just the lowered fat content that makes substitute eggs, which are real eggs, healthful. Eggs are not thoroughly cooked during the preparation of hollandaise sauce, posing a risk of salmonella contamination, a bacteria that some experts think is present in 80 percent of uncooked eggs. Substitute eggs are pasteurized, so they don't pose that risk.*

## Pasta Marinara Sauce

This is a classic Italian marinara sauce. You can make it with three textures, all using the same ingredients. Using a food processor to chop the vegetables and basil leaves makes preparation easier. You can add more tomatoes or a jar of prepared sauce to extend this sauce if necessary (do so near the end of cooking).

*Tools: Large nonstick saucepan*

*Preparation time: 2*

*Yield: 4 servings*

*1 28-ounce can crushed tomatoes or tomato sauce*

*1 large onion, peeled and coarsely chopped*

*2 large cloves garlic, peeled and minced (optional)*

*1 large carrot, coarsely chopped*

*2 stalks celery, including tops, chopped*

*4 to 5 sprigs fresh sweet basil, chopped*

*1 teaspoon dried oregano*

*1 bay leaf*

*1 teaspoon olive oil (optional)*

*¹/₂ teaspoon fennel seed*

*Sugar*

**1** In a large nonstick saucepan, combine the tomatoes, onion, garlic (if desired), carrot, celery, basil, oregano, bay leaf, olive oil (if desired), fennel, and a pinch of sugar. Simmer on medium-low heat, covered, for 25 minutes, stirring occasionally. Remove the bay leaf.

*(continued)*

**2** You can adjust the texture and thickness of the sauce in three ways: Strain it through a colander for a thin sauce, puree the vegetables to make a thick, smooth sauce, or leave the vegetables in pieces for a chunky texture. (The latter two contain more fiber.)

***Nutrition at a glance (per serving):*** *Total fat 0.5 g; Saturated fat 0 g; Protein 3 g; Dietary fiber 3 g; Carbohydrate 15 g; Cholesterol 0 mg; Sodium 366 mg; % of calories from fat 8; Calories 69.*

***Lynn's pasta sauce tips:*** *Whenever you make pasta sauce, you can add those little bits of stuff that are always left in the refrigerator. Tomato sauce can take chopped carrots, broccoli, mushrooms, shallots or leeks, green peppers, zucchini, celery, and shrimp.*

## White Sauce

White sauce is creamy and pale in color. You can use it as a base for many sauces, such as those listed in the sidebar, "Ten different white sauces." Serve it over potatoes, fish, shellfish, or poultry, or with vegetables, such as corn, fennel, potatoes, or broccoli.

***Tools:*** *Nonstick saucepan*

***Preparation time:*** *1*

***Yield:*** *About 2 cups, or 8 servings*

| | |
|---|---|
| *1 cup liquid fat-free non-dairy creamer* | *3 tablespoons flour* |
| *1 cup skim milk* | *Salt (optional) and freshly ground white pepper* |

In a cold nonstick saucepan, whisk together the creamer, milk, flour, and salt (if desired) and white pepper to taste. Cook over medium-high heat for at least 4 minutes so that the flour doesn't taste doughy or pasty.

***Nutrition at a glance (per serving):*** *Total fat 0 g; Saturated fat 0 g; Protein 1 g; Dietary fiber 0 g; Carbohydrate 16 g; Cholesterol 1 mg; Sodium 16 mg; % of calories from fat 1; Calories 71.*

# Ten different white sauces

You can make all manner of delicious lowfat sauces with a white sauce base. Here are some recipes that may become favorites:

✔ **Béchamel or lemon sauce:** Add 1 bay leaf, a pinch of nutmeg, 2 whole cloves, and 1 small finely chopped or minced onion to the basic white sauce recipe and simmer over low heat, covered, for 15 minutes; or bake, covered, in a 350° oven for 20 minutes. Remove the bay leaf and cloves before serving.

✔ **Bordelaise sauce:** While the sauce is cooking, add $1/2$ cup dry red or white wine, 1 tablespoon chopped fresh parsley, 2 tablespoons beef marrow (marrow sautéed for 2 minutes, which adds 2 grams of fat), $1^{1}/2$ teaspoons fresh lemon juice, and black pepper to taste.

✔ **Cheese sauce:** Add 1 cup shredded fat-free or lowfat cheese to the sauce while cooking. Use this sauce for lowfat macaroni and cheese, au gratin potatoes, cheese and rice, broccoli with cheese, cauliflower and cheese, and so on.

✔ **Cream gravy:** Add defatted meat or poultry drippings to the sauce as it cooks.

✔ **Dijonnaise:** Sauté 1 small chopped onion, 1 minced garlic clove, $1/4$ teaspoon thyme, 1 teaspoon basil, one bay leaf, 1 teaspoon Dijon mustard, and 2 tablespoons Madeira. Add to the sauce and simmer for 5 minutes. Remove the bay leaf before serving.

✔ **Dill sauce:** Add 2 tablespoons chopped fresh dill to the white sauce as it cooks.

✔ **Egg sauce:** Add 1 cup cooked and diced substitute eggs and 4 hard-cooked egg whites, chopped, to the sauce while cooking.

✔ **Mornay sauce:** Sauté 2 small chopped onions, leeks, or shallots and 1 tablespoon grated Parmesan cheese. Add to the sauce while cooking.

✔ **Mushroom velouté:** Sauté 6 ounces of chopped mushrooms, 1 small finely chopped onion or 2 shallots, and a pinch of nutmeg. Add this mixture to the sauce while cooking.

✔ **Rosemary:** Add 2 tablespoons finely chopped fresh rosemary, 1 teaspoon chopped fresh or dried thyme, and 1 clove peeled garlic to the sauce while cooking. Remove the garlic before serving.

# Cold sauce recipes

The following cold sauce recipes can satisfy your cravings for sweet, spicy, and tangy flavors without ruining your lowfat eating plan.

## Apple Sauce

After you make your own apple sauce, you'll never use store-bought again; the homemade version is so easy, and the results are spectacular. Apple sauce is such a simple food for all that taste. If you don't have tart apples (such as Granny Smiths, Gravensteins, or Winesaps), add more lemon juice.

***Tools:*** *Large nonstick saucepan or microwaveable bowl*

***Preparation time:*** *2*

***Yield:*** *About 4 cups, or 6 servings*

*6 tart apples, unpeeled, cored, and coarsely chopped*

*¹/₂ cup brown sugar or maple syrup*

*¹/₂ cup raisins*

*3 tablespoons fresh lemon juice*

*¹/₄ teaspoon cinnamon*

*Pinch of nutmeg*

*Pinch of allspice*

*1* Place all the ingredients in a microwaveable bowl or nonstick saucepan and mix well.

*2* If microwaving, lightly cover and microwave on high for 25 minutes, stirring once or twice.

If cooking on the stovetop, cover the saucepan and simmer over low heat for 45 minutes.

***Nutrition at a glance (per serving):*** *Total fat 0.5 g; Saturated fat 0 g; Protein 1 g; Dietary fiber 3 g; Carbohydrate 49 g; Cholesterol 0 mg; Sodium 9 mg; % of calories from fat 2; Calories 189.*

***Lynn's apple sauce tips:*** *Apple sauce should never contain butter. By adding raisins or currants, you can slightly reduce the amount of sugar you use. Adding fresh or dried cranberries lends a tart flavor. (You need to slightly increase the amount of sugar you add.) To dress up the apple sauce, add chopped walnuts or pecans, which slightly increases the fat content but adds fiber and nutrients.*

## Barbecue Sauce

Barbecue sauce that is tangy and sweet is great on preboiled-and-then-grilled chicken legs, chicken wings, vegetables, and Western fried potatoes.

**Preparation time:** *1*

**Yield:** *Just over 2 cups, or 8 servings*

*¹/₂ cup maple syrup or brown sugar*

*1 to 2 tablespoons cider vinegar*

*¹/₄ cup cherry, apricot, jalapeño, or other tart jelly or preserves*

*1 tablespoon Worcestershire sauce*

*1 tablespoon low-sodium soy sauce*

*1 clove garlic, peeled and minced*

*1 medium onion, peeled and chopped*

*1 cup chili sauce or ketchup*

*1 tablespoon chili powder*

*1 tablespoon prepared mustard*

*Several drops hot pepper sauce*

In a small bowl, combine all the ingredients. Mix well.

**Nutrition at a glance (per serving):** *Total fat 0.5 g; Saturated fat 0 g; Protein 1 g; Dietary fiber 1 g; Carbohydrate 31 g; Cholesterol 0 mg; Sodium 591 mg; % of calories from fat 3; Calories 125.*

**Lynn's barbecue sauce tips:** *People in different parts of the United States use different barbecue ingredients. In the West, some use orange zest (peel) for flavor; some Southerners add bourbon. New Orleans barbecue sauce wouldn't be the same without Cajun spices, and many New Englanders add Old Bay Seasoning.*

## Cranberry Sauce

If you like cranberries, you'll eat this as a side dish with many foods, not just as a relish for turkey. I can never get enough, and company loves it. My friend Lillian Pulitzer Smith of New Orleans, a superb home cook, gave it to me. You may want to adjust the sugar depending upon how sweet you like relish; luckily, sugar can be added at any time. You can double the whole recipe easily.

**Tools:** *Large saucepan, food processor*

**Preparation time:** *2*

**Yield:** *1 quart, or 8 servings*

*(continued)*

*1 pound cranberries*

*1 cup sugar*

*6 ounces golden raisins*

*1 large orange*

*2 teaspoons fresh lemon juice*

*2 teaspoons lemon zest (chopped peel)*

*¹/₂ cup cider vinegar*

*¹/₄ teaspoon ground cloves*

*1 teaspoon ground cinnamon*

*1* In a large saucepan, place the cleaned and picked-over berries, sugar, and raisins.

*2* Wash the orange with soapy water and rinse well. Cut into fourths or eighths. Pull out and remove the center pith and as many seeds as possible. Leave the skin on.

*3* Put the orange fourths or eighths (with the skin) into a food processor and process with a couple of pulses until the orange pieces are the size of raisins.

*4* Add the processed orange, lemon juice, lemon zest, vinegar, cloves, and cinnamon to the mixture in the saucepan.

*5* Heat over medium heat until the berries burst, about 30 to 40 minutes, stirring occasionally.

***Nutrition at a glance (per serving):*** *Total fat 0.5 g; Saturated fat 0 g; Protein 1 g; Dietary fiber 3 g; Carbohydrate 53 g; Cholesterol 0 mg; Sodium 4 mg; % of calories from fat 1; Calories 203.*

***Lynn's cranberry sauce tip:*** *You can add ¹/₂ cup chopped nuts, chestnuts, or pecans to this sauce. Adding chestnuts raises the fat content by 0.2 gram per serving; using pecans adds about 4 grams. You can also add ¹/₂ cup brandy. Serve cranberry sauce with fat-free or lowfat sour cream with meat, poultry, beans, blintzes, or pancakes, or make a mold with your cranberry sauce by adding gelatin and chilling. Turn out on a plate and tuck in shiny garden leaves, such as magnolia, ligustrum, holly, or nandina.*

## Cucumber and Chive Sauce for Fish and Poultry

This creamy lemon and herb sauce is perfect for salmon and other fish. After you make it, spoon half of it onto the salmon to pan-cook, and serve the other half with the fish. This sauce is also terrific for a quick turkey or chicken fillet.

***Preparation time:*** *1*

***Yield:*** *1¹/₃ cups, or 10 servings*

*(continued)*

2-inch piece of cucumber, finely chopped (peeled if waxed)

$^1/_4$ cup minced red bell pepper

$^1/_4$ cup snipped fresh chives

1 cup fat-free or lowfat sour cream

$^1/_4$ cup fresh lemon juice

2 tablespoons lemon zest

1 teaspoon dry mustard

Salt (optional) and freshly ground black pepper

In a small bowl, combine all the ingredients and mix well.

**Nutrition at a glance (per serving):** *Total fat 0 g; Saturated fat 0 g; Protein 2 g; Dietary fiber 0 g; Carbohydrate 6 g; Cholesterol 0 mg; Sodium 18 mg; % of calories from fat 4; Calories 30.*

**Lynn's fish and turkey seasoning tips:** *You can flavor and cook both fish and turkey fillets in several lowfat or fat-free liquid sauces, such as salad dressing, mayonnaise, Hellman's Dijonnaise, mustard, soy sauce, tomato sauce, ketchup, barbecue sauce, bouillon dissolved in water, or wine.*

## Plum Sauce

This is a sweet, tangy sauce for dipping or basting chicken, duck, or turkey tenders (pieces of skinned breast, all visible fat removed). Cooking initially thins this sauce, but it thickens as it cooks down.

**Tools:** *Small saucepan*

**Preparation time:** *2*

**Yield:** *Just over 2 cups, or 8 servings*

$^1/_2$ cup brown sugar

1 tablespoon cider vinegar

1 cup canned plums, pitted and chopped, 2 tablespoons juice reserved

2 teaspoons fresh lemon juice

1 tablespoon Worcestershire sauce

1 tablespoon low-sodium soy sauce

1 large clove garlic, peeled and minced

1 medium onion, peeled and finely chopped

1 tablespoon prepared mustard

Hot pepper sauce

**1** In a small saucepan, combine the brown sugar, vinegar, plums and juice, lemon juice, Worcestershire sauce, soy sauce, garlic, onion, mustard, and several drops hot pepper sauce and mix well.

**2** Simmer, covered, over medium-low heat for 15 minutes. Store in the refrigerator. The mixture thickens as it cools. Use hot or cold.

*(continued)*

**Nutrition at a glance (per serving):** *Total fat 0 g; Saturated fat 0 g; Protein 1 g; Dietary fiber 1 g; Carbohydrate 20 g; Cholesterol 0 mg; Sodium 126 mg; % of calories from fat 1; Calories 80.*

**Lynn's sweet sauce tips:** *You can make a quick and tangy sweet sauce for poultry by mixing 1 tablespoon each pepper jelly and mustard and 1 teaspoon low-sodium or regular soy sauce.*

## Tartar Sauce

Tartar sauce is a traditional favorite with fish, and this pretty version is also good as a sandwich spread. If you or your family have a sweet tooth, use sweet pickles; if savory is your preference, try dill pickles.

**Preparation time:** *1*

**Yield:** *About 2 cups, or 8 servings*

*1 cup fat-free or lowfat mayonnaise*

*3 tablespoons skim milk (if needed to thin the mayonnaise)*

*3 tablespoons chopped onions or scallions*

*1 tablespoon fresh lemon juice*

*¹/₄ cup finely chopped sweet or dill pickles*

*¹/₄ cup finely chopped pimento or red bell pepper*

*¹/₄ cup chopped fresh parsley or watercress*

*1 tablespoon Dijon mustard*

In a small bowl, combine all the ingredients and mix well. Chill and serve.

**Nutrition at a glance (per serving):** *Total fat 0 g; Saturated fat 0 g; Protein 0 g; Dietary fiber 1 g; Carbohydrate 7 g; Cholesterol 0 mg; Sodium 298 mg; % of calories from fat 7; Calories 34.*

**Lynn's tartar tips:** *You can add additional ingredients such as a teaspoon of horseradish or drained capers, a few drops of hot sauce, or crushed red pepper (flakes) to tartar sauce. For a slightly different, more refined flavor, use fat-free or lowfat sour cream instead of mayonnaise.*

## A salsa recipe

If you find that your lowfat diet is getting bland, this zesty salsa will perk up your taste buds.

### Colorful Red, Yellow, and Green Salsa

This salsa is not spicy. It has a bright yellow-green speckly color and an unusually good taste because it is made with tiny yellow tomatoes or large yellow tomatoes (yellow tomatoes are sweeter than red). Good with lowfat or fat-free tortilla chips, to spice up a hot or cold soup (as South Americans do), on grilled fish or poultry, or with beans, this is a basic salsa. Garnish with a sprig of cilantro or chopped jalapeño for heat.

**Tools:** *Food processor*

**Preparation time:** *2*

**Yield:** *About 2 cups, or 6 servings*

*¹/₄ cup finely chopped fresh cilantro, including stems*

*2 tablespoons chopped fresh parsley*

*¹/₂ cup chopped celery*

*4 large scallions (white and green parts), chopped*

*2 tablespoons chopped onion*

*1 large clove garlic, peeled and minced*

*2 tablespoons chopped mixed green and red bell pepper*

*1¹/₂ cups lightly processed yellow tomatoes (miniature, or large if possible)*

*2 tablespoons fresh lime juice*

*2 tablespoons fresh lemon juice*

*1 tablespoon fresh orange or tangerine juice*

*1 teaspoon vinegar*

*Several drops of hot pepper sauce*

*Salt (optional)*

In a large bowl, combine all the ingredients. Let sit in the refrigerator to marinate for at least 30 minutes, covered.

**Nutrition at a glance (per serving):** *Total fat 0 g; Saturated fat 0 g; Protein 1 g; Dietary fiber 1 g; Carbohydrate 5 g; Cholesterol 0 mg; Sodium 15 mg; % of calories from fat 8; Calories 20.*

**Lynn's salsa tips:** *To make a smoky-flavored salsa with heat, add 1 or 2 chopped dried jalapeños (chipotles) that have been soaked in water for 30 minutes. (See Figure 16-1 for a variety of hot peppers that you can add to salsa.) Add a 16-ounce can of drained pinto beans to give your salsa more body.*

**Figure 16-1:**
You can
add a
variety of
hot peppers
to salsas
and other
spicy
dishes —
what you
should add
depends
on your
tolerance
of heat.

## A gravy recipe

Are you feeling deprived because you are eating smaller portions of meat and poultry? Adding a luxurious gravy helps you feel satisfied.

### Beef, Chicken, or Turkey Gravy

This gravy is thick and perfect the way gravy should be. It has no fat yet all the flavor. Roasted chickens and turkeys produce great drippings (just be sure to defat them), so you may want to add less water.

**Tools:** *Metal skillet or flat metal cake pan or defatting cup, skillet*

**Preparation time:** *1*

**Yield:** *About $1/2$ to 1 cup, or 4 servings*

*$1/2$ to 1 cup beef, chicken, or turkey drippings*

*1 to 2 tablespoons flour*

*Salt (optional) and freshly ground black pepper*

*1* If you have 10 minutes before serving the meat, place the drippings in a metal skillet or flat metal cake pan, place in the freezer for 10 minutes or so, and remove the congealed fat.

*(continued)*

If time is short and you have less than $1/2$ cup of drippings, add 1 cup water to the drippings, heat to the boiling point, and pour into a defatting cup. Pour off the fat-free liquid to use for the gravy and discard the fat left in the cup.

**2** Place the defatted drippings in a clean skillet. Whisk in the flour. Heat to boiling, lower the temperature to a simmer, and whisk until thick, about 4 minutes. Season with salt (if desired) and pepper to taste.

***Nutrition at a glance (per serving):*** *Total fat 0 g; Saturated fat 0 g; Protein 1 g; Dietary fiber 0 g; Carbohydrate 2 g; Cholesterol 0 mg; Sodium 9 mg; % of calories from fat 16; Calories 12.*

***Lynn's gravy-seasoning tips:*** *You can add finely diced giblets, all visible fat removed, to turkey or chicken gravy. You add a gram or two of fat, but it's mostly muscle meat. Here's where a beef or chicken bouillon cube or beef or chicken flavor granules come in handy. Add bouillon or granules to the hot water in the gravy recipe to extend the flavor.*

# Chapter 17

# Desserts

## In This Chapter

▶ Including delicious desserts in a lowfat eating plan

▶ Putting together quick lowfat desserts

▶ Discovering lowfat dessert options

*T*his chapter can help you change your beliefs about dessert. A dessert doesn't have to be a fat-laden concoction in order to satisfy your sweet tooth and provide a pleasing end to a meal. I explain how to make popular high-fat desserts into lowfat delectables.

In choosing recipes for this chapter, I had a specific goal: desserts that really taste good and are easy to make. Not impossible! Lowfat desserts are a challenge, but the effort is worth it because they taste so good.

## Defatting Desserts

Dessert is both the easiest course to change to lowfat and the most difficult. It's the easiest because you usually have already eaten and don't mind if the dessert isn't a foot-wide slice of tiramisu topped with whipped cream. It's also the easiest because sugar and fruit are often associated with dessert, neither contains fat, and you can make many delicious desserts with them. Fruit is also not particularly high in calories and is one of the most healthful foods, containing fiber, vitamins, and minerals. Although the other common dessert ingredient, sugar, has little nutritional value, it has half as many calories as fat does.

A simple way to reduce the fat in a usually fruit-filled dessert such as pie is to increase the amount of fruit and decrease the amount of crust. Fruit-filled, deep-dish pies with just a top or bottom crust make the transition to lowfat nicely — and not a poor-quality, dry, cardboard crust, either, but a flaky, buttery, delicious crust. Desserts such as crumbles, crisps, cobblers, and tarts make this transition well.

Admittedly, desserts can be difficult to change because we have become used to elaborate restaurant concoctions that resemble a meal's Academy Award-winning ending for a chef. I think these desserts are, if not purpose-fully irresponsible, just plain silly. Recently in a fine dining establishment, I was served a dessert that was a dizzying 7 inches high, stacked on an almond mocha cheesecake base with a teepee of enough white and dark chocolate leaves, butter fudge grapes, and shiny praline spun strings all around it for six people. Can't chefs use their talents and training in ways that don't incapacitate people?

Most fast-food and run-of-the mill restaurants, and even nice little family eateries, serve desserts that are usually extraordinarily high in fat and often, if not as large as my mocha cheesecake, still too large a portion. These desserts may be a delight for some who are not watching their weight, fat intake, or health, but they can be a nightmare for people who don't like to be so tempted.

When served a dessert that is not what you expected (a scoop of ice cream on the cake or whipped cream on the pudding, for example), the trick is to have a little taste and then pass it around the table. If you're ordering for yourself, keep your body in mind and order sorbet or some fresh fruit without cream sauce or whipped cream. Or if your head gets the notion to just go for it, get a slice of fruit pie and eat only the fruit and just a taste of the crust (which is where the fat is).

Those of you who don't want a plain old apple but are scared of butter fudge truffle cheesecake (one serving of which has 55 grams of fat *without* whipped cream) do have other choices. You can make pretty sumptuous desserts lowfat fairly easily. In fact, any of the following desserts can be made lowfat:

- Banana splits
- Brownies
- Cakes
- Cheesecakes
- Cobblers
- Cookies
- Crisps

- Deep-dish pies (with a single crust)
- Hot fudge sundaes
- Parfaits
- Puddings and custards
- Strudels
- Tarts

IMPROVISE

# Ten quickie lowfat dessert assemblies

These ten quickies are all fast-assembly desserts, using ingredients that you buy and assemble. Putting these desserts together takes 10 minutes or less for most.

**Berry parfait:** Place blueberries, nectarines, strawberries, blackberries, or raspberries in a tall glass or bowl, layer them with fat-free or lowfat vanilla frozen yogurt or ice cream, and top it off with fat-free or lowfat whipped topping, additional berries, and a mint leaf.

**Black forest cake with cherries:** Slice a store-bought fat-free or lowfat chocolate cake lengthwise and fill it with fat-free or lowfat whipped topping. Cover with canned cherry pie filling or bananas and another dollop of whipped topping.

**Blueberry fruit yogurt:** Fold together 2 4-ounce containers of fat-free blueberry yogurt, 2 cups fresh blueberries, 1 cup fat-free or lowfat whipped topping, 2 tablespoons granulated sugar, and 1 teaspoon lemon juice. Top with a few fresh berries and a mint sprig.

**Figs and ice cream:** Simmer 10 dried figs, 2 tablespoons granulated sugar, and 1 teaspoon lemon zest in 2 cups water for 25 minutes and serve over fat-free or lowfat ice cream.

**Fruit sauce and pound cake:** Serve slices of store-bought fat-free or lowfat pound cake with a sauce of 2 cups berries (raspberries or blueberries), ¹/₂ cup granulated sugar, and 1¹/₂ tablespoons cornstarch dissolved in 3 tablespoons lemon juice and heated for 3 to 4 minutes until thick, pureed if desired.

**Gingersnap ice cream:** Top several store-bought lowfat or fat-free gingersnaps with one scoop of fat-free or lowfat vanilla or lemon frozen yogurt and a heaping spoonful of fat-free or lowfat whipped topping sprinkled with lemon zest.

**Lemony fresh yogurt cake:** Pour 2 tablespoons lemon juice mixed with 4 ounces fat-free or lowfat lemon yogurt over store-bought fat-free or lowfat lemon cake and top with a sprinkle of crushed lemon sourballs.

**Mocha chocolate pudding and bananas:** Spoon fat-free or lowfat store-bought chocolate yogurt or pudding over fat-free or lowfat coffee ice cream or frozen yogurt and top with banana slices. Add fat-free or lowfat whipped cream or whipped topping and a pinch of instant coffee sprinkled on top.

**Strawberry (or banana) shortcake:** Top a store-bought angel food cake slice with fresh strawberries (or bananas slices rubbed with lemon juice), fat-free or lowfat whipped cream or whipped topping, and a big, ripe strawberry with the leaves still attached.

**Tropical fruit ambrosia:** Carefully mix together 2 small cans drained mandarin oranges or 1¹/₂ cups peeled fresh orange or tangerine sections, 1 cup miniature marshmallows, ¹/₄ cup chopped pecans, 2 sliced bananas, 1 cup chopped fresh pineapple, ¹/₄ cup fresh lemon juice, 2 tablespoons granulated sugar, and 2 cups fat-free or lowfat whipped topping.

With exceptionally tasty fat-free and lowfat ice creams, frozen yogurts, creamers (which have the consistency of cream), whipped creams, and other whipped toppings to tempt you, all without the downside of fat and with fewer calories, you can make some pretty good dessert combinations.

Plus, you can find good lowfat store-bought cookies, brownies, cupcakes, and cakes. Although many fat-free and lowfat desserts still leave something to be desired, combinations of these cakes, toppings, and fruit are simple and fairly tasty. The "ten quickies" listed in the preceding sidebar include several easily assembled desserts using these products.

But if you feel like something special and want to make a really good pie, pudding, or cake, the desserts in this chapter are to die for, and this time the dying is only figurative. You can nibble on Apple Crumble or Pear Crisp or dip into the Sweet Potato Pudding without guilt. And put some nuts on top — they have taste, fiber, and just a small amount of fat, and they add an interesting crunch. Lowfat doesn't mean no fat and no fun. Lowfat means desserts the natural way, the way they were meant to be.

# Delectable Dessert Recipes

Desserts don't have to be high-fat to be lush and satisfying. Make use of all the lower-fat toppings, cream cheeses, ice creams, frozen yogurts, cakes, and cookies, and you don't have to skip the last (and some say best) course of the meal!

## Angel Food Cake with Sauces

This cake is bright white, rich-tasting, and perfect. My testers finished off much of it even before it cooled. The cake doesn't need frosting, but you can serve it with nonfat coffee ice cream and a few raspberries or any of the sauces that follow the cake recipe. The tropical fruit topping for the tapioca pudding (later in this chapter) would be excellent on this cake, too, as would a lowfat chocolate sauce.

**Tools:** *10-inch tube pan*

**Preparation time:** *3*

**Yield:** *10 servings*

*1¹/₄ cups sifted all-purpose flour, sifted before measuring*

*1³/₄ cups granulated sugar*

*1³/₄ cups egg whites (about 12 to 14 whites)*

*1¹/₂ teaspoons cream of tartar*

*¹/₄ teaspoon salt*

*1 teaspoon vanilla extract*

*¹/₂ teaspoon almond extract*

*(continued)*

*1* Preheat the oven to 375°.

*2* Wash with hot, soapy water, rinse, and dry all the tools you're using, plus your hands. (If any oil is present, the whites won't stiffen.)

*3* Sift together the flour and ³/₄ cup of the sugar three times and set aside. In a large mixing bowl, beat the egg whites, cream of tartar, and salt until soft peaks form. Gradually add the remaining 1 cup sugar and continue beating until very stiff peaks form.

*4* Sift about a third of the flour mixture over the egg whites and gently fold it in with a large rubber spatula. Repeat with the remaining flour mixture, ¹/₄ cup at a time. Fold in the vanilla and almond extract.

*5* Spoon the batter into the tube pan. Run a knife gently through the batter in a swirling motion to remove air pockets. Bake in the lower third of the oven for 40 to 50 minutes.

*6* Place a wine bottle on the counter and let the tube pan rest upside down on the bottle neck for 1 hour. Invert and run a thin knife around the edge up and down between the cake and the pan to loosen. (See Figure 17-1.) Serve slices of cake with one of the following sauces if desired.

***Nutrition at a glance (per serving):*** *Total fat 0 g; Saturated fat 0 g; Protein 6 g; Dietary fiber 1 g; Carbohydrate 48 g; Cholesterol 0 mg; Sodium 124 mg; % of calories from fat 1; Calories 216.*

***Lynn's chocolate sauce and juice tips:*** *Hershey's Hot Fudge Topping has no fat if you use 2 tablespoons or less per serving. Yum! Try chocolate and red raspberries or strawberries as a topping. In angel food cake mixes, substitute canned pineapple juice or other juice for the water in the recipe for peppier flavor.*

Place a wine bottle on the counter and let the tube pan rest on the bottle neck for one hour.

Invert and run a thin knife around the edge up and down to loosen.

**Figure 17-1:** Cooling and loosening an angel food cake.

VINO Classic

## Honey Lemon Sauce

This sauce is excellent on a variety of desserts, such as fat-free ice cream, frozen yogurt, or angel food cake. Refrigerate the sauce for a day or two to thicken it even more and serve it over bread pudding or crepes filled with bananas or oranges for a spectacular dessert.

**Tools:** *Nonstick saucepan*

**Preparation time:** *1*

**Yield:** *1¹/₂ cups, or 10 servings*

| | |
|---|---|
| 1 tablespoon finely granulated sugar | ³/₄ cup boiling water |
| 1 tablespoon cornstarch | Dash of nutmeg |
| ¹/₃ cup honey | 2 tablespoons fresh lemon juice |

**1** In a nonstick saucepan, blend the sugar and cornstarch. Stir in the honey and boiling water. Stir over low heat until thickened and clear, and then remove from the heat.

**2** Add the nutmeg and stir until blended. Stir in the lemon juice and serve over slices of cake.

*Nutrition at a glance (per serving):* Total fat 0 g; Saturated fat 0 g; Protein 0 g; Dietary fiber 0 g; Carbohydrate 11 g; Cholesterol 0 mg; Sodium 1 mg; % of calories from fat 0; Calories 43.

## Raspberry Sauce

This sauce has great versatility. You can use it cool and drizzled over angel food cake, on cheesecake or poached pears, on fat-free or lowfat ice cream or frozen yogurt, or warm on pancakes or crepes.

**Tools:** *Nonstick skillet*

**Preparation time:** *1*

**Yield:** *About 2 cups, or 10 servings*

*(continued)*

1 cup fresh or frozen raspberries, partially thawed and drained, juice reserved

1 teaspoon lemon zest

²/₃ cup light corn syrup

2 tablespoons cornstarch

2 tablespoons fresh lemon juice

2 tablespoons water or apple juice

**1** In a nonstick skillet, heat a third of the raspberries over low heat and mash them with a potato masher or fork. Stir in the lemon zest.

**2** Add another third of the berries, but don't mash them, and cook for 2 to 3 minutes until the berries get hot and burst. Check for sweetness and add some sugar if necessary.

**3** Add the final third of the berries and heat for just a minute. Add the corn syrup, mix well, and lower the heat. In a small bowl, mix the cornstarch with the lemon juice and water or apple juice, and add the mixture to the skillet, stirring for just a few minutes or until thick and clear.

***Nutrition at a glance (per serving):*** *Total fat 0 g; Saturated fat 0 g; Protein 0 g; Dietary fiber 1 g; Carbohydrate 20 g; Cholesterol 0 mg; Sodium 26 mg; % of calories from fat 1; Calories 74.*

## Apple Crumble

This dessert convinced my television show director Mark White to work on losing weight when he tasted how delicious a lowfat pastry can be. He lost 100 pounds and now weighs a svelte 195.

The type of apple you use in this recipe makes a huge taste difference. Red or Golden Delicious apples can't stand up to the baking process, so use tart, firm apples, such as Granny Smiths or Gravensteins.

***Tools:*** *7-x-11-inch or 10-inch-square baking pan, large nonstick frying pan*

***Preparation time:*** *3*

***Yield:*** *8 servings*

*(continued)*

*6 tart Granny Smith or Gravenstein apples, cored, seeds removed, and cut into even $^1/_2$-inch slices (peeled or unpeeled)*

*$^1/_2$ cup raisins*

*$^3/_4$ cup granulated sugar*

*$^1/_4$ cup fresh lemon juice*

*$^1/_2$ teaspoon cinnamon*

*$^1/_8$ teaspoon allspice*

*$^1/_4$ cup minute tapioca granules*

*$1^1/_2$ cups fat-free or lowfat granola*

*$^1/_4$ cup chopped walnuts (optional)*

**1** Preheat the oven to 350°.

**2** In a large bowl, toss the apples, raisins, sugar, lemon juice, cinnamon, allspice, and tapioca, mixing completely. Lightly cover the mixture with foil and let it sit for 15 minutes, tossing once or twice to mix. Lightly coat a 7-x-11-inch or 10-inch-square baking pan with no-stick vegetable oil spray and place the apple mixture in the pan.

**3** Lightly coat a large nonstick frying pan with no-stick spray. Add the granola and walnuts (if desired) and lightly spray the mixture. Heat on medium, stirring, for 10 minutes or until the granola is just slightly golden brown. Sprinkle the mixture on the apples and lightly coat with no-stick spray.

**4** Bake covered with foil for 1 hour and 5 minutes. Remove the foil and bake for an additional 10 minutes. Turn off the heat and let the crumble sit for 15 minutes in the oven. Serve hot, warm, chilled, or at room temperature with a scoop of fat-free or lowfat vanilla ice cream or frozen yogurt.

***Nutrition at a glance (per serving):*** *Total fat 1.5 g; Saturated fat 0 g; Protein 2 g; Dietary fiber 4 g; Carbohydrate 62 g; Cholesterol 0 mg; Sodium 36 mg; % of calories from fat 5; Calories 252.*

***Lynn's lowfat tip:*** *Citrus juice or citrus zest added to cooked apples was a common recipe in Martha Washington's* Booke of Cookery *in 1749 — an excellent suggestion when you want extra flavor with less fat. Her apple recipes called for Pippins, a tart, usually green apple.*

## Berry Patch Cobbler

Old-fashioned and tart-sweet, this fruit cobbler is full of fiber and nutrients but has almost no fat. Use any ripe fruit, such as tart cherries, blackberries, peaches, boysenberries, blueberries, or apples — I've made it with each fruit and favor blackberries. You can also make this cobbler with frozen fruit. The crust can be on

*(continued)*

top and tucked in, or on the bottom and wrapped slightly around the fruit. If you're using blackberries or cranberries, increase the sugar by 50 percent. This dish is watery when baked and served hot (just as good); when cool, the juices thicken. Serve the cobbler with fat-free or lowfat whipped cream or milk, ice cream, or vanilla frozen yogurt.

***Tools:*** *Shallow 8-inch square or round baking pan, bowl, or dish; pastry cutter; rolling pin*

***Preparation time:*** *3*

***Yield:*** *9 servings*

***Filling:***

*1¹/₂ pounds berries, peaches, or thinly sliced apples (about 6 cups or 3 pints)*

*²/₃ to 1 cup granulated sugar*

*¹/₄ cup fresh lemon juice*

*¹/₂ teaspoon lemon zest (optional)*

*¹/₃ cup minute tapioca granules*

*¹/₄ teaspoon cinnamon*

***Crust:***

*1 cup all-purpose flour*

*¹/₂ teaspoon salt*

*1 tablespoon canola oil*

*1 tablespoon butter*

*4 to 6 tablespoons skim milk*

*Flour for rolling crust*

*1 teaspoon granulated sugar to sprinkle on top of crust*

***1*** Preheat the oven to 400°.

***2*** Lightly coat a shallow 8-inch square or round baking pan, bowl, or dish with no-stick vegetable oil spray.

***3*** In a large bowl, mix the fruit and sugar and lightly toss. In a smaller bowl, combine the lemon juice, zest (if desired), tapioca, and cinnamon. Let sit, lightly covered with foil or a towel, for 15 minutes, tossing occasionally while you prepare the topping.

***4*** In another large bowl, combine the flour and salt. Put the canola oil and butter in a microwave-safe cup and microwave for 10 to 20 seconds or until just melted but not hot. Add the milk to the buttery oil. Drizzle half the mixture into the flour. With a fork, mix the ingredients. Add the remaining liquid, 2 tablespoons at a time, and mix, cutting with a pastry cutter just until you can press the flour into a ball.

***5*** Lightly sprinkle with flour both a rolling pin and a large sheet of waxed paper (optional) or a smooth counter or large cutting board. Place the dough on the center of the paper. Roll out the dough roughly to the shape of the baking dish, but 4 to 5 inches larger on all sides. (See Figure 17-2 for rolling instructions.) Lightly coat the baking dish with no-stick spray.

*(continued)*

**6** Roll the waxed paper with the dough and, if you're putting the crust on the bottom, place it dough-side-down at one end of the baking dish; then carefully unroll. Lift the waxed paper from the dough in the baking dish, pressing the dough lightly to the dish. Add the fruit filling and loosely wrap by pleating or gently folding the filling with the dough. Leave open a 2- or 3-inch gap in the center. If you're using a top crust, fill the bowl with the fruit and cover with the crust, slitting it eight times with a knife.

**7** Sprinkle the top of the dough area with sugar and then lightly cover the dish with foil. Lower the heat to 350° and bake for 1 hour. Uncover and bake for 15 more minutes.

***Nutrition at a glance (per serving):*** *Total fat 3 g; Saturated fat 1 gram; Protein 2 g; Dietary fiber 3 g; Carbohydrate 44 g; Cholesterol 4 mg; Sodium 140 mg; % of calories from fat 14; Calories 207.*

***Lynn's lowfat tip:*** *Cobblers are traditionally made with a biscuit topping, which can be high in fat. Two lowfat biscuit mixes are available: Lowfat Pioneer, with 0.5 grams total fat, and Reduced-Fat Bisquick, with 2.5 grams total fat.*

## Rolling Out Dough for a Cobbler

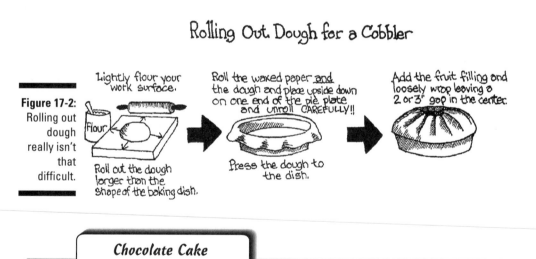

**Figure 17-2:** Rolling out dough really isn't that difficult.

Lightly flour your work surface.

Roll out the dough larger than the shape of the baking dish.

Roll the waxed paper and the dough and place upside down on one end of the pie plate and unroll CAREFULLY!!

Press the dough to the dish.

Add the fruit filling and loosely wrap leaving a 2 or 3" gap in the center.

## Chocolate Cake

A chocolaty chocolate cake that tastes good *and* is low in fat is a real treat. Kids love to help because it is so easy to make. Add some nuts for just a little extra fat, extra crunch, and a few vitamins and minerals (plus lots of taste). If you can get it, use a soft cake flour, such as that made by Lily.

***Tools:*** *8-inch square pan*

***Preparation time:*** *2*

***Yield:*** *12 servings*

*(continued)*

2 cups all-purpose flour or 1³/₄ cups cake flour

1 teaspoon instant (dry) coffee

¹/₃ cup unsweetened cocoa powder

1 teaspoon baking soda

¹/₄ teaspoon salt

1 cup sugar

2 tablespoons canola oil

1 egg white

1 cup nonfat plain yogurt

2 teaspoons vanilla

¹/₄ cup fat-free hot fudge topping

Powdered sugar (optional)

**1** Preheat the oven to 350°. Lightly coat an 8-inch square pan with no-stick vegetable oil spray.

**2** Place the flour, coffee, cocoa, baking soda, salt, and sugar in a large bowl and stir several times to mix. Sift the whole mixture twice, letting it fall back into the bowl.

**3** In a medium bowl, combine the oil, egg whites, yogurt, vanilla, and fudge topping (if the syrup is thick, place in the microwave for 1 minute, or long enough to melt it). Mix together completely.

**4** Pour the liquid ingredients over the dry ingredients and mix thoroughly with a spatula to make sure that everything gets mixed together. Pour the mixture into the pan.

**5** Bake for 30 to 35 minutes. Dust with powdered sugar if desired.

**_Nutrition at a glance (per serving):_** _Total fat 3 g; Saturated fat 0.5 g; Protein 4 g; Dietary fiber 2 g; Carbohydrate 39 g; Cholesterol 0 mg; Sodium 193 mg; % of calories from fat 13; Calories 197._

**_Lynn's lowfat cake tips:_** _Marginally good commercial lowfat and even fat-free frostings are available in vanilla, chocolate, or strawberry. Decorate the cake with chocolate jimmies. With Just Whites (from Deb El Foods, 2 Papetti Plaza, Elizabeth, NJ 07207), you can make an uncooked egg white frosting with confectioners' sugar and vanilla, or use fat-free or reduced-fat cream cheese and sugar for a cream cheese frosting._

### Lime Meringue Pie

Very tart and very tasty, this meringue needs to be made with Just Whites, a some-times-hard-to-find product (see "Lynn's lowfat cake tips" in the preceding recipe). The filling in this pie has all the flavor of a filling made with high-fat and high-cholesterol egg yolks.

_(continued)_

**Tools:** *8-inch pie pan*

**Preparation time:** *2*

**Yield:** *8 servings*

**Crust:**

*1 cup fat-free or lowfat graham cracker crumbs*

**Filling:**

*1¹/₂ cups granulated sugar*

*¹/₃ cup cornstarch*

*1¹/₄ cups water*

*¹/₂ cup substitute eggs*

*¹/₃ cup fresh lime juice*

*1 tablespoon lime zest*

*2 drops green food coloring (optional)*

**Meringue:**

*4 Just Whites egg whites (or 2¹/₂ tablespoons)*

*¹/₂ teaspoon cream of tartar*

*3¹/₂ tablespoons granulated sugar*

*¹/₂ teaspoon vanilla*

*1* Preheat the oven to 350°.

*2* Press the graham cracker crumbs into an 8-inch pie pan and bake for 10 minutes. Remove from the oven and cool.

*3* In a medium saucepan, combine the sugar and cornstarch. Gradually stir in the water. Cook over medium heat, stirring constantly, until the mixture comes to a boil and begins to thicken. Boil for 1 minute. Slowly stir at least half the hot mixture into the substitute eggs and then add back to the hot mixture in the saucepan. Boil 1 minute longer, stirring constantly.

*4* Remove from the heat and continue stirring until smooth. Stir in the lime juice and lime zest, add green food coloring (if desired), and pour the filling into the crust.

*5* Make the Just Whites as directed, adding the sugar, cream of tartar, and vanilla. Cover the lime pie filling with the meringue and brown in the oven for 12 minutes. Cool and chill in the refrigerator.

**Nutrition at a glance (per serving):** *Total fat 1 g; Saturated fat 0.5 g; Protein 4 g; Dietary fiber 1 g; Carbohydrate 62 g; Cholesterol 0 mg; Sodium 158 mg; % of calories from fat 3; Calories 265.*

**Lynn's egg white tip:** *Why use Just Whites and not regular egg whites? So that salmonella, a bacteria often found in uncooked egg products, doesn't make you ill. Browned meringues just aren't cooked long enough to kill the bacteria, but Just Whites are pasteurized.*

## Oatmeal Raisin Cookies

Crisp and delicious, you'll be snacking on these cookies all day. These raisin-filled crunchies are perfect for kids and grownups alike. Make them by yourself, thinking of how much you and everyone will love them, or make them with a friend or the kids. This recipe takes a tip from cookbook author Nancy Bagget on how to flatten the cookies. You can also *not* flatten them and cook oatmeal cookie balls for a slightly softer cookie.

***Tools:*** *Electric mixer, several nonstick baking sheets*

***Preparation time:*** *2*

***Yield:*** *About 60 2-inch cookies*

$2^1/_2$ *cups quick-cooking oats*

*1 cup all-purpose flour*

$^1/_2$ *teaspoon baking soda*

$^1/_2$ *teaspoon baking powder*

$^1/_4$ *heaping teaspoon cinnamon*

$^1/_4$ *teaspoon freshly grated nutmeg, or* $^1/_8$ *teaspoon ground nutmeg*

*3 tablespoons butter, softened*

*2 tablespoons canola, safflower, or walnut oil*

*1 cup dark brown sugar, packed*

*2 tablespoons honey*

$^1/_2$ *teaspoon maple extract*

*1 large egg white*

$^1/_4$ *cup apple sauce*

*2 teaspoons vanilla extract*

$^1/_2$ *cup raisins*

$^1/_4$ *cup chopped walnuts or pecans (optional)*

*1* Preheat the oven to 350°. Lightly coat several nonstick baking sheets with no-stick vegetable oil spray and set aside.

*2* In a medium bowl, combine the oats, flour, baking soda, baking powder, cinnamon, and nutmeg and set aside.

*3* In a large mixer bowl, place the butter and oil and beat on medium speed until smooth. Add the brown sugar, honey, maple extract, egg white, apple sauce, and vanilla and beat until smooth. Beat in the flour mixture. With a large wooden spoon, stir in the oat mixture, raisins, and walnuts or pecans (if desired) until thoroughly mixed.

*4* Lightly spray your hands with no-stick spray. Scoop a teaspoon-sized or 1-inch-round volume of batter into your palms, making a ball. Place the balls on a cookie sheet, spacing them 3 inches apart. Flatten each cookie by pushing the bottom of a lightly sprayed glass on the cookie dough ball, pressing it firmly and as flat as possible into a 2-inch round. (Or leave the cookies in balls, if you prefer.)

*(continued)*

**5** Bake the cookies in the upper third of the oven for 10 minutes. They should be slightly soft. Remove them carefully and let them cool completely before storing.

*Nutrition at a glance (per cookie):* *Total fat 1 g; Saturated fat 0.5 g; Protein 1 g; Dietary fiber 0 g; Carbohydrate 9 g; Cholesterol 2 mg; Sodium 23 mg; % of calories from fat 23; Calories 50.*

*Lynn's lowfat tip:* *Apple sauce can help to take the place of fat, making baked goods more moist when you decrease the fat. But do so cautiously, replacing only one-third of the fat with drained apple sauce.*

## Peach and Blackberry Tart

Fruit tarts are pretty, delightful pies with no top crust; they should have a tart taste. You can bake one large tart or you can bake individual tarts. If you wait until the tart cools, you'll find that it holds together in perfect slices. If you can't wait, the fruit will be freeform and juicy. Top with fat-free or lowfat whipped topping or ice cream.

You can make these fruit tarts with pears and apricots, peaches and blueberries, or apples and a small sprinkle of walnuts, too. The amount of fruit necessary may change slightly. Just be sure to cover the bottom of the pan with fruit.

*Tools:* *Large pie pan, or tart pan, or 4-x-8-inch or 5-x-9-inch glass casserole dish*

*Preparation time:* *3*

*Yield:* *8 servings*

*1 pound peaches (about 4 to 8), peeled and sliced into $^1/_4$-inch to $^1/_2$-inch slices*

*$^1/_2$ cup granulated sugar*

*$^1/_2$ teaspoon cinnamon*

*3 tablespoons fresh lemon juice*

*2 tablespoons water*

*$^1/_3$ cup minute tapioca granules*

*$1^1/_2$ cups fine crumbs from fat-free lemon-flavored cookies or gingersnaps (about 28 cookies)*

*1 pint blackberries, rinsed and drained*

**1** Preheat the oven to 350°.

**2** In a large bowl, place the peaches, sugar, cinnamon, lemon juice, water, and tapioca and toss gently. Lightly cover and let sit for 15 minutes, mixing once or twice to break up the tapioca granules that tend to cluster.

*(continued)*

**3** Meanwhile, lightly coat a tart or pie pan with no-stick vegetable oil spray. Press the cookie crumbs into the pan so that the crust is about $1/4$ inch thick. Go up the sides only $1/2$ to 1 inch, not to the rim. Lightly spray the crumbs with no-stick spray.

**4** Arrange the peach slices touching each other, side by side, facing the same way. Cover the bottom completely and neatly with slices. You can make circles or designs if you want. (See Figure 17-3.)

**5** Nestle the blackberries on the peach slices, spacing them somewhat evenly. Cover with foil, wrapping loosely. Set the tart or pie pan on a cookie sheet and bake in the center of the oven for 1 hour and 15 minutes. Remove from the oven and let cool for several hours to let the tapioca gel.

*Nutrition at a glance (per serving): Total fat 0 g; Saturated fat 0 g; Protein 2 g; Dietary fiber 3 g; Carbohydrate 51 g; Cholesterol 0 mg; Sodium 123 mg; % of calories from fat 1; Calories 216.*

*Lynn's fat-free fruit tip: Nearly all fruits, except for avocados, coconuts, and nuts (which are all technically fruit), are low in fat. In fact, fruits are the lowest in fat (along with most vegetables) of any food.*

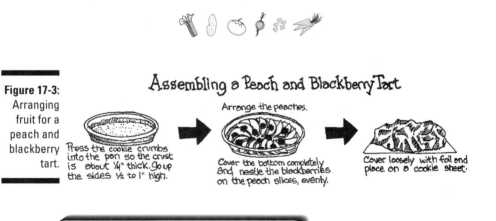

**Figure 17-3:** Arranging fruit for a peach and blackberry tart.

Assembling a Peach and Blackberry Tart

Press the cookie crumbs into the pan so the crust is about $1/4$" thick. Go up the sides $1/2$ to 1" high.

Arrange the peaches.

Cover the bottom completely and nestle the blackberries on the peach slices, evenly.

Cover loosely with foil and place on a cookie sheet.

## Pear Crisp with Yogurt Sauce

Crisps are unstructured, informal, and relaxed, comfortable on good china or on paper plates. Serve at room temperature with an iced beverage in summer, hot with coffee in winter. This easy-to-make, delicious, and homey baked pear recipe works just as well with apples or peaches. It is for breakfast, dessert, or a snack. Pears are high in fiber, too.

*Tools: 8-x-8-inch baking or pie dish, small nonstick saucepan*

*Preparation time: 2*

*Yield: 8 servings*

*(continued)*

**Filling:**

6 Bosc, Anjou, Comice, or Nelis pears, washed, cored, and sliced (peeled or unpeeled)

2 tablespoons fresh lemon juice

1 tablespoon fresh orange juice

1 teaspoon orange zest

$^1/_2$ cup light or dark brown sugar

$^1/_2$ teaspoon ground nutmeg

**Topping:**

$^1/_4$ teaspoon cinnamon

1 tablespoon canola oil or butter

2 tablespoons fresh orange or apple juice

$^1/_4$ cup oat bran

$^1/_4$ cup old-fashioned rolled oats

$^1/_2$ cup fat-free or lowfat granola

2 tablespoons flour

2 tablespoons brown sugar

*1* Preheat the oven to 350°. (Or you can use a microwave.)

*2* Lightly coat an 8-x-8-inch glass (if microwaving) or metal baking or pie dish with no-stick vegetable oil spray. Place the sliced pears in the dish. Sprinkle the lemon juice, orange juice, zest, brown sugar, and nutmeg on the pears.

*3* In a small nonstick saucepan, place the cinnamon, oil or butter, and apple or orange juice and cook, stirring, over medium heat for about 2 minutes until hot (or melted). Add the oat bran, rolled oats, granola, flour, brown sugar, and cook, stirring continuously, on medium heat for about 3 minutes.

*4* Spoon the mixture over the pears, lightly spray the mixture with no-stick spray, and microwave for 25 minutes or bake in the oven for 45 minutes. Check to be sure that the pears are tender but not mushy. Remove from the oven or microwave and let the crisp cool to room temperature. Lay on top of the following creamy yogurt sauce or serve with fat-free vanilla ice cream or frozen yogurt.

### Yogurt Sauce

1 cup plain nonfat yogurt, drained in a clean cloth over the sink for 15 minutes

3 to 4 tablespoons maple syrup or light corn syrup

$^1/_4$ teaspoon maple extract

$^1/_2$ teaspoon orange zest

$^1/_4$ cup confectioners' sugar

Whisk together the ingredients in a small bowl. Drizzle some sauce onto each plate. With a wide spatula, place the pear crisp on top.

***Nutrition at a glance (per serving):*** *Total fat 3 g; Saturated fat 0.5 g; Protein 4 g; Dietary fiber 4 g; Carbohydrate 56 g; Cholesterol 1 mg; Sodium 43 mg; % of calories from fat 10; Calories 251.*

*(continued)*

***Lynn's lowfat tip:*** *You use fat-free or lowfat granola in this recipe because it is usually dry and crisp, which makes for a crisp topping without fat. Some granolas contain chopped apricots, nuts, or dates, and all these flavors add to the dish.*

## Strawberry Cheesecake

Now cheesecake can be a most satisfying dessert and still be lowfat. This high, creamy, deli-style version is a perfect example of why cheesecake doesn't have to have copious amounts of fat to have that great look and taste. I've made over 50 of these, and they're beautiful. Tuck leaves and whole berries with the stems around the plate for an "oh my gosh, this is gorgeous" presentation. Make the recipe the day before to keep the cheesecake from cracking when you decorate it.

***Tools:*** *Small saucepan, 9-inch springform pan, heavy foil, food processor or electric mixer, large ovenproof pan, blender*

***Preparation time:*** *3*

***Yield:*** *16 servings*

***Cheesecake:***

*2 quarts water*

*1 tablespoon unflavored gelatin*

*3 tablespoons fresh orange juice*

*12 fat-free or lowfat graham crackers processed into crumbs, about 1¹/₄ cups*

*1 8-ounce package fat-free cream cheese, softened*

*1 8-ounce package reduced-fat cream cheese, softened*

*2 15-ounce containers fat-free or lowfat ricotta, or 2³/₄ cups*

*¹/₂ cup substitute eggs, or ¹/₄ cup substitute eggs plus 1 egg, beaten*

*3 egg whites*

*1 cup granulated sugar*

*¹/₃ cup flour*

*2 teaspoons orange liqueur or orange zest (optional)*

*2 teaspoons vanilla*

*1¹/₂ pints strawberries (20 to 40 berries), about 20 hulled and the rest left unhulled with pretty leaves*

***Sauce:***

*¹/₂ cup lemonade concentrate*

*2 tablespoons cassis (optional)*

*¹/₂ cup cranberry juice*

*1¹/₂ pints strawberries, hulled and chopped*

*2 tablespoons cornstarch*

*2 tablespoons sugar*

**1** Preheat the oven to 350°.

**2** Bring 2 quarts water to a boil.

*(continued)*

***3*** In a small saucepan, place the gelatin and orange juice and let sit for 1 minute. Cook and stir over low heat only until dissolved, about 1 minute.

***4*** Wrap the outside of a 9-inch springform pan completely with heavy foil, making sure that all the edges are sealed and that the foil has no holes. The foil should stick above the edge of the pan ¹/₄ inch and not wrap into the pan. (See Figure 17-4 for illustrated instructions.)

***5*** Coat the inside of the pan with no-stick vegetable oil spray. Place the graham cracker crumbs in the pan and flatten with the palm of your hand against the bottom and sides of the pan, going up at least 2 inches on the sides.

***6*** In a food processor or with a mixer, whip the cream cheese with the ricotta; then add the gelatin, eggs, egg whites, sugar, flour, orange liqueur or zest (if desired), and vanilla. Pulse to mix.

***7*** Pour the batter into the foil-prepared pan. Place the pan in a larger ovenproof pan (it can be rectangular). Carefully fill the larger pan with enough boiling water to reach halfway up the sides of the springform pan, making sure not to get any water in the cheesecake batter.

***8*** Bake for 1 hour and 10 to 15 minutes until firm but still slightly jiggly. Turn off the oven and let the cake cool in the oven for 1 hour.

***9*** Remove and cool to room temperature; then refrigerate, covered with foil or plastic wrap. Chill the cake in the refrigerator for at least 4 hours. When ready to serve, remove from the springform pan and place the cake on a platter (cheesecakes often crack) by sliding it off, both hands cupping the cake sides (having two people helps). You may want to chill the cake in the refrigerator overnight. Just before serving, decorate by placing strawberries lightly on the top of the baked cheese-cake, stem side down.

***10*** To make the sauce, place the lemonade concentrate, cassis (if desired), cranberry juice, strawberries (and any juice), cornstarch, and sugar in a cool, medium-sized saucepan. Whisk well. Turn on the heat to high, bring to a boil, reduce the heat to a simmer, and cook, stirring, until thickened and clear. Put in a blender or use a hand blender and puree. Strain the sauce. Cool and spoon the thickened sauce over the cheesecake and strawberries just before serving so that the sauce drips down the sides. Decorate the sides with the additional strawberries with leaves.

***Nutrition at a glance (per serving):*** *Total fat 3 g; Saturated fat 2 g; Protein 13 g; Dietary fiber 1 g; Carbohydrate 39 g; Cholesterol 13 mg; Sodium 354 mg; % of calories from fat 12; Calories 245.*

***Lynn's strawberry tips:*** *One medium strawberry contains about 7 calories and some fiber, and a whole dish gives you more vitamin C than you need in a day. Don't wash strawberries or other berries until you're ready to use them, or they'll get mushy.*

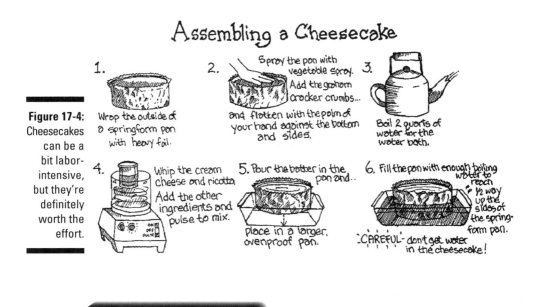

# Assembling a Cheesecake

1.

2. Spray the pan with vegetable spray. Add the graham cracker crumbs...

3. Boil 2 quarts of water for the water bath.

**Figure 17-4:** Cheesecakes can be a bit labor-intensive, but they're definitely worth the effort.

Wrap the outside of a springform pan with heavy foil.

and flatten with the palm of your hand against the bottom and sides.

4. Whip the cream cheese and ricotta. Add the other ingredients and pulse to mix.

5. Pour the batter in the pan and... place in a larger, ovenproof pan.

6. Fill the pan with enough boiling water to reach 1/2 way up the sides of the spring-form pan. -CAREFUL- don't get water in the cheesecake!

## Sweet Potato Pudding

Old-timey delicious and a favorite of kids, this luxurious sweet potato pudding can be served with fat-free or lowfat whipped topping, vanilla ice cream, or frozen yogurt. You can substitute squash or pumpkin for the sweet potatoes if you like. Usually baked in individual custard cups or ramekins, this pudding can also be baked in a large ovenproof soufflé dish. You can add a circle of miniature marshmallows to the top.

**Tools:** *Six individual ramekins or custard cups, large high-sided baking pan*

**Preparation time:** 2

**Yield:** *6 servings*

*2 quarts water*

*2 cups cooked or canned sweet potatoes, drained*

*1 cup liquid fat-free non-dairy creamer*

*$^1/_2$ cup fat-free sweetened condensed milk*

*$^1/_2$ cup substitute eggs*

*$^1/_4$ cup brown sugar, corn syrup, or maple syrup*

*1 tablespoon molasses (optional)*

*$1^1/_2$ teaspoons ground cinnamon*

*$^1/_2$ teaspoon ground ginger*

*$^1/_4$ teaspoon allspice (optional)*

*$^1/_4$ teaspoon ground nutmeg*

*$^1/_8$ teaspoon ground cloves*

*2 teaspoons grated lemon zest*

*$^1/_2$ teaspoon salt (optional)*

*(continued)*

*1* Preheat the oven to 400°. Bring 2 quarts water to a boil.

*2* Lightly coat six individual ramekins or custard cups with no-stick vegetable oil spray.

*3* In a large bowl, combine the sweet potatoes, creamer, milk, eggs, brown sugar, molasses (if desired), cinnamon, ginger, allspice (if desired), nutmeg, cloves, zest, and salt (if desired) and mix well.

*4* Pour into the cups and place the cups in a large, high-sided baking pan. Fill the pan halfway with boiling water, making sure that no water gets into the filled pudding cups.

*5* Carefully place the pan with the water and filled cups in the oven and bake for 10 minutes at 400°. Lower the heat to 350° and bake for 30 minutes more or until a knife inserted in the center comes out clean, indicating that the center is cooked.

*Nutrition at a glance (per serving): Total fat 0 g; Saturated fat 0 g; Protein 5 g; Dietary fiber 2 g; Carbohydrate 58 g; Cholesterol 3 mg; Sodium 71 mg; % of calories from fat 1; Calories 256.*

*Lynn's lowfat tips: Sweet potatoes, as well as winter squashes, such as pumpkin, hubbard, Canada, Boston marrow, butternut, buttercup, and acorn, are full of vitamin A and fiber and have almost no fat. The seeds of the squash are edible and sweet when baked in the squash or toasted. You can eat them as snacks, sprinkled on salads, on the cooked squash as a garnish, or even sprinkle a few on the pudding.*

## Tropical Fruit Tapioca Pudding with Coconut

In this recipe, you lightly poach and thicken tropical fruits and pour them over creamy tapioca. In a pinch, you can use chopped dried apricots or prunes instead. Serve chilled and top with fat-free or lowfat whipped cream or whipped topping. For a special treat, slice a fresh fig, peach, or raspberries and place them around the edge of each plate.

*Tools: Two large saucepans*

*Preparation time: 2*

*Yield: 6 servings*

*(continued)*

### Pudding

*¹/₃ cup granulated sugar*

*3 tablespoons minute tapioca granules*

*2³/₄ cups liquid fat-free non-dairy creamer, skim milk, or fat-free evaporated skimmed milk*

*¹/₄ cup substitute eggs or 1 egg, slightly beaten*

*1 teaspoon vanilla*

In a large saucepan, combine the sugar, tapioca, creamer or milk, and egg and let sit for 5 minutes. Turn the heat to medium and cook, stirring, until the mixture comes to a boil. Remove from the heat, stir in the vanilla, and let sit for 20 minutes, covered (chill to thicken more).

### Tropical Fruit Topping

*¹/₂ cup pineapple syrup or juice from canned pineapple*

*3 tablespoons fresh lemon juice*

*1 teaspoon coconut extract*

*1¹/₂ tablespoons cornstarch*

*³/₄ cup canned pineapple chunks, drained*

*³/₄ cup fresh, bottled, or canned mango, drained and diced*

*¹/₂ cup fresh, bottled, or canned papaya, drained and diced*

*2 bananas, sliced*

*2 tablespoons coconut, toasted in a 350° oven on foil for 2¹/₂ minutes*

**1** In a large, cool saucepan, place the pineapple syrup, lemon juice, coconut extract, and cornstarch and whisk until blended. Add the pineapple, mango, papaya, and banana.

**2** Turn on the heat to medium and, with a soft spatula, gently stir until the fruit and syrup are boiling. Keep stirring until thick, about 1 minute. Pour this mixture on the tapioca and sprinkle the toasted coconut over the top. Chill if desired.

*Nutrition at a glance (per serving):* *Total fat 1.5 g; Saturated fat 1 g; Protein 2 g; Dietary fiber 2 g; Carbohydrate 85 g; Cholesterol 0 mg; Sodium 19 mg; % of calories from fat 3; Calories 358.*

*Lynn's tropical fruit tip:* *If you're trying to thicken or jell anything made with pineapple chunks, such as a sauce or sweet and sour stir-fry, or if you're trying to chill and jell pineapple in a molded gelatin salad or dessert, use only canned pineapple — never fresh. Fresh pineapple contains an enzyme that keeps any food it's in from thickening or jelling, whereas canned pineapple doesn't.*

# Chapter 18

# Beverages

*P*aying attention to the fat in beverages, especially the daily cream in your coffee or tea, can be very beneficial to a lowfat eating plan. This chapter shows clearly how you can accumulate both fat and saturated fat in just small amounts of cream or milk, and how you can make creamy, thick, typically fat-filled beverages (such as milkshakes and eggnog) nearly fat-free but still rich and delicious. I include eight recipes, one the newest craze, a drink called *chai*.

# Don't Be Fat-Fooled by Beverages

Occasionally, you want a milkshake with a fast-food lunch, a latté to soothe you, or an Irish whiskey or cream liqueur to end a festive meal. And plain old coffee with a smidgeon of cream is one of the most popular beverages around. Because beverages are so important in modern culture, casting an eye on their ever-increasing fat content is smart. As if trying to prepare a lowfat meal isn't already enough of a challenge, beverages — especially the ones people drink routinely, such as coffee with cream, latté, cappuccino, milkshakes, cocoa, and chocolate milk — have become a deceptively easy place for hidden fat and calories to reside. But modifying a beverage to make it more healthful without losing taste or appeal is easy.

Don't be lulled into thinking that a little fat in your beverage now and then isn't important. When viewed cumulatively, the total amount of cream you may use daily with just a few cups of coffee totals almost a whole cup. One cup of heavy cream contains 88 grams of fat and 821 calories.

Even people who are dieting and supplementing their diets with liquid protein mixes may not realize that these beverages often contain a great deal of calories and some fat. In fact, I advise people who are trying to gain weight to drink liquid protein mixes or Carnation Instant Breakfast as snacks or with their meals. Doing so is an easy way to increase caloric intake by several hundred calories.

---

## A short history of drinking

When the earth was young, streams, rivers, creeks, brooks, tributaries, and springs of clear, clean water, as well as rains and melting snow, supplied all human thirst needs. Each day in this Paleolithic period, or "golden age" of nutrition, humans ate a varied diet of a little wild game, which, because the animals had to run from predators, was naturally very lean. They supplemented this with vegetables, roots, leaves, fruits, nuts, berries, bugs, and some fish and shellfish. But humankind's main beverage was water. People consumed no dairy products. Our hunter-gatherer forebears had no evidence of heart disease.

Beverages soon began to evolve from water to other liquids. In 8500 B.C., goat's milk became a food source in the Near East. Five thousand years later, in the same region, farmers started raising cattle for milk. The Chinese were drinking wine made from millet, fruits, and berries, and in Ireland, people were beginning to make hard alcohol by fermenting grains.

The Sumerians and Greeks brewed 50 different kinds of beer, although they did not actually invent wine. Mongolian tribes drank mare's milk, and by the second century A.D., and for several centuries thereafter, watered wine was the usual beverage for Europeans.

One entrepreneurial Japanese family began to nationally distribute sake, a rice wine, by the 1600s, although it had already been drunk in villages throughout Japan for at least 1,000 years. By the mid-1800s, beverages were so important in France that a typical family spent a third or more of its income on drink (presumably wine and beer).

You can see that beverage choices throughout the ages have been very personal and important. Choices are just as important today. Now even water comes bottled plain, bottled sparkling, or bottled and flavored both plain and sparkling or carbonated. We enjoy exotic drinks with or without liquor, ranging from sodas, teas, nectars, milks, and juices made not only from common fruits but also from vegetables, such as celery and carrots. Unlikely beverage choices are even made from clams (for Clamato juice), beef bouillon (the base for bull shots), goat's milk, yogurt, malt powder (for malted milks), and spices like ginger (for ginger ale). Hundreds of kinds of leaves, including mint and sassafras, are made into teas.

# Identifying Beverages That Are Usually Low or High in Fat, Saturated Fat, and Cholesterol

As I discussed earlier in this chapter, snappy-sounding beverages can contain hidden amounts of fat, which add up quickly if you consume many high-fat drinks. This section can help you make smart beverage choices — or really appreciate those times when you do indulge!

By themselves, the following common beverages contain no fat. Many *do* contain calories, however. Only those that are marked with an asterisk (*) do not contain calories.

- ✔ Beer
- ✔ Bloody Mary, with or without alcohol
- ✔ Carbonated water*
- ✔ Champagne
- ✔ Chocolate milk (fat-free)
- ✔ Clam juice
- ✔ Clear liqueurs
- ✔ Clear mixed alcoholic drinks
- ✔ Coffee (black)*
- ✔ Club soda*
- ✔ Cream sherry
- ✔ Daiquiri
- ✔ Diet drinks*
- ✔ Fruit juice and punch
- ✔ Ginger ale
- ✔ Lemonade
- ✔ Sangria
- ✔ Screwdriver
- ✔ Seltzer water*
- ✔ Soft drinks
- ✔ Tea (plain)

- Vegetable juice
- Water*
- Wine, wine coolers, and wine spritzers

When made with the usual recipe of whole milk, half-and-half, cream, or regular ice cream, these beverages are high in fat and contain cholesterol and saturated fat. A few, such as eggnog, hot buttered rum, coffee with cream, and Irish whiskey made with whipped cream, contain *a great deal* of fat and calories. Beware!

- Brandy Alexander or brandy cream
- Café au lait
- Cappuccino
- Chocolate milk
- Coffee with cream, regular powdered creamer, or half-and-half
- Egg cream soda
- Eggnog
- Frosted malt
- Hot buttered rum
- Hot cocoa
- Ice cream punch or soda
- Iced coffee (with cream or milk)
- Irish coffee
- Latté
- Malted milk
- Milk punch
- Milkshake
- Protein mixes or liquid supplements
- White Russian
- Yogurt shake

Knowing the ingredients in a beverage can help you decide whether it contains an unacceptable amount of fat. Making wise choices about the beverages you drink can help you avoid thousands of extra calories over the course of a year.

## Kids and milk

Beverages don't *have* to contain fat; ideally, they shouldn't. But people start drinking fatty mother's milk when they're young. Then they graduate to whole milk. Not surprisingly, a study in late 1996 said that nearly one-fourth of American children, slightly more girls than boys, between the ages of six and eight, are obese, and most of these youngsters probably drink whole milk. Experts do say that children should drink whole milk until age two, but not after that. Skim milk is better for most of them. (In some cases, — for example, a child who's not gaining weight — 2 percent milk may be necessary for the additional calories.)

# Cheap, Easy, and Lowfat Coffee Tricks

Are you tired of gray coffee, cappuccino, or latté? The gray color is the result of adding skim milk. But you can find many other ways to add "cream" to your daily coffee, cappuccino (see Figure 18-1), or latté without using a high-fat cream or milk. You can still get the right color, aroma, and taste.

Are you a little suspicious of using a product that isn't milk or cream? For the last 30 years, many restaurants haven't been using real milk or cream for coffee, anyway, except in upscale establishments. If your creamer comes in a little white plastic thimble or it's the dry, powdered type, it isn't cream or even a milk product. Most people are accustomed to the slightly different taste of this creamy substance in coffee or tea. And many non-dairy products are available that taste great. Non-dairy creamers come both lowfat and fat-free, liquid and powdered, and are quickly growing in popularity. They do differ in calorie content. Usually 2 tablespoons contain 20 calories.

**Figure 18-1:**
You can add color, aroma, and flavor to your cappuccino without adding fat.

Lowfat beverage aficionados tell me that they use the following products in their coffee and tea (as do I). I also include comments about taste and texture.

- **Fat-free powdered or nonfat dry milk granules:** These granules are 100 percent milk, and some come in packets. Many brands are available. Dry milk powder has only a slightly sweet taste and is cheaper than fat-free powdered creamers. Dry milk powder tastes just as good and isn't as sweet as dry creamers.

- **Powdered fat-free or lowfat non-dairy creamer:** This is the old office mixture, but dry creamers now come fat-free and lowfat; the old stuff was filled with saturated fat. Many brands are available, although most still contain high amounts of coconut oil or palm oil, oils that are high in saturated fat (the worst fat). Most, such as Carnation, are quite sweet-tasting yet have a pleasant flavor.

- **Fat-free or lowfat ice cream or frozen yogurt in vanilla, chocolate, or coffee flavors:** Ice cream and frozen yogurt cool coffee slightly, are sweet, and taste good. Because they don't taste like yogurt, the frozen yogurts are pretty good, too.

- **Fat-free or lowfat frozen, refrigerated, canister, or dry packaged whipped topping:** These products give coffee a slightly different sweet taste, but it isn't bad, and the whipped topping looks festive. It melts a little weirdly. Don't whip the dry stuff; just use a teaspoon in each cup and let it dissolve.

- **Evaporated skimmed milk:** This product is canned and has a slight caramel flavor — pretty good in coffee.

- **Sweetened condensed fat-free milk:** It's nice and thick and already sweetened. Add a drop of vanilla if you like.

- **Liquid fat-free or lowfat non-dairy creamer, plain or flavored:** You can find this in the refrigerated dairy case. It comes in numerous flavors, most of them awful. Plain tastes the best and is the favorite creamer because it's naturally fairly thick. Farm Rich and Carnation brands are good. People who are allergic to milk favor non-dairy creamer.

- **Soy milk:** It's made from soybeans. Unlike non-dairy creamers, it has some protein. Soy milks come in different levels of fat, so look on the label for the brand with the lowest fat content. People who are allergic to cow's milk favor soy milk, along with non-dairy creamers.

The following tricks make coffee taste richer but still keep it lowfat or fat-free:

- ✔ **Make your instant regular or decaf coffee (or tea) by boiling a cup of skim milk rather than water.** Both tea and instant coffee steep or dissolve in skim milk just fine, and all milk gives a nice, mellow taste. Every skim milk brand tastes slightly different, so if you don't like one, try another.

- ✔ **Brew coffee with skim milk instead of water.** Using milk may screw up your coffeemaker, but all coffeemakers go bad in a year, anyway. I recommended this trick to my TV viewers, and only one letter (out of hundreds) came back saying that a coffeemaker was harmed. It didn't damage mine; in fact, the coffeemaker in which I used only water wore out quicker. Just use milk at your own risk. The coffee tastes great — but the coffeemaker is a little difficult to clean.

# Lowfat but Not Old Hat: Great but Easy Beverage Recipes

People love creamy drinks: cream or ice cream in coffee, cappuccino, café au lait, latté, hot cocoa, milkshakes, and after-dinner drinks like White Russians or Irish whiskey. Fortunately, today you can make each of these creamy concoctions quite deliciously with lowfat or fat-free milk, ice cream, frozen yogurt, and liquid non-dairy creamer. Because these substitutions create very little change in taste or texture, beverages are a good place to continue your lowfat undertaking.

## Chai

A dark combination of silky tea and milk, chai is the trendiest beverage hitting the Pacific Northwest coffee bars. Seasoned with exotic spices and herbs, it is served hot and steamy. Notice that this recipe calls for $^1/_8$ teaspoon of several ingredients. If you don't have a $^1/_8$ teaspoon measuring spoon, just fill your $^1/_4$ measuring spoon halfway.

**Tools:** *Saucepan, strainer, whisk*

**Preparation time:** *2*

**Yield:** *1 serving*

*(continued)*

2 black tea bags, or 2 tablespoons black tea

$^1/_4$ teaspoon cinnamon

$^1/_4$ teaspoon fennel seeds

$^1/_8$ teaspoon nutmeg

$^1/_8$ teaspoon ground cloves

$^1/_8$ teaspoon ground ginger

$^1/_8$ teaspoon ground cardamom

2 to $2^1/_2$ tablespoons honey

1 cup liquid fat-free or lowfat non-dairy creamer, skim milk, or 1 percent milk, or a mixture totaling 1 cup

**1** Boil 1 cup water in a saucepan. As soon as it boils, turn off the heat and add the tea bags or loose tea (in a closed tea strainer), cinnamon, fennel seeds, nutmeg, cloves, ginger, cardamom, and honey. Let the mixture steep for 10 to 15 minutes.

**2** Remove the tea bags or strainer, pour the liquid into a glass, and chill until cold, or for several hours. Strain the mixture, pour it back into a saucepan, add the creamer or milk, and heat until almost boiling, whisking to make it frothy.

***Nutrition at a glance (per serving):*** *Total fat 0.5 g; Saturated fat 0 g; Protein 0 g; Dietary fiber 0 g; Carbohydrate 69 g; Cholesterol 0 mg; Sodium 10 mg; % of calories from fat 1; Calories 299.*

***Lynn's chai notes:*** *In Hindi, chai means tea. A similar drink to the recipe given, again called chai, is consumed in India, Nepal, and surrounding areas. Americanized blends of chai can contain vanilla and sugar instead of honey. Live Chai, a company in Boulder, Colorado, makes a ready-to-drink chai beverage.*

### Chocolate Milkshake or Malted Milkshake

Once a staple in every 1940s and '50s malt shop, drugstore, and grocery store, chocolate malts are making a comeback. Purchase malt powder in a grocery or health-food store. For a plain milkshake, leave out the malt powder. If you like more chocolate flavor, add a tablespoon of chocolate syrup. Many brands, such as Dove, aren't lowfat but, at 4 grams for 2 tablespoons, the amount isn't astronomical. Hershey's Topping makes a thick fat-free syrup.

***Tools:*** *Blender or food processor*

***Preparation time:*** *1*

***Yield:*** *4 servings*

*(continued)*

*1 cup fat-free or lowfat vanilla ice cream*

*3 cups fat-free or lowfat chocolate ice cream*

*1 teaspoon vanilla*

*1 cup liquid fat-free non-dairy creamer*

*$1/4$ cup malted milk powder*

*4 ice cubes*

In a blender or food processor, place the two ice creams, vanilla, creamer, malted milk powder, and ice cubes. Puree at low speed just until smooth. (If you puree too long, it becomes thin.)

**Nutrition at a glance (per serving):** *Total fat 0.5 g; Saturated fat 0 g; Protein 7 g; Dietary fiber 1 g; Carbohydrate 68 g; Cholesterol 9 mg; Sodium 49 mg; % of calories from fat 1; Calories 307.*

**Lynn's flavor tips:** *For a strawberry shake, puree fat-free or lowfat vanilla or a combination of vanilla and strawberry ice cream, sugar, and lots of fresh strawberries in a blender. For a raspberry shake, puree the raspberries first; then strain (discard the seeds) and puree the berries with fat-free or lowfat vanilla ice cream and sugar. You can make a maple shake by pureeing fat-free or lowfat vanilla or praline ice cream, maple extract, and maple syrup.*

## Cocoa

All winter, I make hot, chocolaty, rich-tasting cocoa. When I have marshmallows handy, I float a big, melting one on top, which is pretty indulgent. You can also squirt the top with lowfat or fat-free whipped cream topping and sprinkle on cinnamon or a few chocolate jimmies. Check the sweetness of the finished drink, because some sweetened cocoa needs more sugar than others, and some cocoa isn't sweetened at all.

**Tools:** *Large nonstick saucepan*

**Preparation time:** *1*

**Yield:** *4 servings*

*2 cups skim milk*

*2 cups liquid fat-free or lowfat non-dairy creamer*

*6 tablespoons sweetened cocoa powder (chocolate milk mix)*

*$1/2$ teaspoon vanilla*

*Very small pinch of salt*

*$1/4$ cup sugar*

*4 marshmallows (optional)*

*(continued)*

In a large nonstick saucepan over low heat, combine the milk, creamer, cocoa, and vanilla, whisking until smooth. Heat until hot but not boiling. Stir in the sugar and place the marshmallows (if desired) on top to melt. Pour into four mugs and serve.

***Nutrition at a glance (per serving):*** *Total fat 1 g; Saturated fat 0.5 g; Protein 6 g; Dietary fiber 0 g; Carbohydrate 81 g; Cholesterol 3 mg; Sodium 155 mg; % of calories from fat 2; Calories 358.*

***Lynn's marshmallow tips:*** *Marshmallows have no fat. For a fancy presentation, lightly spray a foil sheet with no-stick vegetable oil spray, place large marshmallows on the sheet, and toast them in an open oven for 30 to 40 seconds several inches from the burner, making sure that they don't completely melt (you'll have to keep an eye on them). Lift them off the sheet with a lightly sprayed spatula and place them on the cocoa (or on sweet potatoes).*

## Eggnog

For a month, from Thanksgiving to New Year's, parties wouldn't be as festive if cupfuls of thick and rich eggnog weren't served. Place the nog-filled bowl on a plate decorated with garlands of flat pine branches, fresh strawberries, or cranberries and tiny miniature red and silver balls, and dust the frothy top with fragrant nutmeg. *This* recipe has no fat or cholesterol.

**Tools:** *Food processor or blender*

**Preparation time:** *1*

**Yield:** *About 24 servings*

*2 quarts fat-free or lowfat (3 percent or less) vanilla ice cream*

*2 cups very cold liquid fat-free non-dairy creamer*

*2 cups skim milk*

*¹/₄ cup finely granulated sugar*

*¹/₄ teaspoon freshly ground nutmeg*

*1 teaspoon vanilla*

*Pinch of salt*

*1 cup substitute eggs*

*¹/₂ cup brandy (optional)*

*¹/₂ cup cognac (optional)*

*¹/₂ cup rum (optional)*

*Or 1¹/₂ cups liquid fat-free non-dairy creamer in the place of alcohols*

*1 pint fat-free or lowfat canister-style whipped cream topping (optional)*

*1 teaspoon freshly ground nutmeg*

**1** In a food processor or blender, in batches if necessary, combine the ice cream, creamer, milk, sugar, nutmeg, vanilla, salt, eggs, and liquors (if desired).

*(continued)*

**2** Pour the mixture into a large punch bowl and top with whipped cream (if desired), blending lightly with a spoon. Sprinkle with additional nutmeg.

**Nutrition at a glance (per serving):** *Total fat 0 g; Saturated fat 0 g; Protein 4 g; Dietary fiber 0 g; Carbohydrate 25 g; Cholesterol 3 mg; Sodium 61 mg; % of calories from fat 1; Calories 121.*

**Lynn's eggnog extras:** *This recipe is very similar to the one used in the White House, except that the eggs aren't raw, and the "cream" isn't filled with fat. You can reduce or increase the recipe's yield easily.*

## Hot or Iced Irish Coffee

Mocha-colored, creamy, and either icy cold or piping hot, Irish coffee has to be served in a glass, and it has to have the perfect balance of cream and strong coffee. This recipe does. For extra richness, add an extra dollop of fat-free ice cream and a sprinkle of cinnamon. Of course, you can enjoy hot or iced coffee without the whiskey if you prefer.

**Preparation time:** *1*

**Yield:** *4 servings*

*Ice to fill glasses (if serving iced)*

*4 cups strongly brewed coffee, or 5 tablespoons instant coffee dissolved in 4 cups boiling skim milk*

*¹/₄ cup finely granulated sugar*

*1 cup liquid fat-free non-dairy creamer*

*¹/₂ cup Irish whiskey*

*1 cup fat-free or lowfat whipped topping*

If serving iced, fill four glasses with ice and fill each glass half-full with coffee. Immediately add the sugar and stir to dissolve. Add to each glass ¹/₄ cup creamer and 2 tablespoons whiskey, adding more ice if necessary. Add the whipped topping.

If serving hot, pour the boiling or hot coffee three-fourths full into each glass. Add the sugar and stir to dissolve. Add 3 tablespoons creamer (instead of ¹/₄ cup for the iced version), 2 tablespoons whiskey, and the whipped topping.

**Nutrition at a glance (per serving):** *Total fat 0 g; Saturated fat 0 g; Protein 0 g; Dietary fiber 0 g; Carbohydrate 41 g; Cholesterol 0 mg; Sodium 25 mg; % of calories from fat 0; Calories 299.*

**Lynn's sugar tips:** *Finely granulated sugar dissolves more easily in very cold beverages. Finely granulating any sugar by using your food processor is easy (and cheaper); however, you can buy it already finely granulated in any market.*

## Pineapple Yogurt Shake

Pineapple lovers adore this shake. Decorate with a pineapple wedge. You may want to blend it in batches, half the ingredients at a time.

**Tools:** *Blender or food processor*

**Preparation time:** *1*

**Yield:** *4 servings*

1 16-ounce can crushed pineapple

2 ripe bananas, cut in half (optional)

1 cup fat-free or lowfat frozen vanilla yogurt or ice cream

4 ounces (or ¹/₂ cup) fat-free or lowfat vanilla or lemon yogurt

2 teaspoons coconut extract

In a blender or food processor, at low speed, combine the pineapple, bananas (if desired), frozen yogurt, yogurt, and coconut extract.

**Nutrition at a glance (per serving):** *Total fat 0 g; Saturated fat 0 g; Protein 4 g; Dietary fiber 1 g; Carbohydrate 31 g; Cholesterol 1 mg; Sodium 51 mg; % of calories from fat 1; Calories 142.*

**Lynn's fruit shake tip:** *For a less creamy consistency, substitute fresh orange juice for the regular yogurt.*

## Root Beer Float

Don't know what a float is? Teenagers from the 1920s to the 1950s drank them at soda shops and drugstores. The name *soda jerk* came from the guy who "jerked" the soda handles. Ice cream sodas and root beer floats are simple and cold, and kids love them. This retro drink is still refreshing on a hot summer night. Use a frosted mug for extra authenticity.

**Preparation time:** *1*

**Yield:** *1 serving*

1 large scoop vanilla fat-free or lowfat ice cream

2 cups cold root beer

*(continued)*

In a very tall glass, place one scoop of ice cream. Pour the root beer over it. Insert a straw and serve immediately.

***Nutrition at a glance (per serving):*** *Total fat 0 g; Saturated fat 0 g; Protein 5 g; Dietary fiber 0 g; Carbohydrate 84 g; Cholesterol 6 mg; Sodium 139 mg; % of calories from fat 0; Calories 352.*

***Lynn's retro drink tips:*** *You can make floats with lemon or cherry sorbet and a citrus soda like Fresca or a cola like Coke or Pepsi. You make a traditional ice cream soda with vanilla ice cream and ginger ale. Just make sure that the ice cream is lowfat or fat-free.*

## Strawberry Banana Shake

So thick and icy-pink, a strawberry shake is a great beverage. One friend tells me that this shake helps her beat the diet blues. She keeps frozen skim milk cubes to make the shake thicker, and occasionally she omits the bananas or doubles the strawberries. You may want to blend the ingredients in batches, half at a time.

***Tools:*** *Blender or food processor*

***Preparation time:*** *1*

***Yield:*** *4 servings*

*1 10-ounce package frozen strawberries, slightly thawed*

*2 ripe bananas, cut in half*

*2 cups fat-free vanilla ice cream*

*2 tablespoons honey*

*¹/₂ cup very cold skim milk*

In a blender or food processor, at low speed, combine the strawberries, bananas, ice cream, honey, and milk. Blend until smooth, about 20 seconds.

***Nutrition at a glance (per serving):*** *Total fat 0.5 g; Saturated fat 0 g; Protein 5 g; Dietary fiber 2 g; Carbohydrate 51 g; Cholesterol 5 mg; Sodium 68 mg; % of calories from fat 2; Calories 220.*

***Lynn's cherry shake tip:*** *To make a cherry shake, puree 20 ounces of frozen cherries (in place of the strawberries) and omit the bananas.*

# Part IV
## The Part of Tens

The 5th Wave · By Rich Tennant

"Well yeah, I think lowfat yogurt is a good substitute for cream, just not in a White Russian."

## In this part . . .

This is the fun part. I offer helpful tips and bits of valuable information in lists of ten. For example, you can find ten myths about fat and the ten most important steps in lowering your fat intake. I also tell you about some great sources of more information on lowfat cooking and eating.

# Chapter 19

# The Ten Most Important Steps in Lowering Your Fat Intake

. . . . . . . . . . . . . . . . . . . . . . . . . . . . . . . . . . . . . . . . . . . .

## In This Chapter

Ten tricks that make eating lowfat easy and effective

. . . . . . . . . . . . . . . . . . . . . . . . . . . . . . . . . . . . . . . . . . . .

Changing your diet is an adaptive process, especially with an addictive, tasty substance like fat. Plus, feel-good foods that are on nearly every menu — beef roasts, pork chops, fried chicken, bacon, cheese, butter, sour cream, whipped cream, candy, cookies, and cakes — are usually fat-filled. So it's hard.

This chapter aims to make eating lowfat a little easier by telling you ten quick things you can do *right now,* and with little effort, to reduce the amount of fat you consume. Remember, it's all the little things you do that count. Train yourself to think lowfat when you eat, shop, and order in restaurants.

## Go fat-free in dairy

Probably the single most important step you can take to reduce the amount of fat you consume is to switch to fat-free (skim) milk, cheese, sour cream, yogurt, ice cream or frozen yogurt, and butter- or margarine-type spreads. The invisible fat you eat in full-fat dairy foods becomes the visible fat you wear on your hips, belly, cheeks, and everywhere else (and the invisible fat that accumulates around your heart and in your arteries).

Reduced-fat dairy products are a start, but to counterbalance the fat in much of the food you eat over which you have no control, such as what you eat in restaurants or when traveling, fat-free should be your goal.

## Discover liquid fat-free non-dairy creamers

Flavored and unflavored liquid fat-free non-dairy creamers are ideal for putting in coffee, tea, cocoa, and desserts. The plain liquid non-dairy type (it's made from soybeans) is a terrific substitute everywhere you use cream, such as in cream soups, casseroles, and milkshakes and on cereals. Unlike high-fat cream, this thick, white liquid doesn't curdle when boiled or baked. You can find it near the milk in quart-sized cartons in the refrigerator case.

## Cut the number of times you eat meat, fish, poultry, and cheese each week

Try to stick to a total of five weekly servings of lean meat or skinned poultry trimmed of all visible fat, and eat high-fat cheese only twice a week. This means eating lots of different versions of pasta marinara or pasta primavera (without cream), rice with mushrooms, wild rice or Spanish rice, couscous or other grains with vegetables, and wonderful, large salads instead.

## Expand the variety of foods you eat

For every high-fat food you give up, add ten new lower-fat treats. Going lowfat isn't a deprivation diet — I'm not saying that you can never eat this or that again. It's an invitation to discover, cook, and taste the hundreds of different varieties of vegetables, fruits, and grains, to try those red lobster mushrooms or that interesting cereal. Lowfat doesn't have to mean no fat (except in a very few items where it makes sense, such as dairy products). Eating different and wonderful new foods is great fun. And it's good for you.

## Pick off, cut off, or spoon off all visible fat

Pick all the fat off bacon, even the bacon in your restaurant BLT (at home I cut it off with scissors). Remove some of the meat (all meat has fat) in a thick meat sandwich. Cut the fat off the meat you leave in the sandwich, yell at the waiter who said that the meat was lean to begin with, and then remove some or all of the cheese. Squish out some of the mayo and ask for extra lettuce, onions, sprouts, and tomatoes.

With chicken, remove the skin, pick off the fat, and doggie-bag the second piece. Get sauces and salad dressings on the side and dip. Slide the whipped cream off the Jell-O for dessert. Give away the ice cream on the pie and eat only the filling. Remove fat like you're a fat detective on a mission. Be a fat-ferreting fanatic. It's your body!

## Buy and cook with very little fat

When you purchase oil, think about what you need it for. Can you buy a smaller amount? Instead of frying in fat, sauté vegetables in no-stick vegetable oil spray, or use water, vegetable juice, diet salad dressing, low-sodium soy sauce, or Worcestershire sauce.

If you buy fat, you'll use fat, and if you use fat, you'll wear fat.

## Shop when hungry, eat when famished, and stop eating when full

Lowfat and fat-free foods look good when you're hungry, so shop for them then. Eat only when you're really hungry (this is when you are supposed to eat) and enjoy it to the max. The moment you feel full, leave the table and take the food to the sink, or immediately summon a waiter to remove your plate if you're at a restaurant. If you don't, you'll get a second wind and continue to nibble when it is no longer satisfying. You'll eat everything on your plate and on everyone else's plate.

Or eat a healthy snack before going out for a big meal.

## Eat smaller portions, especially when eating out

Keep portion sizes for meat, fish, and poultry to 3 ounces a serving (the size of a deck of cards or four stacked dice), and for cheese, to just a few ounces (the size of a ping pong ball). Reducing portion sizes of high-fat and medium-fat foods keeps your fat intake down and your food bill cheaper. A dinner out can be lunch the next day, too.

## Decide what you want to eat before you even look at the menu

Before you go into a restaurant, or at least when you pass through the portal, decide, given the type of establishment, exactly what you want to eat. Then stick to your plan. Don't let hunger, impulse decisions, menu choices, the waiter's description of the specials, or your friends' orders influence your food choice.

In a steak house, skip the steak and instead get a baked potato, vegetables such as asparagus, green beans, or mushrooms, a terrific salad with dressing on the side (or just vinegar and a few drops of oil) or even cole slaw, and fruit for dessert. You'll be plenty full, your body will be nourished, and you won't walk out stuffed full of fat, discouraged, and energy-robbed. If you really have to have meat, order well-done round steak or a small filet, cut it in half, and take the rest home.

## If you fall off the lowfat wagon, just climb back on

This is the most important advice of all. You will fail — we all do. In fact, if you don't fail, you aren't trying hard enough. Push it, eating lowfat as often as possible. When you fail, you get to know how quickly and easily you can adapt to a lower-fat eating plan (everyone is different).

When you fall off and eat three jumbo bags of potato chips and every eclair in the box, don't give up. The only people who win this fat-lowering battle are those who can put each spree behind them and resolve to begin again. At the very next meal, you get a new chance to do it the way you want. Don't worry about results — just do what you can do. Losing weight, lowering your cholesterol, and increasing your energy level take time, and you'll hit a plateau every two or three weeks.

*Don't* say, "I'm a failure, so I may as well eat everything in sight. Because lowfat is too hard and too much trouble, I'll just wallow in this mindset forever." Don't give up on yourself and your health.

You pushed it; you learned your limit. If you start eating lowfat again as soon as possible, pretty soon the binges become fewer, shorter, and smaller, and you're eating the way you want to.

# Chapter 20
# Ten Myths about Fat

*In This Chapter*

Ten common myths about fat, debunked

*W*ith so much media attention being paid to diet and fat, you may find it difficult to sort fact from fiction. The goal of this chapter is to dispel ten of the most common myths about food and fat.

## Fast-food fish sandwiches have little fat

They have plenty. Opt for a grilled chicken breast sandwich, a plain baked potato, or a garden salad instead.

## Fish has less fat than beef

Sometimes. And some fish has *more* fat than beef. It depends on the type of fish and how it's prepared (in fast-food restaurants, fish is fattier than hamburger) and the type of beef and how it's prepared.

## Four glasses a day of 2 percent milk is lowfat and okay

It isn't. Drinking four glasses of 2 percent milk is like eating six slices of bacon, says the Center for Science in the Public Interest. Switch to skim or $1/2$ percent milk instead.

## Oils marked "Lite" contain less fat than regular oils

All oils contain the same amount of fat. *Lite,* which is not a government-regulated term, in this case refers to color. In some cases, *lite* can mean less sodium, but oil has no sodium.

## In terms of heart and artery health, butter is better than margarine

It isn't. Butter and margarine have the same total fat content, but butter contains four times as much saturated fat as margarine. Diet margarine has even less saturated fat than regular margarine, so it's an even better choice for a lowfat eating plan.

## Eating six eggs a day lowers your cholesterol and helps you lose weight

It doesn't. Eating six eggs a day can raise your cholesterol — you're consuming over 1,200 milligrams, after all. Some high-protein diets have been found to lower weight, but high-animal-protein diets are no longer considered healthful.

## Eggs are lowfat

They aren't. An egg contains about 5 grams of fat and 213 to 240 milligrams of cholesterol. Substitute eggs, however, are another story; they're fat-free and cholesterol-free and taste very similar to fresh eggs.

## Heredity has everything to do with fat metabolism, weight gain, heart disease, and overall health

Heredity may have something to do with it, say most experts, but far more important are your choices in diet and exercise. If you don't eat too many calories, you won't gain weight. If your body tends not to remove excess dietary saturated fat well and that fat becomes cholesterol plaque in your arteries, less dietary saturated fat is the primary treatment to lower blood cholesterol, and less total fat is the way to reduce your weight.

## You have to be careful with all these fat-free and lowfat foods to get enough fat in your diet

Probably not in the United States, unless you're anorexic. All foods contain fat, even radishes. Most people consume far more fat than they need.

## If you eat everything in moderation, you'll be fine

Because *moderation* is a relative term, this philosophy is dangerous. What *you* think is moderation may not be moderation in the eyes of your doctor. Instead, stick to a lowfat eating plan and select a variety of foods with the USDA Food Guide Pyramid as your guide.

# Chapter 21

# Ten Terrific Web Sites on Healthy Eating

. . . . . . . . . . . . . . . . . . . . . . . . . . . . . . . . . . . . . . . . . . . . . .

**In This Chapter**

Surfing the Net for lowfat recipes, cooking tips, and nutritional information

. . . . . . . . . . . . . . . . . . . . . . . . . . . . . . . . . . . . . . . . . . . . . .

*T*he World Wide Web is full of information about health and nutrition, and you can find thousands of terrific recipes to suit any palate. If you have Internet access, check out these great sites.

## American Dietetic Association

At `http://www.eatright.org/`, you can find consulting registered dietitians in your area. The site also includes information about the Food Guide Pyramid and lists other nutrition resources.

## Cooking Connections

On this terrific reference site, Rebecca Sewell Homan includes a huge number of links — to recipes from *Gourmet* and *Bon Appetit* magazines, cooking magazines on the Web, cooking with garlic, cooking outdoors, and more. She also includes a recipe finder. Check out Cooking Connections at `http://troy.gc.peachnet.edu/www/rhoman/cook.htm`.

## Cooking Light Online

This site, at `http://pathfinder.com/@@L26UOAYAf5siUTSV/cl/`, features terrific recipes from the popular print magazine *Cooking Light.*

## Cooking with Olivia

Olivia shares healthy recipes and provides a link to chat, a link to a random cooking site, and a catalog of recipes from vegetarian dishes to seafood to desserts, with fat content clearly indicated. You can find her Web site at `http://www.cyberrealm.net/ocasas/`.

# FATFREE: The Low Fat Vegetarian Archive

At http://www.fatfree.com/, you can find a large archive of lowfat and fat-free vegetarian recipes, information about vegetarian nutrition, and links to other lowfat and vegetarian sources on the Internet, including a link to the USDA Nutrient Database, which gives a complete nutrient analysis of a huge number of foods.

# The Gourmet Connection

This online magazine "for gourmet food and health enthusiasts" features articles on food and diet-related topics. You can find this site at http://www.norwich.net/gourmet/link1.htm.

# Health-Enomics Healthy Kitchen

This site, at http://members.aol.com/hgourmet/index.html, offers healthy dinner menus and tips for seasoning foods. It also provides a place for you to post cooking questions and sign up for nutrition consulting services.

# Lifetime Online Healthy Kitchen

This Lifetime site, at http://www.lifetimetv.com/HealthNutrition/HealthyKitchen/index.html, includes a wide variety of recipes, information about healthy eating on the go, tips for purchasing ingredients, ideas for cooking with kids, and more.

# Low-Fat Lifestyle Forum

According to the authors, this forum "is for people who are interested in adopting a low-fat lifestyle or for those who are already living a low-fat lifestyle." The forum, at http://www.wctravel.com:80/lowfat/, includes lowfat cooking tips, dining out tips, product recommendations, cookbook recommendations, links to other related sites, and, of course, recipes.

# Low-Fat Living

Check out http://www.xe.net/lowfat/ for articles, recipes, tips and tricks, advice for dining out, book reviews, and more. You also can post questions that will be answered by a nutritionist (this feature isn't active yet but will be soon).

# Chapter 22

# Ten Healthful Newsletters

*In This Chapter*

Great newsletters that help you keep your body healthy

Several newsletters are excellent, as is *Prevention* magazine (available at newsstands or from Prevention Customer Service, P. O. Box 7319, Red Oak, IA 51591, 800-666-1206).

*Consumer Reports on Health*
Subscription Department
P. O. Box 56360
Boulder, CO 80323-6360
800-234-2188

*Environmental Nutrition*
*The Newsletter of Food, Nutrition, and Health*
P.O. Box 420451
Palm Coast, FL 32142-0451
800-829-5384

*Harvard Health Letter*
P. O. Box 420300
Palm Coast, FL 32142-0300
800-829-9045

*Harvard Heart Letter*
P. O. Box 420234
Palm Coast, FL 32142-0234
800-829-9171

*Harvard Women's Health Watch*
P. O. Box 420234
Palm Coast, FL 32142-0234
800-829-5921

*Health News*
P. O. Box 52924
Boulder, CO 80322-2924
800-848-9155

*The Johns Hopkins Medical Letter — Health After 50*
Subscriptions Dept.
Health After 50
P. O. Box 420235
Palm Coast, FL 32142-0235
904-446-4675

*Mayo Clinic Health Letter*
Subscription Services
P. O. Box 53889
Boulder, CO 80322-3889
800-333-9037

*Nutrition Action Healthletter*
1875 Connecticut Ave. N.W.
Suite 300
Washington, D.C. 20009-5728
circ@essential.org (include postal address); www.cspinet.org
800-237-4874

*Tufts University Health and Nutrition Letter*
P. O. Box 57857
Boulder, CO 80322-7857
800-274-7581

*University of California at Berkeley Wellness Letter*
P. O. Box 420148
Palm Coast, FL 32142
904-445-6414

# Appendix

# Glossary

**Arteriosclerosis:** A disease of the arteries that causes the arteries to become thick and hardened. It is important for the arteries to stay unclogged because they carry blood from the heart to all other parts of the body. Arteriosclerosis is caused mainly by a diet high in saturated fats.

**Atherosclerosis:** The most dangerous form of arteriosclerosis, in which fatty materials that come from the diet and that are made by the body fill up the arteries. When arteries are blocked, blood isn't able to flow freely. This type of arteriosclerosis causes strokes and heart attacks, which occur because of blockage of blood to the brain or to the heart, respectively.

**Calories:** The units in which energy is measured. Calories measure energy from the food you eat, such as the carbohydrates in bread, pasta, fruits, and dairy products, the protein in meats, beans, and dairy products, the fat in oils and butter, and the alcohol in wine and beer. Carbohydrate and protein each provide 4 calories per gram, fat provides 9 calories per gram, and alcohol provides 7 calories per gram. You use the calories (energy) from food to perform all body functions, such as digesting food and breathing, plus all daily activities, such as walking, typing, and swimming.

**Calories from fat:** Every Nutrition Facts panel lists the number of calories from the fat in the food. Calculating calories from fat can be complicated and time-consuming. Limiting your dietary fat by adding up fat grams each day is far easier and more meaningful.

**Cholesterol (blood):** The cholesterol in your blood and in your body is different from the cholesterol in your food. Your body needs cholesterol to work properly, and cholesterol is present in every single cell of your body. Cholesterol is made in your liver, which makes all the cholesterol your body needs. A few people's bodies make too much cholesterol. Additional dietary cholesterol (what you eat) can sometimes be harmful and can affect your blood cholesterol level. A high blood cholesterol level is a risk factor in heart and artery disease. If your total blood cholesterol level is over 200, you should check with your doctor.

**Cholesterol (dietary):** The cholesterol in your food is different from the cholesterol in your blood. Dietary cholesterol is a white, waxy, substance that cannot be tasted, smelled, or seen. The cholesterol you eat comes only from animal products such as meat, cheese, milk, cream, butter, fish, and poultry; all animal products contain cholesterol, except egg whites. A diet too high in cholesterol may cause an elevated blood cholesterol level, although not as much as a high intake of dietary saturated fat does.

**Cholesterol-free:** A nutrient claim on a food package that relates to the cholesterol content of the product. To qualify for this claim, the product must contain 2 milligrams of cholesterol or less and 2 grams or less of saturated fat per RACC and per labeled serving. (See also "RACC.")

**Diet:** Your daily eating plan. Your diet is always the first line of defense in heart and artery disease and weight management, even when combined with drugs. A healthy diet involves selecting foods and recommended numbers of servings from the USDA Food Guide Pyramid. Following the Pyramid can provide you with a diet that is low in fat and high in fiber if you choose lowfat or fat-free foods.

**Dietary fiber:** Like the human skeleton, plants have a structure of fiber that holds them together and upright. When you eat plants or a diet high in fiber, your body cannot digest (or process) the fiber, which is beneficial because fiber helps prevent bowel problems. Fiber may help control blood sugar in people with diabetes, and it may also help lower blood cholesterol (especially if high-fiber foods are substituted for high-saturated-fat or -cholesterol foods). High-fiber foods include beans, fruits, vegetables, and whole grains. Meat, dairy products, and oils contain no fiber.

**Extra lean:** A labeling claim for meat, game meat, poultry, and seafood that contain less than 5 grams of total fat, less than 2 grams of saturated fat, and less than 95 milligrams of cholesterol per RACC (see also "RACC") and per 100 grams. You may not find many beef, pork, or lamb products that are labeled extra lean.

**Fat:** Three types of fat are found in varying amounts in foods: saturated fat, polyunsaturated fat, and monounsaturated fat. Although all foods contain fat, the amount of total fat varies greatly, from minuscule amounts in most fruits and vegetables to small amounts in skinless turkey breast to larger amounts in fatty meats. Products such as oils are 100 percent fat.

**Fat-free:** Fat-free is a regulated claim that can be used on products that contain less than 0.5 grams of fat per RACC (see also "RACC") and per labeled serving. Other similar terms, such as *free of fat, no fat, zero fat, without fat, nonfat, trivial source of fat, negligible source of fat,* and *dietarily insignificant source of fat,* may also be used.

**HDL (high density lipoproteins):** The liver and the intestine make a lipoprotein (HDL) that carries cholesterol from all parts of the body to the liver. An HDL level lower than 35 is considered a risk factor for coronary heart disease.

**Hydrogenation:** Hydrogenation causes oils to harden or become solid by changing the way they are chemically bonded. This process makes liquid margarine hard at room temperature. The more hydrogenated or harder a fat, such as stick margarine, the more saturated it becomes. Butter, which is already solid at room temperature, contains four times as much saturated fat as margarine.

**LDL (low density lipoproteins):** A type of lipoprotein that the body makes by breaking down very low density lipoproteins (VLDL). LDL is the main carrier of cholesterol in the blood. If your cholesterol test shows a large amount of LDL in your blood, you may be at a higher risk for atherosclerosis and coronary heart disease. A desirable LDL level is less than 130 milligrams per deciliter. (See also "VLDL.")

**Lean:** A term used on nutrient labels to describe meat, game meat, poultry, and seafood with less than 10 grams of total fat, less than 4.5 grams of saturated fat, and less than 95 milligrams per RACC (see also "RACC") and per 100 grams.

**Lipids:** Fatty substances, such as cholesterol, triglycerides, and phospholipids, that are found naturally in the blood and in body tissues. Excesses of these substances can lead to heart and artery disease.

**Low cholesterol:** A nutrient label claim that describes foods containing 20 milligrams of cholesterol or less and 2 grams of saturated fat or less per RACC (see also "RACC") and per labeled serving.

**Lowfat:** A nutrient claim found on food labels that is used to describe foods that contain 3 grams of fat or less per RACC (see also "RACC") and per labeled serving. The phrases *low in fat, contains a small amount of fat, low source of fat,* and *little fat* may also be used for this claim.

**Lowfat, high-fiber:** Words that are often used together because reducing fat and increasing fiber in your diet can help you lose weight in a healthful manner.

**Low saturated fat:** A nutrient label claim that describes a food containing 1 gram of saturated fat or less per RACC (see also "RACC") and per labeled serving and 15 percent or less of calories from saturated fat.

**Monounsaturated fat:** A type of fat that apparently does not affect heart or artery disease. Sources include olive oil, olives, canola oil, almonds, and avocados. Although olive oil has more saturated fat than canola oil, both are relatively low in saturated fat. Oils high in monounsaturated fats have the same total fat content and calories as do those that are low in monounsaturated fats.

**Nutrient claim:** A word or phrase on a food label that tells you the amount of a nutrient in a food. The claim can be made only if the food meets government definitions.

**Obesity:** Classified as a weight 20 percent or more above ideal body weight. Another indicator is defined by the Body Mass Index. A Body Mass Index greater than 27 may increase your risk for stroke, heart attacks, diabetes, and cancer.

**Omega-3 fatty acids:** Fish contains a type of polyunsaturated fatty acids called omega-3 fatty acids. Eating fish once or twice a week may reduce the chances of a blood clot forming and may help to lower triglycerides. All fish and shellfish do contain cholesterol in amounts that are comparable to those in meat and poultry, but they have less saturated fat.

**Plaque:** Fatty material and cholesterol build-up on the inner surface of the arteries. Plaque can accumulate all around the inside of an artery until the artery becomes narrow or completely blocked, which can lead to heart attacks or strokes.

**Polyunsaturated fat:** A type of fat found in walnuts, corn oil, safflower oil, sunflower oil, and pumpkin seeds, among other things. Oils that are high in polyunsaturated (and monounsaturated) fats apparently do not increase your risk of heart disease, although they have the same number of calories as those oils that are low in polyunsaturates. Some experts previously thought that these unsaturated fats may lower cholesterol.

**RACC:** Stands for *Reference Amount Customarily Consumed.* It is the basis for the serving sizes found on nutrition labels. The serving size listed on the label may not be what you are used to eating, however. Your serving size changes depending on your age, your sex, and your level of activity.

**Saturated fat:** The type of fat most implicated in artery blockage and cholesterol plaque. It is found mainly in animal products and in a few vegetable products. Small amounts of saturated fat are in canola oil and safflower oil, and slightly more are in corn oil and olive oil. The oils with the highest amounts are coconut, palm, and palm kernel; butter, cheese, and meats also contain large amounts of saturated fat.

**Trans fatty acids:** A type of fat created when oils are hydrogenated (see also "Hydrogenation"). Most foods contain only very small amounts of trans fatty acids. Even with hydrogenation and the resulting trans fatty acids, for example, stick margarine still has one-fourth the saturated fat of the same amount of butter.

**Triglycerides:** Substances that the body makes when it ingests too many calories. Triglycerides also come from the fats found in foods. They are stored in the body as body fat.

**VLDL (very low density lipoproteins):** A type of lipoprotein that carries the triglycerides that the body makes.

# Index

*Lowfat Cooking For Dummies*
about, 1–2
assumptions about reader, 3
conventions, 2–3
icons, 5–6
organization, 4–5
reason for writing, 1
using, 2
Low-Fat Lifestyle Forum Web site, 382
Low-Fat Living Web site, 382
lunch meat, 85

## • M •

Mac and Chili recipe, 269–270
mace, 68
mahi mahi, 218
malt vinegar, 65
Malted Milkshake recipe, 364–365
mangoes, cutting tips, 225
maple syrup, 74
margarine, 98–99, 378
marjoram, 68
marshmallows, 74
tips, 74
toasting, 366
mashed potatoes, 310–311
*See also* potatoes
flavoring, 311
thickening soups and, 192
*Mayo Clinic Health Letter,* 384
mayonnaise, 140, 282
meal plans
comparison, 31–32
daily totals for, 32
meat, 75–94
breakfast, 117
calories, 76–79
canned, 48–49
in casseroles, 191
cholesterol, 76–79
cooking methods, 230–232
cutting consumption of, 374
extra lean, 87
fast-food, 79
fat and, 76–79
fat reduction in, 79–80
hot dogs, 85
lean, 87
lowfat cuts of, 233–234
lowfat soups with, 188–190
lowfat tips, 156
lunch, 85
problems, 229

purchasing, 86–88
saturated fat, 78–79
substitutes, 86
zero-trimming, 87
Meat Loaf recipe, 240
meat recipes, 238–243
Beef Fajitas, 238–239
Lamb and Eggplant with Rice and Tomatoes, 242–243
Meat Loaf, 240
Sweet and Sour Pork, 241–242
Mediterranean Vegetables and Rice (or Orzo) recipe, 311–312
metabolism, 17, 378
microwaving
asparagus, 275
beans, 260–261
fish, 211
meat/poultry, 231
rice, 256
vegetables, 299
milk, 26, 53, 96–98
*See also* dairy products
brewing coffee with, 363
chocolate, 97
fat/calorie comparison, 97
kids and, 106–107, 361
labeling controversy, 98
in soups, 191
soy, 362
switching to lower fat, 108–109
two percent, 96–97, 106, 377
milkshakes, 112, 364–365
millet. *See also* grains
cooking time, 253
defined, 252
mint, 69
mocha chocolate pudding, 337
moderation, 16, 379
molasses, 74
monounsaturated fat, 30, 387
mornay sauce, 326
muffins, oat bran, 136–137
mushroom velouté, 326
mushrooms
breakfast, 119
creamed spinach with, 308
marinated, 143, 167
omelet/egg scramble, 126
in pasta sauce, 322–323
portobello, 146–147
salad, 176
spiced green beans with, 313–314
mustard, 69, 181, 282
myths, about fat, 377–379

## • T •

## • U •

## • V •

# • W •

# • Y •

# • Z •